Living Language

COMMON
USAGE
DICTIONARY

GERMAN-ENGLISH
ENGLISH-GERMAN

THE LIVING LANGUAGE COURSES®

Living Spanish

Living French

Living German

Living Japanese

Living Russian

Living Portuguese (South American)

Living Portuguese (Continental)

Living Hebrew

Living Swahili

Children's Living French

Children's Living Spanish

Advanced Living French

Advanced Living Spanish

Living English for Native Spanish Speakers

Living English for Native French Speakers

Living English for Native Italian Speakers

Living English for Native German Speakers

Living English for Native Portuguese Speakers

Living English for Native Chinese Speakers

Living Language™ Spanish Video

Living Language™ French Video

Living Language™ German Video

Additional Living Language™ conversation manuals
and dictionaries may be purchased separately.

Living Language™

COMMON USAGE DICTIONARY

GERMAN-ENGLISH
ENGLISH-GERMAN

By Genevieve A. Martin
and Theodor Bertram

BASED ON THE DICTIONARY DEVELOPED BY
RALPH WEIMAN
FORMERLY CHIEF OF LANGUAGE SECTION,
U.S. WAR DEPARTMENT

CONTAINING OVER 15,000 BASIC TERMS WITH
MEANINGS ILLUSTRATED BY SENTENCES AND
1000 ESSENTIAL WORDS SPECIALLY INDICATED

Crown Publishers, Inc., New York

Manufactured in the United States of America

Library of Congress Catalog Card Number: 56-9318

ISBN 0-517-55782-7

1985 Updated Edition

15   14   13   12

TABLE OF CONTENTS

INTRODUCTION

The German Common Usage Dictionary lists the most frequently used German words, gives their most important meanings and illustrates their use.

1. The *basic* words are indicated by capitals. These are the words generally considered essential for any reasonable command of the language.

2. Only the most important meanings are given.

3. These meanings are illustrated, wherever necessary, by means of everyday phrases and sentences. Where there is no close English equivalent for a German word or where the English equivalent has several different meanings, the context of the illustrative sentences helps to make the meanings clear.

4. Each important word is followed by the everyday expressions in which it most frequently occurs. The Common Usage Dictionary serves accordingly as a phrase book or conversation guide: it contains thousands of everyday sentences which are of practical importance (for traveling, correspondence, etc.) or which serve as illustrations of the grammatical features of current written and spoken German. The Common Usage Dictionary should, therefore, prove helpful both to beginners who are building up their vocabulary and to advanced students who want to perfect their command of colloquial German.

5. In translating the German phrases and sentences an attempt has been made to give not a mere translation but an equivalent—that is, what an English speaker would say in the same situation. (Literal translations have been added to help the beginner.) The user is thus furnished with numerous examples of how common German expressions (particularly the very idiomatic and the very colloquial ones) can best be translated into English. This feature makes the Common Usage Dictionary especially useful for translation work.

6. The English-German part contains the most common English words and their German equivalents. By consulting the sentences given under the German word in the German-English part the reader can observe whether the German word always translates the English one or whether it does so only in certain cases.

EXPLANATORY NOTES

Literal translations are in parentheses.

Gender is indicated by *m.* for masculine, *f.* for feminine and *n.* for neuter.

Case is indicated by *nom.* for nominative, *gen.* for genitive, *dat.* for dative, *acc.* for accusative.

GERMAN-ENGLISH

A

AB 1. *adv.* off, down, away from, from.
ab heute *from today.*
ab und an *now and then.*
ab und zu *to and fro, now and then.*
von hier ab *from here.*
von nun ab *henceforth.*
2. *separable prefix (implies a movement down or away, imitation, appropriation, deterioration, destruction).*
Das Flugzeug stürzte ins Meer ab. *The plane fell down into the sea.*
Einige alte Häuser werden abgebaut. *Some old houses will be demolished.*
Er hat ihm tau send Mark abgeschmeichelt. *He got a thousand marks from him by flattery.*
Ich schreibe meine Aufgabe ab. *I copy my homework.*
Abart *f.* variety.
abbeissen *to bite off.*
sich die Nägel abbeissen *to bite one's nails.*
abbezahlen *to pay off.*
abbiegen *to turn off.*
Abbild *n.* copy, image.
abbinden *to unbind.*
Abbitte *f.* apology.
abbrechen *to break up, interrupt, deduct, gather.*
Blumen abbrechen *to gather flowers.*
die Arbeit abbrechen *to cease work.*
abdanken *to dismiss, abdicate.*
Der Fürst hat abgedankt. *The prince has abdicated.*
abdrehen *to turn off, switch off.*
Drehen sie das Radio ab! *Turn off the radio!*
abdrucken *to print.*
ABEND *n.* evening.
diesen Abend *this evening.*
Es wird Abend. *It is getting dark.*
heute Abend *tonight.*
Abenteuer *n.* adventure.
auf Abenteuer ausgehen *to look for adventure.*
abenteuerlich *adventurous.*
Abenteurer *m.* adventurer.
ABER *but, however, anyway.*
Ich wollte ausgehen aber das Wetter war zu schlecht. *I wanted to go out but the weather was too bad.*
Das Kind wollte spielen, die Mutter aber wollte nicht. *The child wanted to play but the mother did not want to.*
Der König aber . . . *as for the king . . .*
Nein aber! *I say!*

Nun aber! *But now!*
tausend und aber tausend *thousands and thousands.*
abermals *again, once more.*
abfahren *to set off, depart.*
Der Zug fährt um drei Uhr ab. *The train leaves at three.*
Siefuh rübel ab. *She got the worst of it.*
Abfahrtsort *m.* place of departure.
abfinden *to settle, come to an agreement.*
abführen *to lead away, carry away.*
Abführung *f.* removal.
Abgabe *f.* tax, tribute, delivery.
abgabenfrei *tax free.*
abgabenpflichtig *taxable.*
Abgang *m.* departure, exit.
ABGEBEN *to give, supply, deliver, pay taxes.*
sich mit etwas abgeben *to occupy oneself with a matter.*
Wir können die Waren zu diesem Preis nicht abgeben. *We cannot supply the merchandise on these terms.*
abgehen *to depart, go off.*
Er lässt sich nichts abgehen. *He denies himself nothing.*
von seinem Vorhaben nicht abgehen *to persist in one's plans.*
abgemacht *agreed.*
abgewinnen *to win from.*
abgewöhnen *to disaccustom, give up.*
Ich habe mir das Rauchen abgewöhnt. *I have given up smoking.*
Abgrund *m.* abyss, precipice.
abhalten *to hold off, restrain.*
Lassen Sie sich nicht abhalten. *Don't let me stop you.*
abhängen *to unhang, hang up (phone), disconnect.*
abhängig *sloping, dependent on.*
abheben *to lift off, uncover, become detached.*
Die helle Gestalt hebt sich auf dem dunkeln Hintergrunde vorteilhaft ab. *The light figure is brought into relief against the dark background.*
Abhilfe *f.* relief.
abholen *to get, collect.*
Das Taxi wird mich abholen. *The taxi will pick me up.*
Abkunft *f.* descent, origin.
ablenken *to divert, distract.*
ablesen *to pick up, read off.*
abliefern *to deliver.*
ABMACHEN *to remove, loosen, agree, settle.*
Abgemacht! *Agreed!*

abnehmen *to take off, gather, pick up (phone).*
  Er nimmt seinen Hut ab. *He takes off his hat.*
Abnelgung *f. dislike, antipathy.*
Abort *m. lavatory.*
abräumen *to take away, remove.*
ABREISE *f. departure.*
  eine unvorbergesehene Abreise *an unexpected departure.*
Absage *f. refusal.*
absagen *to refuse, to cancel, call off.*
  eine Gesellschaft absagen lassen *to call off a party.*
  Falls Sie mir nicht absagen, komme ich. *Unless you call it off, I'll come.*
Abscheu *m. aversion, horror.*
abscheulich *horrible, abominable, nasty.*
  Das war abscheulich von ihm. *It was very nasty of him.*
ABSCHIED *m. departure.*
  Abschied nehmen *to take leave.*
  Ich werde Abschied von Ihnen nehmen. *I am going to leave you.*
  Den Abschied bekommen *to be dismissed.*
  Der Offizier hat seinen Abschied genommen. *The officer has been placed on the retired list.*
abschreiben *to copy, to deduct.*
abseits *prep. (gen.) aside, apart, away from.*
ABSICHT *f. intention, purpose, view.*
  in der Absicht *with the intention.*
  Er tat es in böser Absicht. *He did it with a malicious intention.*
absichtlich *on purpose.*
Abstand *m. distance, interval.*
  Er nahm Abstand von seiner Erbschaft. *He gave up his inheritance.*
Absturz *m. fall, crash.*
  Er wurde bei einem Flugzeugabsturz getötet. *He was killed in a plane crash.*
ABTEIL *n. compartment, division, section.*
  Abteil erster Klasse *n. first-class compartment.*
  Nichtraucherabteil *n. non-smoking compartment.*
Abteilung *f. department (in a store).*
  Schuhabteilung *f. shoe department.*
abtrocknen *to dry off, wipe.*
  das Geschirr abtrocknen *to dry the dishes.*
abwärts *downward.*
abwechseln *to vary, change, alternate.*
abwesend *absent.*

Abwesenheit *f. absence.*
abzahlen *to pay off.*
abziehen *to retain, take off, subtract.*
  Der Arbeitgeber zieht die Steuer vom Einkommen ab. *The employer retains taxes from the salary.*
Abzugskanal *m. sewer.*
ach! *Ah! Oh!*
ACHT *eight.*
  heute in acht Tagen *A week from today.*
  achtmal *eight times.*
ACHTE *eighth.*
achten *to esteem, regard, respect.*
ACHTUNG *f. esteem.*
  Achtung! *Beware! Attention!*
achtungsvoll *respectful.*
ACHTZEHN *eighteen.*
ACHTZEHNTE *eighteenth.*
ACHTZIG *eighty.*
ACHTZIGSTE *eightieth.*
ACKER *m. field, soil.*
Ackerbau *m. agriculture.*
ackern *to plough.*
Ackersmann *m. ploughman.*
addieren *to add up.*
Adel *m. nobility, aristocracy.*
Ader *f. vein.*
Adjektiv *n. adjective.*
adlig *noble.*
ADRESSE *f. address.*
  Hier ist meine Adresse. *Here is my address.*
adressieren *to address.*
Adverb *n. adverb.*
Affe *m. monkey.*
Affekt *m. excitement.*
affektiert *affected.*
Agent *m. agent.*
ahnen *to have a presentiment.*
  Es ahnt mir Unglück. *I have a presentiment of evil.*
  Ich habe keine Ahnung. *I don't have the slightest idea.*
ähnlich *similar, like.*
  ähnlich sehen *to look alike*
Ähnlichkeit *f. similarity, resemblance.*
Akademie *f. academy, university.*
Akten *pl. deeds, documents.*
Aktie *f. share, stock.*
aktiv *active.*
Akzent *m. accent, stress.*
Alarm *m. alarm.*
Alkohol *m. alcohol, liquor.*
ALL (aller, alle, alles) *entire, whole, every, each, any.*
  all die Leute *everybody.*
  all und jeder *each and every.*
  alle Tage *every day.*

auf alle Fälle *in any case.*
ohne allen Grund *for no reason at all.*
ALLEIN *alone, single, solitary, apart, lonesome.*
Ich bin allein. *I am lonesome.*
Sie lebt allein. *She lives alone.*
allerart *diverse.*
allgemein *universal.*
Alphabet *n. alphabet.*
ALS *when, than, as, like.*
Als Bismarck starb. *When Bismarck died.*
Sie ist Grösser als ihr Bruder. *She is taller than her brother.*
als ob *as if, as though*
Er tut als ob er die Antwort kenne. *He acts as if he knew the answer.*
so bald als *as soon as*
ALSO *so, thus, in this way.*
"Also sprach Zarathustra .." *"Thus spoke Zarathustra . . ."*
ALT *old, aged, ancient.*
alte Sprachen *ancient languages (classics)*
altehrwürdig *venerable.*
altgläubig *orthodox.*
altmodisch *old-fashioned.*
eine alte Junger *an old maid.*
ALTER *n. age, old age, antiquity.*
Mittelalter *n. Middle Ages.*
älter *older, elder, senior.*
Altertum *n. antiquity.*
Altertumshändler *m. antique dealer.*
älteste *oldest.*
am (an dem) *on, at.*
Amerikaner *m. -in f. American.*
amerikanisch *American.*
AMT *n. office, charge, board.*
In compound words, the suffix amt designates a government office:
das Auswärtige Amt *the Foreign Office.*
Polizeiamt *n. police station*
Zollamt *n. customs.*
in Amt und Würden stehen *to be a person of position.*
amüsant *amusing.*
AMÜSIEREN *to amuse.*
sich amüsieren *to enjoy oneself.*
Ich habe mich in der Gesellschaft sehr amüsiert. *I enjoyed myself at the party.*
AN 1. *prep. (dat. when answering question, Wo?; acc. when answering question, Wohin?, and depending on the idiom).*
an die Arbeit gehen *to go to work.*
an der Arbeit sein *to be at work.*
an der Donau *on the Danube.*
an und für sich *in itself.*

Er starb an seinen Wunden. *He died of his wounds.*
Es ist an mir. *It is my turn.*
Ich gehe an die Tür. *I go to the door.*
Ich weiss, was an der Geschichte dran ist. *I know what the story is.*
soviel an mir liegt *as far as I am concerned.*
2. *separable prefix. (implies movement closer to the speaker, proximity, contact, attraction, climbing, beginning).*
Der Hund ist angebunden. *The dog is tied.*
Der Tag bricht an. *The day begins.*
Er behielt seine Schuhe an. *He kept his shoes on.*
Er zieht seine Jacke an. *He puts his coat on.*
Ich steige langsam den Berg hinan. *I climb the mountain slowly.*
anbehalten *to keep on.*
Ich will meinen Mantel anbehalten. *I'll keep my coat on.*
anbieten *to offer, volunteer.*
Anblick *m. sight, view.*
Andenken *n. memory, souvenir.*
zum Andenken an meine Eltern. *In memory of my parents.*
ANDER *other, another, different, next.*
am anderen Morgen *the next morning.*
anderer Meinung sein *to be of a different opinion.*
ein andermal *another time.*
einen Tag um den andern *every other day.*
etwas anderes *another thing, something different.*
nichts anderes als *nothing but.*
unter anderem *among other things.*
anderenfalls *otherwise.*
anderseits *on the other side.*
andeuten *to indicate.*
Anerbieten *n. offer, proposal.*
Anfall *m. attack, fit.*
Herzanfall *m. heart attack.*
Anfang *m. beginning, start.*
anfangen *(to) begin, start.*
von Anfang, bis zu Ende *from beginning to end.*
Anfrage *f. inquiry.*
anfragen *to inquire.*
anfreunden (sich) *to become friends.*
angemessen *suitable, accurate.*
Angesicht *n. face, countenance.*
von Angesicht zu Angesicht *face to face.*
angesichts *considering, in view of.*
Angewohnheit *f. habit, custom.*

angrenzen *to border.*
Angriff *m. attack.*
  in Angriff nehmen *to set about.*
Angst *f. anxiety.*
ängstigen *to frighten.*
  sich ängstigen vor *to be afraid of.*
  sich ängstigen um *to feel anxious about.*
anhaben *to wear, have on.*
  Ich kann ihm nichts anhaben. *I cannot find any weak spot in him.*
anhalten *to stop, pull up.*
anhören *to listen to.*
Anker *m. anchor.*
anklagen *to accuse.*
ankleiden *to dress.*
anklopfen *to knock at.*
ANKOMMEN *to arrive, approach, reach.*
  Es kommt darauf an, ob Sie Zeit haben. *It depends on whether you have time.*
  Wir müssen es darauf ankommen lassen. *We have to take a chance on it.*
ANKUNFT *f. arrival.*
anmelden *to announce, notify, report.*
Anmut *f. grace, charm.*
anmutig *graceful, charming.*
Annahme *f. acceptance, assumption.*
annehem *to accept, receive, assume, take care of.*
anpassen *to fit, suit, adapt.*
anprobieren *to try on.*
anrechnen *to charge.*
  zu viel anrechen *to overcharge.*
  Ich rechne Ihnen Ihre Hilfe hoch an. *I appreciate your help very much.*
Anrede *f. address.*
anreden *to address, accost.*
  Der Schutzmann redete mich an. *The policeman called me.*
anregen *to incite, stimulate, excite.*
Ansage *f. announcement, notification.*
ansagen *to announce, notify.*
anschauen *to look at, contemplate.*
anschaulich *evident, clear.*
Anschrift *f. address (letter).*
anschuldigen *to accuse.*
ANSEHEN *to look at, consider, regard.*
  dem Ansehen nach *to all appearances.*
  im Ansehen stehen *to be esteemed.*
  vom Ansehen kennen *to know by sight.*
Ansicht *f. view, sight, opinion.*
  nach meiner Ansicht *according to my opinion.*
Ansichtskarte *f. picture postcard.*
Ansprache *f. speech, address.*
Anspruch *m. claim, pretension.*

  Anspruch haben auf *to be entitled to.*
Anstand *m. manners, decency, etiquette.*
  ohne Anstand *without hesitation.*
anständig *decent, respectable.*
ANSTATT (statt)
  1. *prep (gen.) instead of; also conj.*
  Statt eines Regenschirmes nahm er einen Stock. *Instead of an umbrella, he took a stick.*
  Anstatt seine Arbeit zu tun, geht er spazieren. *Instead of doing his work, he takes a walk.*
anstrengen (sich) *to strain, exert.*
anstrengend *tiring, trying, exacting.*
ANTWORT *f. answer.*
ANTWORTEN *to answer.*
anvertrauen *to entrust, confide.*
Anwalt *m. lawyer, attorney.*
anwesend *present.*
Anwesenheit *f. presence.*
Anzahl *f. quantity, amount.*
anzahlen *to pay on account.*
Anzeige *f. notice, advertisement.*
anzeigen *to notify, report, announce.*
  Ich halte es für angezeigt. *I consider it advisable.*
ANZUG *m. suit, dress.*
anzüglich *suggestive, personal.*
Anzüglichkeit *f. suggestive remark.*
anzünden *to light the fire, set fire to.*
APFEL *m. apple.*
  in den sauern Apfel beissen *to swallow a bitter pill.*
APFELSINE *f. orange.*
Apotheke *f. pharmacy.*
Apotheker *m. pharmacist.*
Apparat *m. apparatus, appliance, telephone.*
  Bleiben Sie am Apparat! *Hold the wire!*
Appetit *m. appetite.*
applaudieren *to applaud.*
APRIL *m. April.*
Aquator *m. equator.*
ARBEIT *f. work, job.*
ARBEITEN *to work, manufacture.*
  arbeitsfähig *able-bodied*
  arbeits unfähig *unfit for work*
Arbeiter *m. (-in, f.) worker, laborer.*
  Arbeiterstand *m. working class.*
Arbeitgeber *m. employer.*
Arbeitnehmer *m. employee.*
arbeitsam *industrious, diligent.*
Architekt *m. architect.*
Architektur *f. architecture.*
arg *bad, mischievous.*
  Sie dachte an nichts Arges. *She meant no harm.*

Ärger *m. annoyance, anger, worry.*
ärgerlich *annoying, angry.*
ärgern *to annoy, irritate, bother.*
Argument *n. argument.*
Aristokrat *m. aristocrat.*
Aristokratie *f. aristocracy.*
aristokratisch *aristocratic.*
ARM *m. arm.*
ARM *poor*
Armband *n. bracelet.*
Armbanduhr *f. wrist watch.*
Ärmel *m. sleeve.*
Armlehne *f. arm of chair.*
Armut *f. poverty.*
Arrest *m. arrest.*
ART *f. kind, manner, way, type.*
artig *good, well-behaved.*
Artikel *m. article.*
Arznei *f. medicine (drug).*
Arzneikunde *f. pharmacy (profession of).*
Ast *m. branch (tree).*
Atem *m. breath, suspense.*
    Dieser Kriminalroman halt uns in Atem.
      This detective story keeps us in
      suspense.
atemholen *to take breadth.*
atemlos *breathless.*
atemraubend *breath-taking.*
    Der Film war atemraubend. *The movie*
      was breath-taking.
Athlet *m. athlete.*
atmen *to breathe.*
AUCH *also, too, even.*
    was auch *whatever.*
    wer auch *whoever.*
    wo auch *wherever.*
    Was auch geschieht, Sie sind
      verantwortlich. *Whatever happens,*
      you are responsible.
    Wer auch kommen mag, ich bin nicht
      zu Hause. *Whoever comes, I am not*
      home.
    Wo auch immer er auftauchen mag,
      man wird ihn erkennen. *Wherever he*
      appears, he will be recognized.
AUF 1. *prep. (dat. when answering*
      question, Wo?; acc. when answering
      question, Wohin?, and depending on
      the idiom) on, upon, at, in, to, for,
      during.
    Er kommt auf die Strasse hinab. *He*
      comes down to the street.
    Ich kaufe Gemüse auf dem Markt. *I*
      buy vegetables at the market.
    Ich traf sie auf dem Ball. *I met her at*
      the ball.
    Ich fahre auf das Land. *I drive to the*
      country.
    Sie wohnen auf oliesem Schloss. *They*

      live in that castle.
    Die Jäger gehen auf die Jagd. *The*
      hunters go hunting.
    Der Tag folgt auf die Nacht. *The day*
      follows the night.
    alle bis auf einen *all except one.*
    auf der Rückfahrt von Wien *during the*
      return from Vienna.
    auf Deutsch *in German.*
    auf einmal *suddenly.*
    auf keinen Fall *in no case.*
    auf Wiedersehen! *Good-bye!*
    Liebe auf den ersten Blick *love at first*
      sight.
    2. *adv. up, upwards.*
    auf und ab *up and down.*
    3. *Conj.* auf dass *in order to.*
    auf dass nicht *for fear that.*
    4. *Separable prefix (implies motion*
      upward or outward, opening,
      completion).
    Ich setze meinen Hut auf. *I put my hat*
      on.
    Die Sonne geht auf. *The sun is rising.*
    Bitte, machen Sie das Fenster auf.
      Please open the window.
aufbewahren *to keep, preserve, stock.*
Aufbewahrung *f. preservation, storage.*
aufbrauchen *to use up.*
aufeinander *one on top of the other.*
Aufenthalt *m. stay, residence.*
aufessen *to eat up.*
Auffassung *f. conception, interpretation.*
Aufgabe *f. task, duty, problem.*
aufgeben *to commission, order, lose,*
      give up, resign, check, send.
    die Hoffnung aufgeben *to lose hope.*
    ein Telegramm aufgeben *to send a*
      telegram.
aufhängen *to hang up.*
aufheben *to pick up, rise, abolish.*
aufheitern *to cheer up.*
aufklären *to clear, explain.*
Aufklärung *f. explanation.*
aufmachen *to open, unlock, undo.*
Aufmachung *f. make up.*
aufmerken *to pay attention, attend.*
aufmerksam *attentive.*
Aufmerksamkeit *f. attention.*
Aufnahme *f. taking up, admission,*
      enrollment, snapshot.
aufnahmefähig *receptive.*
Aufnahmeprüfung *f. entrance*
      examination.
aufnehmen *to lift, take up, admit,*
      photograph, record (a voice).
aufpassen *to adapt, fix, pay attention.*
    Aufgepasst! *Attention!*
Aufpasser *m. watcher, spy.*

aufräumen *to arrange, put in order, clean.*

aufrecht *upright, straight.*

aufregen *to stir up, excite.*

aufregend *exciting, seditious.*

Aufregung *f. excitement, agitation.*

Aufsatz *m. main piece, top, ornament, article (newspaper).*

aufschliessen *to unlock.*

Aufschluss *m. opening up, explanation, information.*
  Aufschluss über eine Sache geben *to give some information about something.*

aufschreiben *to write down.*

Aufsehen *n. sensation, attention.*
  Er erregt Aufsehen. *He attracts attention.*

Aufstand *m. tumult, revolt.*

AUFSTEHEN *stand up, rise, get up.*
  aufstehen gegen *to rebel against.*
  Stechen Sie auf! *Get up!*

aufstellen *to set up, erect, draw up, nominate.*
  Eine Behauptung aufstellen *to make a statement.*

Auftrag *m. commission, instruction.*
  im Auftrage von *by order of.*
  einen Auftrag ausführen *to execute a commission.*

auftragen *to carry up, serve up, draw, charge.*
  Et nat mir viele Grüsse an Sie aufgetragen. *He sends you his regards. ("He charged me with many greetings for you.")*

aufwachen *to awake.*

aufwachsen *to grow up.*

Aufwand *m. expenditure, expense.*

aufwärts *upwards.*
  Er schwimmt een Fluss aufwärts. *He swims upstream.*

aufwecken *to awaken.*

aufziehen *to bring up, raise, wind a watch, pull up, tease.*
  Einen aufziehen *to make fun of somebody.*

Aufzug *m. procession, parade, attire, outfit, act (play), elevator.*

AUGE *n. eye.*
  Er versuchte mir Sand in die Augen zu streuen. *He tried to deceive me ("throw dust into my eyes").*
  gure Augen haben *to have good eyesight.*
  grosse Augen machen *to look very surprised.*
  Ich habe kein Auge zugemacht. *I did not sleep a wink.*

  unter vier Augen *privately ("between four eyes").*
  Wir haben ihn aus den Augen verloren. *We lost sight of him.*

Augenarzt *m. oculist.*

Augenblick *m. moment.*
  im Augenblick *for the moment.*

augenblicklich *immediately.*

Augenbraue *f. eyebrow.*

Augenlid *n. eyelid.*

Augenwimper *f. eyelash.*

AUGUST *m. August.*

Auktion *f. auction sale.*

AUS 1. *prep. (dat.) out, out of, for, from, in, upon.*
  Aus den Augen, aus dem Sinn. *Out of sight, out of mind.*
  Er kommt aus dem Theater. *He comes out of the theater.*
  Er hat es aus Liebe getan. *He did it for love.*
  Meine Uhr ist aus Gold. *My watch is made of gold.*
  Sie stammt aus Paris. *She is a native of Paris.*
  2. *adv. out, over, up.*
  von hier aus *from here.*
  von mir aus *for my part.*
  3. *separable prefix. Implies the idea of motion out (in this case also combines with him or her), achievement.*
  Die Vorstellung ist aus. *The performance is over.*
  Ich gehe aus dem Speisezimmer hinaus. *I go out of the dinning room.*

ausbessern *to repair.*

ausbilden *to form, develop, cultivate, educate, train.*

ausbleiben *to stay away, fail to appear, escape.*
  Ihre Strafe wird nicht ausbleiben. *You will not escape punishment.*

Ausblick *m. outlook, prospect.*

ausbrechen *to break out, vomit.*
  in Tränen ausbrechen *to burst into tears.*

Ausbruch *m. outbreak, eruption, escape.*

Ausdauer *f. perseverance, assiduity.*

ausdauern *to hold out, outlast, endure.*

ausdehnen *to expand, prolong.*

ausdenken *to invent, conceive, imagine.*

Ausdruck *m. expression, phrase.*

ausdrücken *to squeeze, express.*
  sich kurz und klar ausdrücken *to express oneself briefly and to the point.*

auseinander *apart, separately.*

ausführen *to take out, export, realize.*

ausführlich adj. detailed, full; in detail, fully.
Erzählen Sie mir alles ausführlich. Tell me everything in detail.

ausfüllen to fill out, stuff.

Ausgabe f. delivery, edition, issue, publication.

Ausgang m. way out, exit, end.

ausgeben to give out, deliver, issue, deal (cards).

ausgehen to go out, come out, run out, proceed, start from, end.
frei ausgehen to go free.
ihm geht die Geduld aus. He is losing his patience.
Wie wird diese Sache ausgehen? How will this matter end?

AUSGEZEICHNET excellent, distinguished.

ausgleichen to make even, equalize, settle, arrange, compensate.

aushalten to bear, suffer, support, hold out, last.

Aushang m. notice (posted); poster.

aushängen to hang out, post a notice.

Aushilfe f. aid (temporary); assistant.

auskleiden to undress.

auskommen to manage, get along.
Es ist schwer mit ihm auszukommen. It is difficult to get along with him.
Ich komme nicht mit dem Papier aus. can't manage with the paper. (I don't have enough of it.)

Auskunft f. information, intelligence.

Auskunftei f. information bureau.

auslassen to leave out, omit, let out.

Auslese f. choice, selection.

auslesen to select, choose, read through.

ausmachen to put out, constitute, come to, settle, amount.
Das macht nichts aus. It does not matter.

Ausmass n. measurement, scale, proportion.
mit solchem Ausmass to such an extent.

ausmessen to measure, survey.

Ausnahme f. exception.
ohne Ausnahme without exception.

auspacken to unpack.

Ausrede f. excuse, pretense.

ausreden to finish speaking, excuse.
einem etwas ausreden to dissuade somebody from something.

ausrichten to execute, deliver, obtain.
Haben Sie es ihm ausgerichtet? Did you give him the message?

Ausruf m. cry, exclamation.

ausrufen to cry out, admonish, proclaim.

ausruhen to rest.

Aussage f. statement, assertion, declaration, evidence.

aussagen to affirm, declare, give evidence.

ausschalten to cut out, switch off.
Schalten Sie den Motor aus! Switch off the motor!

ausscheiden to separate, withdraw.

ausschiffen to disembark, land.

ausschliessen to exclude.

ausschliesslich exclusive.

ausschmücken to decorate, adorn.

ausschneiden to cut out, snipe.

AUSSEHEN to look out, appear.

Aussehen n. look, air.

aussen on the outside, abroad, without.
von aussen from the outside.

aussenden to send out.

AUSSER 1. prep. (dat.) out of, out, besides.
ausser der Jahreszeit out of season
ausser sich beside oneself.
2. with gen. out of.
ausser Landes out of the country.
3. conj. except, unless, but.
Ausser Sonntags, gehe ich jeden Tag in die Schule. I go to school every day except Sunday.

ausserdem besides, moreover.

aussetzen to set out, put out, offer, bequeath.
auszusetzen haben to find fault with.

Aussicht f. view, prospect.

aussinnen to plan, plot, scheme.

aussöhnen to reconcile.

aussondern to separate, select.

Aussprache f. pronunciation, accent.

aussprechen to pronounce, express.

aussuchen to seek out, search.

Austausch m. exchange.

austauschen to exchange.

Auster f. oyster.

austragen to deliver, distribute.

austreten to tread under, trample, retire.

Ausverkauf m. clearance sale.

ausverkaufen to sell out, clear off (a shop).

Auswahl f. choice, assortment, selection.

auswählen to choose, select.

Auswanderer m. emigrant.

auswandern to emigrate.

Auswanderung f. emigration.

auswärtig foreign, abroad.

Ausweg m. way out.

ausweichen *to avoid, evade, shun.*
Ausweis *m. certificate, document, identity card.*
ausziehen *to undress, pull out, extract, move, remove.*
Auszug *m. departure, extract, removal.*
Auto *n. automobile, car.*
Autobahn *n. parkway.*
Autobus *m. bus.*
Axt *f. axe.*

B

Bach *m. brook.*
BACKEN *to bake, fry.*
Bäcker *m. baker.*
Backobst *n. dried fruit.*
Backofen *m. oven.*
Backpulver *n. baking powder.*
BAD *n. bath, spa.*
Badeanstalt *f. baths, swimming pool.*
Badeanzug *m. bathing suit.*
Badehose *f. bathing shorts.*
Bademantel *m. bathrobe.*
Badeort *m. spa.*
Badetuch *n. bath towel.*
Badewanne *f. bathtub.*
Badezimmer *n. bathroom.*
BAHN *f. track, road, way, railway.*
Bahnarbeiter *m. railway man.*
Bahnbeamte *m. railroad official.*
Bahngleis *n. track.*
BAHNHOF *m. station.*
Bahnsteig *m. platform.*
Bahnübergang *m. railroad crossing.*
Balance *f. balance, equilibrium.*
balancieren *to balance.*
BALD *soon, shortly.*
  bald..., bald... *sometimes... sometimes...*
  bald darauf *soon after.*
Balkon *m. balcony.*
Ball *m. ball, dance.*
Ballett *n. ballet.*
Ballon *m. balloon.*
Band *n. ribbon.*
Bande *f. band, gang.*
bändigen *to tame, to break.*
Bandmass *n. tape measure.*
BANK *f. 1. bench, seat.*
  durch die Bank *all, without exception.*
  auf die lange Bank schieben *to postpone, delay.*
  2. bank.
  Geld auf der Bank haben *to have money in the bank.*

Bankanweisung *f. check.*
Bankbeamte *m. bank clerk.*
BAR *bare, naked, devoid of.*
  barfuss *barefoot.*
Bär *m. bear.*
Bargeld *n. cash.*
  bar zahlen *to pay cash.*
barmherzig *merciful.*
Barmherzigkeit *f. mercy.*
Baron *m. (-in, f.) Baron (ess).*
Bart *m. beard, whiskers.*
BAU *m. building, construction, edifice, frame.*
Bauch *m. belly, stomach.*
BAUEN *to build, construct, cultivate.*
  Luftschlösser bauen *to build castles in the air.*
Bauer *m. peasant.*
Bauerhof *m. farm.*
Bauernvolk *n. countryfolk.*
baufällig *dilapidated.*
BAUM *m. tree, pole.*
Baumschule *f. nursery (trees).*
Baumwolle *f. cotton.*
Baustein *m. brick.*
beabsichtigen *to intend.*
beachten *to observe, notice.*
Beachtung *f. consideration, attention.*
beachtenswert *noteworthy.*
Beamte *m. official, civil servant.*
  Zollbeamte *m. customs officer.*
beängstigen *to alarm.*
beanspruchen *to claim, demand.*
beanstanden *to object, reject.*
beantworten *to answer, reply.*
beaufsichtigen *to supervise.*
beben *to tremble.*

  vor Angst beben *to tremble with fear.*
Becher *m. cup, goblet, dice box.*
bedacht *thoughtful, considerate.*
bedanken *to thank.*
Bedarf *m. need, requirement.*
bedauerlich *deplorable, regrettable.*
bedecken *to cover.*
  Der Himmel ist bedeckt *the sky is overcast.*
bedenken *to think, think over, reflect, ponder.*
  sich eines andern bedenken *to change one's mind.*
bedenklich *doubtful.*
Bedenkzeit *f. time for reflection.*
Bedienung *f. service.*
  emschliesslich der Bedienung *service included.*
bedürfen *to need, require.*
Bedürfnis *n. need, want, necessity.*
beeindrucken *to impress.*
beerdigen *to bury.*

Beerdigung *f. funeral.*
befassen *to occupy.*
> Er befasst sich mit Politik. *He is in politics.*

Befehl *m. order, command.*
befehlen *to order, command.*
befestigen *to fasten, fortify.*
befolgen *to obey.*
befreien *to free, liberate.*
Befreier *m. liberator.*
Befreiung *f. liberation.*
befreunden *to befriend.*
> sich befreunden mit *to become friends with.*

befriedigen *to satisfy, content.*
befriedigend *satisfying.*
Befriedigung *f. satisfaction, gratification.*
Befund *m. state, condition, report.*
befürchten *to apprehend, fear.*
Befürchtung *f. apprehension, fear.*
befürworten *to recommend.*
begabt *gifted.*
begeben *(sich) to set about.*
begegnen *to meet, encounter.*
begeistern *to inspire, fill with enthusiasm.*
begeistert *inspired, enthusiastic.*
Begeisterung *f. inspiration, enthusiasm.*
Beginn *m. beginning.*
BEGINNEN *to begin, start.*
beglaubigen *to attest, certify.*
begleiten *to accompany.*
> nach Hause begleiten *to see (someone) home.*

begründen *to found, to prove.*
Behoglichkeit *f. comfort.*
beholten *to keep, retain, remember.*
> Behalten Sie das Kleingeld! *Keep the change!*

behandeln *to handle, deal with.*
beharren *to persist, remain firm.*
> beharren auf *to insist on.*

behaupten *to maintain, assert, affirm.*
Behelf *m. help, expedient.*
behelfen *(sich) to manage, do without.*
BEI 1. *prep. (dat.) at, by, near, with, because of, in case of.*
> bei der Hand *by hand.*
> Bei Feuer, müssen wir die Feuerwehr rufen. *In case of a fire, we must call the fire department.*
> Bei ihrem Charakter wird sie unglücklich werden. *With (because of) her character, she will be unhappy.*
> bei Tage *by day.*
> bei weitem *by far.*
> beim Metzger *at the butcher's.*

> Er arbeitet bei Licht. *He works by light.*
> Hast du Geld bei dir? *Do you have any money on you?*
> Ich kaufe meine Kleider bei Engels. *buy my clothes at Engels.*
> Meine Schwester wohnt bei mir. *My sister lives with me.*

Beichte *f. confession.*
beichten *to confess.*
BEIDE *both.*
> wir beide *both of us.*
> einer von beiden *one of the two.*
> keiner von beiden *neither of them.*
> beiderseits *on both sides, mutually.*

BEIFALL *m. approval, approbation, applause.*
beifolgend *herewith, enclosed.*
beiläufig *accidental, casual; incidentally.*
beilegen *to add, enclose.*
Beileid *n. sympathy.*
> Beileid bezeigen *to console somebody.*

beim *(bei dem) at, by.*
BEIN *n. leg, bone.*
> sich kein Bein ausreissen *to take it easy.*
> Er ist immer auf den Beinen. *He's always on his feet.*

beinahe *nearly, almost.*
beipflichten *to agree with, assent to.*
beisammen *together.*
beiselte *aside, apart.*
BEISPIEL *n. example.*
> zum Beispiel *for example.*
> Das ist ein schlechtes Beispiel. *This is a bad example.*

beispiellos *unheard of.*
beissen *to bite.*
> Der Hund beisst nicht. *The dog does not bite.*

beistehen *to help, stand by.*
beistimmen *to agree with.*
Beitrag *m. contribution, subscription.*
bejahen *to answer in the affirmative, assent, accept.*
bejammern *to lament.*
bejammernswert *deplorable, lamentable.*
bekämpfen *to combat, fight, struggle.*
BEKANNT *well-known, acquainted.*
> bekannt machen mit *to introduce to.*

Bekannte *m. acquaintance, friend.*
Bekanntmachung *f. publication, announcement, notice.*
bekennen *to confess, admit, profess.*
> sich schuldig bekennen *to plead guilty.*

beklagen *to complain, lament.*
BEKOMMEN *to get, receive, catch,*

agree with.
Das ist nicht mehr zu bekommen. *You can't get that any more.*
Es bekommt mit nicht. *It does not agree with me.*
bekräftigen *to confirm, corroborate.*
belächeln *to smile at.*
belachen *to laugh at.*
belästigen *to molest, trouble.*
beleben *to animate, revive.*
Beleg *m. proof, evidence, illustration.*
BELEGEN *to cover, reserve.*
Ich möchte einen Platz belegen. *I want to reserve a seat.*
belegte Brötchen *sandwiches.*
eine Vorlesung belegen *to enroll for a course.*
belehren *to enlighten, instruct.*
eines Besseren belehren *to correct.*
beleidigen *to offend, insult.*
beliefern *to supply.*
belohnen *to reward.*
Belohnung *f. reward.*
belügen *to lie (falsify).*
belustigen *to amuse, entertain.*
Belustigung *f. amusement.*
bemerkbar *noticeable, perceptible.*
bemerken *to notice, observe, remark.*
bemerkenswert *noticeable, noteworthy.*
Bemerkung *f. remark, observation.*
bemitleiden *to pity, be sorry for.*
bemitleidenswert *deplorable.*
benachrichtigen *to inform, advise.*
Benachrichtigung *f. information, advice.*
benachteiligen *to prejudice.*
Benachteiligung *f. prejudice, injury.*
benehmen *to behave.*
Benimm dich nicht wie ein kleines Kind! *Don't behave like a child!*
beneiden *to envy.*
benommen *confused, dizzy.*
benötigen *to require.*
benutzen *to use, employ, utilize.*
beobachten *to observe, watch.*
heimlich beobachten *to shadow.*
BEQUEM *suitable, convenient, lazy.*
Sei nicht so bequem! *Don't be so lazy!*
bequemen *to condescend, comply, submit.*
Bequemlichkeit *f. convenience.*
beraten *to advise.*
Berater *m. adviser.*
beratschlagen *to deliberate.*
berechnen *to calculate, estimate.*
bereden *to talk over, persuade.*
Beredsamkeit *f. eloquence.*
Bereich *m. & n. reach, range, area, zone.*

BEREIT *ready, prepared.*
bereit halten *to keep ready.*
bereitwillig *willing, ready.*
Bereitwilligkeit *f. willingness.*
bereuen *to repent, regret.*
BERG *m. mountain, hill.*
über alle Berge sein *to be out of the woods.*
Mir standen die Haare zu Berge. *My hair stood on end.*
Bergmann *m. miner.*
berichten *to report.*
berichtigen *to correct, amend, settle (a bill).*
Berichtigung *f. correction, amendment.*
berücksichtigen *to consider.*
Berücksichtigung *f. consideration, regard.*
BERUF *m. profession, occupation.*
beruflich *professional.*
berufstätig *working.*
beruhigen *to quiet, calm.*
Beruhigung *f. reassurance, comfort.*
BERÜHMT *famous, celebrated.*
Berühmtheit *f. fame, celebrity.*
besänftigen *to soften, appease, soothe.*
beschädigen *to damage, injure, harm.*
beschäftigen *to occupy, engage, employ.*
Beschäftigung *f. occupation.*
beschäftigungslos *unemployed, out of work.*
Bescheid *m. answer, information.*
Bescheid geben *to inform.*
Ich habe ihm gehörig Bescheid gesagt. *I told him off.*
bescheiden *modest, moderate.*
Bescheidenheit *f. modesty.*
bescheinen *to shine upon.*
bescheinigen *to certify, attest.*
Bescheinigung *f. certificate, receipt.*
beschleunigen *to hasten, accelerate.*
beschränken *to limit, confine, restrict.*
Beschränkrung *f. limitation, restriction.*
beschreiben *to write upon, describe.*
Beschreibung *f. description.*
beschuldigen *to accuse.*
Beschuldigung *f. accusation.*
Beschwerde *f. hardship, trouble, complaint.*
beschweren *(sich) to complain.*
Beschwerdebrüro *n. complaint department.*
beschwichtigen *to calm, pacify, appease.*
Besen *m. broom.*
besetzen *to trim, occupy, set.*
Es ist alles besetzt! *All seats are occupied.*

Besetzt! *Occupied! Busy!*
Besetzung *f. occupation, cast.*
   Die Besetzung ist aussergewöhnlich
   gut. *The cast is outstanding.*
besichtigen *to view, inspect, visit.*
Besichtigung *f. view, inspection.*
besiegen *to conquer, beat, defeat.*
besinnen *to consider, reflect.*
   sich eines Besseren besinnen *to think*
   better of.
besinnlich *contemplative, thoughtful.*
Besitz *m. possession, property, estate.*
besorgen *to take care of, fetch,*
   procure, provide.
Besorgnis *f. fear, alarm.*
Besorgung *f. care, management.*
   Besorgungen machen *to go shopping.*
besprechen *to discuss, talk over,*
   criticize, review.
BESSER *better.*
   umso besser *so much the better.*
bessern *to improve, recover.*
   sich bessern *to improve oneself.*
Besserung *f. recovery, improvement.*
   Gute Besserung! *I hope you will get*
   well soon!
best(er-es) *best.*
beständig *constant, permanent, steady;*
   constantly, all the time.
Beständigkeit *f. constancy, stability.*
bestätigen *to confirm, ratify.*
bestechen *to bribe, corrupt.*
bestechlich *corruptible.*
Bestechung *f. corruption.*
Besteck *n. one setting of silver.*
bestellen *to arrange, order, tell,*
   cultivate.
   Waren bestellen *to order goods.*
   zu sich bestellen *to send for.*
BESTIMMEN *to decide, fix, intend,*
   define, induce.
   bestimmen über *to dispose of.*
   bestimmt! *agreed!*
Bestimmtheit *f. certainty, precision.*
bestrafen *to punish.*
Bestrafung *f. punishment.*
BESUCH *m. visit, company, attendance.*
BESUCHEN *to visit, attend.*
Besucher *m. visitor, spectator,*
   audience.
beteiligen *to give a share, take part,*
   take an interest.
   beteiligt sein *to participate.*
Beteiligung *f. share, participation.*
betonen *to stress, accent, emphasize.*
Betonung *f. stress, emphasis.*
beträchtlich *considerable.*
betreffen *to concern.*
   was mich betrifft *so far as I am*

   concerned.
betreten *to tread on.*
   Betreten des Rasens verboten! *Keep*
   off the grass!
Betrieb *m. management, plant, factory.*
   in Betrieb sein *to be working.*
   ausser Betrieb *not working, closed*
   in Betrieb setzen *to set in motion.*
betrinken *to get drunk.*
betrüben *to grieve, distress.*
Betrug *m. deception, fraud, swindle.*
betrügen *to deceive, defraud, trick.*
BETT *n. bed.*
   das Bett hüten *to be confined in bed.*
   früh zu Bett gehen *to go to bed early.*
Bettdecke *f. blanket, bedspread.*
bettein *to beg.*
Bettlaken *n. sheet.*
Bettler *m. beggar.*
Bettwäsche *f. bed linen.*
beugen *to bend, bow.*
beunruhigen *to disturb, alarm, upset.*
beurlauben *to grant leave, take leave.*
   beurlaubt *absent on leave.*
Beutel *m. bag, purse.*
bevollmächtigen *to empower,*
   authorize.
BEVOR *before.*
bewachen *to watch over.*
bewältigen *to master.*
bewegen *to move, stir.*
Beweggrund *m. motive.*
   Was war der Beweggrund des
   Verbrechens? *What was the motive*
   of the crime?
beweglich *movable, mobile, quick,*
   lively.
BEWEGUNG *f. movement, agitation,*
   motion.
   Einer politischen Bewegung angehören
   to belong to a political party.
Beweis *m. proof, evidence.*
beweisen *to prove, demonstrate.*
Beweisführung *f. demonstration.*
bewerben *to apply for, compete.*
Bewerber *m. applicant, candidate.*
Bewerbung *f. application, courtship.*
bewilligen *to consent, concede.*
bewusst *conscious.*
   sich einer Sache bewusst sein *to be*
   conscious or aware of something.
bewusstlos *unconscious.*
BEZAHLEN *to pay.*
sich bezahlt machen *to pay for itself*
   (be lucrative).
bezaubernd *charming.*
bezichtigen *to charge with.*
Bezug *m. covering, cover, case.*
   in Bezug auf *in regard to.*

Bezug nehmen auf *to refer to.*
unter Bezugnahme auf *with reference to.*
Bibel *f. Bible.*
Bibliothek *f. library.*
Bibliothekar *m. librarian.*
Biene *f. bee.*
Bier *n. beer.*
BIETEN *to offer.*
sich alles bieten lassen *to put up with everything.*
BILD *n. image, picture, illustration, portrait, likeness.*
BILDEN *to form, shape, educate.*
Der Präsident hat ein neues Kabinett gebildet. *The president has formed a new cabinet.*
die bildenden Künste *fine arts.*
Bildseite *f. face, head (coin).*
Bildung *f. formation, constitution.*
billig *just, reasonable, fair, moderate.*
binden *to bind, tie.*
BIS *until, as far as, about.*
zwei bis drei Pfund. *About two or three pounds.*
bis an *(acc.) up to.*
bis in alle Ewigkeit *till the end of time.*
bis auf *(acc.) except for.*
Mir gefällt der Film bis auf das Ende. *like the film except for the ending.*
alle bis auf einen *all except one.*
bis auf weiteres *until further notice.*
bis zu *(dat.) (down) to.*
von dem Kopf bis zu den Füssen *from head to foot.*
bis jetzt *so far.*
bisher *till now.*
bisweilen *sometimes.*
Bischof *m. bishop.*
bisschen *a bit, a little, a while.*
Das ist ein bisschen stark. *That's going a bit too far.*
Er kam ein bisschen spät. *He came a little late.*
Bissen *m. bite, mouthful.*
Bitte *f. request, prayer.*
BITTE *please.*
bitte, bitte schön, bitte sehr. *(In response to a request: Here you are. In response to thanks: You are welcome; don't mention it.)*
Wie, bitte? *I beg your pardon?*
BITTEN *to ask, beg, implore.*
Ich bitte um Entschuldigung. *I beg your pardon, I am sorry.*
bitter *bitter.*
blamieren *to expose to ridicule.*
sich blamieren *to make a fool of oneself.*

BLATT *n. leaf, petal, blade, sheet.*
sich kein Blatt vor den Mund nehmen *to speak plainly.*
Blattern *f. smallpox.*
blättern *to leaf through the pages of a book.*
Blatternimpfung *f. smallpox vaccination.*
BLAU *blue.*
Blech *n. tin.*
Blei *n. lead.*
BLEIBEN *to stay, remain, keep, last.*
bleiben lassen *to leave alone.*
Das bleibt unter uns. *That's between you and me.*
Es bleibt dabei *Agreed.*
sich gleich bleiben *to remain the same.*
stehen bleiben *to stop, stand still.*
bleibend *permanent, lasting.*
bleich *pale, faded, faint.*
bleichen *to bleach.*
Bleistift *m. pencil.*
blenden *to blind, dazzle.*
BLICK *m. glance, look, gaze.*
auf den ersten Blick *at first sight.*
Er warf ihm einen bösen Blick zu. *He gave him a dirty look.*
blind *blind, false.*
ein blinder Alarm *a false alarm.*
Blindheit *f. blindness.*
blinken *to glitter, glimpse, twinkle, signal.*
Blitz *m. lightening, flash.*
blitzen *to lighten, flash, sparkle.*
Block *m. block, log, pad, stocks.*
blond *blond, fair.*
BLOSS *bare, naked, uncovered; merely, only.*
Ich tue es bloss Ihnen zu gefallen. *am only doing it to please you.*
blühen *to bloom.*
BLUME *f. flower.*
Lasst Blumen sprechen! *Say it with flowers!*
Blumenkohl *m. cauliflower.*
Bluse *f. blouse.*
BLUT *n. blood, race, parentage.*
blutarm *anemic.*
Blutdruck *m. blood pressure.*
bluten *to bleed.*
Blutprobe *f. blood-test.*
Blutvergiftung *f. blood-poisoning.*
Boden *m. floor, ground, soil, attic.*
Bogen *m. bow, curve, arch.*
BOHNE *f. bean.*
grüne Bohnen *string beans.*
weisse Bohnen *dried beans.*
Bombardement *n. bombardment.*

bombardieren to bomb.
Bombe f. bomb.
  Atombombe f. atomic bomb.
Bonbon m. & n. candy.
BOOT n. boat.
  Bootsfahrt f. boatride.
Börse f. purse, stock exchange.
Börsenmakler m. stockbroker.
bösartig ill-natured, wicked, malicious.
BÖSE bad, angry, evil.
boshaft malicious, mischievous.
Bote m. messenger.
Botschaft f. news.
Botschafter m. ambassador.
boxen to box.
Brand m. burning, fire, conflagration.
  in Brand geraten to catch fire.
Brandschaden m. damage by fire.
BRATEN m. roast.
  Brathuhn n. roast chicken.
  Bratkartoffeln pl. fried potatoes.
  Bratapfel m. baked apple.
BRATEN to roast, grill, fry.
Brauch m. usage, use, custom.
brauchbar useful, practicable.
BRAUCHEN to use, employ, need.
  Wie lange werden Sie noch brauchen?
    How much more time will it take you?
Brauhaus n. brewery, tavern.
BRAUN brown.
Brause f. shower, douche, spray.
brausen to storm, rage, roar, rush.
  sich abbrausen to take a shower.
Braut. f. fiancee.
  Brautführer m. best man.
  Brautjungfet f. bridesmaid.
  Brautkleid n. wedding dress.
  Brautpaar n. engaged couple.
Bräutigam m. bridegroom.
brav good, honest, excellent.
BRECHEN to break, pick.
  Er spricht ein gebrochenes Deutsch.
    He speaks broken German.
BREIT broad, wide, flat.
  weit und breit high and low.
Breite f. breadth, width, latitude.
Bremse f. brake.
bremsen to put the brakes on.
BRENNEN to burn, brand, bake, roast.
  darauf brennen to be anxious.
  Es brennt in der Stadt. There is a fire
    in town.
Brett n. board, plank, shelf, stage.
  am schwarzen Brett on the board.
BRIEF n. letter.
Briefkasten m. letter-box.
Briefmappe f. attaché case.
Briefmarke f. stamp.
Briefpapier n. stationery.

Brieftasche f. wallet, pocket-book.
Briefträger m. mailman.
Briefumschlag m. envelope.
Brille f. glasses.
BRINGEN to bring, fetch, carry, put,
  take.
  dazu bringen to induce to.
  Er hat sich ums Leben gebracht. He's
    committed suicide.
  es zu etwas bringen to achieve
    something.
  Ich werde das in Ordnung bringen. I'll
    straighten that out.
  um etwas bringen to deprive of.
britisch British.
BROT n. bread.
  Brötchen roll.
  sein Brot verdienen to earn one's
    living.
Brötchen n. roll.
Bruch m. break, fracture, fraction.
Bruchteil m. fraction.
BRÜCKE f. bridge (also dental).
  Er hat alle Brücken hinter sich
    abgebrochen. He has burnt his
    bridges behind him.
BRUDER m. brother.
  Bruderschaft f. fraternity.
Brunnen m. spring, well, fountain.
Brust f. breast, chest, bosom.
Bube m. boy, jack of cards.
BUCH n. book.
Buchdeckel m. cover, binding.
Buchführung f. bookkeeping.
Buchhaltung f. bookkeeping.
Buchhändler m. bookseller.
Buchhandlung f. bookshop.
Büchse f. can.
Büchsenöffner m. can opener.
Buchstabe m. letter, character.
Buchumschlag m. jacket (book).
Bügelbrett n. ironing board.
Bügeleisen n. iron (for pressing).
bügeln to press.
Bühne f. stage, platform.
Bund m. league, confederation.
Bündel m. bundle.
bunt colored, lively, gay.
  Das ist mir zu bunt. I'm fed up with it.
Burg f. castle, citadel.
Bürge f. bail.
bürgen to guarantee, vouch for.
Bürger m. citizen, townsman.
Bürgerkrieg m. civil war.
Bürgermeister m. mayor.
Bürgersteig m. pavement.
BÜRO n. office.
Bütobote m. office boy.
bürokratisch bureaucratic.

Bursch *m. youth, lad, fellow.*
Burschenschaft *f. students'
  association.*
Bürste *f. brush.*
bürsten *to brush.*
Busch *m. bush.*
Busse *f. penitence, repentance.*
  Busse tun *to do penance.*
büssen *to suffer for, expiate.*
Büste *f. bust.*
Büstenhalter *m. brassiere.*
BUTTER *f. butter.*
Butterbrot *n. slice of bread and butter.*

C

Café *n. café.*
Cello *n. cello.*
Cellist *m. cellist.*
Champagner *m. champagne.*
Charakter *m. character, disposition.*
charakteristisch *characteristic.*
Chauffeur *m. chauffeur.*
Chef *m. head, boss, chief.*
Chemie *f. chemistry.*
chemisch *chemical.*
Chinese *m. Chinese (person).*
chinesisch *Chinese.*
Chirurg *m. surgeon.*
Chor *m. choir, chorus.*
Choral *m. chorale.*
Chorgesang *m. choir singing.*
Choristin *f. chorus-girl.*
Chorknabe *m. choir-boy.*
Christ *m. Christian.*
Christenheit *f. Christendom.*
Christentum *f. Christianity.*
Chronik *f. chronicle.*
Cousin *m. (Vetter m.) cousin (man).*
Cousine *f. (Kusine f.) cousin (woman).*
Creme *m. cream (cosmetic).*

D

DA 1. *adv. there, here.*
  2. *conj. when, because, as, since.*
  da sein *to be present.*
  da stehen *to stand near, stand by.*
DABEI *near, near by, close to,
  moreover.*
  dabei bleibt es *there the matter ends.*
dableiben *to stay, remain.*
Dach *n. roof.*

unter Dach und Fach *safe.*
Dachkammer *f. attic.*
DADURCH *through it, by it, thereby.*
  dadurch dass *through the fact that.*
  Er ist dadurch berühmt geworden.
    That made him famous.
DAFÜR *for that, for it, instead of it.*
  dafür sein *to be in favor of.*
  Ich kann nichts dafür. *It is not my
    fault.*
DAGEGEN 1. *adv. against it.*
  nichts dagegen haben *to have no
    objection.*
  2. *conj. on the other hand.*
DAHEIM *at home.*
DAHER *from there.*
  Ich komme gerade daher. *I am just
    coming from there.*
DAHIN *to there.*
  bis dahin *by then.*
  Ich gehe sofort dahin. *I am going there
    right now.*
dahinten *behind.*
damalig *then, of that time.*
Dame *f. lady, queen (cards), checkers.*
  eine Partie Dame spielen *to play a
    game of checkers.*
DAMIT 1. *adv. with it, by it.*
  Was wollte er damit sagen? *What
    does he mean by that?*
  2. *conj. so that, in order to.*
  Ich sage es noch einmal damit Sie es
    nicht vergessen. *I say it once more
    so that you won't forget it.*
  damit nicht *for fear that.*
Dämmerlicht *n. dusk.*
Dämmerung *f. twilight, dawn.*
Dampf *m. vapor, steam.*
Dampfbad *n. steam bath.*
dämpfen *to damp, tone down,
  extinguish, steam (cooking).*
  Dämpfer *m. steamer.*
DANACH *afterwards, after that,
  thereafter.*
  Es sieht danach aus. *It looks like it.*
daneben 1. *adv. near it, next to it, close
  by.* 2. *conj. besides, moreover, at the
  same time, also.*

DANK *m. thanks, gratitude, reward.*
  Gott sei Dank! *Thank God!*
  zum Dank *as a reward.*
DANKBAR *grateful, thankful.*
DANKE! *thank you!*
  Danke schön! *Thank you very much!*
DANKEN *to thank.*
  Nichts zu danken. *Not at all, don't
    mention it.*
DANN *then, thereupon.*
  dann und wann *now and then.*

DARAN (dran) *at it, of that, in it, in that.*
Ich glaube daran. *I believe in it.*
nahe daran sein *to be near, on the point of.*
Wer ist dran? *Whose turn is it?*

DARAUF (drauf) *on, upon it, after that, thereupon.*
darauf aus sein *to be out to, aim at.*
Es kommt darauf an. *It all depends.*
Ich lege keinen Wert darauf. *I'm not interested in it.*

DARAUS (draus) *of it, of that, from this, from that.*
Daraus ist nichts geworden. *Nothing came of it.*

darbieten *to offer, present.*

Darbietung *f. entertainment, performance.*

DAREIN (drein) *into it, therein.*

DARIN (drin) *in it, in that.*
Es ist nichts darin. *There is nothing to it.*

darlegen *to explain.*

Darlegung *f. explanation, exposition.*

Darlehen *n. loan.*

DARÜBER (drüber) 1. *adv. over it, above it, about it.*
Darüber besteht kein Zweifel. *There is no doubt about that.*
darüber hinaus *beyond that.*
2. *conj. meanwhile.*

DARUM (drum) *round it, for it, about it.*
Ich kann mich nicht darum kümmern. *I can't take care of that.*

DARUNTER (drunter) *under it, underneath, among them, by that.*
Was verstehen Sie darunter? *What do you mean by that?*

DAS 1. *neuter article (nom. and acc.). the.*
2. *demons. pron. that.*
3. *rel. pron. which, that.*
das jenige das *the one which.*
dasselbe *the same.*

dasein *to exist, be present.*

Dasein *n. existence, life.*
Kämpf für das Dasein *struggle for life.*

DASS *conj. that.*
dass doch *if only.*

Datum *n. date.*

Dauer *f. length, duration.*
auf die Dauer *for long.*

DAUERN *to last, continue.*
lange dauern *to take a long time.*

Dauerwelle *f. permanent wave.*

Daumen *m. thumb.*

DAVON *for it, from this, from that, of it, of that.*
Was halten Sie davon? *What do you think of it?*

Geben Sie mir ein Paar davon. *Give me a pair of them.*
Das hängt davon ab. *It depends.*

DAVOR *in front of it, of it, of that.*
Sie stehen direkt davor. *They stand right in front of it.*

DAZU *to it, for it, for that purpose.*
Es ist schon zu spät dazu. *It is already too late for that.*
dazu gehören *to belong to it.*
dazu tun *to add to.*

dazwischen *in between.*

Decke *f. cover, blanket.*

Deckel *m. cover, lid.*

DECKEN *to protect, cover, guard, secure.*

Deckung *f. cover, shelter, protection.*
in Deckung gehen *to take cover.*

Defekt *m. defect, deficiency.*

Degen *m. sword.*

DEIN *(poss. adj. fam. form.) your.*

DEIN *(er, e, es) (poss. pron. fam. form.) yours.*

DEM *dat, sing of der and das to the, to this, to whom, to which.*
demnach *then.*
demnächst *soon, shortly.*
demzufolge *accordingly.*
Wie dem auch sei *be that as it may.*

Demokrat *m. democrat.*

Demokratie *f. democracy.*

Demut *f. humility.*

demütig *humble.*

demütigen *to humiliate.*

Demütigung *f. humiliation.*

DEN *acc. sing. of der; dat. pl. of die. the, this, to them, whom, which.*

DENEN *dat. pl. of die (rel. pron.) to whom, to which.*

DENKEN *to think, intend, mean.*
Was denken Sie zu tun? *What do you intend to do?*
denken an *to remember, think of.*
sich denken *to imagine.*
Das kann ich mir schon denken. *I can well imagine.*

Denker *m. thinker.*

DENN *for, because, then.*
es sei denn, dass *unless.*

dennoch *nevertheless.*

deponieren *to deposit.*

DER 1. *masc. article (nom.) the; (fem. (gen. & dat.) of the, to the; pl. (gen.) of the.*
2. *demons. pron. this.*
3. *rel. pron. which, who, that.*
derjenige der *the one who, he who.*
derselbe *the same.*

DEREN *gen. fem. and pl. of die, (rel. pron.) whose.*

DES *gen. sing. of der and das of the.*

DESHALB *therefore, for that reason.*

DESSEN *gen. sing. of der and das pron. whose.*

Detektiv *m. detective.*

deuten *to point out, explain, interpret.*

deutlich *distinct, clear; distinctly, clearly.*

Deutlichkeit *f. distinctness, clearness.*

DEUTSCH *German.*

DEUTSCHE *m. & f. German (person).*

DEUTSCHLAND *n. Germany.*

Deutung *f. interpretation, explanation.*

Devise *f. foreign bill, motto.*

DEZEMBER *m. December.*

Dialekt *m. dialect.*

Diamant *m. diamond.*

Diät *f. diet.*
   Diät leben *to diet.*

DICH *acc. of du. (fam. form) you.*

DICHT *thick, dense, tight, close.*

dichten *to compose, write poetry, invent.*

Dichter *m. poet.*

Dichtung *f. poetry, fiction.*

DICK *thick, stout, fat.*
   Er ist dick geworden. *He got fat.*

Dickkopf *m. blockhead.*

DIE 1. *fem. article (nom. and acc.), the. pl. article (noun. and acc.). the.*
   2. *demons. pron. this.*
   3. *rel. pron. who, which, that.*
   diejenige die *she who, the one which.*
   dieselbe *the same.*

DIEB *m. thief, burglar.*
   Halten Sie den Dieb! *Stop the thief!*

DIENEN *to serve.*
   Womit kann ich dienen? *Can I help you?*

Diener *m. servant.*

Dienerin *f. maid.*

dienlich *serviceable.*

Dienst *m. service, duty, situation, employment.*
   ausser Dienst *off duty.*
   zu Diensten stehen *to be at a person's disposal.*

DIENSTAG *m. Tuesday.*

Dienstbutenzimmer *n. servant's room.*

diensteifrig *zealous.*

Dienstmädchen *n. maid.*

Dienstelle *f. headquarters.*

DIES(er,-e,-es) *this, that.*

DIESMAL *this time.*

DIESSEITS *(gen.) on this side.*

Diktat *n. dictation, treaty.*

DING *n. thing, object.*
   guter Dinge sein *to be in high spirits.*
   vor allen Dingen *first of all.*

Diplom *n. diploma, certificate.*

Diplomatie *f. diplomacy.*

diplomatisch *diplomatic.*

DIR *dat. of du (fam. form) you, to you.*

direkt *direct*

Direktor *m. director.*

Dirigent *m. conductor.*

dirigieren *to conduct, direct.*

diskret *discreet, tactful.*

Diskretion *f. discretion.*

diskutieren *to discuss.*

Distanz *f. distance.*

DOCH *however, anyway, nevertheless, but, still, yet; surely, of course, yes (in answer to a negative question); indicates a well-known fact.*
   Willst du nicht kommen? Doch. *Won't you come? Of course.*
   Habe ich doch gewusst, dass er schwer krank war. *I knew (very well) he was very ill.*
   Ich werde doch gehen. *I will go anyhow.*
   Ja doch! *of course.*
   Sie werden doch zugeben, dass er recht hatte. *But you will admit he was right.*
   Und doch ist es nicht so traurig, wie Sie denken. *And still it is not so sad as you think.*

DOKTOR *m. doctor.*
   den Doktor machen *to take the degree of doctor.*

Doktorarbeit *f. thesis for doctorate.*

Dokument *n. document.*

dokumentieren *to prove.*

Dolch *m. dagger.*

dolmetschen *to interpret.*

Dolmetscher *m. interpreter.*

Dom *m. cathedral.*

Donner *m. thunder.*
   vom Donner gerührt *thunderstruck.*

donnern *to thunder.*

Donnerschlag *m. thunderbolt.*

DONNERSTAG *m. Thursday.*

Donnerwetter *n. thunderstorm.*
   Donnerwetter! *Good heavens!*

doppeldeutig *ambiguous.*

Doppelpunkt *m. colon.*

doppelt *double.*
   Doppelbett, *n. double bed.*
   Doppelzimmer, *n. room with twin beds.*

DORF *n. village.*

Dorn *m. thorn.*

DORT *there, yonder.*
   dorther *from there.*
   dorthin *that way, over there.*

Dose *f. box, can, dose, amount.*

DRAHT *m. wire, cable, line.*

Drängen *to push, press, hurry, urge.*

Nicht drängen! *Do not push!*

draussen *outside, outdoors, abroad.*

drehen *to turn, rotate, revolve.*

DREI *three.*

Dreieck *n. triangle.*

DREISSIG *thirty.*

DREISSIGSTE *thirtieth.*

DREIZEHN *thirteen.*

DREIZEHNTE *thirteenth.*

dringen *to enter, get in, penetrate.*

  dringen auf *to insist on.*

dringend *urgent.*

DRITTE *third.*

Droge *f. drug.*

Drogerie *f. chemist's shop.*

drüben *over there, yonder.*

Druck *m. pressure, compression.*

  in Druck gehen *to go to press.*

drucken *to print.*

Druckknopf *m. push button.*

Drukfehler *m. misprint.*

Dschungel *f. jungle.*

DU *pers. pron. fam. form. you.*

  auf du und du stehen *to be on intimate terms.*

Duft *m. scent, smell, fragrance.*

DUFTEN *to smell sweet, be fragrant.*

duftig *sweet-smelling, fragrant.*

dulden *to endure, bear, suffer.*

dumm *stupid, dull, ignorant.*

  Sei nicht so dumm! *Don't be so stupid!*

  Es wurde mir zu dumm. *I got sick and tired of it.*

Dummheit *f. stupidity, blunder.*

Dummkopf *m. stupid fellow, dunce.*

düngen *to fertilize.*

Dünger *m. fertilizer, manure.*

dunkel *dark, gloomy, vaguely.*

  Ich erinnere mich dunkel . . . *I vaguely remember . . .*

Dunkelheit *f. darkness, obscurity.*

dunkeln *to get dark.*

dünn *thin, weak, rare.*

DURCH 1. *prep. (acc.) through, across, by, by means of, because of.*

  Durch den Krieg wurden viele Städte. *Many cities were destroyed because of the war.*

  Er bestand die Prüfung durch viel Arbeit. *He passed the examination by working hard. (through much work.)*

  Er schickt es durch die Post. *He sends it by post.*

  Ich ging durch den Wald. *I walked through the forest.*

  die ganze Zeit durch *all the time.*

  durch and durch *through and through.*

2. *prefix,*

  a) *inseparable. through, across, around.*

  Die Milchstrasse durchzieht den Himmel. *The milky way goes across the sky.*

  b) *separable, implies the idea of accomplishment.*

  Ich lese das Buch durch. *I read the book to the end.*

durcharbeiten *to work through, study thoroughly.*

durchaus *thoroughly, absolutely.*

  durchaus nicht *not at all, not in the least.*

durcheinander *confusedly, in disorder.*

durchfahren *to drive through.*

Durchfahrt *f. thoroughfare, passage.*

  Keine Durchfahrt! *No thoroughfare!*

durchfechten *to fight out.*

durchfinden *to find one's way through.*

durchführbar *to carry out, accomplish, execute.*

Durchfuhrung *f. accomplishment, execution.*

Durchführung *f. accomplishment, execution, performance.*

Durchgang *m. passageway.*

  Kein Durchgang! *No trespassing!*

durchgehen *to go through, pass through, run away.*

durchhalten *to hold out, carry through.*

durchmachen *to go through, suffer.*

  Sie haben viel durchgemacht. *They have gone through a lot.*

Durchmesser *m. diameter.*

durchnehmen *to work through, go over.*

Durchreise *f. journey through, passing through, transit.*

durchreisen *to travel through, cross.*

Durchreisevisum *n. transit visa.*

durchschauen *to look through.*

Durchschlag *m. collander, strainer, carbon copy.*

durchschlagend *powerful.*

Durchschlagpapier *n. carbon paper.*

durchschneiden *to cut through.*

durchsetzen *to achieve.*

durchsuchen *to search through.*

Durchsuchung *f. search, police raid.*

durchtrieben *cunning, sly, artful.*

Durchzug *m. march through, passage through.*

DÜRFEN *to be allowed to, be permitted.*

  Darf ich, bitte? *May I, please?*

  Darf ich um den nächsten Tanz bitten? *May I have the next dance?*

  Darf man hier rauchen? *Is smoking allowed here?*

dürftig *poor, needy, indigent.*

DÜRR *dry, parched, dried, lean, skinny.*

dürres Holz *dry wood.*
DÜRRE *f. dryness, drought.*
Durst *m. thirst.*
Das macht Durst. *That makes (one) thirsty.*
dürsten *to be thirsty, long for, crave.*
durstig *thirsty.*
Dusche *f. shower-bath.*
duschen *(sich) to take a shower.*
Dutzend *n. dozen.*
dutzendmal *dozens of times.*

E

Ebbe *f. ebb, low tide.*
die Ebbe und die Flut *the ebb and flow.*
EBEN *even, flat, smooth.*
eben erst *just now.*
eben deshalb *for that very reason.*
ebenfalls *likewise, too, also.*
ebenmässig *symmetrical, proportional.*
ebenso *just as, just so, quite as.*
zu ebener Erde *on the ground floor.*
Ebene *f. plain.*
ebnen *to level, smooth.*
Echo *n. echo.*
ECHT *genuine, true, real, legitimate.*
Echtheit *f. legitimacy.*
Ecke *f. corner, angle.*
eckig *triangular, cornered.*
edel *noble, well-born, generous.*
Efeu *n. ivy.*
Effekt *m. effect, stocks.*
Effekthascherei *f. showing off.*
effektvoll *effective.*
Egoismus *m. egoism.*
Egoist *m. egoist.*
egoistisch *egoistic.*
egozentrisch *egocentric.*
EHE *before, until.*
ehemals *formerly.*
eher *sooner, rather.*
Ehe *f. matrimony, marriage.*
Ehefrau *f. wife, spouse.*
Ehegatte *m. husband.*
Ehepaar *n. married couple.*
ehelich *matrimonial, conjugal.*
Ehescheidung *f. divorce.*
Ehescheidungsklage *f. divorce suit.*
Eheschliessung *f. marriage.*
EHRE *f. honor, reputation, respect.*
Meine Ehre steht auf dem Spiel. *My honor is at stake.*
ehren *to honor.*
ehrenamtlich *honorary.*

Ehrenbezeigung *f. mark of respect.*
Ehrenwort *n. word of honor.*
ehrerbietig *respectful.*
Ehrerbietung *f. deference, respect.*
Ehrfurcht *f. respect, awe, reverence.*
Ehrgefühl *n. sense of honor, self-respect.*
Ehrgeiz *m. ambition.*
ehrgeizig *ambitious.*
Ehrlichkeit *f. honesty.*
Ehrlosigkeit *f. dishonesty, infamy.*
Ei *n. (pl. Eier) egg.*
Eigelb *n. egg yolk.*
Eiweiss *n. egg white.*
Rührei *scrambled eggs.*
Spiegeleier *fried eggs.*
Weiche Eier *soft-boiled eggs.*
Eiche *f. oak.*
Eichhörnchen *n. squirrel.*
Eifer *m. zeal, ardor.*
Eifersucht *f. jealousy.*
eifersüchtig *jealous.*
eifrig *eager, keen, zealous.*
EIGEN *own, proper, particular, special, choosy.*
Er ist sehr eigen im Essen. *He is very fussy about his food.*
eigenartig *odd, peculiar, strange, queer.*
eigensinnig *stubborn, obstinate.*
eigentlich *real, actual; actually, really, exactly, just, as a matter of fact, indeed.*
Was heisst das eigentlich? *What does it actually mean?*
Eigentum *n. property.*
eigentümlich *queer, odd, peculiar.*
eignen *(sich) to be suited, qualified.*
EILE *f. hurry, haste, speed.*
Es hat keine Eile. *There's no hurry about it.*
Eile mit Weile. *Haste makes waste.*
EILEN *(sich) to hurry.*
Das eilt sehr. *This is very urgent.*
Das eilt nicht. *There's no hurry.*
eilig *fast, hasty.*
es eilig haben *to be in a hurry.*
Eilzug *m. fast train, express.*
EIN, eine, ein *1. indefinite article. a, an.*
2. number. one.
3. pron. one.
Eines Tages *some day.*
ein für allemal *once for all.*
4. separable prefix (implies the idea of entrance or reduction in volume).
Die Lehrerin trat in das Schulzimmer ein. *The teacher (fem.) entered the classroom.*
Läuft dieser Stoff ein? *Does this material shrink?*

EINANDER *each other, one another.*
Wir haben einander jahrelang nicht
gesehen. *We have not seen each
other for years.*

einarbeiten *to get used to, familiarize
with.*

einatmen *to inhale.*

Einbahnstrasse *f. one-way street.*

einbiegen *to turn into.*
Biegen Sie in diese Strasse ein. *Turn
into this street.*

einbilden *to imagine, fancy, think,
believe.*

Einbildung *f. imagination, conceit,
presumption.*

einbrechen *to break open, through.*
Heute Nacht ist ein Deibe bei ihm
eingebrochen. *Last night a thief
broke into his house.*

Einbrecher *m. burglar.*

Einbruch *m. house-breaking, burglary.*

EINDRUCK *m. impression.*
Er tut es bloss, um Eindruck zu
machen. *He does it only to show off.*

EINFACH *simple, plain, single; simply,
plainly, elementary.*
einfache (Fahrt) *one-way (ticket).*

Einfall *m. falling down, collapse, idea,
whim.*
Wie kommen Sie auf den Einfall?
What gave you the idea?

einfältig *simple.*

Einfluss *m. influence.*

einflussreich *influential.*

Einfuhr *f. importation, import.*

einführen *to introduce, import,
inaugurate.*

Einführung *f. importation.*

Einfuhrzoll *m. import duty.*

Eingabe *f. petition, memorial.*

EINGANG *m. entrance.*
Kein Eingang. *No entrance.*
Verbotener Eingang! *Keep out!*

eingeben *to give, administer, inspire.*

eingebildet *imaginary.*

Eingebung *f. inspiration.*

Eingemachte *n. preserves, jam.*

eingestehen *to admit, confess.*

eingewöhnen *to accustom.*

Einhalt *m. stop.*
Einhalt gebieten *to put a stop to.*

einhalten *to observe, follow, keep to,
meet.*
Wird er den Termin einhalten? *Will he
meet the deadline?*

Einhaltung *f. observance.*

Einheit *f. unity, union, unit.*

einheitlich *uniform.*

einholen *to bring in, collect, gather,*
make up.
einholen gehen *to go shopping.*

einig *in agreement, united, unanimous.*

einigemal *several times.*

einigen *to come to terms, unite, unify.*

Einig (-er, -e, -es) *some, any, a few.*

einigermassen *to some extent,
somewhat.*

Einigkeit *f. harmony.*

Einigung *f. agreement.*

einjagen *to alarm, frighten.*

EINKAUF *m. purchase, buying.*

EINKAUFEN *to buy, purchase, shop.*
Einkaufspreis, *m. cost price.*

Einkommen *n. income.*

Einkommensteuer *f. income tax.*

einladen *to invite.*

EINLADUNG *f. invitation.*

Einlass *m. entrance, admission.*

einlassen *to admit, let in.*

einleben *to settle down, familiarize
oneself.*

einleiten *to begin, initiate, introduce,
institute.*

Einleitung *f. introduction.*

einmachen *to preserve.*

Einmachglas *n. preserves jar.*

EINMAL *once, formerly.*
auf einmal *all at once.*
Es war einmal . . . *Once upon a time
there was . . .*
noch einmal *once more.*

einmengen *to meddle with, interfere.*

einmütig *unanimous.*

Einnahme *f. occupation, capture,
conquest.*

einnehmen *to engage, occupy, receive,
collect, captivate.*

einnehmend *captivating.*

einordnen *to arrange, classify, file.*

einpacken *to wrap up.*

einpflanzen *to plant, inculcate.*

einrahmen *to frame.*

einreden *to persuade, talk someone
into.*

einreichen *to hand in, deliver, present.*

einreihen *to insert, include, arrange.*

Einreise *f. entry into a country.*

Einreiseerlaubnis *f. permit to enter a
country.*

einrichten *to arrange, prepare,
manage, furnish.*
sich einrichten *to plan.*

Einrichtung *f. furniture.*

EINS *one, the same.*
Es kommt auf eins hinaus. *It comes to
the same thing.*

EINSAM *lonely, solitary, lonesome.*

Einsamkeit *f. loneliness, solitude.*

einschälfern *to lull to sleep.*
einschalten *to insert, put in.*
einschenken *to pour in.*
einschlafen *to fall asleep.*
einschlagen *to drive in (nail), break, wrap up.*
  Schlagen Sie mir das, bitte, ein. *Will you please wrap that for me?*
einschliessen *to lock up, enclose.*
einschliesslich *inclusive.*
Einschreibebrief *m. registered letter.*
einschreiben *to enter, note down, register.*
einschreiten *to intervene, proceed.*
einschüchtern *to intimidate.*
EINSEITIG *one-sided, partial.*
einsetzen *to put it, insert.*
  sich einsetzen für *to speak on behalf of.*
Einspruch *m. protest, objection.*
  Einspruch erheben *to object to, protest against.*
EINST *once, one day.*
  einstmals *once, formerly.*
  einstweilen *meanwhile, for the present.*
  einstweilig *temporary.*
einsteigen *to get in.*
  Nach Düsseldorf einsteigen! *(Passengers) to Düsseldorf, all aboard!*
einstellen *to put on, adjust, stop, cease.*
  Arbeit einstellen *to strike.*
  Betrieb einstellen *to close down.*
  sich einstellen auf *to be prepared.*
Einstellung *f. adjustment, enlistment, attitude.*
  Ich verstehe Ihre Einstellung nicht. *I don't understand your attitude.*
einstimmen *to join in.*
einstimmig *unanimous.*
einstudieren *to study, rehearse.*
einteilen *to divide, plan, distribute.*
Einteilung *f. division, distribution, arrangement.*
eintönig *monotonous.*
Eintönigkeit *f. monotony.*
Eintracht *f. harmony, union, concord.*
eintreffen *to arrive, happen.*
  Was ich befürchtete, ist eingetroffen. *What I was afraid of has happened.*
EINTRETEN *to go in, enter.*
  Bitte, treten Sie ein! *Won't you come in, please!*
  eintreten für *to stand up for.*
  eintreten in *to join.*
EINTRITT *entrance, entry.*
  Eintritt verboten! *No admission!*

Eintritt frei! *Admission free!*
Eintrittsgeld *n. admission fee.*
Eintrittskarte *f. ticket.*
EINVERSTANDEN *agreed.*
  einverstanden sein *to agree.*
Einverständnis *n. agreement, consent.*
Einwand *m. objection, protest.*
einwandfrei *faultless, perfect.*
Einwanderer *m. immigrant.*
einwandern *to immigrate.*
Einwanderung *f. immigration.*
einwechseln *to change money.*
einwenden *to object.*
einwilligen *to consent.*
Einwilligung *f. consent.*
Einwurf *m. slit, slot.*
Einzahl *f. singular.*
einzahlen *to pay in.*
Einzahlung *f. payment.*
EINZELN *individual, particular, separate, single.*
  Kann man jeden Band einzeln kaufen? *Can I buy each volume separately?*
  jeder einzelne *each and every one.*
einzlehen *to pull in, draw, move in.*
  Sie sind schon in ihre neue Wohnung eingezogen. *They have already moved into their new apartment.*
EINZIG *only, sole, unique.*
  einzig und allein *solely, entirely.*
  Er ist das einzige Kind. *He is the only child.*
Einzug *m. entry, entrance, moving in.*
EIS *n. ice, ice cream.*
  Eisbahn. *f. rink.*
  Eisschrank, *m. refrigerator.*
  eisig *icy.*
EISEN *n. iron.*
  zun alten Eisen werfen *to junk.*
Eisenbahn *f. railway.*
  Eisenbahnwagen, *m. railway car.*
Eisenwaren *pl. hardware.*
eisern (er, -e,-es) *of iron, inflexible.*
  der eiserne Vorhang *the iron curtain.*
  Er hat einen eisernen Willen. *He has an iron will.*
eitel *vain, conceited, idle.*
Eitelkeit *f. vanity, conceit.*
Elefant *m. elephant.*
elegant *elegant.*
Eleganz *f. elegance.*
Elektriker *m. electrician.*
elektrisch *electric.*
elektrisieren *to electrify.*
Elektrizität *f. electricity.*
Element *n. element.*
elementar *elementary.*
Elend *n. misery, misfortune, distress.*
elend *miserable, ill; miserably.*

Elfenbein n. ivory.
ELFTE eleventh.
Ellenbogen m. elbow.
elterlich parental.
ELTERN pl. parents.
elternlos orphan.
Emigrant m. emigrant.
Empfang m. receipt, reception.
EMPFANGEN to receive, welcome.
Empfänger m. receiver, addressee.
empfänglich susceptible.
Empfangsnahme f. receipt (paper).
empfehlen to recommend.
empfinden to experience, feel perceive.
empfindlich sensitive.
Empfindlichkeit f. sensitiveness.
empören to rouse, excite, shock.
Empörung f. rebellion.
ENDE n. end, result, conclusion,
  extremity.
  am Ende in the end, after all.
  Ende gur, alles gut. All is well that
    ends well.
  letzten Endes finally.
  zu Ende führen to finish.
  zu Ende gehen to come to an end.
ENDEN to end, finish, stop, die.
Endergebnis n. final result.
endgültig final, definite.
endlos endless.
Endstation f. terminus.
Energie f. energy.
energisch energetic, vigorous.
ENG narrow, tight, close, intimate.
  engherzig narrow-minded.
engagieren to engage.
Engel m. angel.
Engländer m. Englishman.
Engländerin f. Englishwoman.
Englisch n. English.
  auf Englisch in English.
Enkel m. 1. ankle. 2. grandson.
Enkelkind n. grandchild.
Enkeltochter f. (Enkelin) grandaughter.
entbehren to be without, lack, miss.
entbehrlich superfluous, spare.
Entbehrung f. privation, want.
entdecken to discover, find out, detect.
Entdecker m. discoverer.
Entdeckung f. discovery.
Ente f. duck.
entehren to dishonor.
enteignen to expropriate, dispossess.
Enteignung f. expropriation.
enterben to disinherit.
entfalten to unfold, develop, display.
entfernen to remove, take away,
  depart.
  sich entfernen to leave.

entfernt far off, far away, distant.
  nicht im entferntesten not in the least.
Entfernung f. distance.
entfliehen to run away, escape.
entfremden to estrange, alienate.
Entfremdung f. estrangement,
  alienation.
entführen to carry off, elope.
Entführung f. abduction, elopement,
  kidnapping.
entgegen toward, opposed to,
  contrary to.
entgegen arbeiten to work against,
  counteract.
entgegengehen to go to meet, face.
entgegengesetzt opposite.
entgegenhalten to object, contrast.
entgegenkommen to come to meet.
  auf halbem Weg entgegenkommen to
    meet halfway.
entgegenkommend obliging, kind,
  helpful.
entgegennehmen to accept, receive.
entgegensehen to look forward to,
  expect.
entgegensetzen (entgegenstellen) to
  oppose, contrast.
entgegentreten to advance toward,
  oppose.
entgegnen to reply, answer.
Entgegnung f. reply.
entgehen to escape, elude.
enthalten to contain, hold, include.
  enthalten sein to be included.
entkommen to escape.
entladen to unload, discharge.
Entladung f. discharge.
entlassen to dismiss.
Entlassung f. dismissal.
entledigen to get rid of, perform,
  execute.
entmutigen to discourage, dishearten.
entnehmen to take from, gather,
  understand.
enträtseln to solve, decipher.
entrüsten to provoke, irritate, make
  angry.
Entrüstung f. anger, indignation.
entsagen to renounce, abandon.
  dem Thron entsagen to abdicate.
entschödigen to compensate.
Entschödigung f. compensation.
Entscheid m. answer.
entscheiden to decide, make up one's
  mind.
  Entscheiden Sie das. You decide that.
entscheidend decisive, critical.
Entscheidung f. decision, judgment,
  sentence, award.

entscheiden *decided, firm, resolute.*

Entschiedenheit *f. determination, certainty.*

entschliessen *to decide, make up one's mind.*
  Ich habe mich anders entschlossen. *I've changed my mind.*

Entschlossenheit *f. determination.*

Entschluss *m. resolution, decision.*

entschuldbar *excusable.*

ENTSCHULDIGEN *to excuse.*
  Entschuldigen Sie, bitte! *Please excuse me!*
  Ich bitte vielmals um Entschuldigung. *am awfully sorry.*
  sich entschuldigen *to apologize. .*

entschwinden *to vanish, disappear.*

entsetzen *to dismiss from, relieve, frighten.*

entsetzlich *terrible, dreadful.*

entsinnen *to remember, recollect, recall.*

entspannen *to relax.*

Entspannung *f. relaxation, rest, recreation.*

entstehen *to arise, originate.*

Entstehung *f. rise, origin, formation.*

entstellen *to distort, misrepresent.*

enttäuschen *to disappoint.*

Enttäuschung *f. disappointment.*

ENTWEDER ... ODER *either ... or.*

entwerfen *to draw up, design.*

entwerten *to depreciate, cancel.*

ENTWICKELN *to develop, explain.*
  einen Film entwickeln *to develop a film (photographic).*

Entwicklung *f. development.*

Entwicklungsjahre *pl. adolescence.*

entwürdigen *to degrade, disgrace.*

Entwurf *m. sketch, draft.*

entziehen *to deprive of, take away from, withdraw.*

entzücken *to delight, charm, enchant.*

entzückend *charming, delightful.*

entzwei *in two, torn, broken.*

entzweien *to estrange, alienate.*

Episode *f. episode.*

Epoche *f. epoch, era.*

ER *he.*
  er selbst *himself.*

erarbeiten (sich) *to get through hard work.*

erbarmen *to feel pity, have mercy.*

erbämlich *pitiful, miserable.*

erbarmungslos *merciless, pitiless.*

Erbe *m. heir.*

Erbe *n. heritage, inheritance.*

erben *to inherit.*

Erbfolge *f. succession.*

erblassen *to turn pale.*

erblicken *to catch sight of, perceive.*

erbrechen *to break open, vomit.*

Erbschaft *f. inheritance, legacy.*

Erbse *f. pea.*

Erbstück *n. heirloom.*

Erbteil *n. portion of inheritance.*

Erdbeben *n. earthquake.*

Erdbeere *f. strawberry.*

Erdboden *m. ground, soil, earth.*

ERDE *f. earth, ground, soil.*
  auf der Erde *on earth.*

Erdgeschoss *n. ground floor.*
  zu ebener Erde *on the ground floor.*

Erdkunde *f. geography.*

erdolchen *to stab.*

Erdteil *m. continent.*

ereignen *to happen, occur, pass.*
  Wann hat sich das ereignet? *When did that happen?*

Ereignis *n. event, occurrence, incident.*

erfahren *to learn, experience.*

Erfahrung *f. experience, information.*
  Wo kann ich das erfahren? *Where can I get this information?*
  aus Erfahrung *by experience.*
  erfahrungsgemäss *from experience.*

erfinden *to find out, discover, invent.*

Erfinder *m. inventor.*

Erfindung *f. invention.*

Erfolg *m. success, result, outcome.*

erfolgen *to result, follow.*

erfolglos *unsuccessful, fruitless.*

erfolgreich *successful.*

erforderlich *necessary, requisite.*

erforschen *to explore, investigate.*

Erforschung *f. exploration, investigation.*

ERFREUEN *to give pleasure, gladden, be pleased, rejoice.*

erfreulich *delightful, gratifying, satisfactory.*

erfreulicherweise *fortunately.*

ERFREUT *glad, pleased, delighted.*
  Sehr erfreut *(in social introductions). How do you do? (Delighted.)*

erfrieren *to die of cold, freeze to death.*

erfrischen *to refresh.*

Erfrischung *f. refreshment.*

ergänzen *to complete, restore.*

Ergänzung *f. completion, restoration.*

ergeben *to produce, yield, result in.*

ergeben *devoted.*
  Ihr ergebener *yours faithfully.*

ergiebig *productive.*

ergreifen *to seize, take hold of.*

ergreifend *moving, touching.*

ergriffen *moved, touched.*

Ergriffenheit *f. emotion.*

erhalten *to receive, obtain, preserve.*
Erhalter *m. supporter.*
erhältlich *obtainable.*
Erhaltungszustand *m. condition, state of preservation.*
erheben *to raise, lift up, collect.*
erhebend *elevating, impressive.*
erheblich *considerable.*
Erhebung *f. raising, elevation, revolt.*
erhitzen *to heat, warm.*
erholen *to recover, get better.*
Erholung *f. recovery, rest, recreation.*
ERINNERN *to remind.*
   Erinneren Sie mich später daran.
   Remind me about it later.
   sich erinnem an *to remember, recall.*
   Ich kann mich nicht mehr daran
   erinnem. *I can't remember it any more.*
Erinnerung *f. remembrance, recollection, memory.*
   Ernnerung wachrufen *to evoke memories.*
   zur Erinnerung *in memory of.*
erkälten *to chill.*
   sich erkälten *to catch a cold.*
erkämpfen *to win by fighting.*
erkennbar *recognizable.*
ERKENNEN *to recognize, perceive, realize.*
   zu erkennen geben *to show, indicate.*
   sich zu erkennengeben geben *to make oneself known.*
erkenntlich *recognizable, grateful.*
Erkenntnis *f. knowledge, perception, understanding.*
ERKLÄREN *to explain, account for, declare.*
ERKLÄRUNG *f. explanation, interpretation, declaration.*
erkranken *to fall ill, be taken ill.*
Erkrankung *f. illness.*
erkundigen *to inquire, make inquiries.*
Erkundigung *f. inquiry.*
ERLAUBEN *to allow, permit, presume.*
   Erlauben Sie, bitte! *Allow me, please!*
Erlaubnis *f. pemission, leave, license.*
erleben *to experience.*
Erlebnis *n. event.*
erledigen *to carry through, wind up, dispatch.*
   erledigt sein *to be dead tired.*
erleichtern *to facilitate, ease, relieve.*
Erleichterung *f. facilitation, relief.*
erlogen *false, untrue, fabricated.*
erlösen *to save, redeem, deliver.*
Erlösung *f. redemption, release, deliverance.*
ermächtigen *to empower, authorize.*
Ermahnung *f. exhortation, admonition.*

ermässigen *to reduce, abate.*
   Ermässigte Preise *reduced prices.*
ermöglichen *to make possible, enable.*
ermorden *to murder, assassinate.*
Ermordung *f. murder, assassination.*
ermüden *to tire out, weary.*
Ermüdung *f. fatigue, weariness.*
ermutigen *to encourage.*
ernähren *to nourish, feed, support.*
Ernährung *f. nourishment, food, support, maintenance.*
ernennen *to nominate, appoint.*
Ernennung *f. nomination, appointment.*
erneuem *to renew, renovate, replace.*
Erneuerung *f. renewal, renovation.*
erniedrigen *to humiliate, depress.*
Erniedrigung *f. humiliation, degradation.*
ERNST *serious, severe, grave; seriously.*
   Sie nimmt die Sache emst. *She takes the matter seriously.*
   ernst meinen *to be serious about something.*
Ernst *m. seriousness, earnestness, gravity.*
   Ernst machen mit *to put into practice.*
   Ernstfall, *m. emergency.*
Ernte *f. harvest, crop.*
Erntearbeit *f. harvesting.*
ernten *to harvest.*
erobern *to conquer, capture.*
eröffnen *to open, start, disclose.*
erörtern *to discuss.*
Erörterung *f. discussion.*
erpressen *to extort, blackmail.*
Erpressung *f. extortion, blackmail.*
erraten *to guess.*
erregbar *excitable, irritable.*
erregen *to excite, stir up.*
Erregung *f. excitement, agitation.*
erreichbar *attainable, within reach.*
erreichen *to reach, attain, get.*
ERSATZ *m. substitute, equivalent, spare.*
   Ersatzreifen *m. spare tire.*
   Ersatzteil *m. spare part.*
erschaffen *to create, produce.*
Erschaffung *f. creation.*
erscheinen *to appear, come out.*
Erscheinung *f. appearance, figure, apparition.*
erschiessen *to shoot; to kill by shooting.*
Erschiessung *f. execution by gunfire.*
erschöpfen *to exhaust.*
   erschöpfend *exhaustive.*
Erschöpfung *f. exhaustion.*
erschrecken *to frighten.*
erschrocken *frightened.*

erschüttern to shake, upset, shock.
Die Nachricht hat uns erschüttert. *We were shocked by the news.*
erschweren to make more difficult, aggravate.
ersetzen to replace, compensate, restore.
ersparen to save, economize.
ERST first, at first, only.
der erste beste *the first that comes.*
eben erst *just now.*
erst als *not till.*
erst recht nicht *certainly not.*
Zum ersten, zum zweiten, zum dritten! *Going, going, gone!*
Erstaufführung f. opening night.
erstaunen to astonish.
erstaunlich astonishing.
erstenmal (zum) for the first time.
erstens firstly.
erstgeboren first-born.
ersticken to suffocate.
erstmalig first, for the first time.
Ertrag m. produce, yield, profit, returns.
erträglich bearable, endurable.
ertränken to drown.
ertrinken to be drowned.
erübrigen to save, spare.
erwachen to awake.
erwachsen to grow up.
die Erwachsenen *the grown-ups, adults.*
erwägen to consider, weigh.
erwähnen to mention.
ERWARTEN to wait for, await, expect.
Erwartung f. expectation, hope.
in Erwartung Ihrer Antwort *looking forward to your reply.*
erwartungsvoll expectant, full of hope.
erweitern to widen, expand.
Erweiterung f. widening, expansion.
Erwerb m. acquisition, gain, profit.
erwerben to acquire, gain.
erwerbslos unemployed, out of work.
Erwerbslosenunterstützung f. unemployment relief.
ERZÄHLEN to tell, relate, narrate.
Erzählung f. story, tale, narrative.
erzeugen to breed, produce, procreate.
Erzeugnis n. product.
Deutsches Erzeugnis. *Made in Germany.*
Erzeugung f. procreation, production.
erziehen to raise, educate, train.
erzieherisch educational.
Erziehung f. education, upbringing.
Erziehungswesen n. educational system.
erzürnen to get angry.

erzwingen to force, extort.
ES it.
essbar edible.
ESSEN to eat, dine.
Essen n. food, dinner, meal.
Essenszeit f. mealtime.
Essig m. vinegar.
Esslöffel m. tablespoon.
Esswaren pl. provisions, victuals.
Esszimmer n. dining room.
Etage f. floor.
Etagenwohnung f. flat.
ETWA nearly, about, by chance.
ETWAS some, something, any, anything, a bit, somewhat.
EUCH acc. and dat. of ihr (fam. form pl.) you, to you.
EUER poss. adj. (fam. pl. form) your.
EUER(ER,-E,-ES) poss. pron.)pl. fam. form) yours.
euerseits on your part.
euresgleichen like you, of your kind.
euretwegen for your sake, on account of you.
Europa n. Europe.
evakuieren to evacuate.
evangelisch Protestant.
Evangelium n. Gospel.
EWIG eternal, forever, all the time.
Ewigkeit f. eternity.
exakt exact.
Examen n. examination.
Examensarbeit f. thesis, paper.
examinieren to examine.
Excellenz f. Excellency.
Exemplar n. sample.
exemplarisch exemplary.
exerzieren to drill.
Existenz f. existence.
existieren to exist, live.
Experiment n. experiment.
experimentieren to experiment.
Export m. export.
Exporteur m. exporter.
exportieren to export.
Extrablatt n. special edition.
Extrakt m. extract.
exzentrisch eccentric.

F

Fabel f. fable, story, plot.
fabelhaft fabulous.
Fabrik f. factory, mill, plant.
Fabrikanlage f. plant.
Fabrikant m. manufacturer.

Fabrikarbeiter *m. factory worker.*
Fabrikat *n. product (manufactured).*
Fabrikation *f. making.*
fabrizieren *to manufacture.*
Fach *n. compartment, shelf, drawer.*
  Was ist Ihr Fach? *What's your line?*
Fächer *m. fan.*
Fachkenntnis *f. technical knowledge.*
Fachmann *m. expert, specialist.*
Fackel *f. torch.*
Faden *m. thread.*
  an einem Faden hängen *to hang by a thread.*
FÄHIG *able.*
  fähig sein *to be able, capable.*
Fähigkeit *f. capability.*
Fahne *f. flag, banner.*
Fahnenflucht *f. desertion.*
Fahnenflüchtige *m. deserter.*
Fahrbahn *f. road, track.*
fahrbar *passable, navigable.*
Fähre *f. ferry.*
FAHREN *to drive, ride, go, travel.*
  Fahren Sie rechts! *Keep to the right!*
  Fahrendes Volk *n. tramps.*
  mit dem Schiff fahren *to sail.*
  spazieren fahren *to go for a ride.*
Fahrer *m. driver.*
Fahrgast *m. passenger.*
Fahrgeld *n. fare.*
Fahrkarte *f. ticket (transportation).*
Fahrkartenschalter *m. ticket window.*
fahrlässig *careless, negligent.*
Fahrlässigkeit *f. carelessness, negligence.*
Fahrplan *m. timetable.*
  fahrplanmässig *on schedule.*
Fahrrad *n. bicycle.*
Fahrschein *m. transportation ticket (bus).*
Fahrstrosee *f. highway.*
Fahrstuhl *m. lift, elevator.*
  Fahrstuhlführer, *m. elevator boy, attendant.*
FAHRT *f. ride, journey, trip.*
  Hin-und Rückfahrt *round trip.*
  in voller Fahrt *at full speed.*
  Was kostet die Fahrt, bitte? *How much is the fare, please?*
Fahrzeug *n. vehicle, vessel.*
Fakultät *f. faculty.*
FALL *m. fall, drop, case, accident.*
  auf jeden Fall, auf alle Fälle *in any case.*
  auf keinen Fall! *On no account!*
  Gesetzt den Fall Dass . . . *Supposing that . . .*
Falle *f. trap.*
FALLEN *to fall.*
  fallen lassen *to let fall, drop.*

im Felde fallen *to be killed in action.*
in den Rücken fallen *to attack from behind.*
in Ohnmacht fallen *to faint.*
Das Fest fällt auf einen Sonntag. *The holiday falls on a Sunday.*
Das fällt nicht weiter ins Gewicht. *That is of no further consequence.*
falls *in case, in the event.*
Fallschirm *m. parachute.*
FALSCH *wrong, incorrect, false.*
  Sie hat falsche Zähne. *She has false teeth.*
  Das Geld ist falsch. *The money is counterfeit.*
  falsch verstehen *to misunderstand.*
fälschen *to falsify, forge.*
Fälscher *m. forger.*
Falschheit *f. falseness, falsehood.*
Falschspieler *m. cheat (at cards).*
Fälschung *f. forgery.*
Falte *f. pleat, fold, wrinkle.*
falten *to fold.*
familiär *familiar, intimate.*
FAMILIE *f. family.*
Familienname *m. last name.*
Fanatiker *m. fanatic.*
Fang *m. catch, capture, prey.*
fangen *to catch, capture.*
FARBE *f. color, paint.*
  farbenblind *color blind.*
färben *to color, dye.*
  sich die Haare färben *to dye one's hair.*
farbig *colored.*
farblos *colorless, pale.*
Fasching *m. carnival.*
Fass *n. barrel, cask.*
  Das schlägt dem Fass den Boden aus. *That's the last straw.*
Fassade *f. front (of a building).*
FASSEN *to catch, seize, hold, apprehend, grasp, comprehend.*
  Fassen Sie sich kurz! *Make it short!*
  ins Auge fassen *to consider.*
Fassung *f. setting, composure.*
  aus der Fassung bringen *to upset, disconcert.*
fast *almost, nearly.*
faul *lazy, rotten, lazy.*
  Das ist eine faule Sache. *This is a shady business.*
faulen *to rot, be lazy.*
Faulheit *f. laziness.*
Faulpelz *m. idler, lazybones.*
Faust *f. fist.*
  auf eigene Faust *on one's own responsibility.*
  faustdick hinter den Ohren haben *to be sly.*

Fausthandschuh *m. mitten, boxing glove.*

FEBRUAR *m. February.*

FEDER *f. pen, feather.*
Federhalter *m. penholder.*
federleicht *light as a feather.*

Federvieh *n. poultry.*

Fee *f. fairy.*

feenhaft *fairylike.*

fegen *to sweep.*

Fehl *m. blame.*

fehl *wrong.*
fehl am Platze sein *to be out of place.*

Fehlbetrag *m. deficit.*

FEHLEN *to miss, make a mistake, lack, be absent.*
es an nichts fehlen lassen *to spare no pains.*
Sie werden mir sehr fehlen. *I'll miss you very much.*
Was fehlt Ihnen? *What's the matter with you?*

FEHLER *m. fault, defect, mistake, blunder.*
Das ist mein Fehler. *That is my fault.*

Fehlgriff *m. mistake.*

Fehlschlag *failure.*

Feier *f. festival, celebration, ceremony, party.*

feierlich *solemn, festive, ceremonious.*

Feierlichkeit *f. solemnity, ceremony.*

feiern *to celebrate.*
Sie feiern ihre goldene Hochzeit. *They are celebrating their golden anniversary.*

Feierstunde *f. leisure hour, festive hour.*

Feiertag *m. holiday.*

feige *cowardly.*

Feigheit *f. cowardice.*

feil *for sale, mercenary.*
feil bieten *to offer for sale.*
feil halten *to have for sale.*

FEIN *fine, thin, delicate, refined, distinguished, elegant.*

Feind *m. enemy.*

feindlich *hostile.*

feinfühlig *sensitive.*

Feingefühl *n. tact.*

Feinheit *f. fineness, grace, elegance, refinement, subtlety.*

Feinschmecker *m. gourmet.*

FELD *n. field, plain, ground, square.*
Schlachtfeld, *n. battlefield.*

Feldstecher *m. binoculars.*

Feldzug *m. campaign.*

Fell *n. skin, hide, coat, fur (animals).*
Diese Katze hat ein schönes Fell. *This cat has a beautiful fur.*

Fels *m. rock, cliff.*

felsenfest *firm as a rock.*

felsig *rocky, craggy.*

FENSTER *n. window.*

Fensterbank *f. window-sill.*

Fensterflügel *m. window-sash.*

Fensterrahmen *m. window-frame.*

Fensterscheibe *f. window pane.*

Ferien *pl. holidays, vacation.*

FERN *far, distant, remote.*
von fern *from afar, from a distance.*

Ferne *f. distance.*

ferner *further, furthermore, besides.*

Ferngespräch *n. long-distance phone call.*

Fernglas *n. binoculars, field glass.*

fernmündlich *by telephone, over the telephone.*
Das Telegramm wurde mir femmündlich durchgegeben. *The telegram was given to me over the phone.*

Fernsehen *n. television.*

Fernsprechbuch *n. telephone directory.*

Fernsprecher *m. telephone.*

Fernsprechstelle *f. telephone booth.*

FERTIG *ready, ready-made, finished, done.*
fertigbringen *to bring about, accomplish.*
sich fertig machen *to get ready.*
Werden Sie damit fertig werden? *Will you be able to manage this by yourself?*

FEST *n. festival, feast.*

FEST *firm, hard, rigid, steady, solid, stiff, stable, firmly, stiffly, fully.*
eine feste Stellung *a permanent post.*
fester Schlaf *sound sleep.*

festbinden *to tie, bind, fasten.*

Festessen *n. banquet.*

festfahren *to get stuck.*

Festhalle *f. banqueting hall.*

festhalten *to hold tight.*

festigen *to make firm.*

Festigkeit *f. solidity, firmness.*

festlegen *to fix, lay down, invest.*

festlich *festive, solemn.*

Festlichkeit *f. festivity.*

festmachen *to fasten, attach, fix, settle.*

Festnahme *f. arrest, seizure.*

festsetzen *to fix, set, settle.*
Der Preis wird auf hundert Mark festgesetzt. *The price has been fixed at one hundred marks.*

festsitzen *to be stuck, fit tightly.*

Festspiel *n. festival performance.*

Feststellung *f. statement, determination, identification.*

Festtag *m. holiday, feast.*

Festung f. fortress, stronghold.
FETT fat, plump, fertile, rich, greasy.
Fett n. grease, fat.
fettig fatty, greasy.
Fetzen m. rag, scrap.
FEUCHT damp, humid, muggy.
FEUER n. fire, firing, bombardment.
　Feuer! Fire!
　Feuer fangen to catch fire.
　Feuer geben to give a light.
feuerfest fireproof.
Feuergefahr f. danger of fire.
feuergefährlich inflammable.
Feuerlöscher m. fire-extinguisher.
Feuerung f. fuel.
Feuerversicherung f. fire insurance.
Feuerwache f. fire station.
Feuerwerk n. firework.
Feuerzeug n. lighter.
Fieber n. fever, temperature.
　Fieber messen to take the
　　temperature.
fieberhaft feverish.
Fiebermesser n. thermometer.
fiebern to be feverish, have a
　temperature.
Fieberthermometer n. clinical
　thermometer.
Fieberwahn m. delirium.
Figur f. figure, form, shape.
Filiale f. branch.
FILM m. film, picture, movie.
Filmaufnahme f. shooting of film.
filmen to film.
Filmstreifen m. filmstrip.
Filter m. filter.
filtern to filter, strain.
Filz m. felt.
filzig stingy.
Finanz f. finance.
Finanzamt n. revenue office.
finanziell financial.
finanzieren to finance, support.
FINDEN to find, discover, meet with,
　think, consider.
Finder m. finder.
findig clever, ingenious.
Findigkeit f. cleverness.
FINGER m. finger.
Fingerabdruck m. fingerprint.
Fingerfertigkeit f. dexterity, skill.
Fingerhut m. thimble.
Fingerspitze f. tip of the finger.
Fingerspitzengefühl n. flair.
Fingerzeig m. hint, tip.
finster dark, gloomy, obscure.
Finte f. feint, trick.
Firma f. firm, business.
FISCH m. fish.

FISCHEN to fish.
Fischer m. fisherman.
Fischerei f. fishing, fishery.
Fischgräte f. fish-bone.
Fischhändler m. fishmonger.
FLACH flat, plain, level.
Fläche f. surface, plain, area.
Flachland n. flat country, plain.
Flagge f. flag.
flaggen to deck with flags.
Flamme f. flame.
FLASCHE f. bottle.
Flaschenbier n. bottled beer.
Flaschenhals m. neck of a bottle.
Flaschenöffner m. bottle opener.
flatterhaft fickle, inconsistent.
Flatterhaftigkeit f. fickleness.
flattern to flutter; wave.
FLECK m. place, spot, stain.
　vom Fleck kommen to get on, make
　　headway.
Flecken m. spot, stain.
fleckenlos spotless.
fleckig spotted, stained.
Flegel m. boor, impertinent person.
flegelhaft rude, insolent.
Flegeljahre pl. teens.
flehen to implore, beseech.
flehentlich fervent.
FLEISCH n. flesh, meat, pulp.
Fleischbrühe f. meat broth.
Fleischer m. butcher.
fleischig fleshy, plump.
fleischlos meatless.
FLEISS m. diligence, industry.
　mit Fleiss on purpose.
fleissig diligent, industrious.
flicken to patch, mend, repair.
Flieder m. lilac.
Fliege f. fly.
FLIEGEN to fly, rush.
　in die Luft fliegen to blow up.
Flieger m. airman, aviator, pilot.
Fliegeralarm m. air raid alarm.
fliehen to run away, flee.
fliessen to flow, run.
　fliessendes Wasser running water.
　fliessend sprechen to speak fluently.
flink quick, agile, nimble.
Flinte f. shotgun, rifle.
　die Flinte in das Korn werfen to give up.
Flirt m. flirtation.
flirten to flirt.
Flitter m. tinsel.
Flitterwochen pl. honeymoon.
Floh m. flea.
Flöte f. flute.
flöten to play the flute.
flott afloat, floating.

Flotte *f. fleet, navy.*
Fluch *m. curse, imprecation.*
fluchen *to curse, swear.*
Flucht *f. flight, escape.*
flüchten *to flee, escape.*
flüchtig *careless, passing, superficial.*
  Er ist nur ein flüchtiger Bekannter. *He is only a passing acquaintance.*
Flüchtling *m. fugitive.*
FLUG *m. flight (aerial).*
Flugblatt *n. pamphlet.*
Fluggast *m. air passenger.*
Flughafen *m. airport.*
Flugplatz *m. airfield.*
Flugwesen *n. aviation, aeronautics.*
Flugzeug *n. airplane.*
Flugzeuglührer *m. pilot.*
Flugzeugträger *m. aircraft carrier.*
Flur *f. field, meadow.*
Flur *m. hall, corridor.*
FLUSS *m. river.*
flüssig *liquid, fluid.*
Flüssigkeit *f. fluidity.*
Flusslauf *m. course of a river.*
flüstern *to whisper.*
Flut *f. tide, flood.*
fluten *to stream, flow.*
FOLGE *f. sequence, succession.*
  Folge leisten *to comply with.*
Folgeerschelnung *f. consequence, effect.*
FOLGEN *to follow, succeed, obey, mind.*
  daraus folgt *hence follows.*
folgendermassen *as follows.*
folgern *to infer, conclude, deduce.*
Folgerung *f. inference, conclusion, deduction.*
folglich *consequently.*
folgsam *obedient, docile.*
Folgsamkeit *f. obedience, docility.*
Folter *f. torture.*
foltern *to torture.*
fordern *to demand, ask, claim, require.*
Forderung *f. demand, claim, challenge.*
Form *f. form, shape.*
Formalität *f. formality.*
Format *n. size, weight, importance.*
Formel *f. formula.*
formell *formal.*
formen *to form, shape.*
förmlich *formal, ceremonious, regular.*
Formlosigkeit *f. formlessness, shapelessness.*
Formular *n. form.*
formuliaren *to formulate, define.*
formvoilendet *perfect in form.*
forschen *to investigate, search.*
Forschung *f. inquiry, investigation.*

Förster *m. forester, gamekeeper.*
FORT *adv. and separable prefix (implies movement away from speaker, or continuation). away, off, gone, on (going on).*
  in einem fort *on and on.*
  und so fort *and so forth.*
fortan *henceforth, from this time.*
Fortbildung *f. further study.*
fortfahren *to drive away, remove, continue.*
  Bittte, fahren Sie fort! *Please go on!*
fortführen *to lead away, go on, continue.*
fortgehen *to go away.*
fortgesetzt *continuous, incessant.*
fortschreiten *to advance, proceed, make progress.*
Fortschritt *m. progress.*
fortschrittlich *progressive.*
fortsetzen *to continue, carry on, pursue.*
Fortsetzung *f. continuation, pursuit.*
  Fortsetzung folgt *to be continued.*
Fracht *f. freight.*
Frachtdampfer *m. freighter.*
FRAGE *f. question, inquiry, problem.*
  das ist noch die Frage *that remains to be seen.*
  eine Frage stellen *to ask a question.*
  ohne Frage *undoubtedly.*
FRAGEN *to ask, inquire.*
  fragen nach *to ask for.*
  nichts danach fragen *not to care about something.*
  sich fragen *to wonder.*
  Es fragt sich, ob es der Mühe wert ist. *It is a question whether it is worth the trouble.*
Fragezeichen *n. question mark.*
fraglich *in question, questionable, doubtful.*
fraglos *unquestionable.*
FRAU *f. woman, wife, Mrs.*
  gnädige Frau *Madam.*
  Inre Frau Gemahlin *your wife.*
Frauenarzt *m. gynecologist.*
FRÄULEIN *n. young lady, girl, Miss.*
fraulich *womanly.*
frech *impudent, insolent.*
Frechheit *f. impudence, insolence.*
FREI *free, vacant, open, liberal, spontaneous, frank; freely, frankly, at ease.*
  die freie Zeit *leisure, spare time.*
  Es ist mein freier Tag. *This is my day off.*
  Ist dieser Platz frei? *Is this seat taken?*
  unter freiem Himmel, im Freien

outside, in the open air.
Freibillet *n. complimentary ticket.*
Freidenker *m. freethinker.*
frelen *to court, woo.*
Freier *m. suitor.*
freigeben *to set free, release, open (to the public).*
freigebig *liberal, generous.*
Freigebigkeit *f. liberality, generosity.*
Freigeist *m. freethinker.*
freihalten *to hold, treat.*
Freiheit *f. freedom.*
freilassen *to release, set free.*
Freilassung *f. release.*
Freimut *m. frankness, candor.*
freimütig *frank, candid.*
freisprechen *to acquit, absolve.*
Freispruch *m. acquittal.*
Freistelle *f. scholarship, free place.*
FREITAG *m. Friday.*
freiwillig *voluntary, spontaneous.*
Freiwillige *m. volunteer.*
FREMD *strange, foreign, unknown, exotic.*
  fremdes Gut other people's property.
fremdartig *strange, odd.*
FREMDE *m. foreigner, tourist, foreign country.*
  in der Fremde abroad.
Fremdeniührer *m. tourist guide.*
Fremdenverkehr *m. tourist traffic.*
Fremdsprache *f. foreign language.*
Frendwort *n. foreign word.*
Fressen *n. animal food, feed.*
fressen *to eat (animals), feed.*
FREUDE *f. joy, delight, pleasure, cheer.*
  Freude haben an to enjoy, delight in.
  freudestrahlend beaming with joy.
freudelos *joyless, cheerless.*
freudig *joyful, cheerful.*
freuen *to please, delight.*
  sich freuen to be pleased, rejoice.
  Es freut mich sehr, Sie kennenzulemen.
  I am very glad to meet you.
  sich freuen auf to look forward to.
FREUND *m. -in f. friend.*
FREUNDLICH *friendly, kind, obliging, pleasant.*
Freundlichkeit *f. friendliness.*
Freundschaft *f. friendship.*
freundschaftlich *friendly, serviceable.*
FRIEDE *m. peace.*
Friedensbruch *m. breach of peace.*
Friedensvertrag *m. peace treaty.*
Friedhof *m. churchyard, cemetery.*
friedlich *peaceful.*
friedliebend *peace-loving.*
frieren *to freeze, be cold, get cold.*
  Mich friert (es). I am cold.

FRISCH *fresh, bright, lively, new.*
  auf frischer Tat in the very act of.
  frisch gestrichen wet paint.
  frische Eier fresh eggs.
  frische Wäsche clean linen.
FRISÖR *m. barber, hairdresser.*
frisieren *to fix one's hair.*
  sich frisieren lassen to have one's hair done.
Frisur *f. hairdressing, hairdo.*
froh *glad, happy.*
frohgemut *cheerful.*
FRÖHLICH *merry, happy.*
  Fröhliche Weihnachten! Mer
  Christmas!
Fröhlichkeit *f. cheerfulness.*
Frohsinn *m. cheerfulness.*
fromm *pious, religious, godly.*
Front *f. front (military).*
Frosch *m. frog.*
Frost *m. frost, cold, chill.*
frösteln *to shiver, feel chilly.*
FRUCHT *f. fruit, crop, produce.*
fruchtbor *fruitful, fertile.*
Fruchtbarkeit *f. fruitfulness, fertility.*
fruchtbringend *fruit-bearing, productive, fertile.*
fruchten *to bear fruit, to have effect.*
Fruchtsaft *m. fruit juice.*
FRÜH *early in the morning.*
  heute früh this morning.
  morgen früh tomorrow morning.
Frühe *f. morning, dawn.*
  in aller Frühe very early.
früher *earlier, sooner, former.*
  früher oder später sooner or later.
frühestens *at the earliest.*
FRÜHLING *m. Spring.*
FRÜHSTÜCK *n. breakfast.*
frühstücken *to breakfast.*
Fuchs *m. fox.*
fügen *to join, put together, add, submit.*
fügsam *yielding, submissive.*
Fügung *f. dispensation, coincidence.*
fühlbar *tangible, perceptible.*
FÜHLEN *to feel, sense, be sensitive to.*
  sich gut fühlen to feel well.
FÜHREN *to lead, conduct, direct, handle, carry.*
  Wer führt? Who is ahead?
  Er führt immer das grosse Wort. He is always bragging.
  Er führt etwas im Schilde. He is up to something.
Führer *m. leader, driver, pilot, guidebook.*
Führerschein *m. driving license.*
Führung *f. leadership, command, direction, management, behavior, conduct.*

Führungszeugnis *n. reference, certificate.*
FÜLLEN *to fill, stuff.*
  sich füllen *to fill up.*
  Das Stadion füllt sich langsam. *The stadium is slowly filling up.*
Fund *m. finding.*
Fundament *n. foundation.*
fundieren *to lay a foundation.*
FÜNF *five.*
FÜNFTE *fifth.*
FÜNFZEHN *fifteen.*
FÜNFZEHNTE *fifteenth.*
FÜNFZIG *fifty.*
FÜNFZIGSTE *fiftieth.*
Funk *m. wireless, radio (communications medium).*
Funke *m. spark.*
funkeln *to sparkle.*
Funker *m. telegraphist.*
Funkspruch *m. radiogram.*
FÜR *prep. (acc.) for, by, to.*
  ein für allemal *once for all.*
  Er Schritt für Schritt vorwärts. *He walks forward step by step.*
  Ich arbeite für mich. *I work for myself.*
  Ich habe Karten für das Theater. *I have tickets for the theater.*
  Stück für Stück *piece by piece.*
  Tag für Tag *day by day.*
  was für ein? *what kind of?*
FURCHT *f. fear, fright, dread, anxiety.*
furchtbar *awful, horrible, terrible; awfully, terribly.*
fürchten *to fear.*
fürchterlich *terrible, horrible, frightful.*
furchtlos *fearless, intrepid.*
Furchtlosigkeit *f. fearlessness, intrepidity.*
furchtsam *timid, nervous.*
Furchtsamkeit *f. timidity.*
Fürst *m. (-in f.) prince(ss).*
Fürwort *n. pronoun.*
FUSS *m. foot, base, bottom.*
  auf eigenen Füssen stehen *to be independent.*
  auf freien Fuss setzen *to set at liberty*
  Er lebt auf grossem Fuss. *He is living in grand style.*
  Ich stehe mit ihm auf gutem Fuss. *I am on good terms with him.*
  zu Fuss *on foot.*
Fussball *m. soccer.*
Fussbank *f. footstool.*
Fussgänger *m. pedestrian.*
  nur für Fussgänger *for pedestrians only.*
Fusspur *f. footprint.*
Fusstapfe *f. footstep.*
Fusstritt *m. kick.*

Futter *n. 1. food, feed (animals). 2. sheath, lining.*
Futterseide *f. silk for lining.*

G

Gabe *f. present, gift, talent.*
Gabel *f. fork.*
gähnen *to yawn, gape.*
GANG *m. walk, stroll, walk, aisle, course, gear, hall, errand.*
  in Gang setzen *to start, set.*
  in vollem Gang *in full swing.*
Gans *f. goose.*
Gänseblümchen *n. daisy.*
GANZ *all, whole, entire, complete; in full, wholly, entirely, thoroughly, altogether.*
  die ganze Stadt *the whole town.*
  ganz anders *quite different.*
  ganz besonders *more especially.*
  ganz gleich *all the same, no matter.*
  ganz und gar *wholly.*
  ganz und gar nicht *not at all.*
  im ganzen *on the whole.*
  im grossen und ganzen *on the whole.*
  von ganzem Herzen *with all my heart.*
GAR *done, cooked through; fully, very, quite, even.*
  gar kein. . . *no. . .whatsoever.*
  gar nicht *not at all.*
  gar nichts *nothing at all.*
Garage *f. garage.*
Garderobe *f. wardrobe, cloakroom.*
Garderobenmarke *f. check (cloakroom).*
Garderobennummer *f. check (cloakroom).*
Gardine *f. curtain.*
Garn *n. yarn, thread.*
garnieren *to trim, garnish.*
Garnitur *f. trimming, outfit.*
garstig *nasty, ugly.*
GARTEN *m. garden.*
Gartenhaus *n. summer house.*
Gartenlaube *f. garden house (pavilion).*
Gärtner *m. gardener.*
Gas *n. gas.*
Gashahn *m. gas tap.*
Gasleitung *f. gas pipes, gas supply.*
Gasse *f. narrow street, alley.*
GAST *m. visitor, guest.*
gastfreundlich *hospitable.*
Gastfreundschaft *f. hospitality.*
Gastgeber *m. host.*
Gasthaus *n. inn, hotel.*

Gasthof *m. inn, hotel.*
gastlich *hospitable.*
Gastspiel *n. guest performance.*
Gastwirt *m. innkeeper.*
Gasuhr *f. gas meter.*
Gatte *m. husband.*
Gattin *f. wife.*
Gaumen *m. palate.*
Geächtete *m. outlaw.*
Gebäck *n. pastry, cookie.*
Gebärde *f. gesture, movement.*
gebärden (sich) *to behave, conduct oneself.*
Gebäude *n. building, structure, edifice.*
GEBEN *to give, present, produce, yield.*
  Das gibt mir zu denken. *That makes me wonder.*
  es gibt *there is, there are.*
  gegeben werden *to play (in theater).*
  Was wird heute in Theater gegeben? *What's playing tonight at the theater?*
Gebet *n. prayer.*
Gebiet *n. district, territory, area, field.*
gebieten *to order, command.*
Gebirge *n. mountain chain.*
gebirgig *mountainous.*
Gebiss *n. set of teeth, denture.*
Gebot *n. order, command, law.*
Gebrauch *m. use, customs, rites.*
gebrauchen *to use, make use of.*
gebräuchlich *usual, in use.*
Gebühr *f. duty, tax, fee, rate.*
gebühren *to be due, proper.*
gebührenfrei *tax-free.*
gebührenpflichtig *taxable.*
gebührlich *suitable, proper.*
GEBURT *f. birth, origin, extraction.*
Geburtshelferin *f. midwife.*
Geburtjahr *n. year of birth.*
Geburtsschein *m. birth certificate.*
Geburtstag *m. birthday.*
Gedächtnis *n. memory, remembrance.*
  aus dem Gedächtnis *from memory.*
GEDANKE *m. thought, idea.*
  sich Gedanken machen *to worry.*
  Wie kommen Sie auf den Gedanken? *What gives you that idea?*
gedankenlos *thoughtless.*
Gedankenlosigkeit *f. thoughtlessness.*
Gedeck *n. cover (at table), set of table linens.*
gedeihen *to grow, develop, succeed.*
gedenken *to intend, think of.*
Gedenkfeier *f. commemoration.*
Gedicht *n. poem.*
gediegen *pure, solid.*
Gedränge *n. crowd, throng.*
gedruckt *printed.*
Geduld *f. patience, endurance.*

gedulden (sich) *to have patience.*
geduldig *patient.*
Gefahr *f. danger, risk.*
gefährden *to endanger, expose to danger.*
gefährlich *dangerous, perilous.*
gefahrlos *safe, secure, without danger.*
gefahrvoll *dangerous, perilous.*
GEFALLEN *to please, suit.*
  Das gefällt mit. *I like that.*
  sich gefallen lassen *to submit, put up with.*
gefällig *pleasant, agreeable.*
Gefangene *m. prisoner, captive.*
  Kriegsgefangene *m. prisoner of war.*
Gefangenschaft *f. captivity, confinement.*
Gefangensetzung *f. capture, arrest.*
Gefängnis *n. prison, jail.*
Gefäss *n. container, receptacle.*
gefasst *composed, collected, calm.*
  sich gefasstmachen auf *to be prepared for.*
Geflügel *n. birds, poultry, fowl.*
Geflüster *n. whispering.*
Gefolge *n. suite, entourage.*
GEFÜHL *n. feeling, sentiment, sense, emotion, sensation.*
gefühllos *numb, heartless.*
Gefühllosigkeit *f. numbness, heartlessness.*
gefühlvoll *tender, sentimental.*
gegebenenfalls *eventually, possibly.*
GEGEN *prep. (acc.) against, about, around, toward, for, to, compared with.*
  Die Soldaten kämpfen gegen den Feind. *The soldiers fight against the enemy.*
  Er schwamm gegen den Strom. *He swam against the current.*
  Es ist gegen neun Uhr. *It is about nine o'clock.*
  gegen voriges Jahr *compared with last year.*
  gegeneinander *against each other.*
  Waren gegen Geld tauschen *to exchange goods for money.*
GEGEND *f. country, region, district.*
Gegenseite *f. opposite side.*
gegenseitig *reciprocal, mutual.*
Gegenstand *m. subject.*
gegenstandlos *pointless.*
Gegenteil *n. contrary, opposite.*
  im Gegenteil *on the contrary.*
gegenüber *opposite.*
Gegenwart *f. present, presence.*
gegenwärtig *present.*
Gegenwert *m. equivalent.*
Gegner *m. opponent, adversary, enemy.*

Gehalt m. content.
Gehalt n. salary.
gehaltlos worthless.
gehaltvoll valuable, substantial.
gehässig spiteful, malicious.
Gehässigkeit f. spite, malice.
geheim concealed, hidden, clandestine.
GEHEIMNIS n. secret, mystery.
geheimnisvoll mysterious.
Gehelmpolizei f. secret police.
GEHEN to go, walk, pass, move, leave;
  run, work (machinery).
  an die Arbeit gehen to go to work.
  Das geht nicht. That won't do.
  Es geht mir gut, danke. I am fine,
    thank you.
  Es geht nichts über gutes Bier. There
    is nothing like good beer.
  Es geht um Tod und Leben. It is a
    matter of life and death.
  gehen auf (nach) to face on, look out on.
  gehen lassen to let go, give up.
  sich gehen lasen to let oneself go.
  Wie geht es Ihnen? How are you?
Gehilfe m. assistant, clerk, helper.
Gehirn n. brain.
GEHÖR n. hearing; ear (mus.).
gehorchen to obey.
GEHÖREN to belong to, be owned by.
  Das gehört nicht zur Sache. That's
    beside the point.
  Dazu gehört Zeit. That takes time.
gehorsam obedient.
Geige f. violin.
geigen to play the violin.
GEIST m. spirit, genius, mind.
geistesabwesend absent-minded.
Geistesgegenwart f. presence of mind.
geisteskrank of unsound mind, insane.
geistesschwach feeble-minded.
geistig spiritual, intellectual, mental.
geistlich religious, spiritual.
geistlos spiritless, lifeless, dull.
geistreich ingenious, spiritual, witty.
Geiz m. stinginess, avarice.
geizig avaricious, stingy.
Geizkragen m. miser.
Gelände n. country, countryside.
Geländer n. railing, banister.
gelangen to reach, arrive, attain to.
gelassen calm, collected.
Gelassenheit f. calmness, composure.
geläufig fluent, familiar, current.
gelaunt disposed.
  gut gelaunt in good humour.
  schlecht gelaunt cross, bad-tempered.
Geläute n. chime, ringing of bells.
GELB yellow.
gelblich yellowish.

Gelbsucht f. jaundice.
GELD n. money.
  Bargeld, n. cash.
  Kleingeld, n. change.
Geldentwertung f. inflation.
Geldschein m. paper money.
Geldschrank m. safe.
Geldstück n. coin.
Geldtasche f. purse.
Gelee m. jelly.
gelegen 1. situated. 2. convenient.
  Er kam gerade zu gelegener Zeit. He
    came just at the right time.
Gelegenheit f. opportunity, occasion,
  chance.
Gelegenheitskauf m. bargain.
gelegentlich occasional, accidental.
gelehrig docile, teachable.
Gelehrigkeit f. docility.
Gelehrsamkeit f. learning, erudition.
gelehrt learned, scholarly, erudite.
Gelehrte m. scholar, savant.
Geleise n. track.
Geleit n. escort, convoy.
geleiten to accompany, escort, convoy.
Geleitwort n. motto.
Gelenk n. joint, articulation.
Geliebte m. & f. lover, mistress,
  beloved.
gelingen to succeed, manage.
gelten to matter, mean, be worth, have
  influence, be valid.
  Das gilt nicht. That does not count.
  gelten als to be considered as.
Geltungstrieb m. desire to dominate.
gemächlich comfortable.
Gemahl m. husband.
Gemahlin f. wife.
gemäss suitable.
GEMEIN ordinary, general, low, vulgar,
  common.
  der Gemeine the private soldier.
  Es war gemein von ihm. It was mean
    of him.
  gemeinhaben mit to have in common
    with.
Gemeinde f. community, congregation,
  parish, municipality.
Gemeinheit f. vulgarity, baseness, bad
  trick.
gemeinnützig beneficial to the
  community.
Gemeinschaft f. community.
  in Gemeinschaft mit together with.
GEMÜSE n. vegetables.
Gemüsehändler m. greengrocer.
Gemüt n. soul, mind, heart, feelings.
Gemütlich good-natured, cozy.
Gemütlichkeit f. comfort, coziness.

GENAU *close, tight, exact, accurate.*
  Er nimmt es sehr genau. *He is very particular.*
  Nehmen Sie es nicht zu genau! *Don't take it too literally!*
Genaulgkeit *f. exactness, accuracy, precision.*
General *m. general.*
genesen *to recover, get better.*
Genesung *f. recovery, convalescence.*
genial *full of genius.*
Genilität *f. originality.*
Genick *n. nape (of neck).*
Genie *n: genius.*
genieren *to trouble, inconvenience, bother.*
geniessbar *eatable, drinkable.*
geniessen *to eat, enjoy, have the benefit of.*
Genosse *m. companion.*
GENUG *sufficient, enough.*
Genugtuung *f. satisfaction, compensation.*
Geographie *f. geography.*
GEPäCK *n. luggage, baggage.*
Gepäckabfertigung *f. luggage office, cloakroom.*
Gepäckannahme *m. luggage counter.*
Gepäckaufbewahrung *f. luggage counter.*
Gepäckausgabe *f. luggage office.*
Gepäckschein *m. receipt for registered baggage.*
Gepäckstück *n. bag, parcel.*
Gepäckträger *m. porter.*
GERADE *direct, upright, straight, honest; just, exactly, directly.*
  nun gerade *now more than ever.*
  geradeus *straight on.*
Gerät *n. tool, implement, utensil.*
geraten *to succeed, turn out well.*
  aneinander geraten *to come to blows.*
  Ihm gerät nichts. *He never succeeds in anything.*
  in Brand geraten *to catch fire.*
geräumig *roomy, spacious.*
Geräusch *n. noise.*
geräuschlos *noiseless.*
geräuschvoll *noisy.*
GERECHT *just, fair, equitable.*
Gerechtigkeit *f. justice, righteousness, fairness.*
Gerede *n. talk, humor.*
Gereiztheit *f. irritation.*
Gericht *n. dish, course, judgment.*
  Jüngstes Gericht. *Last Judgment.*
  vor Gericht *in court.*
Gerichtshof *m. court of law.*
gering *small, little, unimportant.*

nicht im geringsten *not in the least.*
geringfügig *unimportant.*
Gerippe *n. skeleton.*
GERN *gladly, with pleasure, readily, easily.*
  gern essen *to like (to eat something).*
  Gern geschehen! *Don't mention it!*
  gern haben *to like (a person or object).*
  gern tun *(or any verb of action) to like (to do something).*
  Ich esse gern Eisbein mit Sauerkraut. *like pig's knuckles with sauerkraut.*
  Sie har ihn gern. *She likes him.*
  Tanzen Sie gern? *Do you like to dance?*
Geruch *m. smell, scent, odor.*
geruchlos *odorless.*
Gerücht *n. rumor, report.*
Gerüst *n. scaffold, stage.*
GESANG *m. song, singing.*
  Gesanglehrer *m. singing teacher.*
GESCHäFT *n. business, transaction, commerce, commercial firm, store.*
geschäftlich *commercial.*
Geschäftsführer *m. manager.*
Geschäftsmann *m. business man.*
geschäftsmässig *commercial.*
Geschäftsviertel *n. shopping district.*
Geschäftszeit *f. office hours.*
GESCHEHEN *to happen, occur, be done.*
  Es geschieht ihm recht. *It serves him right.*
  Es ist um mich geschehen. *I am done for.*
  geschehen lassen *to allow, permit.*
Geschenk *n. present, gift.*
GESCHICHTE *f. story, history.*
Geschichtsbuch *n. history book.*
Geschick *n. fate, destiny.*
geschickt *clever, capable.*
Geschirr *n. crockery, dishes, china.*
GESCHLECHT *n. sex, gender, kind, species, race, family, stock.*
geschlechtlich *sexual.*
GESCHMACK *m. taste, flavor.*
  Geschmack finden an *to like.*
geschmacklos *insipid, in bad taste.*
Geschmacklosigkeit *f. bad taste.*
geschmackvoll *tastefull.*
Geschrei *n. shouting, screaming, clamor.*
Geschwätz *n. idle talk.*
geschwätzig *talkative.*
geschwind *quick, fast, swift, prompt, speedy.*
Geschwindigkeit *f. quickness, rapidity.*
  Geschwindigkeitsgrenze 60 km. *Speed limit 60 kilometers.*

Geschwister *pl. brother(s) and sister(s).*

Geselle *m. fellow, companion, journeyman.*

Geselligkeit *f. sociability, social life.*

GESELLSCHAFT *f. society, association, company.*

(jemanden) Gesellschaft leisten *to keep (someone) company.*

in Gesellschaft *socially.*

Gesellschafter *m. partner.*

Gesellschaftsanzug *m. evening clothes.*

Gesellschaftskleidung *f. evening clothes.*

Gesellschaftskleidung erwünscht. *Evening dress requested.*

Gesellschaftsspiel *n. party game.*

Gesetz *n. law, statute.*

Gesetzbuch *n. code.*

gesetzlich *legal, lawful.*

gesetzwidrig *unlawful, illegal.*

GESICHT *n. vision, sight, hallucination. appearance, face.*

Das steht Ihnen gut (zu Gesicht). *It is very becoming to you.*

Gesichter schneiden *to make faces.*

Sie lachte übers ganze Gesicht. *She was all smiles.*

Gesichtszug *m. feature.*

Gesinnung *f. mind, way of thinking.*

gesinnungslos *unprincipled.*

gesinnungstreu *loyal.*

Gesinnugswechsel *m. change of opinion.*

gesittet *well-mannered.*

gespannt *stretched, strained.*

Gespenst *n. ghost.*

gespenstig *ghostly.*

Gespött *n. mockery, derision.*

GESPRÄCH *n. talk, conversation, discourse.*

gesprächig *talkative.*

Gesprächsstoff *m. topic of conversation.*

Gestalt *f. form, figure, shape, build, frame, manner, fashion.*

gestalten *to form.*

Geständnis *n. confession.*

gestehen *to confess, admit.*

Gesträuch *n. shrubs, bushes, shrubbery.*

Gesuch *n. application, petition, request.*

GESUND *healthy, well, sound, natural.*

gesunder Menschenverstand *common sense.*

Gesundheit *f. health*

Gesundheit! *God bless you!*

gesundheitlich *hygienic, sanitary.*

gesundheitshalber *for the sake of health.*

Getränk *n. drink, beverage.*

Getreide *n. grain.*

Getreidehalm *m. corn stalk.*

Getreidespeicher *m. granary.*

Getümmel *n. bustle, tumult.*

Gewächs *n. plant.*

gewachsen *equal to.*

Er ist der Arbeit gewachsen. *He is equal to the task.*

Er ist seinem Gegner gewachsen. *He is a match for his opponent.*

Gewächshaus *n. conservatory (greenhouse).*

gewagt *risky.*

Gewähr *f. security, surety.*

gewähren *to grant.*

jemanden gewähren lassen *to let a person do as he pleases.*

GEWALT *f. power, authority, force, violence.*

in der Gewalt haben *to have command of, master.*

mit aller Gewalt *with all one's might.*

sich in der Gewalt haben *to have self-control.*

Gewaltherrschaft *f. despotism.*

gewaltsam *violent.*

gewalttätig *brutal, violent.*

gewandt *agile, skillful, clever.*

gewärtig *expecting, expectant.*

Gewebe *n. weaving, web, tissue, fabric.*

Gewehr *n. rifle, weapon.*

Gewerbe *n. trade, business, profession.*

Gewerbeschein *m. trade license.*

Gewerbeschule *f. trade, technical school.*

gewerbsmässig *professional.*

Gewicht *n. weight.*

ins Gewicht fallen *to weigh with.*

gewichtig *weighty, important.*

Gewinn *m. winning.*

Gewinnanteil *m. dividend.*

gewinnbringend *profitable, lucrative.*

GEWINNEN *to gain, earn, win, produce, extract.*

es über sich gewinnen *to bring oneself to.*

Gewinner *m. winner.*

gewinnsüchtig *greedy (for victory).*

Gewirr *n. confusion, mess.*

GEWISS *certain, sure, fixed; certainly, indeed, of course, no doubt.*

Gewiss! *Surely!*

In gewissem Sinne hat er recht. *In a sense he is right.*

gewissenlos *unscrupulous.*

gewissenmassen *to some extent, so to speak, as it were.*

Gewissheit f. certainty.
Gewitter n. thunderstorm.
gewittern to thunder.
Gewitterregen m. deluge.
GEWÖHNEN to accustom.
  sich an etwas gewöhnen to get used
  to something.
Gewohnheit f. habit.
gewöhnlich usual, ordinary, common.
gewöhnt accustomed.
Gewölbe n. vault.
Gewühl n. turmoil, crowd.
Gewürz n. spice, seasoning, condiment.
gewürzig spiced.
geziert affected.
giessen to pour, water, spill.
Gift n. poison.
giftig poisonous, venomous.
Gipfel m. summit, peak, top.
Gipfelpunkt m. limit.
Giraffe f. giraffe.
Gitter n. railing, fence, grating.
Glanz m. brightness, glamour.
glänzen to shine, glitter, gleam.
glänzend shining, lustrous.
Glanzleistung f. (top) record.
glanzvoll brilliant, splendid, glorious.
GLAS n. glass, jar, pitcher.
gläsern of glass, vitreous.
GLATT even, smooth, slippery, flat;
  smoothly, slippery.
Glatteis n. slippery ice.
Glauben m. faith, confidence, trust,
  belief.
GLAUBEN to believe, trust, think,
  suppose.
  Sie können ihm aufs Wort glauben.
  You can take his word for it.
glaubhaft credible, likely, probable.
gläubig believing, faithful.
gläublich credible, likely.
glaubwürdig credible, reliable,
  authentic.
Glaubwürdigkeit f. credibility,
  authenticity.
GLEICH same, similar, alike, even,
  level, direct, equal, like, equivalent;
  equally, just, at once, immediately.
  es einem gleich tun to rival a person.
  Es ist mir gleich. It is all the same to
  me.
  gleich darauf immediately afterwards.
  Gleich und gleich gesellt sich gern.
  Birds of a feather flock together.
gleichberechtigt entitled to the same
  rights.
GLEICHEN to be equal, resemble.
gleichfalls likewise.
gleichförmig uniform.

gleichgesinnt congenial.
Gleichgewicht n. equilibrium, balance,
  poise.
gleichgültig indifferent, unconcerned.
Gleichgültigkeit f. indifference.
Gleichheit f. equality, identity, similarity.
gleichmässig proportional.
Gleichstrom m. direct current.
gleichviel no matter, just the same.
gleichwertig equivalent.
gleichzeitig simultaneous.
Gletscher m. glacier.
Glied n. limb, member.
gliedern to articulate, arrange, classify.
glitzern to glitter, glisten, twinkle.
Globus m. globe.
Glocke f. bell, clock.
Glockenspiel n. chime.
Glockenturm m. steeple.
GLÜCK n. fortune, good luck,
  prosperity.
  etwas auf gut Glück tun to take a
  chance on something.
  Glück haben to be lucky.
  Glück im Spiel, Unglück in der Liebe.
  Lucky at cards, unlucky in love.
  Glück wünschen to congratulate.
  Viel Glück! Good luck! Many happy
  returns!
glucken to succeed, be lucky.
GLÜCKLICH fortunate.
  Glückliche Reise! Have a pleasant trip!
glücklicherweise fortunately.
Glücksfall m. chance.
Glücksspeil n. game of chance.
Glückwunsch m. congratulations, good
  wishes.
Glühbirne f. electric bulb.
glühen to glow.
glühend glowing, fervent.
Glühwurm m. glowworm.
Glut f. glow, heat.
Gnade f. favor, mercy.
  auf Gnade und Ungnade at discretion.
Gnadengesuch n. petition for
  clemency.
GNÄDIG merciful, gracious.
  gnädige Frau Madam.
GOLD n. gold.
golden gold, of gold, golden.
Goldgrube f. gold mine.
goldig shining like gold.
  jedes Wort auf die Goldwaage legen
  to weigh one's words carefully.
Golf m. golf.
gönnen to wish well, allow, permit; not
  to begrudge.
Gönner m. patron.
Gotik f. Gothic.

GOTT m. God.
  Gott sei Dank! *Thank God!*
  leider Gottes *unfortunately.*
  Um Gottes willen! *For Heaven's sake!*
Götterdämmertun f. twilight of the Gods.
Gottesdienst m. public worship, service (church).
göttlich divine, godlike.
Grab n. tomb, grave.
Grabstein m. tombstone.
Grad m. degree.
Graf m. count.
Gräfin f. countess.
Gram m. sorrow, grief.
grämen to grieve, worry.
Gramm n. gram. (1,000 grams equal 1 kilogram.)
Grammatik f. grammar.
GRAS n. grass.
grässlich terrible, horrible.
Gräte f. fish-bone.
Gratulant m. congratulator, well-wisher.
gratulieren to congratulate.
GRAU gray.
grauen to be afraid, shudder, dread.
  Es graut mir vor. *I am afraid.*
grauenhaft horrible, ghastly.
grauenvoll awful, dreadful.
Grauhaar n. gray hair.
grausam cruel.
Grausamkeit f. cruelty.
grausig gruesome, ghastly.
Grazie f. grace, charm.
graziös gracious.
greifbar tangible, palpable.
greifen to seize, grasp, catch, touch, strike.
  ineinander greifen *to interlock.*
Greis m. old man.
Greisenalter n. old age.
Greisin f. old woman.
Grenze f. frontier, boundary, limit.
grenzenlos boundless, infinite.
Grenzverkehr m. traffic at or across the frontier, frontier trading.
Griff m. grip, grasp, hold, catch.
Grimm m. anger, rage.
grimmig furious, grim.
Grippe f. grippe.
grob clumsy, thick, rough, coarse.
Grobheit f. coarseness, rudeness.
Groil m. resentment, anger.
grollen to be resentful, angry.
GROSS big, tall, large, great, huge, grand.
  die grossen Ferien *the summer vacation.*
  gross tun *to boast.*

gross ziehen *to bring up.*
grosse Kinder *grown-up children.*
grosser Buchstabe *capital letter.*
im grossen und ganzen *on the whole.*
grossartig great, grand.
GRÖSSE f. size, dimension, largeness, tallness, celebrity, star.
Grosseltern pl. grandparents.
Grosshandel m. wholesale trade.
grossjährig of age.
Grossmacht f. great power.
grossmütig generous, magnanimous.
Grossmutter f. grandmother.
grosspurig arrogant.
Grossstadt f. big town.
Grossstädter m. inhabitant of a large town.
grössenteils for the most part, largely.
Grossvater m. grandfather.
grosszügig generous, on a large scale.
Grün n. green, verdure.
GRÜN green (adj.).
  im Grünen *in country surroundings.*
  vom grünen Tisch aus *only in theory.*
GRUND m. ground, bottom, cause, reason.
  im Grunde *after all.*
  auf den Grund gehen *to investigate.*
  Aus welchem Grunde? *For what reason?*
Grundbesitz m. real estate.
gründen to found, establish, promote.
Grundgedanke m. fundamental idea.
Grundlage f. foundation.
grundlegend fundamental.
gründlich thorough, solid, profound.
Gründlichkeit f. thoroughness, solidity.
Grundsatz m. principle.
grundsätzlich fundamental.
Grundstück n. piece of land, lot.
Gründung f. foundation, establishment.
grünen to grow green, sprout.
Gruppe f. group.
GRUSS m. greeting; salute (military).
GRÜSSEN to greet, salute.
  grüssen lassen *to send one's regards.*
gültig valid, available, good, current.
Gültigkeit f. validity; currency (monetary).
Gummi m. rubber, eraser.
Gummiabsatz m. rubber heel.
Gummiband n. rubber band.
Gummimantel m. raincoat.
Gummischuh m. galosh.
Gunst f. kindness, favor.
  zu Gunsten von *in favor of.*
günstig kind, favorable.
Gurke f. cucumber.
Gürtel m. belt, girdle.

Gusstein *m. sink.*
Gut *n. property, good, estate, farm.*
GUT *good, pleasant, kind, full; well, pleasantly, kindly.*
  es gut haben *to be well off.*
  Gute Besserung! *I hope you get well soon!*
  Guten Morgen! *Good morning!*
  kurz und gut *in short.*
  Schon gut! *All right!*
Gutachten *n. expert opinion, estimate.*
Gutachter *m. assessor, surveyor.*
gutartig *good-natured.*
Güte *f. kindness.*
Güterzug *m. freight train.*
gutgelaunt *in a good temper, in good spirits.*
gutgläubig *credulous.*
Guthaben *n. balance, credit.*
gutheissen *to approve, sanction.*
gutherzig *kind-hearted.*
gütig *kind, good.*
gutmachen *to make amends for.*
gutmütig *good-natured.*
Gutmütigkeit *f. good nature.*
Gutsbesitzer *m. landowner, gentleman farmer.*
Gutschein *m. token, voucher.*
gutwillig *willing, voluntary.*
Gymnasialbildung *f. classical education.*
Gymnasiast *m. high-school boy.*
Gymnasium *n. high-school.*
Gymnastik *f. gymnastics.*

H

HAAR *n. (Haare pl.) hair.*
  sich die Haare machen *to do one's hair.*
  Haare auf den Zähnen haben *to stand up (to opponents).*
  um ein Haar *nearly, narrowly.*
  kein gutes Haar an einem lassen *to pull a person to pieces.*
  sich in die Haare geraten *to come to blows.*
  Lassen Sie sich darüber keine grauen Haare wachsen! *Don't let that give you gray hair!*
haaren *to shed hair (animals).*
Haarnadel *f. hairpin.*
Haarspalterei *f. hair-splitting.*
Haarwasser *n. hair tonic.*
Habe *f. property, belongings.*
  Hab und Gut *good and chattel.*
  habhaft werden *to obtain possession.*

HABEN *to have, own, possess, get.*
  Den wievielten haben wir heute? *What is the date today?*
  nichts auf sich haben *to be of no consequence.*
  Recht haben *to be right.*
  unter sich haben *to be in charge of.*
  Was hast du? *What is the matter with you?*
  zu haben sein *to be obtainable.*
Habgier *f. greed, avarice.*
habgierig *greedy, avaricious.*
Habseligkeiten *pl. belongings.*
hacken *to chop, mince.*
Hafen *m. port, harbor.*
Hafenstadt *f. seaport.*
Haft *f. custody, arrest, detention.*
haftbar *responsible, liable.*
haften *to stick to, cling to.*
  haften für *to answer for (bear the responsibility).*
Häftling *m. prisoner.*
haftpflichtig *liable, responsible.*
  mit beschränkter Haftung *with limited liability.*
Haftung *f. liability, responsibility.*
Hagel *m. hail.*
Hagelschlag *m. hailstorm.*
HAHN *m. rooster, cock.*
Hai *m. shark.*
Haken *m. hook, mark.*
HALB *half.*
  auf halbem Wege *midway, halfway.*
  ein halbes Pfund *half a pound.*
  halb durchgebraten *medium done (meat).*
  halb so viel *half as much.*
  halb zwei *half past one.*
halbieren *to halve, bisect.*
Halbinsel *f. peninsula.*
Halbmond *m. crescent moon, half-moon.*
Halbwelt *f. demi-monde.*
Hälfte *f. half.*
  Kinder zahlen die Hälfte. *Children pay half price.*
Halle *f. hall, hangar.*
HALS *m. neck, throat.*
  Es hängt mir schon zum Hals heraus. *I am sick and tired of it already.*
  Hals über Kopf *headlong.*
  um den Hals fallen *to embrace.*
Halsband *n. necklace.*
halsbrecherisch *dangerous.*
Halsschmerzen *pl. sore throat.*
Halstuch *n. scarf.*
Halt *m. stop, halt, hold, footing.*
  Halt! *Stop!*
haltbar *lasting, durable.*

Haltbarkeit *f. durability.*
HALTEN *to hold, support, observe, keep, celebrate, last, stop, endure, continue, follow.*
  an sich halten *to restrain oneself.*
  Et hält sich für sehr klug. *He thinks he is very clever.*
  halt machen *to stop.*
  halten für *to consider, think.*
  es halten mit *to side with.*
  Halten Sie sich rechts! *Keep to the right!*
  halten von *to think of.*
  schwer halten *to be difficult.*
  sein Wort halten *to keep one's word.*
  viel halten auf *to think highly of.*
  Was halten Sie von ihr? *What do you think of her?*
Haltestelle *f. stop, station.*
haltlos *without support, unsteady, unprincipled.*
Haltung *f. behavior, attitude, self-control.*
Hammer *m. hammer.*
HAND *f. hand, palm.*
  auf Händen tragen *to spoil.*
  bei der Hand sein *to be ready.*
  die Hand im Spiel haben *to have a finger in the pie.*
  einem die Hand geben *to shake hands with someone.*
  Hand und Fuss haben *to be to the purpose.*
  mit Händen und Füssen *with might and main (tooth and nail).*
  unter der Hand *secretly.*
  von der Hand gehen *to work well.*
  von der Hand weisen *to decline.*
  zur Hand *handy.*
Handarbeit *f. manual work, labor.*
HANDEL *m. trade, business, affair.*
  Handel treiben *to trade.*
  handelseinig werden *to come to terms.*
handeln *to act, do.*
  handeln mit *to trade with.*
  handeln von *to deal with.*
  sich handeln um *to be about, be a matter of.*
Handelskammer *f. chamber of commerce.*
Handfertigkeit *f. manual skill.*
Handfesseln *f. handcuffs.*
Handgelenk *n. wrist.*
Handgemenge *f. hand-to-hand fighting.*
Handgepäck *n. hand luggage.*
handgreiflich *obvious, manifest.*
  handgreiflich werden *to use one's fists.*
handhaben *to handle, manage.*

Handkoffer *m. suitcase.*
Händler *m. trader, dealer.*
handlich *handy.*
Handlung *f. act, action, deed, business.*
Handlungsweise *f. way of acting, method of dealing.*
Handschrift *f. handwriting.*
Handschuh *m. glove.*
Handstreich *m. surprise attack.*
Handtasche *f. handbag.*
Handtuch *n. towel.*
Handwerk *n. handicraft, trade.*
  einem das Handwerk legen *to stop a person's activities.*
hängen *to hang, suspend, fix, attach.*
  hängen bleiben *to be caught.*
hänseln *to tease.*
Harm *m. grief, sorrow, insult, injury.*
harmlos *harmless.*
Harmlosigkeit *f. harmlessness, innocence.*
Harmonie *f. harmony.*
harmonieren *to harmonize, agree.*
HART *hard, firm, solid.*
  hartherzig *hard-hearted.*
  harthörig *hard of hearing.*
Härte *f. hardness, roughness, cruelty, severity.*
hartnäckig *obstinate, stubborn.*
Hase *m. hare.*
Hasenbraten *m. roast hare.*
Hass *m. hate, hatred.*
hassen *to hate.*
hässlich *ugly, nasty.*
Hässelichkeit *f. ugliness.*
Hast *f. hurry, haste.*
hastig *hurried, hasty.*
Haube *f. hood, cap.*
  unter die Haube bringen *to marry off.*
Hauch *m. breath, slight breeze.*
hauchen *to breathe.*
Haufen *m. heap, pile.*
häufen *to heap, pile, accumulate.*
häufig *frequent, abundant.*
HAUPT *n. chief, head.*
Hauptbahnhof *m. main station.*
Hauptmann *m. captain.*
Hauptperson *f. principal person, leading character (theater).*
Hauptpostamt *n. general post office.*
Hauptquartier *n. headquarters.*
Hauptsache *f. main thing.*
hauptsächlich *principal.*
Hauptstadt *f. capital.*
Hauptverkehrszeit *f. rush hours.*
Hauptwort *n. substantive, noun.*
HAUS *n. house, home, building.*
  das Haus bestellen *to put one's affairs in order.*

das Haus hüten *to be confined to the house.*
nach Hause gehen *to go home.*
von Haus aus *originally.*
zu Hause *at home.*
Hausangestellte *m. & f. servant.*
Hausarbeit *f. housework.*
Hausaufgabe *f. homework.*
Häuschen *n. small house.*
Hausflur *m. hall, corridor.*
Hausfrau *f. housewife.*
Haushalt *m. household.*
haushalten *to keep house, to economize.*
Haushälterin *f. housekeeper.*
Hausherr *m. master.*
Hauslehrer *m. private tutor.*
häuslich *domestic.*
Häuslichkeit *f. family life, domesticity.*
Hausmeister *m. janitor.*
Hausschuh *m. slipper.*
Haussuchung *f. police raid.*
Haustier *n. domestic animal.*
Haustüre *f. front door.*
Hauswirt *m. landlord.*
HAUT *f. skin, hide, coat.*
aus der Haut fahren *to lose one's patience.*
sich seiner Haut wehren *to defend oneself.*
Hautfarbe *f. complexion.*
heben *to lift, raise.*
Heer *n. army.*
Hefe *f. yeast.*
Heft *n. handle, notebook, pamphlet, number.*
heften *to pin, fasten, stitch, fix.*
heftig *violent, strong.*
Heftigkeit *f. violence, vehemence, intensity.*
heikel *delicate, ticklish, difficult.*
HEIL *unhurt, intact, safe, cured.*
heilbar *curable.*
heilen *to cure.*
heilig *holy, godly, sacred.*
Heiligabend *Christmas Eve.*
heilkräftig *curative.*
Heilmittel *n. remedy.*
heilsam *curative.*
Heilsarmee *f. Salvation Army.*
Heilung *f. healing, cure.*
Heilverfahren *n. medical treatment.*
HEIM *n. home.*
heim *homeward.*
Heimat *f. native country, homeland.*
heimatlos *homeless.*
Heimatstadt *f. home town.*
Heimkehr(-kunft) *f. homecoming.*
heimlich *secret, private, comfortable;*

secretly, privately.
Heimsuchung *f. trial, misfortune.*
Heimtücke *f. malice.*
heimtückisch *malicious, insidious.*
Heimweg *m. way home, return.*
Heimweh *n. homesickness.*
Heimweh haben *to be homesick.*
HEIRAT *f. marriage.*
heiraten *to marry, get married.*
Heiratsantrag *m. proposal.*
heiser *hoarse.*
heiser sein *to be hoarse, have a sore throat.*
Heiserkeit *f. hoarseness, sore throat.*
HEISS *hot.*
HEISSEN *to call, name, be called.*
das heisst *that is.*
es heisst *they say.*
Ich heisse Anna. *My name is Ann.*
Wie heisst das auf Englisch? *What is that called in English?*
heiter *gay, cheerful.*
Heiterkeit *f. brightness, clearness, serenity, cheerfulness.*
heizbar *with heating.*
heizen *to heat.*
Heizkissen *n. electric pad.*
Heizkörper *m. radiator.*
Heizung *f. heating, firing, radiator.*
Held *m. hero.*
HELFEN *to support, help, assist.*
Ich kann mir nicht helfen. *I can't help it.*
Helfer *m. helper, assistant.*
Helfershelfer *m. accomplice ("helper's helper")*
HELL *bright, shining, clear, light, fair, pale, sheer.*
Helle *f. clearness, brightness.*
hellhörig *keen of hearing.*
Helm *m. helmet.*
HEMD *n. shirt.*
Hendbrust *f. shirt front, dicky.*
hemmen *to check, stop, hinder, restrain.*
Hemmung *f. inhibition, check, stoppage restraint.*
hemmungslos *free, unrestrained.*
HER 1. *adv. here, from, since, ago.*
von Alters her *of old, long ago.*
2. *separable prefix (implies the idea of a movement toward the speaker)*
Kommen Sie her! *Come here!*
herab *down, downward.*
herablassen *to lower, let down, condescend.*
Herablassung *f. condescension.*
herabsehen *to look down upon.*
herabsetzen *to lower, degrade, reduce (price).*

Herabsetzung *f. lowering, degradation; reduction (price).*

heran *on, up, near, along.*

heranbilden *to train, educate.*

herankommen *to come near.*
die Dinge an sich herankommen lassen *to bide one's time.*

heranwachsen *to grow up.*

HERAUF *up, upwards.*

heraufgehen *to go up.*
Kommen Sie herauf! *Come up!*

HERAUS *out, from within.*
Sie kommen heraus. *They are coming out.*

herausbekommen *to get back (money); find out.*
auf eins herauskommen *to be all one.*

herausnehmen *to take out, extract.*

herausstellen *to turn out, appear.*

herbel *here, near, hither.*

herbeischaffen *to bring near, procure, produce.*

HERBST *m. autumn.*

herbstlich *autumnal.*

Herd *m. hearth, fireplace.*

Herdplatte *f. hot plate.*

HEREIN *in.*
Kommen Sie herein (Herein!) *Come in!*
Hier herein, bitte! *This way, please!*

hereinfallen *to be taken in, disappointed.*

herkommen *to come near, approach, originate.*

Herkunft *f. origin, descent.*

HERR *m. master, gentleman, lord, sir, Mr.*
Meine Damen und Herren *Ladies and gentlemen.*
Ist der Herr Doktor zu sprechen? *Can I see the doctor?*
eigener Herr sein *to stand on one's own feet.*
Herr werden *to master, overcome.*
Herr im Hause sein *to be the master of the house.*

herrichten *to arrange.*

herrisch *imperious, dictatorial.*

Herrschaft *f. power, rule, command, master and mistress (of an estate).*

herrschen *to rule, govern, prevail, exist.*

Herrscher *m. ruler, tyrant, dictator.*

herrschsüchtig *fond of power, tyrannical.*

herüber *across, to this side.*

herüberkommen *to come over.*

HERUM *around, round, near, about.*
rundherum *all around.*

herumdrehen *to turn round.*

herumführen *to lead.*

herumreichen *to hand around.*

herumtreiben *(sich) to run around.*

HERUNTER *down, off.*

herunterkommen *to come down.*
Komm gleich herunter! *Come down right away!*

heruntersetzen *to lower.*

hervor *out, forth.*

hervorbringen *to produce, yield.*

hervorheben *to make prominent.*

hervorragen *to stand out, project.*

hervorragend *prominent, excellent.*

hervortun (sich) *to distinguish oneself.*

HERZ *n. heart, feeling, mind, courage.*
ans Herz legen *to recommend to someone's care.*
ins Herz schliessen *to become fond of.*
sich ein Herz fassen *to take courage.*
sich zu Herzen nehmen *to take to heart.*
unter dem Herzen tragen *to be expecting a child.*
von Herzen gern *with the greatest pleasure.*
Was haben Sie auf dem Herzen? *What's on your mind?*

herzleidend *suffering from heart trouble.*

herzlich *hearty, cordial.*
mit herzlichen Grüssen *with kindest regards.*

herzlos *heartless.*

Herzschlag *m. heart beat, heart failure.*

Heu *n. hay.*

Heufieber *n. hay fever.*

Heuchelei *f. hypocrisy.*

heucheln *to feign, pretend.*

Heuchler *m. hypocrite.*

HEUTE *today.*
heute abend *tonight.*
heute früh; heute morgen *this morning.*
heute vor acht Tagen *a week ago.*
heutzutage *nowadays.*

Hexe *f. witch.*

Hier *here.*
hier und da *here and there.*

hierauf *hereupon.*

hierdurch *through this, this way, thereby.*

hierher *here, hither.*

hierherum *hereabout.*

hiermit *herewith, with this.*

hiernach *after this, thereupon.*

hierüber *over here, about this.*

hiervon *hereof, from this.*

hierzu *to this, moreover.*

hierzulande *in this country.*

HILFE *f. help, assistance, support, relief.*

Hilfe leisten *to help, assist.*
erste Hilfe *first aid.*
hilflos *helpless.*
hilfreich *helpful, charitable.*
hilfsbedürftig *indigent, needing help.*
HIMMEL *m. sky, heaven.*
aus allen Himmeln fallen *to be bitterly disappointed.*
Himmelsrichtung *f. quarter, direction, point of compass.*
himmlisch *heavenly, celestial.*
HIN 1. *adv. there, thither.*
hin und her *to and fro.*
hin und her überlegen *to turn over in one's mind.*
hin und wieder *now and then.*
2. *separable prefix (implies the idea of a movement away from the speaker).*
Gehen Sie hinaus. *Go out.*
hinab *down, downward.*
HINAUF *up, upward.*
hinaufarbeiten *to work one's way up.*
Er geht die Treppe hinauf. *He goes up the stairs.*
HINAUS *out, outside, past.*
darüber hinaus *beyond that.*
Ich schicke die Kinder hinaus. *I am sending the children outside.*
hinausgehen *to go out.*
hinauskommen *to come out.*
auf eins hinauskommen *to come to the same thing.*
hinausschieben *to defer, postpone, put off.*
hinauswerfen *to throw out, expel.*
hoch hinauswollen *to aim high.*
hinausziehen *to draw out, put off.*
Hinblick *m. look at or toward.*
im Hinblick auf *with regard to.*
hinbringen *to take, bring, carry.*
hinderlich *in the way, hindering, obstructive.*
hindern *to prevent, hinder, hamper.*
hindurch *through, throughout, across.*
HINEIN *in, into.*
Ich gehe in das Zimmer hinein. *I go into the room.*
hineingehen *to go into.*
hinfahren *to convey, carry, drive to.*
Hinfahrt *f. trip there.*
hinfallen *to fall down.*
hinfällig *frail, weak.*
hinfällig werden *to fail, come to nothing.*
hinfort *henceforth, in the future.*
Hingabe *f. surrender, devotion.*
hinhalten *to put off.*
hinlänglich *sufficient, adequate.*
hinnehmen *to take, accept.*

hinsehen *to look at.*
hinsetzen *to set down, sit down.*
hinsichtlich *with regard to.*
hinstellen *to place, put down, lie down.*
hinten *behind, in the rear, at the back.*
HINTER 1. *prep. (dat. when answering question, Wo?; acc. when answering question, Wohin? and depending on the idiom) behind, back, after.*
Hinter dem Haus ist eine Garage. *There is a garage behind the house.*
Sie hat schon viel hinter sich. *She has been through a lot.*
hinter sich bringen *to get over, cover.*
Hinterbliebene *m. & f. survivor.*
hintereinander *one after the other.*
zwei Tage hintereinander *two days running.*
Hintergedanke *m. underlying thought, unacknowledged motive.*
Hintergrund *m. background.*
Hinterhalt *m. ambush.*
hinterhältig .. *cious, devious.*
hinterher *behind, afterwards.*
hinterlassen *to leave, leave behind.*
Hat er keine Nachricht für mich hinterlassen? *Hasn't he left a message for me?*
hinterlegen *to deposit.*
Hinterlist *f. artifice, fraud, trick.*
hinterlistig *artful, cunning.*
Hinterrad *n. backwheel.*
hinters *hinter das.*
ins Hintertreffen geraten *to be handicapped.*
Hinüber *over, across, over there, to the other side.*
HINUNTER *down, downward, downstairs.*
Sie geht die Treppe hinunter. *She walks down the stairs.*
Hinweg *m. way there.*
hinweg *away, off.*
hinwegkommen (über) *to get over.*
hinwegsetzen (über) *to disregard.*
Hinweis *m. indication, hint, reference, direction.*
hinweisen *to show, indicate, refer.*
hinwerfen *to throw down.*
hinzu *to, near, there.*
hinzufügen *to add.*
hinzuziehen *to include, consult.*
Hirn *n. brain.*
Hitze *f. heat.*
hitzig *hot, hot-headed.*
HOCH *high, tall, lofty, great, noble.*
Es geht hoch her. *Things are getty pretty lively.*
Hände hoch! *Hands up!*

41

hoch anrechnen *to value greatly.*
Hoch lebe ...! *Long live ...!*
hochleben lassen *to toast.*
hochachten *to esteem, respect.*
Hochachtung *f. esteem, respect.*
hochachtungsvoll *yours faithfully.*
Hochbetrieb *m. intense activity.*
Hochdeutsch *n. high German, standard German.*
hochalten *to cherish, raise.*
Hochhaus *n. skyscraper.*
hochherzig *high-minded, magnanimous.*
Hochmut *m. pride, arrogance.*
hochmütig *arrogant, proud.*
Hochschule *f. university, college.*
Hochsommer *m. midsummer.*
Hochspannung *f. high tension.*
Vorsicht! Hochspannung! *Caution! High tension wires!*
HOCHST *highest, utmost, extreme, maximum; very, extremely.*
Hochstapelei *f. swindling.*
Hochstapler *m. swindler.*
höchstens *at best, at most.*
Höchstgeschwindigkeit *f. top speed, speed limit.*
Höchstgrenze *f. limit.*
Höchstleistung *f. maximum output, record performance.*
höchstwahrscheinlich *most likely.*
hochtrabend *high-sounding.*
Hochverrat *m. high treason.*
Hochzeit *f. wedding, marriage.*
Hochzeitreise *f. honeymoon trip.*
HOF *m. yard, court, farm.*
den Hof machen *to pay court to.*
HOFFEN *to hope.*
hoffentlich *it is to be hoped.*
Hoffnung *f. hope.*
sich falsche Hoffnungen machen *to have illusions.*
hoffnungslos *hopeless.*
hoffnungsvoll *hopeful.*
HÖHE *f. height, altitude, latitude, top, summit, amount.*
auf der Höhe sein *to be up to date, to be in top form.*
auf der Höhe von *at the altitude of.*
aus der Höhe *from on high.*
Das ist die Höhe. *That is the limit.*
in (der) Höhe von *in the amount of.*
Höhensonne *f. ultraviolet light.*
höher *higher, superior.*
HOHL *hollow, concave, dull.*
Höhle *f. hole, cave.*
Hohlraum *m. empty space, cavity.*
Hohn *m. scorn, sneer, mockery, insult.*
höhnen *to mock, defy.*
höhnisch *scornful, sneering.*

HOLEN *to get, take, fetch.*
sich Rat holen *to consult.*
HÖLLE *f. hell.*
höllisch *hellish, infernal.*
HOLZ *n. wood, timber, lumber.*
hölzern *wooden.*
Honig *m. honey.*
horchen *to listen, lend an ear, listen in, spy.*
Es horcht jemand. *Somebody is listening in.*
HÖREN *to hear, listen, attend, obey, understand.*
schwer hören *to be hard of hearing.*
Horizont *m. horizon.*
Horn *n. horn, bugle.*
Horoskop *n. horoscope.*
ein Horoskop stellen *to cast horoscope.*
Hörspiel *n. radio play.*
Hose *f. trousers, pants.*
Sie hat die Hosen an. *She wears the pants.*
Hosenträger *pl. suspenders.*
Hotel *n. hotel, inn.*
hübsch *pretty, charming, nice.*
Huf *m. hoof.*
Hügel *m. hill.*
HUHN *n. hen.*
gebratenes Hühnchen *roast chicken.*
junges Huhn *young chicken.*
Huld *f. grace, favor, charm.*
huldigen *to pay homage.*
Humor *m. sense of humor.*
humoristisch *humorous.*
HUND *m. dog.*
Hundert *n. hundred.*
zu Hunderten *by hundreds.*
HUNDERT *one hundred (adj.)*
HUNGER *m. hunger.*
Hunger haben *to be hungry.*
Hungerkut *f. reducing diet.*
hungern *to be hungry, starve.*
Hungersnot *f. famine.*
hungrig *hungry.*
husten *to cough.*
Hustensirup *m. cough syrup.*
HUT *m. hat.*
unter einen Hut bringen *to reconcile.*
hüten *to guard, keep, beware.*
das Zimmer hüten *to be confined to one's room.*
Hütte *f. hut.*

I

ICH *I, self, ego.*
Ideal *n. ideal.*

Idealist m. idealist.
Idee f. idea, notion.
identifizieren to identify.
identisch identical.
IHM dat. of er, es (pers. pron., masc. and neut.) to him, to it.
IHN acc. of er (pers. pron. masc.) him, it.
IHNEN (ihnen) dat. of sie (pers. pron. pl). to them.
IHNEN (ihnen) dat. of Sie (pers. pron. sing. polite form) to you.
IHR dat. of sie (pers. pron. fem.) to her, to it.
IHR (ihr) poss. adj. (fem. and pl.) her, its, their.
IHR (ihr) poss. adj. (sing. polite form) your.
IHR(ER,-E,-ES) poss, pron. (fem. and pl.) hers, its, theirs.
poss. pron. (sing. polite form) your.
ihretwegen on her (its, their) account, for her sake.
ihretwegen on your account, for your sake.
illustrieren to illustrate.
imitieren to imitate.
IMMER always, ever.
auf immer forever.
immer mehr more and more.
immer wieder again and again.
immerfort continually, constantly.
wer auch immer whoever.
immerhin for all that, still, nevertheless.
immerzu all the time, continually.
impertinent impertinent, insolent.
imponieren to impress.
Import m. imports, importation.
Impuls m. impulse.
impulsiv impulsive.
IN prep. (dat. answering question, Wo?; acc. answering question, Wohin?) in, into, to, at.
Die Besucher gehen in die Oper. The spectators go to the opera.
Der Lehrer sitzt in dem Zimmer. The teacher is sitting in the room.
Der Lehrer tritt in das Zimmer ein. The teacher goes into the room.
Der Sänger singt in der Oper. The singer sings at the opera.
Goethe wurde in Frankfurt geboren. Goethe was born in Frankfort.
im Februar in February.
im Kreise in a circle.
Inbegriff m. embodiment, essence.
inbegriffen including, inclusive, included.
INDEM while, by, on, since.

indirekt indirect.
indiskret indiscreet, tactless.
Indiskretion f. indiscretion.
Industrie f. industry.
Industrielle m. manufacturer, producer.
Infektionskrankheit f. infectious disease.
infolge in consequence of, as a result of.
infolgedessen because of that, consequently, hence.
Ingenieur m. engineer.
Inhaber m. holder, proprietor, occupant.
Inhalt m. contents, area, extent, volume, capacity.
inhaltlich with regard to the contents.
Inhaltsangabe f. summary, table of contents.
inhaltsleer empty, meaningless.
inhaltsreich full of meaning, significant.
Inhaltsverzeichnis n. contents, table of contents, index.
inmitten in the midst of.
innen within, inside, in.
INNER interior, internal, inner.
innerhalb within, inside.
innerlich inward, internal, interior.
innig hearty, intimate.
Innigkeit f. cordiality, intimacy.
ins in das.
insbesondere particularly.
Inschrift f. inscription, legend.
Insekt n. insect.
INSEL f. island.
Inserat n. advertisement.
inserieren to advertise.
insgesamt all together, collectively.
insofern in so far, as far as that goes.
insowelt in so far.
Instandhaltung f. upkeep.
inständig instant, urgent.
Instinkt m. instinct.
instruieren to instruct, brief.
Instrument n. instrument.
intelligent intelligent.
Intelligenz f. intelligence, understanding, intellect.
interessant interesting.
Interesse n. interest, advantage.
interessieren to interest.
international international.
interviewen to interview.
Inventar n. inventory, stock.
investieren to invest.
inzwischen in between, in the meantime.
IRGEND any, some.
wenn irgend möglich if at all possible.
irgendetwas something.

irgendjemand *somebody.*
irgendwann *sometime.*
irgendwie *somehow.*
irgendwo *somewhere.*
irgendwoher *from some place or other.*
irgendwohin *to somewhere or other.*
ironisch *ironical.*
irre *astray, wrong, confused, insane.*
  irre werden an *to lose confidence in.*
IRRE *f. wandering, mistaken course.*
  in die Irre gehen *to lose one's way, go
    astray.*
  Irre machen *to confuse.*
irren, *to err, wander, lose one's way, be
    mistaken, be wrong.*
  sich irren *to be mistaken.*
  Irren ist menschlich *To err is human.*
Irrenanstalt *f. lunatic asylum.*
irritieren *to irritate.*
Irrsinn *m. madness, insanity.*
irrsinnig *mad, insane.*
Irrtum *m. error, mistake.*
  Sie sind im Irrtum. *You are mistaken.*
irrtümlich *erroneous, wrong.*
Italiener *m. Italian (person).*
Italienisch *n. Italian (language).*
Italienisch *Italian.*

J

JA *yes, really, indeed, certainly.*
  Da sind Sie ja! *So there you are!*
  Sie wissen ja, dass ich nicht gehen
    kann. *But you know that I can't go.*
  ja sogar *even.*
Jacke *f. jacket.*
Jackenkleid *n. lady's suit.*
JAGD *f. hunt, pursuit, hunting, shooting.*
  auf die Jagd gehen *to go hunting.*
Jagdschein *m. hunting license.*
jagen *to chase, pursue.*
Jäger *m. hunter, huntsman, sportsman.*
jäh *sudden, quick, steep.*
JAHR *n. year.*
  ein halbes Jahr *six months.*
Jahrestag *m. anniversary.*
Jahreswende *f. New Year, turn of the
    year.*
JAHRESZEIT *f. season.*
jahrhundert *n. century.*
jährlich *yearly, annual.*
Jahrmarkt *m. fair.*
Jahrtausand *n. thousand years,
    millennium.*
Jahrzehnt *n. decade.*
Jähzorn *m. sudden anger, violent
    temper.*

jähzorning *hot-tempered, irascible.*
Jammer *m. misery, wailing.*
  Was für ein Jammer! *What a pity!*
jammern *to lament, wail, moan.*
JANUAR *m. January.*
Japaner *m. Japanese (person).*
japanisch *Japanese (language).*
jauchzen *to exult, shout, rejoice.*
JAWOHL *of course, indeed.*
JE *each, ever, at all times.*
  je zwei *two at a time.*
  Sie erhielten je ein Pfund. *They
    received a pound each.*
  je nach *according to.*
  je nachdem *according as.*
  Je eher umso (desto) besser. *The
    sooner, the better.*
jedenfalls *at all events, in any case.*
JEDER (jede, jedes) *every, each,
    either, any.*
jedermann *everyone, everybody.*
jederzeit *at any time, always.*
jedesmal *every time.*
  jedesmal wenn *whenever, as often as.*
jedoch *however, nevertheless.*
jeher *von jeher at all times, from times
    immemorial.*
jemals *at any time.*
jemand *somebody, someone.*
JENER (jene, jenes) *that, that one, the
    former, the other.*
  jenseitig *opposite, on the opposite
    side.*
JENSEITS 1. *adv. beyond, on the other
    side, yonder.*
  2. *prep. (gen.). that side, on the other
    side.*
jetzig *present, actual.*
JETZT *now, at present.*
Joch *n. yoke.*
Jod *n. iodine.*
Journalist *m. journalist.*
Jubel *m. rejoicing, jubilation.*
Jude *m. Jew.*
jüdisch *Jewish.*
JUGEND *f. youth, young people.*
Jugendfreund *m. friend of youth.*
jugendlich *youthful.*
Jugendliche *m. & f. young boy or girl.*
Jugendliebe *f. first love.*
Jugendzeit *f. youth, young days.*
JULI *m. July.*
JUNG *young, youthful.*
Junge *m. boy, lad.*
jungenhaft *boyish.*
jünger *younger.*
Jungfrau *f. virgin, maid, maiden.*
  alte Jungfer *old maid.*
Junggeselle *m. bachelor.*

Jüngling *m. young man.*
JUNI *m. June.*
Jura *pl. law.*
  Jura studieren *to study law.*
Jurist *m. law-student, lawyer.*
Justiz *f. administration of the law.*
Juwel *n. jewel.*
Juwelier *m. jeweler.*

K

Kabarett *n. cabaret.*
Kabine *f. cabin.*
Kachel *f. glazed tile.*
KAFFEE *m. coffee.*
Kaffeekanne *f. coffee-pot.*
Käfig *m. cage.*
kahl *bald, bare, naked.*
kahlköpfig *bald-headed.*
Kai *m. wharf.*
Kaiser *m. emperor.*
Kalb *n. calf.*
Kalbfleisch *n. veal.*
  Kalbsbraten *m. roast veal.*
Kalender *m. calendar.*
kalkulieren *to calculate.*
KALT *cold, indifferent.*
kaltblütig *cold-blooded.*
Kälte *f. coldness, indifference.*
Kamel, *n. camel.*
Kamera *f. camera.*
Kamerad *m. friend, comrade, fellow.*
Kameradschaft *f. fellowship,*
  comradeship.
Kamin *m. chimney, fireplace.*
Kamm *m. comb.*
kämmen *to comb.*
Kammer *f. small room, chamber*
  (government).
Kammermusik *f. chamber music.*
KAMPF *m. fight, combat, conflict,*
  struggle.
  Kampf ums Dasein *struggle for a*
  living.
KÄMPFEN *to fight.*
Kanal *m. canal, sewer.*
Kanarienvogel *m. canary bird.*
Kandidat *m. candidate.*
kandidieren *to be a candidate.*
Kaninchen *n. rabbit.*
Kanne *f. jug, pot, pitcher.*
Kanone *f. cannon.*
Kante *f. edge, corner.*
kantig *edged, angular.*
Kantine *f. canteen, mess.*
Kanzel *f. pulpit.*

Kapelle *f. chapel, band.*
Kapital *n. capital.*
Kapitalsanlage *f. investment.*
Kapitalismus *m. capitalism.*
Kapitalist *m. capitalist.*
kapitalkräftig *wealthy.*
Kapitän *m. captain.*
Kapitel *n. chapter.*
kapitulieren *to capitulate.*
Kaplan *m. chaplain.*
kaputt *broken, ruined, out of order.*
Karfreitag *m. Good Friday.*
Karikatur *f. caricature.*
Karneval *m. carnival.*
Karotte *f. carrot.*
Karriere *f. career, gallop.*
KARTE *f. card, ticket, map, menu.*
  Karten legen *to tell one's fortune.*
Kartenspiel *n. card game, pack of*
  cards.
KARTOFFEL *f. potato.*
  Kartoffelpüree *n. mashed potatoes.*
  Bratkartoffeln *pl. fried potatoes.*
  Kartoffelsalat, *m. potato salad.*
Karton *m. cardboard, box.*
Karwoche *f. Passion Week.*
KÄSE *m. cheese.*
Kaserne *f. barracks.*
Kasse *f. cash-box.*
  Zahlen Sie, bitte, an der Kasse.
  Please pay the cashier.
Kassenschein *m. receipt.*
kassieren *to receive money.*
Kassierer *m. cashier.*
Kastanie *f. chestnut.*
Kasten *m. box, chest, mailbox.*
Katalog *m. catalog.*
Katastrophe *f. catastrophe.*
katastrophal *catastrophic.*
Katholik *m. Roman Catholic.*
katholisch *Roman Catholic. (adj.).*
Katze *f. cat.*
kauen *to masticate, chew.*
  Kaugummi, *n. chewing-gum.*
KAUF *m. buy, purchase.*
  mit in Kauf nehmen *to put up with.*
KAUFEN *to buy, purchase.*
  sich etwas kaufen *to buy oneself*
  something.
Käufer *m. buyer.*
Kaufhaus *n. store, warehouse,*
  department store.
Kaufladen *m. store, shop.*
Kaufmann *m. shopkeeper, merchant.*
KAUM *hardly, scarcely, barely.*
Kavalier *m. cavalier, gentleman.*
keck *bold, daring, impudent.*
Keckheit *f. boldness.*
Kegel *m. ninepin.*

kegeln *to bowl.*
Kehle *f. throat.*
Kehlkopf *m. larynx.*
KEHREN *turn, to sweep.*
  sich kehren an *to pay attention to; to mind.*
  kehrtmachen *to face about, turn back.*
KEIN *adj. no, not one, not any.*
KEIN (ER,-E,-ES) *pron. none, neither.*
  keiner von beiden *neither of them.*
keinerlei *of no sort.*
KEINESWEGS *on no account, not at all.*
Kelch *m. cup, goblet, chalice.*
Keller *m. cellar.*
KELLNER *m (-in, f.) waiter, (waitress).*
KENNEN *to know, be acquainted with.*
  kennenlernen *to meet, become acquainted with.*
Kenner *m. connoisseur.*
Kennkarte *f. identity-card.*
kenntlich *recognizable, distinguishable.*
KENNTNIS *f. knowledge, information.*
  in Kenntnis setzen *to inform.*
  zur Kenntnis nehmen *to take note of.*
Kennzeichen *n. identification.*
Kern *m. kernel, corn, seed, stone (fruit).*
Kerze *f. candle, sparking plug.*
Kessel *m. boiler, kettle.*
Kette *f. chain, necklace.*
Kettenhund *m. watch dog.*
keuchen *to pant, puff.*
Keuchhusten *m. whooping cough.*
Keule *f. club, leg (of lamb, etc.)*
keusch *pure, modest, chaste.*
Keuschheit *f. modesty, purity, chastity.*
Kiefer *m. jaw.*
Kilogramm *n. kilogram (2.204 pounds).*
Kilometer *m. kilometer (.621 miles).*
Kilometerzähler *m. mileage recorder.*
KIND *n. child.*
  kleines Kind *baby (infant).*
  von Kind auf *from childhood on.*
Kindergarten *m. kindergarten, nursery school.*
Kinderlähmung *f. infantile paralysis.*
kinderlos *childless.*
Kindermädchen *n. nursemaid.*
Kinderstube *f. nursery.*
Kinderwagen *m. baby carriage.*
Kindheit *f. childhood.*
kindisch *childish.*
kindlich *childlike, filial.*
Kinn *n. chin.*
Kino *n. cinema, picture show, movies.*
Kirche *f. church, service.*
Kirchhof *m. cemetery.*
Kirchtum *m. church steeple.*
Kirsche *f. cherry.*
Kissen *n. cushion, pillow.*

Kissenbezug *m. cover, pillow-case.*
Kiste *f. box, chest, case.*
kitzeln *to tickle.*
kitzlig *ticklish.*
Klage *f. lament, complaint.*
klagen *to lament, complain, sue.*
Kläger *m. plaintiff.*
kläglich *lamentable, deplorable.*
klamm *numb, stiff, tight.*
klammern *to fasten, clasp, cling to.*
Klang *m. sound, tone, ringing of bell.*
Klangfarbe *f. timbre.*
klanglos *soundless.*
klangvoll *sonorous.*
Klappstuhl *m. camp stool or chair.*
Klapptisch *m. folding table.*
Klaps *m. slap.*
KLAR *clear, limpid, pure, plain, evident.*
  klar und deutlich *distinctly, plainly.*
  klar zum Gefecht *ready for action.*
  klar legen (stellen) *to clear up, explain.*
  sich klar darüber sein *to realize.*
Klarinette *f. clarinet.*
Klarinettist *m. clarinetist.*
KLASSE *f. class, form, order.*
Klassenlehrer *m. class-teacher.*
Klassenzimmer *n. classroom.*
Klassik *f. classical art, classical period.*
Klatsch *m. smack, crack, gossip.*
klatschen *to clap, lash, applaud.*
  Beifall klatschen *to applaud.*
Klavier *n. piano.*
Klavierspieler *m. pianist.*
kleben *to stick, glue.*
Klee *m. clover, shamrock.*
KLEID *n. dress, frock, gown.*
  die Kleider *pl. garments.*
kleiden *to dress, clothe, suit, become.*
  Er ist immer gut gekleidet. *He is always well-dressed.*
Kleiderbügel *m. coathanger.*
Kleiderbürste *f. clothes brush.*
Kleiderschrank *m. wardrobe.*
Kleidung *f. dress, clothes, clothing.*
KLEIN *little, small, tiny, minor.*
  klein schneiden *to cut in pieces.*
  klein schreiben *to write with small letters.*
  von klein auf *from infancy on.*
KLEINGELD *n. change (monetary).*
kleingläubig *of little faith.*
Kleinholz *n. sticks, firewood.*
Kleinkram *m. trifle.*
Kleinstadt *f. small provincial town.*
kleinstädtisch *provincial.*
klettern *to climb.*
Klima *n. climate.*
klimatisch *climatic.*

klimmen *to climb.*
Klingel *f. bell.*
klingeln *to ring.*
Klinke *f. doorknob; handle.*
klipp *snapping sound, snap of the fingers.*
  klipp und klar *quite clear.*
klirren *to clink, jingle.*
klopfen *to beat, knock, tap.*
Kloster *n. monastery, convent.*
Klub *m. club.*
Klubsessel *m. lounge chair, easy chair.*
KLUG *intelligent, sensible, clever.*
  Ich werde nicht klug daraus. *I can't figure it out.*
Klugheit *f. intelligence.*
Klumpen *m. lump.*
KNABE *m. boy, lad.*
Knall *m. bang, detonation, crack.*
knapp *narrow, tight, close, poor.*
  knapp werde *to run short of.*
Knappheit *f. narrowness, conciseness.*
Knecht *m. servant, farmhand, slave.*
Knechtheit *f. servitude, slavery.*
kneifen *to pinch, nip.*
Kneipe *f. tavern, public house.*
Knie *n. knee.*
Kniehosen *pl. breeches, shorts.*
knistern *to rustle, crackle.*
KNOCHEN *m. bone.*
knöchern *of bone, bony.*
Knopf *m. button, knob, head.*
knöpfen *to button.*
Knopfloch *n. buttonhole.*
Knospe *f. bud.*
knospig *full of buds.*
Knoten *m. knot.*
knurren *to growl, rumble.*
knusprig *crisp.*
Koch *m. cook.*
Kochbuch *n. cookbook.*
KOCHEN *to cook, boil.*
Kochgeschirr *n. pots and pans.*
Köchin *f. cook.*
Kochlöffel *m. ladle.*
Kochtopf *m. saucepan, pot, casserole.*
Koffer *m. trunk, bag, suitcase.*
Kognak *m. cognac, brandy.*
Kohl *m. cabbage.*
Kohle *f. coal, carbon.*
  auf Kohlen sitzen *to be on tenterhooks.*
Kohleneimer *m. coal bucket.*
Koje *f. cabin, berth.*
Kollege *m. colleague.*
Kolonialwaren *pl. groceries.*
Kolonialwarenhandlung *f. grocery store.*
Komiker *m. comedian.*

komisch *comical.*
Komma *n. comma.*
kommandieren *to command, order.*
KOMMEN *to come, arrive, get, result, happen, occur.*
  Das kommt davon. *That's the result.*
  Das kommt nicht in Frage. *This is out of the question.*
  Es kommt darauf an. *It depends.*
  kommen lassen *to send for.*
  kommen sehen *to foresee.*
  nicht dazu kommen *to have no time to.*
  Wann komme ich an die Reihe? *When will it be my turn?*
  Wie kommt es, dass *how is it that.*
  zu sich kommen *to recover.*
kommend *next.*
  kommende Woche *next week.*
Kommentar *m. commentray.*
Kommode *f. commode.*
Komödiant *m. comedian, actor, hypocrite.*
Komödie *f. comedy.*
Kompass *m. compass.*
komplett *complete; completely.*
Kompliment *n. compliment.*
komponieren *to compose.*
Komponist *m. composer.*
Konditor *m. pastry cook.*
Konditorei *f. pastry-shop, cafe.*
Konfekt *n. candy, chocolates, sweets.*
Konfektion *f. ready-made clothes.*
Konferenz *f. conference.*
Konfession *f. confession.*
Konflikt *m. conflict.*
KÖNIG *m. king.*
königlich *royal.*
Konkurrent *m. rival.*
Konkurrenz *f. competition.*
konkurrieren *to be in competition with, compete.*
Konkurs *m. bankruptcy.*
KÖNNER *to be able to, be possible, understand.*
  Das kann sein. *It may be.*
  Das kann nicht sein. *It is impossible.*
  Ich kann nicht mehr. *I am exhausted.*
  Er kann nichts dafür. *It is not his fault.*
konsequent *consistent.*
Konsequenz *f. consistency.*
konservativ *conservative.*
Konservatorium *n. academy of music.*
Konserve *f. canned goods.*
konstruieren *to construct.*
Konstrukteur *m. constructor.*
Konsul *m. consul.*
Konsulat *n. consulate.*
Kontinent *m. continent.*

Konto n. account (financial).
Kontoauszug m. statement (account).
Kontrakt m. contract.
Kontrast m. contrast.
Kontrolle f. control.
Kontrolleur m. controller.
kontrollieren to control.
Konversationslexikon n. encyclopedia.
Konzert n. concert.
KOPF m. head, brains, intellect, heading.
  auf den Kopf stellen to turn upside down.
  aus dem Kopf by heart.
  einem den Kopf waschen to give a person a dressing-down.
  Es ist mir über den Kopf gewachsen. It was too much for me.
  im Kopf behalten to remember.
  Kopf oder Schrift heads or tails.
  nicht auf den Kopf gefallen sein to be no fool.
  sich den Kopf zerbrechten to rack one's brains.
  sich etwas aus dem Kopf schlagen to dismiss something from one's mind.
  sich in den Kopf setzen to take into one's head.
  über den Kopf waschen to be too much for.
  vor den Kopf stossen to hurt, offend.
Kopfarbeit f. brain work.
Kopfkissen n. pillow.
Kopfsalat m. lettuce.
kopfscheu timid.
Kopfschmerzen pl. headache.
  Ich habe Kopfschmerzen. I have a headache.
Kopfweh n. headache.
Korb m. basket.
  Hahn im Korbe sein to be cock of the walk.
Kork m. cork, stopper.
  Korkzieher m. corkscrew.
Korn n. grain.
  aufs Kom nehmen to aim at.
KÖRPER m. body.
körperlich bodily, physical.
Körperpflege f. physical culture, care of the body.
Körperwärme f. body heat.
korrekt correct.
Korrespondenz f. correspondence.
Korridor m. corridor.
korrigieren to correct.
Kosmetik f. cosmetics.
Kost f. food, board.
kostbar precious, costly, valuable.
Kostbarkeit f. preciousness,

object of valor.
Kosten f. costs, expenses.
  auf seine Kosten kommen to recover expenses, be satisfied with the deal.
KOSTEN to cost, require, taste.
Kostenanschlag m. estimate.
kostenlos free.
kostenpflichtig liable for the cost.
Kostenpunkt f. expenses.
köstlich precious, valuable, delicious.
kostspielig expensive.
Kostüm n. costume, tailored suit.
Kostümfest n. fancy dress ball.
Kotelett n. cutlet, chop.
Krabbe f. shrimp, crab.
Krach m. crash, noise, quarrel.
  mit Ach und Krach with difficulty, just barely.
KRAFT f. strength, energy, power.
  ausser Kraft setzen to annul, abolish.
  Das geht über meine Kräfte. That's too much for me.
  in Kraft treten to come into force, effect.
  nach bestern Kräften to the best of one's ability.
  zu Kräften kommen to regain one's strength.
kräftig robust, strong.
kraftlos weak, feeble.
Kragen m. collar.
KRANK ill, sick.
  sich krank lachen to split one's sides (with laughter).
  krank werden to be taken ill.
Kranke m. patient.
Krankenauto n. ambulance.
Krankenhaus n. hospital.
Krankenschwester f. nurse.
Krankheit f. illness, disease.
Kranz m. wreath, garland.
kraus crisp, curly.
  die Stirne krausziehen to knit one's brow.
Kraut n. cabbage.
Krawatte f. necktie.
Krebs m. crawfish, cancer.
Kredit f. credit.
KREIS m. circle, social group.
  einen Kreis ziehen to describe a circle.
  sich im Kreise drehen to turn around, rotate.
kreisen to circle, revolve, circulate.
Kreislauf m. circulation, course, revolution.
KREUZ n. cross; clubs (cards)
  das Kreuz schlagen to cross oneself.
  das Rote Kreuz the Red Cross.
  kreuz und quer in all directions.

Kreuzung *f. crossing.*
  Eisenbahnkreuzung. *Railroad crossing.*
Kreuzverhör *n. cross-examination.*
Kreuzworträtsel *n. crossword puzzle.*
kriechen *to creep, crawl.*
KRIEG *m. war.*
  im Krieg *in wartime.*
  Krieg führen *to make war.*
Kriegsgefangene *m. prisoner of war.*
Kriegsschauplatz *m. theater of war.*
Kriminalpolizei *f. criminal investigation*
  department.
Kriminalroman *m. detective-story.*
Kritik *f. criticism.*
Kritiker *m. critic.*
kritiklos *uncritical, undiscriminating.*
kritisch *critical.*
kritisieren *to criticize.*
Krone *f. crown.*
Kronleuchter *m. chandelier.*
Krug *m. pitcher, jar.*
Krümel *n. crumb.*
krümeln *to crumble.*
krumm *crooked, curved, bent.*
krümmen *to bend.*
Krümmung *f. curve.*
Krüppel *m. cripple.*
Krystall *n. crystal.*
KÜCHE *f. kitchen, cooking.*
Kuchen *m. cake, pastry.*
Kuchenbäcker *m. pastry-cook.*
Küchenherd *m. stove.*
Kugel *f. bullet, ball, globe, sphere.*
Kuh *f. cow.*
  Er ist bekannt wie eine bunte Kuh. *He*
  is well-known everywhere ("like a
  colorful cow").
KÜHL *cool, fresh, chilly.*
Kühlanlage *cold storage plant.*
Kühle *f. coolness, freshness.*
kühlen *to cool.*
Kühler *m. radiator (car).*
Kühlschrank *m. refrigerator.*
Kühlung *f. cooling, freshness.*
kühn *bold, daring, audacious.*
Kühnheit *f. boldness, audacity.*
Kulisse *f. wing.*
kultivieren *to cultivate.*
Kultur *f. culture.*
Kummer *m. grief, sorrow.*
kummervoll *sad, sorrowful.*
Kunde *f. customer, client, news.*
Kundgebung *f. demonstration.*
kundig *well-informed, experienced.*
kündigen *to give notice.*
Kundschaft *f. intelligence.*
künftig *in the future.*
KUNST *f. art.*
Kunstausstellung *f. art exhibition.*

Kunstgalerie *f. art gallery.*
kunstgerecht *correct.*
Kunsthandel *m. fine art trade.*
Kunsthändler *m. art dealer.*
Künstler *m. artist.*
künstlich *artificial, false.*
Kunstmaler *m. painter.*
Kunstseide *f. artificial silk.*
Kunststoff *m. plastics.*
Kunststück *n. feat, trick.*
KUR *f. treatment, cure.*
Kurgast *m. visitor, patient.*
Kurhaus *n. casino.*
kurios *odd, strange.*
Kurort *m. health resort.*
Kurs *m. course, rate of exchange.*
Kurve *f. curve, bend, turn.*
  Gefährliche Kurve! *Dangerous curve!*
KURZ *short, brief, abrupt; in short,*
  briefly.
  den Kürzem ziehen *to be the loser.*
  in kurzem *soon, shortly.*
  kurz darauf *shortly after.*
  kurz oder lang *sooner or later.*
  kurz und bündig *concisely, briefly.*
  kurz und gut *in short.*
  vor kurzem *recently.*
  zu kurz kommen *to come off badly.*
Kürze *f. shortness, brevity.*
kürzen *to shorten, abridge.*
kurzgefasst *concise.*
Kurzgeschichte *f. short story.*
kürzlich *lately, recently.*
Kurzschrift *f. shorthand.*
kurzsichtig *shortsighted.*
Kürzung *f. shortening, abbreviation.*
Kuss *m. kiss.*
  Mit Grüssen und Küssen *With love*
  and kisses.
küssen *to kiss.*
Küste *f. coast, shore.*
Kuvert *n. envelope, cover, wrapping.*

L

Laborant *m. laboratory assistant.*
Laboratorium *n. laboratory.*
lächeln *to smile.*
  höhnisch lächeln *to sneer.*
Lachen *n. laugh, laughter.*
LACHEN *to laugh.*
lächerlich *laughable, ridiculous.*
  lächerlich machen *to ridicule.*
lachhaft *ridiculous.*
Laden *m. shop, store, shutter.*
Ladeninhaber *m. shopkeeper.*

Ladenschluss *m. closing time.*
Ladentisch *m. counter.*
Lage *f. situation, position, site, condition, storage.*
Lager *n. bed, couch, layer, support.*
Lageraufnahme *f. inventory.*
Lagergeld *n. storage fee.*
Lagerhaus *n. warehouse.*
lagern *to lie down, camp.*
lahm *lame, paralyzed.*
Laie *m. layman.*
Laken *n. sheet.*
LAMPE *f. lamp, light.*
Lampenfieber *n. stagefright.*
Lampenschirm *m. lamp-shade.*
LAND *n. land, mainland, ground.*
  an Land gehen *to land, go ashore.*
  aufs Land gehen *to go to the country.*
  ausser Landes gehen *to go abroad.*
landen *to land, put ashore.*
Landesbrauch *m. national custom.*
Landesfarben *pl. national colors.*
Landessprache *f. national language.*
Landestracht *f. national costume.*
Landesverrat *m. high treason.*
Landesverweisung *f. expulsion, banishment, exile.*
Landhaus *n. country house.*
Landkarte *f. map.*
Landschaft *f. landscape, scenery.*
landschaftlich *provincial.*
Landstrasse *f. highway, highroad.*
Landung *f. landing, disembarkation.*
Landwirtschaft *f. farming, agriculture.*
landwirtschaftlich *agricultural.*
LANG *long, tall.*
  auf lange Sicht *long-dated.*
  auf die lange Bank schieben *to put off.*
  den lieben langen Tag *the livelong day.*
  einen Tag lang *for a day.*
  Es dauert lange. *It takes long.*
  über kurz oder lang *sooner or later.*
langatmig *long-winded, lengthy.*
Länge *f. length, duration.*
  der Länge nach *lengthwise.*
  in die Länge ziehen *to drag on, spin out*
langen *to suffice, last, be enough.*
  langen nach *to reach for.*
Längengrad *degree of longitude.*
länger *longer.*
  Je länger, je lieber. *The longer, the better.*
  schon länger *for some time.*
Longeweile *f. boredom.*
langfristig *long-dated.*
LÄNGS *prep. (gen.) along.*
  Der Weg läuft längs des Stromes. *The road runs along the river.*
langsam *slow, tardy.*
  Langsam fahren! *Slow down!*
Langsamkeit *f. slowness.*
längst *long ago, long since.*
  schon längst *for a very long time.*
  am längsten *the longest.*
  längstens *at the latest, at the most.*
langweilen *to bore.*
  sich zu Tode langweilen *to be bored to death.*
langwierig *lengthy.*
Lärm *m. noise, din, row.*
LASSEN *to let, allow, permit, suffer, omit, abandon.*
  aus dem Spiel lassen *to leave out of the question.*
  Das muss man ihm lassen. *One must credit him with that.*
  es beim alten lassen *to let things remain as they are.*
  holen lassen *to send for.*
  Lass das! Don't!
  Lass nur! *Never mind!*
  Ich habe den Wagen waschen lassen. *I had the car washed.*
  machen (waschen, reinigen, richten, usw.) lassen *to have made (washed, cleaned, fixed, etc.).*
  mit sich reden lassen *to be reasonable.*
  sein Leben lassen *to lose one's life.*
  sich sagen lassen *to be told, take advice.*
  sich Zeit lassen *to take time.*
  warten lassen *to keep waiting.*
lässig *lazy, idle, indolent.*
Last *f. load, weight, burden, charge.*
lästig *troublesome, annoying, irksome.*
Lastwagen *m. cart, truck, van.*
Laterne *f. lantern, lamp.*
Laub *f foliage, leaves.*
Laubwald *n. forest.*
Laubwerk *n. foliage.*
Lauer *f. ambush.*
lauern *to wait for.*
Lauf *m. race, course, run, current.*
  in vollem Lauf *at full gallop.*
  freien Lauf lassen *to give vent to.*
Laufbahn *f. career.*
LAUFEN *to run, flow, go on.*
  laufen lassen *to let things go.*
  auf dem laufenden sein *to be up to date, abreast.*
laufend *running.*
Laufjunge *m. errand-boy.*
Laune *f. mood, whim.*
  guter Laune sein *to be in good mood.*
launisch *moody.*

Laut *m. sound, tone.*
LAUT 1. *adj. loud, noisy, audible.*
  laut werden *to become known, get about.*
  2. *prep. (gen.) according to, in accordance with*
  laut Befehls *by order.*
  laut Rechnung *as per account.*
lauten *to sound.*
läuten *to ring, toll.*
lautlos *silent.*
Lautlosigkeit *f. silence.*
Lautsprecher *m. loudspeaker.*
lauwarm *lukewarm.*
LEBEN *n. life, lifetime, living.*
  am Leben bleiben *to survive.*
  am Leben sein *to be alive.*
  auf Leben und Tod *a matter of life and death.*
  einem Kind das Leben schenken *to give birth to a child.*
  ins Leben rufen *to originate, start.*
LEBEN *to live, be alive, dwell, stay.*
lebendig *living, lively.*
Lebendigkeit *f. liveliness, animation.*
Lebensgefahr *f. danger, risk of one's life.*
lebensgefährlich *highly dangerous.*
Lebenslage *f. position.*
lebenslänglich *for life, perpetual.*
Lebenslauf *m. curriculum vitae, background.*
Lebensmittel *n. food, provisions.*
lebensmüde *tired of life.*
Lebensraum *m. living space.*
Lebensunterhalt *m. livelihood, living.*
Lebenswandel *m. life, conduct.*
Lebensweise *f. mode of life.*
Leber *f. liver.*
lebhaft *lively, vivacious.*
Leck *n. leak.*
lecken *to lick.*
LEDER *n. leather.*
LEER *empty, vacant, blank, idle.*
  mit leeren Händen *with empty hands.*
Leere *f. emptiness, void, vacuum.*
  leerlauf *m. neutral (gear).*
leeren *to empty.*
LEGEN *to put, lay, place, lie down, calm down.*
Lehne *f. back of chair.*
lehnen *to lean against, rest upon.*
  sich lehnen *to lean back.*
Lehnstuhl *m. armchair.*
Lehramt *n. teacher's post.*
Lehrberuf *m. teaching profession.*
Lehrbuch *n. text book.*
Lehre *f. instruction, precept, advice, warning.*

LEHREN *to teach, instruct.*
LEHRER *m. (-in, f.) teacher.*
Lehrfach *n. teaching profession.*
lehrhaft *didactic.*
Lehrjahre *pl. years of apprenticeship.*
lehrreich *instructive.*
Leib *m. body, belly, womb.*
Leibgericht *n. favorite dish.*
Leibschmerzen *m. pl. stomach-ache, colic.*
Leiche *f. corpse.*
LEICHT *easy, light, slight, mild, careless, frivolous; easily.*
  etwas leicht nehmen *to take it easy.*
  leicht möglich *very probable.*
leichtfertig *thoughtless, frivolous.*
Leichtfertigkeit *f. thoughtlessness, frivolity.*
leichtgläubig *credulous.*
Leichtsinn *m. carelessness, thoughtlessness.*
leichtsinnig *careless, thoughtless.*
LEID *n. grief, sorrow, pain, harm.*
  Er tut mir leid. *I am sorry for him.*
  Es tut mir leid. *I am sorry about it.*
  sich ein Leid antun *to commit suicide.*
  zu meinem Leidwesen *to my regret.*
leiden *to suffer, bear, endure, stand.*
  leiden können, leiden mögen *to like.*
  Sie leidet schwer darunter. *It's making her very miserable.*
Leidenschaft *f. passion.*
leidenschaftlich *passionately.*
leidenschaftslos *dispassionate.*
leider *unfortunately.*
  leider nicht *unfortunately not.*
Leihbibliothek *f. lending library.*
leihen *to lend.*
Leine *f. leash.*
Leinwand *f. linen, screen.*
leise *soft, gentle, dim.*
  mit leiser Stimme *in a low voice.*
Leiste *f. strip.*
leisten *to perform, carry out, accomplish.*
  es sich leisten können *to be able to afford something.*
leistungsfähig *capable, fit, efficient.*
Leistungsfähigkeit *f. capacity for work, efficiency, power.*
leiten *to lead, conduct, manage, direct.*
Leiter *m. leader, manager, principal, head.*
Leitung *f. direction, management, guidance, line, pipe.*
Leitungswasser *n. tap water.*
Lektion *f. lesson (in a book).*
lenkbar *docile, tractable.*
lenken *to direct, conduct, drive, steer.*

lernbegierig *anxious to learn.*
LERNEN *to learn, study.*
Lesebuch *reader (book).*
LESEN *to read, lecture.*
lesenswert *worth reading.*
Leser *m. reader (person).*
leserlich *legible.*
LETZT *last, latest, final, extreme.*
  in letzter Zeit *lately, recently.*
  letzte Neuheit *latest novelty.*
  letzten Endes *after all.*
  letzten Sonntag *last Sunday.*
  letztes hergeben *to do one's utmost.*
  zu guter Letzt *finally, in the end.*
letztens *lately, of late.*
Leuchte *f. lamp, light.*
leuchten *to light, shine, beam, glow.*
Leuchter *m. candlestick.*
Leuchtturm *m. lighthouse.*
Leuchtuhr *f. luminous clock or watch.*
Leuchtzifferblatt *m. luminous dial.*
leugnen *to deny, disavow.*
LEUTE *pl. people, persons, folk.*
Leutnant *m. second lieutenant.*
leutselig *affable.*
Lexikon *n. dictionary.*
LICHT *n. light, candle, illumination.*
  Bitte, machen Sie das Licht an. *Please turn on the light.*
  Licht anzünden *to turn on the light.*
  Licht auszünden *to turn off the light.*
  in ein falsches Licht setzen *to misrepresent.*
  Mir ging ein Licht auf. *It dawned on me.*
licht
  am lichten Tage *in broad daylight.*
  lichte Augenblicke *sane moments.*
lichtempfindlich *sensitive to light.*
lichten *to thin out, clear (forest).*
Lichterglanz *m. brightness.*
Lichtpouse *f. photostatic copy.*
Lichtreklame *f. luminous sign, illuminated advertisement.*
LIEB *dear, nice, beloved, agreeable.*
  Es ist mir lieb. *I am glad.*
  es wäre mir lieb *I should like.*
Liebchen *n. darling, love, sweetheart.*
LIEBE *f. love, affection, charity.*
  aus Liebe *for love.*
  mir zu Liebe *for my sake.*
LIEBEN *to love, like, be in love.*
liebenswürdig *amiable, kind.*
Liebenswürdigkeit *f. amiability, kindness.*
lieber *dearer, rather.*
Liebeserklärung *f. declaration of love.*
Liebesgeschichte *f. love story.*
Liebespaar *n. lovers, couple.*

liebgewinnen *to grow fond of.*
liebhaben *to love.*
Liebhaber *m. (-in, f.) lover; amateur.*
Liebhaberei *f. fancy, liking; hobby.*
liebkosen *to caress, fondle.*
Liebkosung *f. caress, petting.*
lieblich *lovely, charming.*
Liebling *m. darling, favorite.*
Liebreiz *m. charm, attraction.*
Liebschaft *f. love affair.*
Liebste *m. & f. dearest, beloved, lover, sweetheart.*
LIED *n. song, air.*
Liederbuch *n. song-book, hymn-book.*
liederlich *slovenly, immoral, dissolute.*
lieferbar *available.*
Lieferfrist *f. term of delivery.*
liefern *to deliver, yield, produce.*
Lieferung *f. delivery, supply.*
Lieferzeit *f. time (or term) of delivery.*
LIEGEN *to lie, rest, be situated, stand.*
  Das liegt an mir. *It is my fault.*
  Mir liegt daran. *I am interested in the matter.*
  Mir liegt nichts daran. *I don't care for it.*
liegenlassen *to leave.*
Likör *m. liqueur, cordial.*
Limonade *f. lemonade.*
lindem *to soften, ease, soothe.*
Linderung *f. relief.*
Linie *f. line, descent, branch (of a family).*
  in erster Linie *first of all.*
LINK *left, wrong side of a cloth, reverse of a coin.*
linkisch *award, clumsy.*
LINKS *to the left, on the left.*
  Gehen Sie nach links! *Go to the left!*
  Sie liess ihn ganz links liegen. *She gave him the cold shoulder.*
linkshändig *left-handed.*
Linnen *n. linen*
Linse *f. lentil.*
Lippe *f. lip.*
Lippenstift *m. lipstick.*
List *f. cunning, craft.*
Liste *f. list, roll, catalogue.*
listig *cunning, crafty, sly, astute.*
Liter *m. liter (1.056 quarts).*
literarisch *literary.*
Literatur *f. literature, letters.*
Litfasssäule *f. billboard.*
Lizenz *f. license, permit.*
Lob *n. praise.*
loben *to praise.*
lobenswert *praiseworthy.*
lobpreisen *to praise.*
Loch *n. hole, gap.*

Locke *f. lock, curl.*
locken *to entice, allure.*
Löffel *m. spoon.*
  Esslöffel, *m. tablespoon.*
Loge *f. box (theater).*
Logik *f. logic.*
logisch *logical.*
Lohn *m. compensation, reward, wages.*
Lohnempfänger *m. wage-earner.*
lohnen *to reward.*
  Es lohnt sich. *It is worth while.*
Löhnung *f. pay.*
lokal *local, suburban.*
Lokomotive *f. engine (of a train).*
Los *n. lot, chance.*
LOS
  1. *adv. loose, slack, free.*
  Hier ist viel los. *There's plenty going on here.*
  Mit ihm ist nicht viel los. *He is not up to much.*
  Was ist los? *What's up?*
  2. *separable prefix (implies the idea of separation or quick movement).*
  Du kannst die Hunde lo skoppeln. *You can untie the dogs.*
  Eins, zwei, drei, los! *One, two, three, go!*
losbinden *to untie, unloosen.*
löschen *to put out, extinguish.*
losgehen *to set out, become loose, go off.*
loskommen *to get away.*
loswerden *to get rid of.*
Löwe *m. lion.*
LUFT *f. air, breath, breeze.*
  aus der Luft greifen *to invent.*
  frische Luft schöpfen *to take the air.*
  in die Luft sprengen *to blow up.*
  keine Luft bekommen *not to be able to breathe.*
  luftdicht *air-tight.*
lüften *to air.*
luftig *airy, breezy.*
Luftkrankheit *f. airsickness.*
  luftkrank sein *to be airsick.*
Luftkurort *m. health resort.*
luftleer *airless.*
  luftleerer Raum *vacuum.*
Luftpost *f. air mail.*
Luftraum *m. atmosphere.*
Lüge *f. lie, untruth, falsehood.*
lügen *to lie (falsify).*
Lunge *f. lung.*
Lungenentzündung *f. pneumonia.*
Lupe *f. magnifying glass.*
Lust *f. pleasure, joy, delight, inclination, lust.*
  Lust haben *to be inclined to.*

lustig *gay, funny, jolly.*
  sich lustig machen *to make fun of.*
Lustspiel *n. comedy.*
Luxus *m. luxury.*
Lyrik *f. lyrics.*

M

Machart *f. style, description, kind, sort.*
MACHEN *to make, do manufacture, cause, amount to.*
  Das lässt sich machen. *This is feasible.*
  Das macht nichts. *That does not matter.*
  Was macht Ihre Erkältung? *How is your cold?*
MACHT *f. strength, might, power, authority.*
mächtig *strong, mighty, powerful.*
machtlos *powerless.*
MÄDCHEN *n. girl, servant.*
  Mädchen für alles *general servant.*
mädchenhaft *girlish, maidenly.*
Mädchenname *m. maiden name.*
Magen *m. stomach.*
  Ich habe einen verdorbenen Magen. *I have an upset stomach.*
Magenverstimmung *f. stomach upset.*
mager *thin, scanty.*
Magerkeit *f. leanness, skimpiness.*
mähen *to mow, cut, reap.*
MAHL *n. meal.*
mahlen *to grind, mill.*
Mahnbrief *m. request to pay.*
mahnen *to remind, admonish, exort.*
Mahnung *f. reminder, warning.*
MAI *m. May.*
Maiglöckchen *n. lily of the valley.*
Mais *m. corn, maize.*
Major *m. major.*
MAL *n. 1. landmark, monument, mark. 2. time, turn.*
  dieses Mal *for once.*
  ein für alle Mal *once and for all.*
  mit einem Mal *suddenly.*
  zum ersten Mal *for the first time.*
mal *times, once, just.*
  Danke vielmals *thank you very much.*
  Viermal drei ist zwölf. *Three times four is twelve.*
malen *to paint, portray, represent.*
  sich malen lassen *to have one's portrait made.*
Maler *m. painter.*
malerisch *pictorial, picturesque.*

MAN *one, they, people, you.*
  man hat mir gesagt dass.... *I was told that....*
  Man sagt so. *So they say.*
MANCHE *many, some.*
manch(er,-e,-es) *many a.*
mancherlei *various, diverse.*
manchmal *sometimes.*
Mangel *m. need, want, absence, lack.*
  aus Mangel an *for want of.*
mangelhaft *faulty, defective.*
mangeln *to want, be wanting.*
  es mangelt mir an *I am short of.*
Manier *f. manner, style.*
manierlich *polite, civil, mannerly.*
MANN *m. man; husband.*
  mit Mann und Maus *with every soul.*
  wenn Not am Mann ist *if the worst comes to the worst.*
Mannesalter *n. manhood.*
mannhaft *manly.*
männlich *male, manly.*
Manschette *f. cuff.*
Manschettenknopf *m. sleeve link.*
MANTEL *m. coat.*
Mappe *f. document case, writing case.*
Märchen *n. fairy tale.*
märchenhaft *fabulous, legendary.*
Marine *f. navy.*
Mark *f. mark (coin).*
markant *characteristic, striking.*
Marke *f. mark, sign, postage stamp, token.*
MARKT *m. market, market place.*
Markthalle *f. market-hall.*
Marktplatz *m. market place.*
Marmelade *f. jam.*
Marmor *m. marble.*
Marmorplatte *f. marble slab.*
Marsch *m. march.*
marschieren *to march.*
MÄRZ *m. March.*
Marzipan *m. & n. marzipan.*
MASCHINE *f. machine, engine, typewriter.*
  auf der Maschine schreiben *to typewrite.*
Maske *f. mask, disguise.*
Maskenball *m. fancy dress ball.*
Maskerade *f. masquerade.*
MASS *n. measure, dimension, size, degree, proportion, moderation.*
  in hohem Mass *in a high degree.*
  Mass nehmen *to measure.*
  Masse und Gewichte *pl. weights and measurements.*
  nach Mass gemacht *made to measure.*
Massarbeit *f. made to measure (to order).*

MASSE *f. crowd, mass, quantity.*
massenhaft *in large quantities, wholesale.*
massgebend *standard.*
massgeblich *standard.*
masshalten *to observe moderation, keep within limits.*
mässig *reasonable, moderate, poor, mediocre.*
mässigen *to observe moderation, restrain.*
Mässigkeit *f. moderation, frugality.*
masslos *boundless, without limit.*
Massregel *f. measure, step.*
Massstab *m. yard, measure, scale.*
Material *n. material, substance.*
materialisieren *to materialize.*
materialistisch *materialistic.*
Mathematik *f. mathematics.*
Matratze *f. mattress.*
Matrose *m. sailor.*
matt *weak, soft, dull; mate(chess).*
  mattsetzen *to mate (chess).*
Mauer *f. wall.*
mauern *to build with stones.*
Maultier *n. mule.*
Maurer *m. mason, bricklayer.*
Maus *f. mouse.*
Mechanik *f. mechanics.*
Mechaniker *m. mechanic.*
mechanisch *mechanical.*
Medikament *n. medicament.*
Medizin *f. medicine, remedy.*
Mediziner *m. medical student.*
MEER *n. sea, seashore.*
Meerenge *f. channel.*
Meeresspiegel *m. sea-level.*
Mehl *n. flour.*
Mehlspeise *f. pudding.*
MEHR *more.*
  desto mehr *all the more.*
  immer mehr *more and more.*
  je mehr ... desto *the more ... the more.*
  mehr als *more than.*
  nicht mehr *no more, any more, any longer.*
  nie mehr *never again.*
  nur mehr *only, nothing but.*
  um so mehr als ... *all the more as.*
Mehrbetrag *m. surplus.*
mehrere *several.*
mehreres *several things.*
mehrfach *manifold, numerous.*
Mehrheit *f. majority.*
mehrmals *several times, again and again.*
Mehrzahl *f. majority, plural.*
Meile *f. mile (1.609 kilometers).*

MEIN *poss. adj. my.*
MEINEN *to mean, think, believe, suppose.*
  Was meinen Sie damit? *What do you mean by that?*
  Was meinen Sie dazu? *What do you think about it?*
  Wie meinen Sie? *I beg your pardon?*
MEIN(er,-e-es) *poss. pron. mine.*
meinerseits *for my part, as far as I am concerned.*
meihesgleichen *my equals, people like me.*
meinethalben *for my sake, for all I care.*
meinetwegen *for my sake, for me, on my account, as far as I am concerned.*
meinetwillen (um-) *for my sake.*
MEINUNG *f. meaning, opinion, view.*
  einem die Meinung sagen *to give someone a piece of one's mind.*
  meiner Meinung nach *to my mind, in my opinion.*
meist *most, mostly.*
  die meisten *most people.*
MEISTENS *mostly.*
MEISTER *m. master.*
Meisterschaft *f. championship.*
Meistersinger *mastersinger.*
Meisterstück *n. masterpiece.*
Meisterwerk *n. masterpiece.*
Meldeamt *n. registration office.*
melden *to report, announce, inform, apply.*
Meldezettel *m. registration form.*
Meldung *f. news, announcement, advice, notification.*
melken *to milk.*
Melodie *f. melody, tune.*
Menge *f. quantity, amount, lots, multitude.*
  in Mengen *in abundance, plenty of.*
mengen *to mix, meddle, interfere.*
MENSCH *m. man, human being, person.*
  Es kam kein Mensch. *Not a soul came.*
  seit Menschengedenken *within the memory of man; immemorial.*
  Was für ein Mensch ist er? *What sort of a person is he?*
Menschenalter *n. generation.*
menschenmöglich *humanly possible.*
Menschheit *f. human race.*
menschlich *human.*
Menschlichkeit *f. human nature.*
merkbar *noticeable.*
merken *to perceive, notice, observe, note.*
  sich nichts merken lassen *to appear*

to know nothing.
merklich *noticeable.*
Merkmal *n. characteristic, sign, mark.*
merkwürdig *characteristic, strange, peculiar, remarkable.*
merkwürdigerweise *strangely enough, strange to say.*
Merkwürdigkeit *f. strangeness, peculiarity.*
Messe *f. mass; fair; mess (officers').*
MESSEN *to measure, survey, take the temperature of a patient.*
  Blicken messen *to eye.*
  messen mit *to compete with.*
  nicht messen können mit *to be no match*
MESSER *n. knife.*
Messergriff *m. knife handle.*
Messerstich *m. stab (with a knife).*
Messing *brass.*
Metall *n. metal.*
Meter *n. meter (39.37 inches).*
Meterma *n. tape-measure.*
Methode *f. method.*
Metzter *m. butcher.*
Metzgerei *n. butcher's shop.*
Meuterei *f. mutiny.*
MICH *acc. of ich (pers. pron) me, myself.*
Miene *f. expression (facial), air, countenance.*
  gute Miene zum bösen Spiel machen *to put up a brave show.*
MIETE *f. rent, lease.*
  Die Miete ist fällig. *The rent is due.*
  zur Miete wohnen *to be a tenant.*
mieten *to rent.*
Mieter *m. tenant.*
mietfrei *rent free.*
Mietshaus *n. apartment house.*
Mietvertrag *m. lease.*
Mikrofan *n. microphone.*
Mikroskop *n. microscope.*
mikroskopisch *microscopic.*
MILCH *f. milk.*
Milchgeschäft *n. dairy.*
Milchgesicht *n. baby face.*
Milchglas *n. opalescent glass.*
Milchladen *m. dairy.*
Milchstrasse *f. Milky Way.*
Milchzahn *m. milk tooth.*
MILD *mild, soft, gentle, mellow, kind, charitable.*
MILDE *f. gentleness, kindness.*
mildern *to soften, extenuate.*
  Mildemde Umstände *extenuating circumstances.*
mildtätig *kind, generous.*
Militär *n. army, service.*

Militärdienst *m. active service.*

militärisch *military.*

Militarismus *m. militarism.*

MILLIARDE *f. billion.*

MILLION *f. million.*

Millionär *m. millionaire.*

MINDER *less, minor, inferior.*

minderbemittelt *of moderate means.*

Minderheit *f. minority.*

minderjährig *minor (age).*
minderjährig sein *to be a minor.*

Minderjährigkeit *f. minority (age).*

minderwertig *inferior.*

Minderwertigkeitsgefühl *n. inferiority complex.*

MINDEST *least.*
nicht im mindesten *not in the least, by no means.*

mindestens *at least.*

Mindestlohn *m. minimum wage.*

Mine *f. mine.*

Mineral *n. mineral.*

Minister *m. minister.*

Ministerium *n. ministry.*

Ministerpräsident *m. prime minister.*

MINUTE *f. minute.*
minutenlang *for several minutes.*

MIR *dat. of ich (pers. pron.) to me, me, myself.*

mischen *to blend, mix, meddle, shuffle (cards).*
sich mischen *to interfere.*

Mischung *f. blend, mix.*

missachten *to disregard, disdain.*

Missachtung *f. disregard, disdain.*

missbilligen *to disapprove.*

Missbilligung *f. disapproval.*

missbrauchen *to misuse, abuse.*

missen *to do without.*

Misserfolg *m. failure.*

Missetat *f. misdeed, crime.*

Missetäter *m. criminal.*

missfallen *to displease.*

Missgeschick *n. bad luck, misfortune.*

missglücken *to fail.*

missgönnen *to grudge.*

missgünstig *envious, jealous.*

Misstrauen *n. distrust, mistrust.*

misstrauen *to distrust, mistrust.*

misstrauisch *suspicious.*

missvergnügt *displeased.*

missverstehen *to misunderstand.*

MIT *prep. (dat.) with, at, by.*

Der Patient hat mit gutem Appetit gegessen. *The patient has eaten with a good appetite.*
mit anderen Worten *in other words.*
mit der Post *by post.*
mit der Zeit *gradually.*

Mit fünf Jahren spielte er schon Klavier. *At the age of five, he already played the piano.*
Wir sind mit der Eisenbahn gereist. *We traveled by train.*
2. *separable prefix (implies accompaniment or participation).*
Kommen Sie mit? *Are you coming along?*

mitarbeiten *to collaborate, cooperate, contribute.*

Mitarbeiter *m. collaborator.*

Mitbesitzer *m. joint proprietor.*

mitbringen *to bring along.*

Mitbürger *m. fellow citizen.*

miteinander *with each other, together, jointly.*

mitempfinden *to sympathize with.*

Mitgefühl *n. sympathy.*

Mitgift *f. dowry.*

Mitglied *n. member.*

mitkommen *to accompany, come along, keep up.*

Mitleid *n. sympathy, pity, mercy.*

Mitleidenschaft *f. compassion.*
in Mitleidenschaft ziehen *to affect.*

mitleidig *compassionate.*

mitleidlos *pitiless.*

mitmachen *to take part in, go through.*
Sie hat sehr viel mitgemacht. *She went through a lot.*

mitnehmen *to take along, affect.*
Ihr Tod hat ihn sehr mitgenommen. *Her death affected him deeply.*

mitschuldig *implicated (in a crime).*

Mitschuldige *m. & f. accomplice.*

mitspielen *to join in a game; to accompany (music).*

MITTAG *m. noon, midday; south.*
zu Mittag essen *to have lunch.*

Mittagessen *n. lunch.*

mittags *at noon.*

Mittagspause *f. lunch hour.*

MITTE *f. middle, centre, mean, medium.*
Er ist Mitte Dreissig. *He is in his middle thirties.*
goldene Mitte *golden mean.*

mitteilen *to impart, communicate.*

Mitteilung *f. information, communication, intelligence.*

Mittel *n. means; remedy, cure, medicine.*
Er ist ohne irgendwelche Mittel. *He is penniless.*

Mittelalter *n. Middle Ages.*

Mitteleuropa *n. Central Europe.*

mittellos *without means.*

mittelmässig *average, mediocre.*

Mittelmeer *n. Mediterranean.*

Mittelstand *m. middle class.*
MITTEN *midway, in the middle of.*
  mitten auf (in) *in the midst of.*
  mittendrin *right in the middle of.*
  mittendurch *right across, right through.*
MITTERNACHT *f. midnight.*
mitternachts *at midnight.*
mittlerweile *meanwhile, in the meantime.*
MITTWOCH *m. Wednesday.*
mitunter *sometimes, now and then.*
Mitwelt *f. our age, our generation.*
Mitwisser *m. confident, one in on the secret.*
MÖBEL *n. piece of furniture.*
Möbel *pl. furniture.*
Möbelhändler *m. furniture dealer.*
Möbelstück *n. piece of furniture.*
möblieren *to furnish.*
Mode *f. fashion.*
Modell *n. model, pattern, mold.*
modern *modern.*
Modeschau *f. fashion show.*
modisch *fashionable.*
MÖGEN *to want, wish, be able, be allowed; to like, care for.*
  Das mag ich nicht: *I don't like that.*
  Das mag sein *that may be so.*
  Er ist faul, er mag nicht lernen. *He is lazy, he does not want to learn.*
  Ich möchte nicht. *I don't want to.*
  Ich möchte wissen. *I'd like to know.*
  wie dem auch sein mag *be that as it may.*
  lieber mögen *to prefer.*
  Ich möchte lieber auf dem Land leben. *I'd rather live in the country.*
möglich *possible, practicable, feasible, likely.*
  alles mögliche *all sorts of things, everything possible.*
  möglichst wenig *as little as possible.*
  möglichst schnell *as quickly as possible.*
  Nicht möglich! *It can't be!*
  sein möglichstes tun *to do one's utmost.*
möglicherweise *possibly, perhaps.*
Möglichkeit *f. possibility, chance.*
Mole *f. pier.*
Moment *m. moment.*
  Einen Moment! *One moment!*
Momentaufnahme *f. snapshot.*
Monarchie *f. monarchy.*
MONAT *m. month.*
monatelang *for months.*
monatlich *monthly.*
Mönch *m. monk.*
MOND *m. moon.*

Mondschein *m. moonlight.*
Monolog *m. monologue.*
MONTAG *m. Monday.*
Moor *n. swamp.*
Moos *n. moss.*
Mop *m. mop.*
moppen *to mop.*
Moral *f. morality, morals, moral.*
moralisch *moral.*
moralisieren *to moralize.*
Mord *m. murder.*
  Selbstmord, *m. suicide.*
Mordanschlag *m. murderous attack.*
Mörder *m. murderer.*
MORGEN *m. morning, dawn, daybreak; the following day.*
  früh morgens *early in the morning.*
  Guten Morgen. *Good morning.*
  heute morgen *this morning.*
  morgens *in the morning.*
morgen *tomorrow.*
  morgen früh *tomorrow morning.*
  morgen in acht Tagen *a week from tomorrow.*
  Morgen ist auch ein Tag. *Tomorrow is another day.*
Morgengrauen *n. dawn of the day, break of the day.*
morgenländisch *from the Middle East.*
Morgenrock *m. robe.*
Motor *m. motor, engine.*
Motorboot *n. motor boat.*
Motorpanne *f. engine trouble.*
Motorrad *n. motorcycle.*
Matte *f. moth.*
Mücke *f. mosquito (gnat).*
Mückenstich *m. mosquito bite.*
MÜDE *tired, weary.*
  müde werden *to get tired.*
Müdigkeit *f. weariness, fatigue.*
MÜHE *f. labor, toil, effort.*
  sich Mühe geben *to take pains.*
  der Mühe wert *worth while.*
  mit Müh und Not *only just, barely.*
  Mühe machen *to give troubles.*
mühelos *easy, effortless.*
Mühevoll *laborious, difficult.*
Mühle *f. mill.*
Müller *m. miller.*
MUND *m. mouth.*
  den Mund halten *to keep one's mouth shut.*
  den Mund vollnehmen *to brag.*
  Er ist nicht auf den Mund gefallen. *He has a ready tongue.*
  nach dem Mund reden *to flatter.*
  Sie leben von der Hand in den Mund. *They live from hand to mouth.*
Mundwinkel *m. corner of the mouth.*

Munition *f. ammunition.*

munter *wide-awake, alive, gay.*

Münze *f. coin, medal.*

Sie nimmt alles für bare Münze. *She takes everything at its face value.*

mürrisch *morose, sullen.*

Museum *n. museum.*

Musik *f. music.*

musikalisch *musical.*

Muskel *m. muscle.*

Muskelkater *m. stiffness and soreness.*

MÜSSEN *to have to, be obliged to, must, ought to.*

Alle Menschen müssen sterben. *All human beings must die.*

Man Müsste es ihr eigentlich sagen. *Somebody really ought to tell her.*

Sie müssen nicht, wenn Sie nicht wollen. *You don't have to if you don't want to.*

Muster *n. sample, model, design, pattern.*

mustergültig *exemplary, perfect.*

musterhaft *exemplary, standard.*

mustern *to examine.*

Musterung *f. examination.*

MUT *m. courage, fortitude, state of mind.*

jemandem den Mut nehmen *to discourage someone.*

Mut fassen *to summon up courage.*

Mut machen *to encourage.*

mutig *brave.*

mutlos *despondent.*

MUTTER *f. mother.*

Muttermal *n. birthmark.*

Muttersprache *f. mother tongue.*

Mütze *f. cap.*

N

NACH 1. *prep. (with dat.) after, toward, according to, like, past, by, in.*

dem Namen nach kennen *to know by name.*

der Sage nach *according to the legend.*

Der Vater schickt die Kinder nach Hause. *The father sends the children home.*

einer nach dem andren *one after another, one at a time.*

Es ist zehn nach fünf. *It is ten after five.*

Es sieht nach Schnee aus. *It looks like snow.*

Gehen Sie nach links. *Turn left.*

meiner Meinung nach *in my opinion.*

Nach dem Essen ruht er sich aus. *He rests after meals.*

nach und nach *little by little*

2. *adv. after, toward, according to.*

3. *separable prefix (implies coming after, following, imitation.)*

Der Schutzmann lief dem Dieb nach. *The policeman ran after the thief.*

Kannst du diese Arbeit nachmachen? *Can you copy this work?*

nachahmen *to imitate.*

nachahmenswert *worthy of imitation.*

Nachahmung *f. imitation.*

Nachbar *m. neighbor.*

Nachbarsschaft *f. neighborhood.*

nachdem *conj. after.*

Nachdem er sie verlassen hatte, weinte sie. *After he left, she cried.*

nachdenken *to reflect, think.*

nachdenken über *to think over.*

nachdenklich *thoughtful.*

Nachdruck *m. stress, emphasis, reprint, reproduction.*

Nachdruck verboten. *Reproduction forbidden.*

nachdrücklich *strong, emphatic.*

nacheifern *to emulate.*

nachforschen *to inquire into, investigate.*

Nachfrage *f. inquiry, demand.*

nachgeben *to yield, give way.*

nachgehen *to follow, investigate, inquire.*

Nachgeschmack *m. after-taste.*

nachher *afterwards, later.*

Nachhilfe *f. aid, help, coaching.*

Nachkomme *m. descendant.*

nachkommen *to come later, follow on.*

Nachkriegszeit *f. postwar period.*

nachlässig *negligent, careless.*

Nachlässigkeit *f. negligence, carelessness.*

nachlaufen *to run after.*

nachlesen *to look up (in a book).*

nachmachen *to imitate, copy, counterfeit, duplicate.*

NACHMITTAG *m. afternoon.*

nachmittags *afternoons, in the afternoon.*

Nachnahme *f. cash on delivery.*

Nachname *m. surname.*

nachprüfen *to test, check, verify.*

Nachricht *f. news, information, account, report, message.*

Ist eine Nachricht für mich da? *Is there a message for me?*

nachsagen *to repeat after.*

nachsehen *to revise, check, examine.*
nachsenden *to send after.*
Nachsicht *f. indulgence.*
nachsichtig (-sichtsvoll) *indulgent, lenient.*
nächst *nearest, next, closest, following.* prep. (dat.) *next to, next after.*
Nächstenliebe *f. love for one's fellow men; charity.*
NACHT *f.night.*
  bei Nacht, des Nachts *at night.*
  über Nacht *during the night.*
  über Nacht bleiben *to stay overnight.*
  zu Nacht essen *to eat supper.*
Nachteil *m. disadvantage, loss, damage, injury.*
  im Nachteil sein *to be at a disadvantage.*
Nachthemd *n. nightgown.*
Nachtigall *f. nightingale.*
Nachtisch *m. dessert.*
Nachtrag *m. supplement.*
nachtragen *to add.*
nachträglich *additional, further.*
Nachweis *m. proof, evidence.*
nachweisen *to prove.*
Nachwirkung *f. after-effect.*
Nachwuchs *m. after-crop, rising generation.*
Nacken *m. nape of the neck.*
nackt *naked, nude, bare, plain.*
Nadel *f. needle, pin.*
NAGEL *m. nail.*
  an den Nagel hängen *to give up.*
  den Nagel auf den Kopf treffen *to hit the nail on the head.*
Nagelfeile *f. nail file.*
Nähe *f. nearness, proximity, vicinity.*
  in der Nähe *near to, close at hand.*
NAHE *near, close to, imminent, approaching.*
  nahe daran sein *to be about.*
  zu nahe treten *to hurt one's feelings, offend.*
nahen *to draw near, approach.*
nähen *to sew, stitch.*
näher *nearer, closer, more intimate, further.*
Nähere *n. details, particulars.*
Näherin *f. seamstress.*
nähern *to bring near, place near.*
nahestehen *to be closely connected, be friends with.*
Nähgarn *n. sewing thread.*
Nähmaschine *f. sewing machine.*
Nähnadel *f. sewing needle.*
Nährboden *m. fertile soil.*
nähren *to feed, nurse, nourish.*
  sich nähren von *to live on.*

Nahrung *f. nourishment, food.*
Nahrungsmittel *pl. food, foodstuffs.*
NAME *m. name, appellation, character.*
  dem Namen nach *by name.*
  im Namen *(with gen.) on behalf of.*
namenlos *nameless.*
Namenstag *m. saint's day, name day.*
nämlich *namely, same, very.*
Narbe *f. scar.*
Narkose *f. anesthetic.*
Narr *m. fool, jester.*
  zum Narren halten *to make a fool of.*
narren *to fool.*
NASE *f. nose.*
  Der Zug fuhr mir vor der Nase weg.
    missed the train by a hair.
  Sie schlug ihm die Tür vor der Nase zu.
    She slammed the door in his face.
NASS *wet, damp.*
  Die Strasse ist nass. *The street is wet.*
  Bei Nässe glatt. *Slippery when wet.*
  nass werden *to get wet.*
Nation *f. nation.*
national *national.*
Nationalhymne *f. national anthem.*
NATUR *f. nature, disposition, constitution.*
Naturalismus *m. naturalism.*
naturalistisch *naturalistic.*
Naturgeschichte *f. natural science.*
natürlich *natural, unaffected.*
  Natürlich! *Of course!*
Natürlichkeit *f. naturalness, simplicity.*
Naturschutzgebiet *n. national park.*
naturtreu *lifelike.*
Nebel *m. fog, mist, haze.*
Nebelhaft *nebulous.*
nebelig (neblig) *misty, foggy.*
Nebelregen *m. drizzle.*
Nebelwetter *n. foggy weather.*
NEBEN 1. prep. (dat. when answering question, Wo?, acc. when answering question, Wohin?). *next, next to, beside, among, besides.*
2. adv. *next to, beside, among.*
  Setzen Sie sich neben mich! *Sit down next to me!*
  Er sass neben dem Mädchen. *He was seated next to the girl.*
  neben anderen Dingen *among other things.*
nebenan *next door.*
Nebenanschluss *m. extension (telephone).*
nebenbei *on the side, by the way, adjoining.*
  nebenbei bemerkt (gesagt) *by the way, incidentally.*

Nebenberuf m. additional occupation, side-line.
Nebenbuhler m. rival.
Nebenbuhlerschaft f. rivalry.
nebeneinander next to each other, side by side.
Nebeneingang m. side entrance.
Nebeneinnahme f. additional income.
Nebenerzeugnis n. by-product.
Nebenfluss m. tributary.
Nebengebäude n. additional building, annex.
Nebengeräusch n. static (radio).
nebenher (nebenhin) by the side of.
Nebenkosten f. incidentals, extra.
Nebenlinie f. branch, secondary railroad line.
Nebenmensch m. fellow-creature.
Nebenperson f. secondary character (theater).
Nebenrolle f. secondary part (theater).
Nebensache f. matter of secondary importance.
nebensächlich unimportant, immaterial.
Nebensatz m. subordinate clause (grammar).
Nebenstrasse f. side-street.
Nebenzimmer n. next room.
necken to tease.
Neffe m. nephew.
Negative n. negative.
Neger m. (-in, f.) Negro.
negieren to deny.
NEHMEN to take, accept, receive.
  Abschied nehmen to say good-bye.
  Anstoss nehmen to object.
  es sich nicht nehmen lassen to insist on something.
  es genau nehmen to be pedantic.
  etwas zu sich nehmen to eat something.
  genau genommen strictly speaking.
  Nehmen Sie Platz! Sit down!
  sich in Acht nehmen to be careful.
Neid m. envy, jealousy.
neidisch jealous, envious.
Neige f. slope, decline.
  auf die Neige gehen to be on the decline, come to an end.
neigen to incline, bow.
  geneigt sein to be inclined.
Neigung f. slope, declivity, inclination, taste.
NEIN no.
Nektar m. nectar.
Nelke f. carnation.
NENNEN to name, call, mention.
  ein Ding beim rechten Namen nennen to call a spade a spade.

nennenswert worth mentioning.
Nennwort n. noun.
Nerv m. nerve.
  auf die Nerven fallen to drive mad.
Nervenheilanstalt f. mental hospital.
nervenkrank neurotic, neurasthenic.
Nervenschwäche f. nervous debility, neurasthenia.
nervös nervous.
Nervosität f. nervousness.
Nerz m. mink.
Nest n. nest.
NETT nice, neat, pretty.
Netz n. net, network.
NEU new, fresh, recent, modern, latest.
  Was gibt's Neues? What's new?
Neubau m. new building, reconstruction.
neuerdings recently, lately.
Neuerung f. innovation.
Neugier f. curiosity.
neugierig curious.
Neuheit f. novelty.
Neuhochdeutsch n. modern high German.
Neuigkeit f. news.
NEUJAHR n. New Year.
  Glückliches Neujahr! Happy New Year!
neulich recently, the other day.
NEUN nine.
NEUNTE ninth.
NEUNZEHN nineteen.
NEUNZEHNTE nineteenth.
NEUNZIG ninety.
NEUNZIGSTE ninetieth.
neutral neutral.
Neuzeit f. modern times.
neuzeitlich modern.
NICHT not.
  auch nicht not even.
  ganz und gar nicht not in the least.
  gar nicht not at all.
  nicht einmal not even.
  nicht mehr no longer, no more.
  Nicht wahr? Isn't it?
  noch nicht not yet.
Nichtachtung f. disregard.
Nichte f. niece.
NICHTS nothing, not anything.
  gar nichts nothing at all.
  Es macht nichts. It doesn't matter.
  Ich will nichts mehr davon hören. I don't want to hear another word about that.
  mir nichts, dir nichts quite coolly.
  nichts als nothing but.
  nichts anderes nothing else.
nichtsdestoweniger nevertheless.
nichtssagend meaningless, insignificant.

Nichtstuer m. idler.
Nichtstun n. idling.
nie never.
  fast nie hardly ever.
NIEDER down, low, mean.
  auf und nieder up and down.
niedergeschlagen downhearted,
  depressed.
Niedergeschlagenheit f. depression.
Niederlage f. defeat, warehouse.
niedertreten to trample.
niedrig low, inferior, humble.
NIEMALS never.
NIEMAND nobody.
Niere f. kidney.
nimmer never.
nimmermehr nevermore, by no means.
nirgends nowhere.
nirgendwo nowhere.
NOCH still, yet, besides.
  noch dazu in addition.
  noch ein another.
  noch einmal once more.
  noch einmal so twice as.
  noch etwas something else.
  noch immer still.
  noch nicht not yet.
  noch nie never before.
  weder ... noch neither ... nor.
nochmals once again.
Norden m. North.
  nach Norden in the direction of the
  North.
nordisch northern, nordic.
nördlich northern.
nordöstlich northeastern.
Nordpol m. North Pole.
Nordsee f. North Sea.
Norm f. standard, rule.
normal normal.
NOT f. distress, want.
  mit Not only just, narrowly.
  ohne Not without real cause.
  seine liebe Not haben mit to have a
  hard time with.
  zur Not if need be.
Notar m. notary.
notariell attested by a notary.
Notausgang m. emergency exit.
Notbehelf m. expedient.
Notbremse f. emergency brake.
Note f. note (music, bank, dipl.); mark
  (school); (-n, pl., music).
Notfall m. emergency.
notgedrungen compulsory, forced.
nötig necessary, needful.
  nötig haben to need.
nötigenfalls if need be.
notleidend poor, distressed.

Notlüge f. white lie.
notwendig necessary.
Notwendigkeit f. necessity.
Novelle f. short story, short novel.
NOVEMBER m. November.
nüchtern empty, sober, insipid.
Nüchternheit f. emptiness, sobriety,
  insipidity.
null null.
  null und nichtig null and void.
Null f. zero.
numerieren to number.
  numerierte Platz m. reserved seat.
NUMMER f. number, part, ticket, size,
  issue.
  Seine Nummer ist besetzt. His line is
  busy.
  Welche Nummer tragen Sie? What
  size do you wear?
  die letzte Nummer the last issue
  (magazine).
NUN now, well, then.
  von nun an henceforth, from now on.
NUR only, sole, merely, just, possibly.
  nur mehr still more.
  Nur zu! Go on!
  wenn nur if only.
  wer nur immer whoever.
Nuss f. nut.
Nussbaum m. walnut tree.
Nussknacker m. nutcracker.
nutzbar useful, necessary.
nutzbringend profitable.
Nutzen m. profit, benefit.
nützen to be of use, be profitable,
  serve.
  Es nützt nicht! It's no use!
nützlich useful.
Nützlichkeit f. usefulness, utility.
nutzlos useless.
Nutzlosigkeit f. uselessness, futility.
Nylon n. nylon.

O

OB whether, if.
  Wir möchten wissen ob sie kommen.
  We want to know whether they are
  coming.
  als ob as if, as though.
OBEN above, up, upstairs, on top.
  auf...oben at the top of.
  dort oben up there.
  nach oben upwards.
  oben auf on top of.
  von oben bis unten from top to bottom.

von oben herab behandeln *to treat in a condescending manner.*
obendrein *into the bargain, in addition.*
ober *upper, supreme, above.*
das obere Bett *the upper berth.*
Ober *m. waiter.*
Herr Ober! *Waiter!*
Oberbefehlshaber *m. commander-in-chief.*
Oberfläche *f. surface, area.*
oberflächlich *superficial, superficially.*
oberhalb *upstairs, above.*
Oberhemd *n. shirt.*
Oberkellner *m. headwaiter.*
Oberkörper *m. upper part of the body.*
Oberlippe *f. upper lip.*
Oberst *m. colonel.*
oberst *highest, top.*
Oberstleutnant *m. lieutenant colonel.*
obgleich *although.*
Oboe *f. oboe.*
Obrigkeit *f. authority.*
obschon *although.*
Obst *n. fruit.*
Obstgarten *m. orchard.*
Ochs *m. ox.*
öde *dull, empty.*
ODER *or.*
oder aber *instead.*
entweder oder *either or.*
Ofen *m. stove, furnace.*
offen *open, free, vacant, frank, sincere.*
auf offender Strecke *on the road.*
offen gestanden *frankly.*
offenbar *obvious, evident.*
Offenbarung *f. disclosure, revelation.*
Offenheit *f. frankness, sincerity.*
offenherzig *frank, sincere.*
offensichtlich *obvious, apparent.*
öffentlich *public.*
Öffentlichkeit *f. publicity.*
offiziell *official.*
Offizier *m. officer.*
öffnen *to open, dissect.*
Öffnung *f. opening, gap, dissection.*
OFT *often, frequently.*
öfter *more often.*
je öfter ... desto *the more ... the more.*
des öfteren *frequently.*
öfters *quite often.*
oftmals *often, frequently.*
OHNE *prep. (acc.) without, but, for, except.*
Er ging ohne ein Wort zu sagen. *He left without saying a word.*
ohne dass *without (conj.)*
ohne dass er mich angeredet hatte *without his having spoken to me.*

ohne weiteres *right off.*
ohne zu *without (before verb).*
ohne zu antworten *without answering.*
ohnehin *besides, apart.*
Ohnmacht *f. faintness, unconsciousness, faint.*
ohnmächtig *powerless, unconscious, helpless.*
ohnmächtig werden *to faint.*
OHR *n. ear, hearing.*
di Ohren steif halten *to keep one's courage.*
ganz Ohr sein *to be all ears.*
Ohrring *m. earring.*
OKTOBER *m. October.*
ÖL *n. oil.*
Ölbaum *m. olive tree.*
Ölbild *n. oil painting.*
ölen *to oil, lubricate.*
Ölfarbe *f. paint.*
ölig *oily.*
Olive *f. olive.*
Omelette *n. omelet.*
ONKEL *m. uncle.*
OPER *f. opera, opera house.*
Operation *f. operation.*
Operette *f. operetta.*
Opfer *n. sacrifice, martyr, victim.*
opfern *to sacrifice.*
Opferung *f. sacrifice.*
Optiker *m. optician.*
Optimismus *m. optimism.*
optimistisch *optimistic.*
Orange *f. orange.*
Orchester *n. orchestra.*
Orden *m. order, decoration.*
ordentlich *in order, neat, tidy.*
ordnen *to put in order, arrange.*
ORDNUNG *f. order, arrangement.*
Das finde ich ganz in Ordnung. *I think it is quite all right.*
in Ordnung bringen *to settle, straighten out.*
Ist alles in Ordnung? *Is everything all right?*
nicht in Ordnung *out of order.*
Organ *n. organ (body).*
organisieren *to organize.*
organisch *organic.*
Organist *m. organist.*
Orgel *f. organ (music).*
original *original.*
ORT *m. place, spot, locality.*
Wir fanden alles wieder an Ort und Stelle. *We found everything back in place.*
örtlich *local.*
Osten *m. East, Orient.*
nach Osten *in the direction of the East.*

Osterfest n. Easter.
Ostern n. East.
Österreicher m. Austrian.
österreichisch Austrian.
östlich eastern.
Ostsee f. Baltic sea.
ostwärts eastward.
Ozean ocean.

P

Paar n. pair, couple.
paar few, some, even, matching.
  ein paar a few, several.
  ein paarmal several times.
paaren to pair, couple.
Pächter m. farmer, tenant, householder.
Päckchen n. small parcel.
packen to seize, grasp, pack.
packend thrilling, absorbing.
Paddelboot n. canoe.
paddeln to paddle.
Paket n. parcel.
Paketannahme f. parcel-receiving office.
Pakt m. pact, agreement.
Palast m. palace.
Palme f. palm.
panieren to bread.
Panik f. panic.
Panne f. breakdown, trouble (motor).
Pantoffel m. slipper, mule.
  unter dem Pantoffel stehen to be henpecked.
Pantoffelheld m. henpecked husband.
Panzer m. armor, tank.
panzern to armor, plate.
Pagagei m. parrot.
PAPIER n. paper, identification paper, document.
  zu Papier bringen to write down, put on paper.
Papierbogen m. sheet of paper.
Papiergeld n. paper money.
Papierhandlung f. stationery store.
Papierkorb m. wastepaper basket.
Pappe f. cardboard.
Papst m. Pope.
Parade f. parade, review.
Paradies n. paradise.
paradiesisch paradisiacal.
parallel parallel.
Parfum n. perfume.
PARK n. park, grounds.
parken to park.
  Parkverbot! No parking!
Parkplatz m. parking place.

Parlament n. parliament.
Parodie f. parody.
Partei f. party, faction, tenant, side.
  Partei nehmen für to take the side of.
Parterre n. ground floor.
Partie f. part, section.
Partner m. partner.
Partnerschaft f. partnership.
Pass m. pass, passage, passport.
Passagier m. passenger.
Passamt n. passport division.
Passant m. passer-by.
PASSEN to fit, suit, be convenient, be suitable.
  zu einander passen to match, harmonize.
PASSEND suitable, convenient.
passieren to go through, pass, cross, happen.
  Was ist passiert? What happened? (What's the trouble?)
passiv passive.
Passkontrolle f. examination of passport.
Pastete f. pie, pastry.
Pastor m. pastor, minister, clergyman.
Pate m. godfather.
Patenkind n. godchild.
Patent n. letters patent.
Patentamt n. patent office.
patentieren to patent.
pathetisch pathetic.
Patient m. patient.
Patin f. godmother.
Patriot m. patriot.
patriotisch patriotic.
Pauke f. kettledrum.
Pause f. pause, interval, break, rest (music).
pausieren to pause.
Pech n. pitch, bad luck.
pechschwarz pitch-black.
Pechsträhne f. run of ill luck.
Pechvogel m. unlucky person.
Pedal n. pedal.
Pedant m. pedant.
pedantisch pedantic.
Pein f. pain, agony, torture.
peinigen to torment, harass.
Peiniger m. tormentor.
Peinigung f. torment, torture.
peinlich painful, embarrassing.
Peinlichkeit f. painfulness; carefulness, embarrassment.
Peitsche f. whip, lash.
Pellkartoffeln pl. potatoes in their jackets.
PELZ m. fur, pelt, skin, hide, fur coat.
Pelzhändler m. furrier.

Pelzmantel *m. fur coat.*
Pension *f. pension; boarding-house.*
  Er erhält eine Pension. He receives a
  pension.
  in Pension sein *to board.*
Pensionat *n. boarding-school.*
pensionieren *to pension off.*
per a, *per.*
  per Post *by post.*
  per Adresse *care of.*
Periode *f. period.*
Perle *f. pearl, bead.*
perlen *to sparkle.*
Perlenkette *f. pearl necklace, string of
  pearls.*
PERSON *f. person, personage,
  character (theater).*
  in Person *in person.*
Personal *n. staff, employees,
  personnel.*
Personalbeschreibung *f. personal
  description of a person.*
Personalien *pl. particulars about a
  person.*
Personenaufzug *m. passenger
  elevator.*
Personenkraftwagen *m. motor-car.*
Personenzug *m. passenger train.*
persönlich *personal; personally.*
Persönlichkeit *f. personality.*
Perücke *f. wig.*
pessimistisch *pessimistic.*
Pest *f. plague, pestilence, epidemic.*
Petersilie *f. parsley.*
Pfad *m. path.*
Pfadfinder *m. (-in, f.) boy (girl) scout.*
Pfahl *m. pole, stake, pile, post.*
Pfand *n. pledge, security, forfeit.*
pfänden *to seize, take in pledge.*
Pfandhaus *n. pawnshop.*
Pfandleiher *m. pawnbroker.*
Pfandschein *m. pawn ticket.*
Pfanne *f. pan.*
Pfannkuchen *m. pancake.*
Pfarrer *m. priest, pastor, minister.*
Pfarrgemeinde *f. parish.*
Pfau *m. peacock.*
PFEFFER *m. pepper.*
Pfefferkuchen *m. spiced cakes,
  gingerbread.*
Pfefferminz *n. & f. peppermint.*
pfeffern *to season with pepper.*
Pfeife *f. whistle, pipe.*
pfeifen *to whistle, pipe.*
Pfeil *m. arrow.*
Pfeiler *m. pillar, post.*
PFERD *n. horse.*
Pfiff *m. whistle, whistling, trick.*
Pfingsten *n. & f. Pentecost, Whitsuntide.*

Pfirsich *m. peach.*
PFLANZE *f. plant.*
pflanzen *to plant.*
Pflanzenkunde *f. botany.*
Pflaster *n. plaster, pavement.*
Pflasterstein *m. paving-stone.*
PFLAUME *f. plum.*
  gedörrte Pflaume *f. prune.*
Pflaumenmus *n. plum jam.*
PFLEGE *f. care, attention, nursing.*
Pflegeeltern *pl. foster parents.*
Pflegekind *n. foster child.*
pflegen *to care for, cherish, nurse,
  cultivate.*
PFLICHT *f. duty, obligation.*
Pflichteifer *m. zeal.*
Pflichtgefühl *n. sense of duty.*
pflichtgemäss *conformable to one's
  duty.*
pflücken *to pick, gather, pluck.*
Pflug *m. plough.*
pflügen *to plough.*
Pförtner *m. gatekeeper.*
Pfote *f. paw.*
Pfui! *Shame!*
Pfund *n. pound.*
Pfütze *f. puddle.*
Phänomen *n. phenomenon.*
Phantasie *f. imagination, fancy.*
phantasieren *to daydream, imagine.*
Phantast *m. dreamer, visionary.*
phantastisch *fantastic, fanciful.*
Philosoph *m. philosopher.*
Philosophie *f. philisophy.*
philosophieren *to philosophize.*
Photoapparat *m. camera.*
Photograph *m. photographer.*
Photographie *f. photography.*
photographieren *to photograph.*
Physik *f. physics.*
Pianist *m. pianist.*
Piano *n. piano.*
Picknick *n. picnic.*
Pietät *f. reverence, piety.*
pietätlos *irreverent.*
Pikkoloflöte *f. piccolo.*
Pilger *m. pilgrim.*
pilgern *to go on a pilgrimage.*
Pille *f. pill.*
Pilot *m. pilot.*
Pilz *m. mushroom.*
  Giftpilz, *m. poisonous mushroom.*
Pinsel *m. brush, paintbrush.*
pinseln *to paint.*
Pirat *m. pirate.*
Pistole *f. pistol.*
Plage *f. plague.*
plagen *to plague, torment.*
  sich plagen *to struggle,*

overwork oneself.
Plakat *n. placard, poster.*
  Keine Plakate. *Post no bills.*
Plakatsäule *f. sign post.*
Plan *m. plan, map, design; intention.*
planen *to plan, scheme.*
Planet *m. planet.*
planlos *without any fixed plan.*
planmässig *according to plan; methodical.*
Planung *f. planning, plan.*
Planwirtschaft *f. economic planning.*
Plastik *f. plastic art, sculpture.*
plastisch *plastic.*
Platin *n. platinum.*
plätschern *to splash.*
PLATT *flat, level, insipid, dull.*
Plattdeutsch *n. Low German.*
Platte *f. plate, tray; record (phonograph)*
  kalte Platte *cold meats.*
PLATZ *m.place, spot, room, seat; square (street).*
  Platz machen *to make room.*
  Bitte, nehmen Sie Platz. *Please have a seat.*
  am Platz sein *to be opportune.*
Platzanweiser *m. (-in, f.) usher.*
Plätzchen *n. little place; cookie.*
platzen *to burst, explode, crack.*
Platzmangel *m. lack of space.*
Plauderei *f. chat, small talk, conversation.*
PLAUDERN *to chat, talk, gossip.*
PLÖTZLICH *sudden; suddenly.*
plump *heavy, shapeless, tactless, clumsy.*
Plumpheit *f. shapelessness, heaviness, clumsiness.*
plumpsen *to plump down.*
Plunder *m. trash.*
plündern *to plunder, pillage.*
Plünderung *f. plundering, sack.*
Plural *m. plural.*
Pöbel *m. mob, populace.*
pöbelhaft *vulgar, low.*
pochen *to knock, beat, throb.*
Pocken *f. pl. smallpox.*
Pockenimpfung *f. smallpox vaccination.*
Podium *n. platform, rostrum.*
Poesie *f. poetry.*
Poet *m. poet.*
poetisch *poetical.*
Pol *m. pole.*
polar *polar, arctic.*
Polarforscher *m. polar explorer.*
Pole *m. Pole (native of Poland).*
polieren *to polish.*
Politik *f. politics, policy.*

Politiker *m. politician.*
politisch *political.*
politisieren *to talk politics.*
Politur *f. polish.*
POLIZEI *f. police.*
  Rufen Sie die Polizei! *Call the police!*
Polizeiamt *n. police-station.*
Polizeiaufsicht *f. police control.*
Polizeilich *m. police officer.*
polizeilich *of the police.*
Polizeistreife *f. police raid.*
Polizeistunde *f. curfew.*
polizeiwidrig *contrary to police regulations.*
Polizist *m. policeman, constable.*
polnisch *Polish.*
Polster *n. cushion, pillow, bolster, pad.*
Polstermöbel *pl. upholstered furniture.*
Polstersessel *m. easy chair.*
Polsterung *f. upholstery, padding, stuffing.*
Pomade *f. pomade.*
Pomp *m. pomp.*
pomphaft *pompous, magnificent.*
pompös *pompous, magnificent.*
populär *popular (political).*
Pore *f. pore.*
porös *porous.*
Portemonnaie *n. purse.*
Portion *f. portion, helping, ration, order.*
Porto *n. postage.*
portofrei *postfree, prepaid.*
portopflichtig *liable to postage fee.*
Porträt *n. portrait, likeness.*
porträtieren *to portray, paint a portrait.*
Porträtmaler *m. portrait painter.*
Porzellan *porcelain, china.*
Porzellanservice *n. set of china.*
positiv *positive.*
Posse *f. farce, trick.*
POST *f. post, mail, post office.*
Postamt *n. post office.*
Postanweisung *f. money order.*
Postbeamte *m. post-office clerk.*
Postbote *m. postman.*
Posten *m. post, situation.*
  auf dem Posten sein *to feel well.*
Postkarte *f. postcard.*
postlagernd *general delivery.*
postlich *postal.*
Postschliessfach *n. post-office box.*
postwendend *by return mail.*
Pracht *f. splendor.*
Prachtausgabe *f. deluxe edition.*
prächtig *magnificent, splendid, lovely.*
prachtvoll *splendid, gorgeous, magnificent.*
prahlen *to brag, boast.*
Prahlerei *f. boasting, bragging.*

prahlerisch *boastful, ostentatious.*
praktisch *clever, handy, useful.*
　Praktischer Arzt *general practitioner.*
praktizieren *to practice (a profession).*
prall *blazing, tight, tense.*
　in der prallen Sonne *in the full glare of
　　the sun.*
Prämie *f. premium.*
prämieren *to award a prize to.*
Präposition *f. preposition.*
präsentieren *to present.*
Präsident *m. president.*
Präsidium *n. chair, presidency*
prassen *to feast, revel.*
präzis *precise, exact, punctual.*
Präzision *f. precision.*
predigen *to preach.*
Prediger *m. preacher, minister.*
Predigt *f. sermon, lecture.*
PREIS *m. price, cost, rate, praise.*
　um jeden Preis *at any cost.*
　um keinen Preis *not at any price.*
　zum festem Preis *at fixed price.*
Preisangabe *f. quotation of prices.*
Preisausschreiben *n. prize
　competition.*
Preisbewerber *m. competitor.*
Preiselbeere *f. cranberry.*
preisen *to praise, extol, glorify.*
Preiserhöhung *f. rise in prices.*
Preisgabe *f. surrender, abandonment.*
preisgeben *to surrender, give up,
　abandon, sacrifice.*
Preislage *f. price range.*
Preisrichter *m. arbiter, judge.*
Preissturz *m. fall in prices.*
Preisträger *m. prize-winner.*
Preistreiberei *f. forcing up of prices.*
preiswert *reasonable, cheap.*
Premiere *f. first night.*
Presse *f. press.*
Pressestimme *f. press comment,
　review.*
Priester *m. priest.*
Prima *f. highest class of secondary
　school.*
prima *prime, first-rate.*
primitiv *primitive.*
Prinz *m. (-essin, f.) prince(ss).*
Prinzip *n. principle.*
　aus Prinzip *as a matter of principle.*
prinzipiell *on principle.*
PRIVAT *private, privately.*
Privatrecht *n. civil law.*
Probe *f. trial, experiment, test,
　probation; rehearsal (theater).*
　auf die Probe stellen *to put to the test.*
　Probe ablegen *to give proof of.*
Probeabzug *m. proof.*

proben *to rehearse.*
probeweise *on approval, on trial.*
Probezeit *f. time of probation.*
probieren *to try, taste.*
　Darf ich das anprobieren? *May I try
　　this on?*
Problem *n. problem.*
problematisch *problematic.*
Produkt *n. product.*
Produktion *f. production.*
Produzent *m. producer, manufacturer.*
produzieren *to produce, show off,
　exhibit.*
Professor *m. professor.*
Professur *f. professorship.*
Prognose *f. forecast.*
Programm *n. program.*
Projekt *n. project.*
Projektionsapparat *m. projector.*
Proklamation *f. proclamation.*
Prokura *f. procuration, power of
　attorney.*
prolongieren *to prolong.*
Promenade *f. promenade.*
Propaganda *f. propaganda.*
Prophet *m. prophet.*
prophetisch *prophetic.*
prophezeien *to prophesy.*
Prophezeiung *f. prophecy.*
Proportion *f. proportion.*
Prosa *f. prose.*
Prosit! *To your health!*
Prospekt *m. prospect.*
Protest *m. protest.*
　Protest erheben *to protest.*
Protestant *m. Protestant.*
protestantisch *Protestant.*
Protestantismus *m. Protestantism.*
protestieren *to protest.*
Protokoll *n. ticket (police); protocol.*
Proviant *m. provision.*
Provinz *f. province.*
provinziell *provincial.*
Provision *f. provision, brokerage.*
Prozent *n. per cent.*
Prozentsatz *m. percentage.*
prozentual *expressed as percentage.*
PROZESS *m. lawsuit, process,
　proceedings, trial.*
　im Prozess liegen *to be involved in a
　　law suit.*
　kurzen Prozess machen mit *to dispose
　　of quickly.*
prozessieren *to be involved in a
　lawsuit.*
Prozession *f. procession.*
PRÜFEN *to test, investigate, inspect,
　examine.*
Prüfer *m. examiner.*

Prüfling *m. examinee.*
PRÜFUNG *f. investigation, examination.*
eine Prüfung ablegen *to take an*
examination.
Prunk *m. splendor, ostentation.*
prunkvoll *gorgeous, splendid.*
Psychiater *m. psychiatrist.*
Psychiatrie *f. psychiatry.*
psychisch *psychic.*
Psychologe *m. psychologist.*
Psychologie *f. psychology.*
psychologisch *psychological.*
Psychopath *m. psychopath.*
Publikum *n. public.*
Pudel *m. poodle.*
pudelnass *drenched, soaked.*
Puder *m. toilet powder.*
pudern *to powder.*
Puls *m. pulse.*
Pulsschlag *m. pulse-beat.*
Pult *n. desk.*
Pulver *n. powder, gunpowder.*
Pulverfass *n. powder barrel.*
auf dem Pulverfass sitzen *to sit on top*
of a volcano.
PUNKT *m. point, dot, spot.*
der springende Punkt *the salient point.*
Punkt ein Uhr *at one o'clock sharp.*
pünktlich *on time, punctual, prompt.*
Pünktlichkeit *f. punctuality.*
Puppe *f. doll, puppet.*
Putz *m. trimming, ornament, dress.*
putzen *to clean, polish.*
Putzfrau *f. charwoman.*
Putzlappen *m. duster, flannel, polishing*
cloth.
Pyjama *n. & m. pajamas.*

Quadrat *n. square.*
Quäker *m. Quaker.*
Qual *f. torment, torture, pain.*
Quälen *to torment, worry, torture,*
bother.
Quäler *m. tormentor.*
Quälerei *f. tormenting, torture.*
Quälgeist *m. nuisance (person).*
qualifizieren *to qualify.*
Qualität *f. quality.*
qualitativ *qualitative.*
Qualitätsware *f. high-class article.*
Qualm *m. dense smoke.*
qualmen *to smoke (chimney).*
qualmig *smoky.*
qualvoll *very painful, agonizing.*

Quarantäne *f. quarantine.*
unter Quarantäne stellen *to*
quarantine.
Quecksilber *n. mercury.*
Quelle *f. spring, fountain.*
quellen *to gush, well, flow.*
Quellwasser *n. spring water.*
quer *cross, lateral, oblique; across,*
obliquely.
kreuz und quer *all over.*
querfeldein *across country.*
Querschnitt *m. cross-section.*
Querstrasse *f. crossroad.*
Quertreiberei *f. intrigue.*
quetschen *to squeeze, smash.*
Quetschung *f. contusion.*
Quetschwunde *f. bruise.*
quietschen *to scream, squeal.*
quittieren *to receipt.*
Quittung *f. receipt.*
Quote *f. quota, share.*

Rabatt *m. discount.*
Rabbiner *m. rabbi.*
Rache *f. revenge.*
rächen *to revenge, avenge.*
sich rächen *take revenge, get*
revenge.
Deine Faulheit wird sich an dir rächen.
You will have to suffer for your
laziness.
Rachsucht *f. thirst for revenge.*
rachsüchtig *revengeful.*
RAD *n. wheel, bicycle.*
radfahren *to cycle.*
Radfahrer *m. cyclist.*
Radfahrweg *m. cycle track.*
Radiergummi *m. eraser.*
Radierung *f. etching.*
Radio *n. radio.*
Radreifen *m. bicycle tire.*
raffiniert *refined.*
Rahm *m. cream.*
Rahmen *m. frame.*
Rakete *f. rocket.*
Rampe *f. ramp, platform; limelight.*
ramponieren *to damage.*
RAND *m. edge, brim, border, margin.*
ausser Rand und Band sein *to be out*
of hand.
Schreiben Sie es an den Rand! *Write*
it in the margin!
Randbemerkung *f. marginal note.*
Rang *m. rank, order, quality, class.*

den Rang ablaufen *to get the better of.*

ersten Ranges *first class, first rate.*

erster Rang *first balcony, dress circle.*

zweiter Rang *second balcony, upper circle.*

Rangabzeichen *n. badge of rank.*

Rangordnung *f. order of precedence.*

Rangstufe *f. degree.*

rar *rare, scarce.*

Rarität *f. rarity, curiosity.*

rasch *quick, swift, speedy.*

rascheln *to rustle.*

rasen *to rave, rage, speed.*

rasend *raving, raging.*

rasend machen *to make mad.*

Raserei *f. raving, fury, rage.*

Rasierapparat *m. safety razor.*

elektrischer Rasierapparat *electric razor.*

rasieren *to shave.*

sich rasieren *to shave (oneself).*

sich rasieren lassen *to get shaved.*

Rasierklinge *f. razor blade.*

Rasiermesser *n. razor.*

Rasierpinsel *m. shaving brush.*

Rasierzeug *n. shaving things.*

Rasse *f. race, breed.*

rassig *thoroughbred.*

rassisch *racial.*

Rast *f. resting, recreation, rest, repose.*

rasten *to rest.*

rastlos *restless, indefatigable.*

Rastlosigkeit *f. restlessness.*

RAT *m. counsel, advice, consultation, remedy.*

Rat schaffen *to devise means.*

um Rat fragen *to ask advice.*

zu Rat ziehen *to consult.*

Rate *f. installment.*

raten *to advise, guess, solve.*

ratenweise *by installments.*

Ratgeber *m. adviser.*

Ration *f. ration.*

rationell *rational; economical.*

ratlos *at a loss, helpless.*

Ratlosigkeit *f. helplessness, perplexity.*

Ratschläge *m. counsel, advice.*

ratschlägen *to deliberate.*

Rätsel *n. riddle, enigma, puzzle.*

Es ist mir ein Rätsel. *It puzzles me.*

rätselhaft *mysterious, enigmatic.*

Ratte *f. rat.*

Raub *m. robbery, plundering.*

auf Raub ausgehen *to go on the prowl.*

rauben *to rob, plunder.*

Räuber *m. robber, thief.*

Raubmord *m. murder and robbery.*

Raubtier *n. beast of prey.*

Raubvogel *m. bird of prey.*

Rauch *m. smoke.*

RAUCHEN *to smoke.*

Rauchen Verboten! *No Smoking!*

Raucher *m. smoker.*

räuchern *to smoke, cure, fumigate.*

Räucherwaren *pl. smoked meats and fish.*

Rauchtabak *m. tobacco.*

Rauchzimmer *n. smoking room.*

RAUH *uneven, rough, raw, hoarse, harsh.*

Rauheit *f. roughness, harshness.*

RAUM *m. place, room, space.*

Raum geben *to give way, indulge.*

räumen *to clear away, remove, clean, evacuate.*

Rauminhalt *m. volume, capacity.*

räumlich *relating to space, spatial.*

Räumlichkeit *f. room, premises, space.*

Raummangel *m. lack of room.*

Räumung *f. removal, evacuation.*

Raupe *f. caterpillar.*

Raupenschlepper *m. caterpillar tractor.*

Rausch *m. drunkenness, intoxication, frenzy.*

rauschen *to rustle, rush, roar.*

Rauschgift *n. narcotic.*

Reaktion *f. reaction.*

Rebe *f. grape, vine.*

Rebell *m. rebel.*

rebellieren *to rebel.*

Rechen *m. rake.*

Rechenmaschine *f. calculating machine.*

Rechenschuft *f. account.*

Rechenscheiber *m. slide rule.*

RECHNEN *to count, reckon, calculate.*

RECHNUNG *f. sum, account, bill, calculation.*

auf eigene Rechnung *at one's own risk.*

auf Rechnung setzen *to charge, put to one's account.*

in Rechnung ziehen *to take into account.*

laut Rechnung *as per invoice.*

Meine Rechnung, bitte. *Please bring me the check.*

Sind Sie auf Ihre Rechnung gekommen? *Did you get your money's worth? (Was it worth while?)*

Rechnungsprüfer *m. auditor.*

RECHT *n. right, privilege, title, claim, law.*

alle Rechte vorbehalten *all rights reserved.*

an den Rechten kommen *to meet*

one's match.

mit vollem Recht   *for good reasons.*

nach dem Rechten sehen   *to see to things.*

Recht behalten   *to be right in the end.*

Recht geben   *to agree with.*

Recht haben   *to be right.*

Recht sprechen   *to administer justice.*

von Rechts wegen   *by rights, according to the law.*

zu Recht bestehen   *to be valid.*

RECHT   *right, all right, right-hand, correct, proper, genuine, lawful.*

Das ist mir recht.   *That's all right with me.*

Das ist nur recht und billig.   *That's only fair.*

die rechte Hand   *the right hand.*

erst recht   *all the more now, now more than ever.*

erst geschieht ihm recht.   *It serves him right.*

es recht machen   *to suit, please.*

Man kann es nicht allen recht machen.   *You cannot please everybody.*

schlecht und recht   *not bad.*

zur rechten Zeit   *in time.*

Rechte   *f. right hand.*

Rechteck   *n. rectangle.*

rechteckig   *rectangular.*

rechterhand   *on the right hand.*

rechtfertigen   *to justify.*

sich rechtfertigen   *to justify oneself.*

Rechtfertigung   *f. justification.*

rechthaberisch   *dogmatic.*

rechtlich   *just, lawful, legitimate.*

Rechtlichkeit   *f. integrity, honesty.*

rechtmässig   *lawful, legitimate.*

RECHTS   *to the right, on the right.*

Biegen sie rechts ab!   *Turn to the right!*

nach rechts   *to the right.*

Nehmen Sie die erste Strasse rechts.   *Take the first turn to your right.*

Rechts Halten!   *Keep to the right!*

Rechts um!   *Right turn!*

Rechtsanspruch   *m. legal claim.*

Rechtsanwalt   *m. lawyer, counsel.*

Rechtsbeistand   *m. legal adviser.*

rechtschaffen   *honest, upright; very, extremely.*

Rechtschreibung   *f. spelling.*

Rechtsfall   *m. lawsuit.*

Rechtsgelehrte   *m. jurist.*

rechtsgültig   *legal, valid.*

Rechtspruch   *m. verdict.*

rechtsungültig   *illegal, invalid.*

rechtsverbindlich   *legally, binding.*

Rechtsweg   *m. legal proceedings, law.*

rechtswidrig   *illegal.*

Rechtswissenschaft   *f. jurisprudence.*

rechtzeitig   *in good time.*

recken   *to stretch, extend.*

Redakteur   *m. editor.*

Redaktion   *f. editors, editorial staff.*

redaktionell   *editorial.*

REDE   *f. talk, discourse, speech, conversation, rumor.*

Davon ist keine Rede!   *That's out of the question!*

Davon ist nicht dir Rede!   *That's not the point!*

eine Rede halten   *to make a speech.*

in die Rede fallen   *to interrupt.*

nicht der Rede wert   *not worth mentioning.*

Rede stehen   *to answer for.*

Wovon ist die Rede?   *What is it all about?*

zur Rede stellen   *to call to account.*

Redefluss   *m. flow of words.*

Redefreiheit   *f. freedom of speech.*

redegewandt   *fluent, eloquent.*

REDEN   *to talk, speak, converse, make a speech.*

begeistert reden   *to rave, enthuse.*

mit sich reden lassen   *to listen to reason.*

nicht zu reden von   *to say nothing of.*

von sich reden machen   *to cause a stir.*

Redensart   *f. phrase, idiom, nonsense.*

Redner   *m. orator, speaker.*

redselig   *talkative.*

reduzieren   *to reduce.*

Reederei   *f. steamship company.*

Referenz   *f. reference.*

reformieren   *to reform.*

Regal   *n. shelf.*

rege   *active, brisk.*

Regel   *f. rule, regulation, principle.*

in der Regel   *as a rule.*

regelmässig   *regular, proportional.*

regeln   *to arrange, regulate.*

geregelt   *regular, well ordered.*

regelrecht   *regular, correct, proper.*

REGEN   *m. rain, shower.*

Auf Regen folgt Sonnenschein.   *The calm follows the storm. ("After rain follows sunshine.")*

Regenbogen   *m. rainbow.*

regendicht   *waterproof.*

Regenmantel   *m. raincoat.*

Regenschirm   *m. umbrella.*

Regenzeit   *f. rainy season.*

Regie   *f. production (theater); administration, management.*

regieren   *to rule, govern, reign.*

Regierung   *f. government, reign, rule.*

Regierungsbeamte *m. government official.*

Regiment *n. regiment, government.*

Regisseur *m. stage manager.*

Register *n. register, index, table of contents.*

registieren *to register.*

REGNEN *to rain.*

  Es regnet in Strömen. *It's raining cats and dogs.*

regnerisch *rainy.*

regsam *active, agile, quick.*

Regsamkeit *f. agility, activity, quickness.*

Regung *f. movement.*

Reh *n. deer.*

Rehbraten *m. roast venison.*

Reibeisen *n. grater.*

Reiben *to rub, grate, grind.*

  wundreiben (sich) *to chafe.*

REICH *rich, wealthy, well off, plentiful, abundant.*

Reich *n. empire, kingdom.*

  Deutsche Reich *n. Germany.*

  Österreich *n. Austria.*

reichen *to give, present, hand.*

reichhaltig *full, rich abundant.*

Reichhaltigkeit *f. fullness, richness.*

reichlich *plentiful, abundant, copious.*

Reichsautobahn *f. state road.*

Reichtum *m. wealth, abundance.*

Reichweite *f. range, reach.*

Reif *m. frost.*

REIF *ripe, mature, mellow.*

Reifen *m. tire.*

reifen *to ripen, mature.*

Reifenpanne *f. flat tire, blowout.*

Reifenschaden *m. flat tire, blowout.*

Reifeprüfung *f. final comprehensive examination.*

Reifezeugnis *n. final certificate, diploma.*

reiflich *maturely, carefully.*

REIHE *f. row, range, series, sequence.*

  ausser der Reihe *out of one's mind.*

  der Reihe nach *successively, in rotation.*

  Er ist an der Reihe. *It is his turn.*

Reihenfolge *f. succession, sequence.*

reihenweise *in rows.*

reihum *in turns, by turns.*

Reim *m. rhyme.*

reimen *to rhyme.*

REIN *clean, plain, sheer, pure, genuine, tidy.*

  aus reinem Trotz *out of sheer obstinacy.*

Reinfall *m. failure, let down.*

Reingewinn *m. net profit.*

Reinheit *f. purity, pureness.*

REUNIGEN *to clean, clense, purify.*

Reinigung *f. cleaning, cleansing.*

Reinigungsanstalt *f. cleaner's.*

reinlich *clean, neat, tidy.*

Reinlichkeit *f. cleanliness, neatness, tidiness.*

Reis *m, rice.*

REISE *f. trip, journey, voyage.*

  Glückliche Reise! *Have a nice trip!*

Reisebüro *n. tourist office.*

Reiseführer *m. guidebook.*

REISEN *to travel.*

REISENDE *m. passenger, traveler.*

Reisescheck *m. traveler's check.*

reissen *to tear, pull, drag.*

  an sich reissen *to seize, hold up, snatch up.*

  in Stücke reissen *to tear to pieces.*

  sich reissen um *to fight for.*

reissend *ravenous, rapid, torrential.*

  reissende Strom *m. torrent.*

Reissverschluss *m. zipper.*

reiten *to ride a horse.*

Reiter *m. horseman, cavalryman.*

Reithose *f. riding pants.*

Reitschule *f. riding school.*

REIZ *m. charm, attraction; irritation; incentive.*

Reizbar *sensitive, irritable.*

reizen *to irritate, excite, provoke, tempt.*

reizend *charming.*

reizlos *unattractive.*

reizvoll *charming, attractive.*

REKLAME *f. publicity, advertisement.*

  Reklame machen *to advertise.*

rekonstruieren *to reconstruct.*

Rekord *m. record, competition.*

Rekrut *m. recruit.*

Rektor *m. university president.*

relativ *relative, relating to.*

Religion *f. religion.*

religiös *religious.*

Rennbahn *f. racecourse.*

RENNEN *to run, race.*

Rennfahrer *m. racing cyclist.*

Rennstall *m. racing stable.*

renovieren *to renovate, redecorate.*

Rentamt *n. revenue office.*

Rente *f. revenue, pension.*

Reparation *f. reparation.*

Reparatur *f. repair.*

  Wegen Reparatur geschlossen. *Closed for repairs.*

Reparaturwerkstätte *f. repair shop.*

Reportage *f. commentary, eye-witness account.*

repräsentieren *to represent.*

Republik *f. republic.*

Republikaner *m. Republican.*
republikanisch *republican.*
Reserve *f. reserve.*
Reserverad *n. spare wheel.*
reservieren *to reserve.*
Respekt *m. respect.*
respektabel *respectable.*
respektieren *to respect.*
respektlos *without respect, irreverent.*
respektvoll *respectful.*
Rest *m. rest, remains, remnant.*
restaurieren *to repair, restore (work of art).*
Restbestand *m. remainder, residue.*
restlos *complete, without anything left over.*
Resultat *n. result, answer.*
retten *to save, preserve, rescue, deliver.*
Rettung *f. rescue, saving, escape.*
Rettungsboot *n. lifeboat.*
Rettungsring *m. lifebelt.*
Reue *f. repentance.*
reuen *to repent, regret.*
  Es reut mich. *I regret.*
reumütig *repentant, penitent.*
Revier *n. hunting ground, district.*
  Polizeirevier *n. district police station.*
Revolte *f. revolt, insurrection.*
Revolution *f. revolution.*
revolutionär *revolutionary.*
Revolver *m. revolver.*
Rezept *n. recipe, prescription.*
rezitieren *to recite.*
Rheumatismus *m. rheumatism.*
rhythmisch *rhythmical.*
Richter *m. judge.*
RICHTIG *right, correct, true, real, straight.*
  Das ist nicht sein richtiger Name. *That's not his real name.*
  Meine Uhr geht richtig. *My watch is right.*
  Richtig! *Quite right!*
Richtigstellung *f. rectification.*
Richtung *f. direction, line, course, tendency.*
riechen *to smell.*
Riemen *m. strap.*
Riese *m. giant.*
riesenhaft *gigantic, colossal.*
Rind *n. ox, cow, cattle.*
Rinde *f. bark, rind of cheese, crust.*
Rinderbraten *m. roast beef.*
Rindfleisch *n. beef.*
Ring *m. ring, circle.*
ringen *to struggle, wrestle.*
Ringkampf *m. wrestling match.*
Ringkämpfer *m. wrestler, athlete.*

Ringrichter *m. umpire.*
rings *round, around.*
ringsum (-her) *all around.*
Rinne *f. gutter, channel.*
rinnen *to flow, run.*
Rinnstein *m. gutter.*
Rippe *f. rib.*
riskant *risky.*
riskieren *to risk.*
Riss *m. tear, hole, gap, crack.*
Ritter *m. knight, cavalier.*
Rittergut *n. estate, manor.*
ritterlich *chivalrous, gallant.*
Rivale *m. rival.*
Rock *m. coat(man's); skirt.*
rodeln *to sled.*
Rodelschlitten *m. sled.*
roden *to root out, clear (forest, garden).*
ROH *raw, crude, coarse, rare (steak).*
Rohmaterial *n. raw material.*
Rohr *n. pipe, tube.*
Röhre *f. tube, valve.*
Rolle *f. roll, cylinder; part (theater).*
  aus der Rolle fallen *to misbehave.*
  die Rollen verteilen *to cast (a play).*
Rollenbesetzung *f. cast.*
Roller *m. rolling sea.*
Rollmops *m. herring.*
Rollschuh *m. rollerskate.*
  Rollschuh laufen *to rollerskate.*
Rollstuhl *m. wheelchair.*
Rolltreppe *f. escalator.*
Roman *m. novel, fiction.*
Romanschriftsteller *m. novelist.*
Romantik *f. romanticism.*
Romantiker *m. romanticist.*
romantisch *romantic.*
röntgen *to x-ray.*
Röntgenaufnahme *f. X-ray photograph.*
Röntgenbild *n. X-ray photograph.*
Röntgenstrahlen *pl. X-rays.*
rosa *pink, rose-colored.*
Rose *f. rose.*
Rosenkohl *m. Brussels sprouts.*
Rosine *f. raisin.*
Rost *m.* 1. *rust.*
  2. *grate.*
Rostbraten *m. roast beef.*
rösten *to roast, grill, toast.*
Rostfleck *m. ironmold.*
rostfrei *stainless.*
  rostfreier Stahl *stainless steel.*
rostig *rusty.*
ROT *red, ruddy.*
  rot werden *to blush.*
rotblond *auburn.*
Röte *f. red, redness, blush.*
Rotkohl *m. red cabbage.*
Rotstift *m. red pencil.*

Rotwein m. red wine.
Rübe f. sugar beet.
  die rote Rübe the red beet.
Rubin m. ruby.
Rückantwort f. reply.
Rückblick m. glance back, retrospect.
RÜCKEN m. back, rear.
  den Rücken kehren to turn one's
   back.
  in dem Rücken fallen to attack from
   the rear.
  Rücken gegen Rücken back to back.
rücken to move, push, move away.
Rückendeckung f. rear, cover,
  protection.
rückerstatten to refund.
Rückfahrkarte f. return ticket.
Rückfahrt f. return trip.
Rückfall m. relapse.
rückfällig relapsing.
Rückflug m. return flight.
Rückfrage f. query, search back.
Rückgabe f. return.
Rückgang m. decline, falling off.
rückgängig retrogressive.
  rückgängig machen to cancel.
Rückgrat spine, backbone.
Rückhalt m. reserve, support.
rückhaltlos unreserved, without
  reserve.
Rückkehr f. return.
Rückkunft f. return.
Rücklehne f. back (of chair).
Rückmarsch m. retreat.
Rückporto n. return postage.
Rückreise f. return trip.
Rückschlag m. reverse, setback,
  reaction.
Rückschritt m. step back, relapse.
Rückseite f. back, reverse side.
Rücksicht f. regard, consideration.
rücksichtslos inconsiderate, reckless.
rüsichtsvoll considerate.
Rücksitz m. back seat.
Rücksprache f. discussion, consultation.
  Rücksprache nehmen to discuss, talk
   over.
Rückstand m. arrears, residue.
rückständig backward, old-fashioned.
Rückstrahler m. rear reflector.
Rücktritt m. retirement, resignation.
Rückwand f. back wall.
rückwärts backwards; back.
Rückwärtsgang m. reverse gear.
Rückweg m. way back, return.
rückwirkend retroactive, retrospective.
Rückwirkung f. reaction, retroaction.
Rückzahlung f. repayment.
Rückzug m. withdrawal, retreat.

Ruder n. oar, rudder, helm.
  ans Ruder kommen to come into
   power.
Ruderboot n. rowboat.
rudern to row.
Ruf m. reputation, cry, call.
  im Rufe stehen to be reputed,
   generally considered as.
RUFEN to call, shout.
  Soll ich sie rufen lassen? Shall I send
   for her?
  wie gerufen kommen to come at the
   right moment.
Rufname m. Christian name.
Rüge f. censure, reprimand.
rügen to censure, reprimand.
RUHE f. rest, repose, calm.
  Angenehme Ruhe! Sleep well!
  in aller Ruhe very calmly.
  Lassen Sie mich in Ruhe! Leave me
   alone!
  Nichts bringt ihn aus der Ruhe.
   Nothing upsets him.
  Ruhe! Silence! Quiet!
  sich zur Ruhe setzen to retire.
  zur Ruhe gehen to go to bed.
ruhelos restless.
RUHEN to rest, sleep, stand still.
  ruhen auf to rest on, be based on.
Ruhestätte f. resting-place.
Ruhestellung f. at-ease position
  (standing).
Ruhestörer m. brawler, rioter.
RUHIG still, quiet, silent, calm,
  composed.
  Bleiben Sie ruhig sitzen! Don't get up!
  Sei ruhig! Be quiet!
Ruhm m. fame, glory.
rühmen to praise.
  sich rühmen to boast, brag.
rühmlich glorious, praiseworthy.
ruhmlos inglorious, obscure.
Rührei n. scrambled egg.
rühren to move, touch, stir.
rührend touching, moving, pathetic.
rührig active, quick.
rührselig sentimental, emotional.
Rührung f. emotion, feeling.
Ruine f. ruin.
ruinieren to ruin.
RUND round, circular, plump.
  rund heraus flatly.
  rund (her)um all around.
Rundblick m. panorama.
RUNDE f. circle, lap, beat.
  die Runde machen to make a round.
runden to make round, round.
Rundfahrt f. circular tour.
Rundfrage f. inquiry, questionnaire.

RUNDFUNK *m. radio, wireless, broadcasting.*
im Rundfunk gehört *heard over the radio.*
Rundfunkgerät *n. wireless set.*
Rundfunkhörer *m. listener (radio).*
Rundgang *m. round (military), stroll.*
rundlich *round, rounded.*
Rundschreiben *n. circular letter.*
Rundung *f. rounding, curve.*
Russ *m. soot.*
Russe *m.* (**Russin** *f.) Russian (person).*
russig *sooty.*
russisch *Russian.*
Russische *n. Russian (language).*
rüsten *to arm, prepare for war.*
rüstig *strong, robust, vigorous.*
Rüstung *f. preparation, equipment, armor.*
Rutsch *m. slide, glide, landslip.*
rutschen *to slide, slip, skid.*
rutschig *slippery.*

S

Saal *m. large room, hall.*
Saat *f. seed.*
Säbel *m. saber.*
sabotieren *to sabotage.*
Sachbearbeiter *m. expert.*
sachdienlich *relevant, pertinent.*
SACHE *f. thing, subject, business, case, cause, point, subject.*
bei der Sache sein *to pay attention.*
gemeinsame Sache machen *to make common cause with.*
zur Sache *to the point.*
Sachen *pl. things, clothes.*
seine sieben Sachen *all one's belongings.*
sachgemäss *appropriate, suitable.*
Sachkunde *f. expert knowledge.*
sachkundig *expert, competent.*
Sachlage *f. state of affairs.*
sachlich *factual, essential, objective.*
Sachlichkeit *f. reality, objectivity.*
Sachschaden *m. damage to property.*
sachte *soft, gentle, slow.*
Sachverhalt *m. facts of the case.*
Sack *m. sack, bag, pocket, purse.*
Sackgasse *f. blind alley, dead end.*
säen *to sow.*
Saft *m. juice, liquid, sap.*
Apfelsinensaft *m. orange juice.*
saftig *juicy, succulent.*
saftlos *dry.*

Sage *f. legend, tale.*
Säge *f. saw.*
SAGEN *to say, tell, mean.*
Das hat nichts zu sagen. *That does not matter.*
Das ist leichter gesagt als getan. *That's easier said than done.*
Er hat es mir ins Ohr gesagt. *He whispered it in my ear.*
Gesagt, getan. *No sooner said than done.*
man sagt *they say.*
sagen lassen *to send word.*
sage und schreibe *precisely.*
sich etwas gesagt sein lassen *to be warned.*
unter uns gesagt *between you and me.*
Was sagen Sie dazu? *What do you say to that?*
Was wollen Sie damit sagen? *What do you mean by that?*
sagenhaft *legendary, fabulous, mythical.*
Sägewerk *n. sawmill.*
Sahne *f. cream.*
Saison *f. season (social).*
Saisonausverkauf *m. clearance sale.*
Saite *f. string, chord.*
Saiteninstrument *n. stringed instrument.*
Salat *m. salad.*
grüner Salat *lettuce.*
Salbe *f. salve, ointment.*
salben *to anoint.*
Salmiakgeist *m. ammonia.*
Salon *m. drawing room.*
salutieren *to salute.*
SALZ *m. salt.*
salzen *to salt, season.*
Salzgurke *f. pickled cucumber.*
salzhältig *containing salt.*
salzig *salted, salty.*
Same *m. seed.*
SAMMELN *to collect, gather, accumulate.*
Sammelplatz *m. assembly.*
Sammelstelle *f. assembly.*
Sammler *m. collector.*
Sammlung *f. collection.*
SAMSTAG *m. Saturday.*
Samt *m. velvet.*
samt *together with.*
samt und sonders *one and all.*
sämtlich *altogether, all of them.*
Sanatorium *n. sanatorium.*
SAND *m. sand.*
Sandale *f. sandal.*
Sandboden *m. sandy soil.*

sandig *sandy.*

SANFT *soft, tender, delicate, gentle, smooth.*

Sanftheit *f. softness.*

Sänftigen *to soften, appease.*

Sanftmut *f. gentleness.*

sanftmütig *gentle, meek.*

Sänger *m. (-in, f.) singer.*

Sanitäter *m. medical aid (person).*

Sardelle *f. anchovy.*

Sardine *f. sardine.*

Sarg *m. coffin.*

sarkastisch *sarcastic.*

Satiriker *m. satirist.*

satirisch *satirical.*

SATT *full, satisfied, saturated.*
    Ich habe es satt. *I've enough of it, I'm fed up with it.*
    nicht satt werden *never to be tired of.*

Sattel *m. saddle.*
    in allen Sätteln gerecht sein *to be good at everything.*

satteln *to saddle.*

sättigen *to satisfy, saturate.*

Satz *m. set, clause, sentence (grammar); proposition (philo.); phrase (music); sediment.*

Satzbau *m. sentence structure.*

Satzzeichen *n. punctuation mark.*

sauber *clean, neat, tidy.*

Sauberkeit *f. tidiness, cleanliness.*

säuberlich *clean, neat.*

säubern *to clean, clear.*

Säuberung *f. cleaning.*

Sauce *f. sauce, gravy.*

SAUER *sour, acid, pickled.*

Sauerbraten *m. sauerbraten.*

Sauerkraut *n. sauerkraut.*

säuerlich *acid, acidulous.*

säuern *to acidify.*

Sauerstoff *m. oxygen.*

Sauerstoffgerät *n. oxygen apparatus.*

saugen *to suck, absorb.*

säugen *to suckle, nurse.*

Säugling *m. infant, baby.*

Säule *f. pillar, column.*

Saum *m. edge, border, hem.*

Säure *f. acid, sourness, tartness, acidity.*

säurehaltig *containing acid.*

Saxophon *n. saxophone.*

schäbig *shabby, worn out.*

Schäbigkeit *f. shabbiness.*

Schach *n. chess.*
    Schach bieten *to defy.*

Schachbrett *n. chessboard.*

Schachfeld *n. square of a chessboard.*

schachmatt *checkmate.*

Schachpartie *f. chess game.*

Schachtel *f. box.*

SCHADE *too bad.*
    Es ist schade! *It is a pity!*
    Wie schade! *What a pity!*
    zu schade für *too good to.*

Schaden *m. damage, harm, injury, bias.*
    Durch Schaden wird man klug. *You learn by your mistakes.*
    zu Schaden kommen *to suffer damage.*

SCHADEN *to hurt, damage, injure, prejudice.*
    Es schadet nichts. *It doesn't matter.*

Schadenersatz *m. compensation.*

Schadenfreude *f. malicious joy.*

schadenfroh *rejoicing over another's misfortune.*

schadhaft *damaged, defective, dilapidated.*
    sich schadlos halten *to get even with.*

schädlich *harmful, bad.*

Schaf *n. sheep.*

Schäfchen *n. lamb.*
    sein Schäfchen ins Trockene bringen *to feather one's nest*

Schäfer *m. shepherd.*

Schäferhund *m. sheep-dog.*

schaffen *to create, produce, accomplish, make, do.*
    einem zu schaffen machen *to give trouble.*
    sich zu schaffen machen *to be busy.*
    wie geschaffen für *as though cut out for.*

schaffend *creative, working.*

Schaffner *m. conductor, (train) guard.*

Schal *m. shawl, scarf.*

Schale *f. skin, peel, rind, shell.*

schälen *to peel, shell, bark, skin.*

Schalk *m. rogue.*

schalkhaft *roguish.*

Schall *m. sound.*

schalldicht *soundproof.*

Schalleffekt *m. sound effect.*

schallen *to sound, resound.*

Schallehre *f. acoustics.*

Schallplatte *f. record (phonograph).*

Schaltanlage *f. switch, gear.*

schalten *to deal with, use, direct, change gears.*

Schalter *m. switch, ticket-window.*

Schaltjahr *n. leap year.*

Schaltung *f. gear change, connection.*

Scham *f. shame, modesty.*

schämen (sich) *to be ashamed.*

Schamgefühl *n. sense of shame.*

schamhaft *modest, bashful.*

schamlos *shameless, impudent.*

Schamlosigkeit *f. shamelessness, impudence.*

schamrot *blushing red.*
Schamröte *f. blush.*
schandbar *infamous.*
Schande *f. shame, disgrace.*
schänden *to spoil, disfigure, dishonor, rape.*
schändlich *shameful, disgraceful.*
Schändlichkeit *f. infamy.*
Schandtat *f. crime, misdeed.*
SCHARF *sharp, keen, harsh, pointed, piercing, acute, strong, quick.*
  Behalten Sie ihn scharf im Auge! *Keep a sharp eye on him!*
  Ich bin nicht so scharf darauf. *I am not so keen on that.*
Scharfblick *m. penetrating glance.*
Schärfe *f. sharpness, rigor, acuteness.*
schärfen *to sharpen.*
scharfkantig *sharp-edged.*
Scharfsicht *f. keenness of sight, perspicacity.*
scharfsichtig *keen-sighted, penetrating.*
Scharlach *m. scarlet fever.*
SCHATTEN *m. shadow, shade, spirit, phantom.*
  in den Schatten stellen *to overshadow.*
  Sie folgt mir wie ein Schatten. *She follows me like a shadow.*
Schattenseite *f. shady side.*
schattieren *to shade.*
schattig *shady.*
Schatz *m. treasure.*
Schatzamt *n. treasury.*
Schatzanweisung *f. treasury bond.*
schätzen *to value, estimate, judge.*
schätzenswert *estimable.*
Schatzmeister *m. treasurer.*
Schätzung *f. estimate, taxation.*
schätzungsweise *approximately.*
SCHAU *f. sight, view, show, exhibition.*
  zur Schau stellen *to exhibit, display.*
Schauder *m. shudder, shivering, horror, terror, fright.*
schauen *to see, behold, gaze, view.*
Schauer *m. horror, terror, awe, thrill.*
schauerlich *awful.*
schauern *to shudder, shiver.*
  mich schaudert bei *I shudder at.*
Schauerroman *m. thriller.*
Schaufel *f. shovel, scoop.*
schaufeln *to shovel.*
Schaufenster *n. show-window.*
Schaukasten *m. show case.*
Schaukel *f. swing.*
schaukeln *to swing, rock.*
Schaukelstuhl *m. rocking chair.*
schaulustig *curious.*
SCHAUSPIEL *n. spectacle, scene, play, drama.*

Schauspieler *m. (-in, f.) actor (actress)*
Schauspielkunst *f. dramatic art.*
Schaustellung *f. exhibition.*
Schaustück *n. specimen.*
Schaum *m. foam.*
  zu Schaum schlagen *to beat up.*
Schäumen *to foam.*
schaumig *foamy, frothy.*
Scheck *m. check.*
Scheckbuch *n. check book.*
Scheckformular *n. blank check.*
Scheckinhaber *m. bearer.*
Scheibe *f. (window) pane, disk, slice, target.*
Scheibenwischer *m. window-wiper.*
Scheide *f. boundary, limits, frontier.*
scheiden *to separate, divide, part, divorce.*
  sich scheiden lassen *to get a divorce.*
Scheidewand *f. partition.*
Scheidung *f. separation, divorce.*
Scheidungsklage *f. divorce suit.*
SCHEIN *m. appearance, air, look; shine; ticket, receipt.*
  Der Schein trügt. *Appearances are deceiving.*
scheinbar *apparent.*
Scheinbild *n. phantom, illusion.*
SCHEINEN *to shine; seem; look.*
scheinheilig *hypocritical.*
Scheintod *m. suspended animation.*
Scheinwerfer *m. reflector, search light, headlight (car).*
Scheitel *m. top, crown, summit.*
scheitern *to fail.*
Schelle *f. door bell, little bell.*
Schema *n. order, arrangement, model.*
schematisch *systematic, mechanical.*
Schenkel *m. thigh.*
schenken *to give, present with, grant.*
  geschenkt bekommen *to get as a present.*
Schenker *m. donor.*
Schenkung *f. donation, gift.*
Schere *f. scissors.*
Scherz *m. joke, jest, pleasantry.*
scherzen *to joke, make fun of.*
scherzhaft *joking.*
Scherzwort *n. joke.*
SCHEU *shy, timid.*
  scheu werden *to shy.*
scheuen *to avoid, shun.*
  sich scheuen *to shy away.*
scheuern *to scrub, rub, clean, chafe.*
Schicht *f. layer, bed, coat, shift.*
Schichtwechsel *m. change of shift.*
Schick *m. elegance, smartness, chic.*
SCHICKEN *to send, dispatch.*
  schicken nach *to send for.*
  sich schicken in *to put up with.*

schicklich *proper, decent.*
Schicksal *n. fate, destiny, lot.*
Schiebefenster *n. sash-window.*
SCHIEBEN *to move, push, shove.*
  schieben auf *to lay the blame on.*
Schiebetür *f. sliding door.*
Schiebung *f. profiteering.*
Schiedsrichter *m. umpire.*
schief *oblique, crooked, askance.*
Schiefer *m. slate, splinter.*
Schieferdach *n. slate roof.*
Schiene *f. rail, track, splint.*
schiessen *to shoot, flash, fire.*
SCHIFF *n. boat, ship, vessel.*
  zu Schiff *on board, by boat.*
schiffbar *navigable.*
Schiffbruch *m. shipwreck.*
Schiffchen *n. small boat, shuttle.*
schiffen *to ship, sail.*
Schiffer *m. sailor.*
Schiffsbesatzung *f. crew.*
Schiffskörper *m. hull.*
Schiffsladung *f. cargo.*
Schiffswerft *m. wharf, dock.*
Schild *n. shield, coat of arms, sign.*
  im Schilde führen *to have something*
  up one's sleeve.
schildern *to relate, describe.*
Schilderung *f. description.*
Schimmel *m. mold, mildew.*
schimmelig *moldy.*
Schimmer *m. glitter.*
schimmern *to glitter, gleam.*
Schimpf *m. disgrace, insult.*
schimpfen *to kick, gripe, scold.*
  schimpfen mit *to scold.*
schimpflich *disgraceful.*
Schimpfwort *n. invective.*
SCHINKEN *m. ham.*
  Eier mit Schinken *ham and eggs.*
Schirm *m. umbrella, shelter,*
  lampshade.
Schlacht *f. combat, battle.*
schlachten *to slaughter, kill, butcher.*
Schlächter *m. butcher.*
Schlachtfeld *n. battlefield.*
Schlachthaus *n. slaughterhouse.*
Schlachtschiff *n. battleship.*
SCHLAF *m. sleep.*
  im Schlaf liegen *to be asleep.*
Schlafanzug *m. pajamas.*
Schläfchen *n. nap.*
SCHLAFEN *to sleep.*
  schlafen gehen *to go to bed.*
Schlafenszeit *m. bedtime.*
schlaff *slack, loose, relaxed.*
Schlaffheit *f. laxity.*
Schlafkrankheit *f. sleeping sickness.*
schlaflos *sleepless.*

Schlaflosigkeit *f. insomnia.*
Schlafmittel *m. narcotic.*
Schläfrig *sleepy.*
Schlafsaal *m. dormitory.*
Schlafwagen *m. sleeping-car.*
Schlafwandler *m. sleepwalker.*
Schlafzimmer *n. bedroom.*
SCHLAG *m. blow, stroke, striking*
  (clock).
  zwei Fliegen auf einen Schlag treffen
  to kill two birds with one stone.
Schlagader *f. artery.*
Schlaganfall *m. stroke, fit.*
SCHLAGEN *to beat, knock, hit, strike,*
  throb.
  sich schlagen *to fight.*
  sich geschlagen geben *to give up.*
  schlagen nach *to take after.*
  eine geschlagene Stunde *a whole*
  hour.
schlagfertig *quick at repartee.*
Schlagfertigkeit *f. quickness at*
  repartee.
Schlagsahne *f. whipped cream.*
Schlagwort *n. slogan.*
Schlagzeile *f. headline.*
Schlagzeug *n. percussion instrument.*
Schlamm *m. mud, ooze.*
schlammig *muddy, oozy.*
Schlange *f. snake.*
  Schlange stehen *to make a line.*
Schlangernbiss *m. snake bite.*
schlank *slim, slender.*
Schlankheit *f. slimness, slenderness.*
schlapp *weak, tired, limp, flabby.*
  schlapp machen *to collapse.*
schlau *sly, cunning.*
Schlauberger *m. sly fox.*
Schlauch *m. hose, tube.*
Schlauheit *f. slyness, cunning.*
Schlaukopf *m. sly fox.*
SCHLECHT *bad, poor, inferior, ill,*
  wicked.
  mir ist schlecht *I feel sick.*
  schlecht machen *to run down.*
  schlecht und recht *somehow.*
  schlecht werden *to spoil (food).*
schlechtgelaunt *in a bad temper.*
Schlechtigkeit *f. badness, wickedness.*
schleichen *to creep, drag, sneak.*
  sich davon schleichen *to steal away.*
  wie die Katze um den heissen Brei
  schleichen *to beat around the bush*
  ("to creep like the cat around the hot
  roast")
schlicht *simple, plain, even.*
schlichten *to make simple, smooth.*
Schlichtheit *f. simplicity.*
Schliesse *f. clasp, fastening.*

SCHLIESSEN *to close, lock, shut, break up.*
in die Arme schliessen *to embrace.*
geschlossen *enclosed.*
Schliessfach *n. locker.*
schliesslich *final, finally, after all.*
Schliessung *f. closing.*
schlimm *bad, sore.*
schlimmstenfalls *if the worst comes to the worst.*
Schlinge *f. knot, loop.*
sich aus der Schlinge ziehen *to get out of a difficulty.*
Schlips *m. necktie (coll.).*
Schlitten *m. sled, sleigh.*
Schlittenfahrt *f. sleigh driving.*
Schlittschuh *m. skate.*
Schlittschuh laufen *to skate.*
Schlittschuhläufer *m. skater.*
SCHLOSS *n. castle, lock.*
Schlosser *m. locksmith.*
Schluck *m. gulp, draught.*
Schluckauf *m. hiccup.*
schlucken *to gulp, swallow.*
Schlucker *m. hiccup.*
armet Schlucker *poor wretch.*
Schlummer *m. slumber.*
schlummern *to slumber.*
Schlüpfer *m. panties.*
SCHLUSS *m. closing, shutting, conclusion.*
Schlüssel *m. key, code.*
Schlüsselbund *m. bunch of keys.*
Schlüsselloch *n. keyhole.*
Schlusslicht *n. tail light.*
Schlusswort *n. summary, last word.*
Schmach *f. disgrace, dishonor, humiliation.*
schmachten *to languish.*
schmachvall *disgraceful, humiliating.*
schmackhaft *tasty, savory.*
schmähen *to abuse.*
schmählich *disgraceful.*
SCHMAL *narrow, thin, slender, poor.*
Hier ist Schmalhans Küchenmeister. *We are on short rations here.*
schmälern *to diminish, lessen.*
Schmalz *n. drippings.*
SCHMECKEN *to taste, try.*
Es schmeckt gut. *It tastes good.*
Es schmeckt mit nicht. *I don't like it.*
schmecken nach *to taste of.*
Wie schmeckt's? *How do you like it?*
Schmeichelei *f. flattery.*
schmeichelhaft *flattering.*
Schmeichelkatze *f. wheedler.*
schmeicheln *to flatter.*
Schmeichler *m. flatterer.*
schmeichlerisch *flattering.*

schmelzen *to melt.*
SCHMERZ *m. pain, ache, hurt, sorrow.*
SCHMERZEN *to hurt, pain, grieve.*
Schmerzensgeld *n. smart money, compensation.*
schmerzerfült *deeply affected.*
schmerzhaft *painful.*
schmerzlich *grievous, sad.*
schmerzlos *painless.*
schmerzstillend *soothing.*
Schmetterling *m. butterfly.*
Schmied *m. blacksmith.*
Schmiede *f. forge.*
schmieden *to forge, hammer.*
schmiegen *to bend.*
schmiegsam *flexible, supple.*
Schmiegsamkeit *f. flexibility.*
schmieren *to spread, grease, smear.*
Schminke *f. rouge, paint, make up.*
schminken *to make up, paint the face.*
Schmöker *m. bad novel, trashy book.*
schmollen *to sulk.*
Schmorbraten *stewed steak.*
SCHMUCK *m. jewelry, ornament, decoration.*
schmücken *to decorate, adorn.*
Schmuckstück *n. piece of jewelry.*
Schmuggel *m. smuggling.*
schmuggeln *to smuggle.*
schmunzeln *to grin.*
Schmutz *m. dirt, mud.*
schmutzen *to dirty.*
Schmutzfleck *m. stain, spot.*
schmutzig *dirty.*
Schnabel *m. beak, bill.*
schnarchen *to snore.*
schnaufen *to breathe heavily, pant.*
Schnecke *f. snail.*
wie eine Schnecke kriechen *to go at a snail's pace.*
SCHNEE *m. snow.*
Schneeball *m. snowball.*
Schneefall *m. snowfall.*
Schneeflocke *f. snowflake.*
schneeglöckchen *n. snowdrop.*
Schneekette *f. non-skid chain (automobile).*
Schneeschuh *m. ski.*
schneetreiben *n. blizzard.*
schneeweiss *snow-white.*
SCHNEIDEN *to cut, carve.*
sich schneiden *to cut oneself.*
schneidend *sharp, bitter.*
Schneider *m. tailor.*
schneien *to snow.*
SCHNELL *quick, fast, swift, prompt, speedy.*
Schnelligkeit *f. rapidity, velocity.*
Schnellzug *m. express train.*

77

Schnippchen n. snap of the fingers.
  ein Schnippchen schlagen to play a
  trick.
Schnitt m. cut, cutting, incision.
  der goldene Schnitt A medial section.
Schnittblumen pl. cut flowers.
Schnittmuster n. cut pattern.
Schnittwunde f. cut.
schnitzen to carve, cut.
Schnupfen m. (head) cold.
schnupfen to take snuff.
Schnur f. string, cord.
  über die Schnur hauen to kick over
  the traces.
Schnurrbart m. moustache.
schnurren to hum, buzz, purr.
schnurstracks immediately.
Schock m. shock.
Schokolade f. chocolate.
SCHON already, all right, very, yet,
  even, indeed, certainly.
  Schon gut! All right!
  Wenn schon! So what!
SCHÖN beautiful, handsome, fine, nice,
  fair, noble.
  Danke schön (Schönen Dank).
  Thanks.
  Das wäre noch schöner! That's all we
  need!
  die Schönen Künste the fine arts.
  schön tun to flatter.
  Schönen Gruss an Ihre Frau. Best
  regards to your wife.
  Schönsten Dank. Many thanks.
  sich schön machen. to smarten
  oneself.
schonen to spare, save, look after.
schonend careful, considerate.
Schöngeist m. wit; esthete.
schöngeistig esthetical.
Schönheit f. beauty.
Schönheitsmittel n. cosmetic.
Schönheitspflege f. beauty treatment.
Schonung f. indulgence.
schonungslos pitiless.
schöpfen to draw, create.
Schöpferkraft f. creative, power.
Schöpflöffel m. strainer.
Schornstein m. chimney, funnel.
Schoss m. lap.
Schotte m. Scotsman.
schottisch Scottish.
schräg diagonally.
Schräge f. slant, slope.
Schramme f. scratch, scar.
schrammen to scratch.
Schrank m. wardrobe.
Schranke f. fencing, enclosure, gate.
  sich in Schranken halten to keep
  within bounds.

schrankenlos boundless, without limits.
Schrankkoffer m. wardrobe trunk.
Schraube f. screw, propeller, bolt.
schrauben to screw, turn, wheel.
Schraubenschlüssel m. wrench.
Schraubenzieher m. screwdriver.
SCHRECK (EN) m. scare, fright, fear,
  dread, horror.
  in Schrecken setzen to terrify.
schrecken to frighten.
Schreckgespenst n. terrible vision.
schreckhaft timid, easily frightened.
schrecklich terrible, awful.
Schreckschuss m. false alarm.
Schrei m. scream, cry.
SCHREIBEN to write, spell.
  auf der Maschine schrieben to type.
  sage und schreibe precisely.
Schreiberei f. writing, correspondence.
Schreibfehler m. slip of the pen.
Schreibmappe f. writing case, portfolio,
  blotter.
Schreibmaschine f. typewriter.
Schreibpapier n. note paper.
Schreibstube f. office.
Schreibwaren pl. stationery.
Schreibwarengeschäft n. stationery
  store.
Schreibwarenhändler m. stationer.
Schreibwarenhandlung f. stationery
  store.
SCHREIEN to scream, shout, yell.
schreiend loud, gaudy.
Schreier m. shouter, bawler.
Schreiner m. carpenter, cabinetmaker.
Schreinerei f. cabinetmaker's.
SCHRIFT f. writing, handwriting, script.
schriftlich in writing, written.
Schriftführer m. secretary (association
  or politics).
Schriftsteller m. writer (author).
SCHRITT m. step, stride.
  auf Schritt und Tritt everywhere, all
  the time.
  Schritt fahren! Drive slowly!
  Schritt für Schritt step by step.
  Schritt halten to keep pace with.
schrubben to scrub.
Schrubber m. scrubber.
schrumpfen to shrink, contract.
Schrumpfung f. shrinking, contraction.
Schubfach n. drawer.
Schublade f. drawer.
schüchtern bashful, timid.
Schüchternheit f. bashfulness, timidity.
Schuft m. scoundrel.
SCHUH m. shoe.
  einem etwas in die Schuhe schieben
  to put the blame on someone.
Schuhanzieher m. shoehorn.

Schuhkrem *f. shoe-polish.*
Schuhmacher *m. shoemaker.*
Schuhputzer *m. bootblack.*
Schuhriemen *m. shoelace.*
Schuhsohle *f. sole of a shoe.*
Schuhwichse *f. boot polish.*
Schularbeit *f. lesson, homework.*
Schulbesuch *m. attendance at school.*
Schulbildung *f. schooling, education.*
SCHULD *f. obligation, debt, cause,*
  blame.
  in jemandes Schuld stehen *to have an*
    obligation.
  Schuld sein *to be guilty of.*
  Schulden machen *to make debts.*
  Schuld geben *to accuse.*
schuldbewusst *guilt-conscious.*
Schuldbrief *m. bond.*
schulden *to owe.*
Schuldenmacher *m. contractor of*
  debts.
schuldig *owing, due, obliged, guilty.*
  Dank Schuldig sein *to be indebted.*
  Geld schuldig sein *to owe money.*
  keine Antwort schuldig bleiben *never*
    to be at a loss for an answer.
Schuldigkeit *f. duty, obligation.*
schuldlos *innocent.*
Schuldner *m. debtor.*
Schuldschein *m. bond, promissory*
  note.
SCHULE *f. school, academy, courses.*
  die Schule schwänzen *to cut classes.*
  Schule machen *to find followers.*
schulen *to school, train, teach.*
Schüler *m. student, pupil.*
Schulferien *pl. m. (-in, f.) school*
  holidays.
schulfrei *having a holiday.*
Schulfreund *m. school friend.*
Schulgeld *n. school fees.*
Schulmappe *f. schoolbag, satchel.*
Schulmeister *m. schoolmaster, teacher.*
schulmeistern *to teach school,*
  censure.
Schulstunde *f. school lesson.*
Schulter *f. shoulder.*
Schulung *f. school training.*
Schulzeugnis *n. school certificates.*
Schuppe *f. scale (fish).*
Schürze *f. apron.*
Schuss *f. shot, report, round.*
schussbereit *ready to shoot.*
Schusswaffe *f. firearm.*
Schussweite *f. range.*
Schusswunde *f. bullet wound.*
schütteln *to shake.*
schütten *to pour in.*
SCHUTZ *m. shelter, protection, refuge.*
  im Schutz der Nacht *under cover of*

  the night.
  in Schutz nehmen *to defend.*
  Schutz suchen *to take shelter.*
Schütze *m. rifleman, private soldier.*
schützen *to protect.*
  sich schützen *to protect oneself.*
Schutzengel *m. guardian angel.*
Schutzhaft *f. protective custody.*
Schutzimpfung *f. vaccination.*
schutzlos *defenseless, unprotected.*
Schutzmann *n. policeman.*
Schutzpockenimpfung *f. vaccination*
  against smallpox.
Schutztruppe *f. colonial force,*
  occupation forces.
SCHWACH *weak, frail, faint, feeble.*
Schwäche *f. weakness, debility.*
schwächen *to weaken.*
Schwächheit *f. weakness, feebleness.*
schwächlich *weak, delicate.*
Schwächlichkeit *f. delicacy, infirmity.*
Schwachsinn *m. imbecility.*
Schwachsinnig *imbecile.*
Schwager *m. brother-in-law.*
Schwägerin *f. sister-in-law.*
Schwalbe *f. swallow.*
Schwamm *m. sponge, mushroom.*
Schwan *m. swan.*
schwanger *pregnant.*
Schwank *m. prank, short anecdote,*
  farce.
schwanken *to rock, toss, sway.*
Schwankung *f. variation.*
Schwanz *m. tail, end.*
Schwarm *m. crowd, multitude.*
schwärmen *to swarm, riot.*
Schwärmer *m. enthusiast, fanatic.*
Schwärmerei *f. enthusiasm.*
schwärmerisch *enthusiastic, fanatic.*
Schwarte *f. rind, skin.*
SCHWARZ *black, dark, dirty, gloomy.*
  ins Schwarze treffen *to hit the bull's*
    eye.
  schwarz auf weiss *in black and white.*
  Sie sieht immer alles schwarz. *She*
    always sees the dark side of things.
Schwarzbrot *n. black bread.*
Schwarze *m. Negro.*
Schwarzhandel *m. black market.*
Schwarzwald *m. Black Forest.*
Schwatz *m. chat, talk.*
Schwatzbase *f. chatterbox.*
schwatzen *to chatter, gossip.*
Schwätzer *m (-in, f.) gossip.*
schwatzhaft *talkative.*
Schwatzhaftigkeit *f. loquacity.*
Schwebe *f. suspense.*
  in der Schwebe sein *to be undecided.*
Schwebebahn *f. suspension railway.*
schweben *to be suspended, pending.*

auf der Zunge schweben *to have on the tip of the tongue.*
in Gefahr schweben *to be in danger.*

Schwede *m. Swede.*

schwedisch *Swedish.*

Schwefel *m. sulphur.*

Schweigen *n. silence.*

schweigsam *silent, taciturn.*

Schweigsamkeit *f. taciturnity.*

Schwein *n. pig, hog.*

Schweinebraten *m. roast pork.*

Schweinefleisch *n. pork.*

Schweiss *m. sweat, perspiration.*

Schweisstropfen *m. bead of perspiration.*

Schweizer *m. Swiss.*

schweizerisch *Swiss.*

schwelgen *to feast, celebrate.*

Schwelle *f. threshold.*

schwellen *to swell, rise, grow.*

Schwellung *f. swelling, tumor, growth.*

SCHWER *heavy, hard, difficult, serious, strong; heavily, seriously, strongly.*
etwas schwer nehmen *to take something to heart.*
schwer fallen (halten) *to be difficult.*

schwerblütig *melancholy.*

schwerfällig *heavy, clumsy.*

Schwerfälligkeit *f. heaviness, clumsiness.*

Schwergewicht *n. heavyweight.*

schwerhörig *hard of hearing.*

Schwerhörigkeit *f. deafness.*

Schwerkraft *f. force of gravity.*

Schwerkriegsbeschädigte *m. disabled soldier.*

schwerlich *hardly, scarcely, with difficulty.*

Schwermut *f. melancholy, sadness.*

schwermütig *melancholy, sad.*

Schwerpunkt *m. center of gravity.*

Schwert *n. sword.*

Schwerverbrecher *m. criminal, gangster.*

schwerwiegend *serious, grave.*

SCHWESTER *f. sister, hospital nurse.*

schwesterlich *sisterly.*

Schwiegereltern *pl. parents-in-law.*

Schwiegermutter *f. mother-in-law.*

Schwiegersohn *m. son-in-law.*

Schwiegertochter *f. daughter-in-law.*

Schwiegervater *m. father-in-law.*

schwierig *difficult.*

Schwierigkeit *f. difficulty.*

Schwimmanstalt *f. swimming-pool.*

SCHWIMMEN *to swim, float, sail.*

Schwimmhose *f. swimming shorts.*

Schwimmweste *f. life jacket.*

Schwindel *m. swindle; dizziness.*

Schwindelanfall *m. fit of dizziness.*

schwindeln *to swindle, cheat; be dizzy.*
Mir schwindelt. *I feel dizzy.*

Schwindler *m. swindler.*

schwindlig *dizzy.*

schwingen *to swing, sway, oscillate, vibrate.*

Schwingung *f. oscillation.*

Schwips *m. Smack! Slap!*
einen Schwips haben *to be tipsy.*

schwören *to swear, take an oath.*

schwül *sultry, muggy.*

Schwung *f. swing (push), vault.*
in Schwung bringen *to set going.*

schwungvoll *energetic.*

Schwur *m. oath.*
Schwur leisten *to take an oath.*

SECHS *six.*

SECHSTE *sixth.*

SECHZEHN *sixteen.*

SECHZEHNTE *sixteenth.*

SECHZIG *sixty.*

SECHZIGSTE *sixtieth.*

See *m. lake.*

SEE *f. sea, seaside.*
an die See gehen *to go to the seaside.*
in See stechen *to put to sea.*

Seebad *n. seaside resort.*

seefest *seaworthy.*
Seefest sein *to be a good sailor.*

Seegang *m. heavy sea, swell.*

Seehund *m. seal.*

seekrank *seasick.*
seekrank sein *to be seasick.*

Seekrankheit *f. seasickness.*

SEELE *f. soul, mind, spirit.*
jemandem aus der Seele sprechen *to express a person's thoughts.*
Sie sind mit Leib und Seele dabei. *They are in it with heart and soul.*

seelisch *spiritual, mental, emotional.*

Seemann *m. sailor.*

Seemeile *f. nautical mile (1.852 kilometers).*

Seenot *f. distress (at sea).*

Seewasser *n. sea-water.*

Segel *n. sail, canvas.*

Segelboot *n. sailboat.*

Segelflugzeug *n. glider.*

segeln *to sail.*

Segelschiff *n. sailboat.*

Segen *m. blessing.*

segnen *to bless.*

SEHEN *to see, look, behold, contemplate.*
darauf sehen *to watch carefully.*
gut sehen *to have good eyesight.*
Ich kenne sie nur vom Sehen. *I know her only by sight.*
schlecht sehen *to have poor eyesight.*

sehen nach *to look after.*

sehenswert *worth seeing, remarkable.*

Sehenswürdigkeit *f. point of interest.*

Sehkraft *f. eyesight.*

Sehne *f. sinew, ligament.*

SEHNEN *to long, yearn for.*

sehnlich *ardent, longing.*

Sehnsucht *f. longing, yearning.*

sehnsüchtig *longing, yearning.*

SEHR *very; very much.*
 Bitte sehr. *You are quite welcome.*

seicht *shallow.*

SEIDE *f. silk.*

Seidenpapier *n. tissue paper.*

Seidenraupe *f. silkworm.*

seidig *silky.*

Seife *f. soap.*

Seifenflocken *pl. soapflakes.*

Seifenpulver *n. soap powder.*

Seil *n. rope, line.*

Seilbahn *f. cable.*

Sein *n. being.*

SEIN *to be, exist.*
 es sei denn, dass *unless.*

SEIN *poss. adj. his, her, its.*

SEIN(ER, -E, -ES) *poss. pron. his, hers.*
 die Seinen *one's own people.*

seinetwegen *because of him, for his sake.*

SEIT *prep. (with dat.) since, for.*
 Ich warte seit einer Stunde. *I have been waiting for an hour.*
 seit kurzer Zeit *lately.*
 seit meiner Ankunft *since my return.*
 Seit Wann? *Since when?*

Seitdem *conj. since, since that time.*

SEITE *f. side, page, party, member.*
 auf die Seite *aside, away.*
 auf die Seite gehen *to step aside.*
 Schwache Seite *weakness.*
 Seite an Seite *side by side.*
 zur Seite stehen *to stand by, help.*

Seitenflügel *m. side, aisle, wing.*

Seitenstrasse *f. side street.*

Seitenzahl *f. number of pages.*

seither *since then.*

seitlich *lateral, collateral.*

seitwärts *sideways, aside.*

Seke *m. champagne.*

Sekretär *m. (-in, f.) secretary.*

SEKUNDE *f. second (time, music, fencing).*

Sekundenzeiger *m. second hand (on clocks).*

selbe (der, die, das) *same.*

selber *self.*
 ich selber *myself.*

SELBST 1. *adj. or pron. self.*
 Ich habe es selbst getan. *I did it myself.*

Das versteht sich von selbst. *That goes without saying.*
 2. *adv. even.*
 Ich habe alles zu Hause gelassen, selbst mein Geld. *I left everything at home, even my money.*

selbständig *independent.*

Selbstbeherrschung *f. self-control.*

selbstbewusst *self-assured.*

Selbstbewusstsein *n. self-assurance.*

Selbsterhaltung *f. self-preservation.*

Selbsterkenntnis *f. self-knowledge.*

selbstgefällig *self-satisfied, complacent.*

Selbstgefühl *n. self-respect.*

Selbstgespräch *m. monologue, soliloquy.*

selbstherrlich *autocratic.*

Selbstkostenpreis *m. cost price.*

selbstlos *unselfish, disinterested.*

Selbstlosigkeit *f. selfishness.*

Selbstmörder *m. suicide.*

selbstredend *self-evident, obvious.*

Selbstsucht *f. selfishness, egoism.*

selbstsüchtig *selfish, egoistic.*

SELBSTVERSTÄNDLICH *evident.*

Selbstvertrauen *n. self-confidence.*

selbstzufrieden *self-satisfied.*

selig *blessed.*

Seligkeit *f. happiness, bliss.*

Sellerie *f. celery.*

SELTEN *rare, unusual.*

Seltenheit *f. rarity, scarcity.*

SELTSAM *strange, unusual, odd.*

Selterwasser *n. soda-water.*

Semester *n. term, session.*

Seminar *n. training college.*

Senat *m. senate.*

senden *to send, broadcast, transmit.*

Sender *m. transmitter.*

Senderaum *m. studio.*

Sendung *f. mission, transmission.*

Senf *m. mustard.*

Senkel *m. lace (shoe).*

senken *to lower, dip, sink.*
 sich senken *to settle.*

sensationell *sensational.*

Sensationslust *f. desire to cause a sensation.*

Sentimentalität *f. sentimentality.*

SEPTEMBER *m. September.*

Serie *f. series, issue.*

Service *n. service set.*

Servierbrett *n. tray.*

servieren *to serve, wait at a table.*

Serviette *f. table napkin.*

Sessel *m. armchair.*

sesshaft *settled, established.*

SETZEN *to put, set, place, fix, erect, put up, sit down.*

alles daran setzen *to risk everything.*
gesetzt den Fall, dass *suppose that.*
in Freiheit setzen *to set free.*
Setzen Sie sich! *Sit down!*
sich etwas in den Kopf setzen *to get an idea into one's head.*
sich in Verbindung setzen mit *to get in touch with.*
unter Druck setzen *to put pressure on.*
Seuche *f. epidemic.*
seufzen *to sigh.*
sezieren *to dissect.*
SICH *oneself, himself, herself, itself, yourself, yourselves, themselves, each other, one another.*
sich selbst *itself, oneself, etc.*
SICHER *secure, safe, certain, positive, surely.*
aus sicherer Hand *on good authority.*
seiner Sache sicher sein *to be certain of a thing.*
sicher gehen *to be on the safe side.*
sicher stellen *to put in safe keeping.*
sicher wissen *to know for certain.*
Sicherheit *f. safety, security.*
in Sicherheit bringen *to secure.*
Sicherheit leisten *to give security.*
sicherheitshalber *for safety's sake.*
Sicherheitsnadel *f. safety-pin.*
Sicherheitsschloss *n. safety-lock.*
sicherlich *surely, certainly.*
sichern *to protect.*
Sicherung *f. protection.*
SICHT *f. sight, visibility.*
sichtbar *visible, apparent.*
sichten *to sight; to sift, sort.*
SIE (sie) *pers. pron. 3rd pers. sing. (fem. nom. & acc.); 3rd pers. pl. (m., f., n., nom. & acc.) she, her, it; they, them.*
SIE (sie) *pers. pron. 2nd pers, polite form (nom. & acc.) you.*
Sieb *n. collander, strainer.*
sieben *to sift, strain.*
SIEBEN *seven.*
SIEBENTE *seventh.*
SIEBZEHNTE *seventeenth.*
SIEBZIG *seventy.*
siebzigst *seventieth.*
siech *sickly, ailing, infirm.*
siedeln *to settle, colonize.*
SIEG *m. victory, triumph.*
Siegel *n. seal.*
Sieger *m. victor, winner.*
siegesgewiss *certain or confident of victory.*
siegreich *victorious.*
Signal *n. signal.*
Signalhupe *f. siren.*
signalisieren *to signal.*

Signatur *f. mark, sign, characteristic.*
Silbe *f. syllable.*
Silber *n. silver.*
Silberpapier *n. silver paper.*
Silversterabend *m. New Year's Eve.*
SINGEN *to sing.*
Singstimme *f. singing voice, vocal part.*
sinken *to sink, drop, fall.*
SINN *m. sense, faculty, mind, understanding, intellect.*
anderen Sinnes werden *to change one's mind.*
in gewissem Sinn *in a way, in a sense.*
im Sinn haben *to intend.*
sich etwas aus dem Sinn schlagen *to dismiss a thing from one's mind.*
Sinnbild *n. symbol, emblem, allegory.*
sinnbildlich *symbolic.*
sinnen *to think, reflect, meditate.*
sinnlich *sensual, sensuous, material.*
sinnlos *senseless, absurd.*
Sinnlosigkeit *f. senselessness, foolishness.*
sinnreich *sensible, clever.*
Sippschaft *f. kinship, relatives.*
Sirene *f. siren.*
Sitte *f. custom, habit.*
Sittengesetz *n. moral law, moral code.*
Sittenlehre *f. moral, philosophy, ethics.*
sittenlos *immoral, dissolute.*
sittlich *moral.*
sittsam *modest.*
Sittsamkeit *f. modesty.*
SITZ *m. seat, residence.*
SITZEN *to sit, fit, adhere.*
etwas auf sich sitzen lassen *to put up with.*
sitzen bleiben *to remain seated.*
sitzen lassen *to leave.*
Sitzgelegenheit *f. seating accommodation.*
Sitzplatz *m. seat.*
Skandal *m. scandal.*
Skelett *n. skeleton.*
skeptisch *sceptical.*
Ski *m. ski.*
skilaufen *to ski.*
Skiläufer *m. skier.*
Skispringen *n. ski-jumping.*
Skizze *f. sketch.*
skizzieren *to sketch.*
Sklave *m. slave.*
sklavisch *slavish, servile.*
Skrupel *m. scruple.*
SO *so, thus, in this way, like that, anyhow.*
Ach so! *Oh, I see!*
So? *Is that so? Indeed? Really?*
so...auch, *however.*
so bald ais *as soon as.*

so . . . doch   *yet, nevertheless.*
so ein   *such a.*
so etwas   *a thing like that.*
so gut wie   *as if, practically.*
so oder so   *this way or that way.*
so. . .so   *though. . .yet.*
so wie   *as, the way*
Sock   *f. sock.*
Sockenhalter   *m. garter (man's).*
sodann   *then.*
sodass   *so that.*
soeben   *just, just now.*
sofern   *so far as.*
sofort   *immediately, at once.*
sogar   *even.*
sogenannt   *so-called.*
sogleich   *at once, immediately.*
Sohle   *f. sole.*
sohlen   *to resole.*
SOHN   *m. son.*
solange   *so, as long as.*
SOLCH   *such, the same.*
   solch ein   *such a.*
Soldat   *m. soldier.*
Solist   *m. soloist.*
SOLLEN   *ought, shall, to have to, must,*
   be supposed to, be said to.
   Du sollst nicht töten.   *Thou shalt not*
      kill.
   Di Schüler sollen fleissig sein.
      Students must be industrious.
   Er soll ein Millionär sein.   *They say he*
      is a millionaire.
   Sollte er nicht zu Hause sein?   *Is it*
      possible that he is not at home?
   Sollte er telefonieren?   *Should he*
      telephone?
   Was soll das heissen?   *What is the*
      meaning of that?
   Was soll es bedeuten?   *What does that*
      mean?
somit   *consequently.*
SOMMER   *m. summer.*
   Sommernachtstraum   *m. Midsummer*
      Night's Dream
Sommerfrische   *f. health-resort.*
Sommersprosse   *f. freckle.*
Sondereausgabe   *f. special edition.*
SONDERBAR   *strange, peculiar.*
sonderbarenweise   *strange to say.*
sondergleichen   *unequaled, unique.*
Sonderling   *m. strange character.*
Sondermeldung   *f. special*
   announcement. .
SONDERN   *but (in a negative sentence).*
   Ich wollte nicht ausgehen, sondern zu
      Hause bleiben.   *I did not want to go*
      out but to stay home.
   nicht nur. . .sondern auch   *not*

   only. . .but also.
   Sie war nicht nur schön, sondern auch
      gut.   *She was not only beautiful but*
      kind as well.
SONNABEND   *m. Saturday.*
SONNE   *f. sun.*
Sonnenaufgang   *m. sunrise.*
Sonnenblume   *f. sunflower.*
Sonnenbrand   *m. sunburn.*
Sonnenbrille   *f. sunglasses.*
Sonnenstrahl   *m. sunbeam.*
Sonnenuntergang   *m. sunset.*
sonnig   *sunny.*
SONNTAG   *m. Sunday.*
sonntags   *on Sunday.*
SONST   *else, moreover, besides,*
   otherwise, formerly.
   Sonst noch etwas?   *Anything else?*
   sonst jemand   *anybody else.*
   sonst nichts   *nothing else.*
   sonst niemand?   *No one else?*
   sonst und jetzt   *formerly and now.*
   Was konnte ich sonst tun?   *What else*
      could I do?
   Wenn es sonst nichts wäre!   *If that*
      were all it was!
   wie sonst   *as usual.*
sonstwie   *in some other way.*
sonstwo   *elsewhere.*
Sopran   *m. soprano.*
SORGE   *f. grief, sorrow, anxiety, worry,*
   trouble, care.
   einem Sorgen machen   *to worry*
      someone.
   sich Sorgen machen   *to worry.*
   Sorge tragen   *to see about something.*
SORGEN   *to care for, look after, take*
   care of, provide.
   sich sorgen um   *to be concerned*
      about.
   sorgen für   *to look after.*
Sorgenkind   *n. delicate child.*
sorgenvoll   *worried.*
Sorgfalt   *f. carefulness, care, accuracy.*
sorgfältig   *careful, painstaking.*
sorglich   *thoughtful.*
sorglos   *carefree, careless.*
Sorglosigkeit   *f. light-heartedness.*
SORTE   *f. kind, sort, brand, grade.*
sortieren   *to sort, arrange.*
Souffleur   *m. prompter.*
SOVIEL   *as much as, so far as.*
soweit   *as far as.*
sowenig   *as little as.*
sowie   *as soon as.*
sowieso   *anyway, anyhow.*
sozial   *social.*
Sozialismus   *m. Socialism.*
Sozialist   *m. Socialist.*

sozialistisch *socialistic.*
Sozialwissenschaft *f. sociology.*
Sozius *m. partner.*
Spähen *to be on the look out, patrol.*
Spalier bilden *to line.*
Spalt *m. crack, slot, gap.*
spalten *to split, divide.*
  sich spalten *to split.*
Spaltholz *n. firewood sticks.*
Spange *f. buckle, brooch.*
Spanier *m. (-in, f.) Spaniard.*
spanisch *Spanish.*
Spanische *n. Spanish (language).*
Spanne *f. short space of time, margin.*
SPANNEN *to put up, stretch, pull, tighten.*
  gespannt sein *to be anxious, curious.*
  Ich bin auf die Antwort gespannt. *I am curious to know the answer.*
spannend *fascinating, absorbing, thrilling.*
Spannung *f. tension, strain, suspense, voltage.*
Sparbüchse *f. money-box (piggy bank).*
Spareinlage *f. savings deposit.*
Spargel *m. asparagus.*
Sparkasse *f. savings bank.*
spärlich *scarce, frugal, thin.*
Spärlichkeit *f. scarcity.*
SPARSAM *economical, thrifty.*
Sparsamkeit *f. economy, thrift.*
Spass *m. joke, fun.*
spassen *to joke.*
Spassmacher *m. joker.*
SPAT *late, belated, backward.*
  Besser spät als nie. *Better late than never.*
  zu spät kommen *to be late.*
  Wie spät ist es? *What time is it?*
Spaten *m. spade.*
später *later, afterwards.*
  späterhin *later on.*
spätestens *at the latest.*
Spatz *m. sparrow.*
SPAZIEREN *to walk about, stroll.*
  spazieren gehen *to go for a walk.*
Spazierfahrt *f. drive.*
Spaziergang *m. walk.*
Spazierganger *m. walker, stroller.*
Speck *m. bacon.*
Speckschwarte *f. rind of bacon.*
Spediteur *m. mover, shipper, forwarding agent.*
Speicher *m. storage room.*
speichern *to store.*
SPEISE *f. food, meal.*
Speiseeis *n. ice cream.*
Speisekarte *f. menu.*
Speisenfolge *f. menu.*
Speisesaal *m. dining room.*

Speisewagen *m. dining car.*
Spekulant *m. speculator.*
spekulieren *to speculate.*
Spende *f. gift, present, donation.*
spenden *to dispense, bestow, administer.*
Spender *m. giver, donor, benefactor.*
spendieren *to pay for.*
Sperre *f. gate, closing, barrier.*
sperren *to close, shut, block, barricade.*
  ins Gefängnis sperren *to put in prison.*
Sperrguthaben *n. blocked account.*
Sperrholz *n. plywood.*
Spesen *f. pl. charges, expenses.*
Spezialarzt *n. specialist.*
spezialisieren *to specialize.*
speziell *special, particular.*
spezifisch *specific.*
spezifizieren *to specify.*
Spiegel *m. mirror.*
Spiegelbild *n. reflected image.*
spiegelglatt *smooth as a mirror.*
spiegeln *to shine, glitter.*
  sich spiegeln *to be reflected.*
SPIEL *n. game, deck of cards, playing, play, sport, touch (music).*
  auf dem Spiel stehen *to be at stake.*
  aufs Spiel setzen *to risk.*
  Lassen Sie mich aus dem Spiel. *Leave me out of this.*
  leichtes Spiel haben *to have no difficulties.*
  seine Hand im Spiel haben *to have a finger in the pie.*
  sein Spiel treiben mit *to make game of.*
Spieldose *f. musical box.*
SPIELEN *to play, act, perform, gamble, pretend.*
  Was spielt man heute abend? *What's playing tonight?*
Spielerei *f. trifle.*
Spielplan *m. program, repertory.*
Spielsachen *pl. toys.*
Spielverderber *m. kill-joy.*
Spielzeug *n. toy.*
Spiess *m. lance, spear, pike.*
Spiessbürger *m. bourgeois.*
Spinat *m. spinach.*
Spinne *f. Spider.*
spinnen *to spin.*
Spinngewebe *n. cobweb.*
Spinnrad *n. spinning wheel.*
Spion *m. spy.*
Spionage *f. spying, espionage.*
Spionageabwehr *f. counterespionage.*
spionieren *to spy.*
Spiritus *m. spirits, alcohol.*
SPITZ *pointed, sharp, acute, caustic.*
Spitze *f. point, tip (tongue), top, head,*

lace, sarcasm.
etwas auf die Spitze treiben *to carry to extremes.*
SPITZEN *to sharpen, point.*
seine Ohren spitzen *to prick one's ears.*
Spitzenleistung *f. record, maximum.*
Spitzenlohn *m. maximum pay.*
Spitzentanz *m. toe-dance.*
spitzfindig *pointed, sharp, sarcastic, subtle.*
Spitzfindigkeit *f. subtlety.*
spitzig *pointed, sharp, sarcastic.*
Spitzname *m. nickname.*
Splitter *m. splinter, chip.*
splittern *to splinter, split.*
spontan *spontaneous.*
Sporn *m. spur.*
Sport *m. sport.*
Sport treiben *to go in for sports.*
Sportfunk *m. radio sports news.*
Sportler *m. sportsman.*
sportlich *sporting, athletic.*
Sportname *m. nickname.*
Spott *m. mockery, ridicule.*
Spöttelei *f. chaff, raillery.*
spötteln *to laugh, sneer at.*
spotten *to mock, make fun, defy.*
spöttisch *mocking, scoffing, sarcastic.*
SPRACHE *f. language, speech, talk.*
mit der Sprache herausrücken *to come out something.*
zur Sprache bringen *to bring up a subject.*
zur Sprache kommen *to be mentioned.*
Sprachfertigkeit *f. fluency.*
sprachgewandt *fluent.*
sprachkundig *proficient in languages.*
Sprachlehre *f. grammar.*
sprachlich *linguistic.*
sprachlos *speechless.*
Sprachschatz *m. vocabulary.*
Sprachschnitzer *m. blunder, mistake.*
Sprachstörung *f. speech defect.*
SPRECHEN *to speak, talk, say, converse, discuss.*
Der herr Doktor ist nicht zu sprechen. *The doctor is busy.*
gut zu sprechen sein auf *to be kindly disposed to.*
Ich bin für niemanden zu sprechen. *I am in to no one.*
sich herumsprechen *to be whispered about town.*
Sie sprechen nicht miteinander. *They are not on speaking terms.*
Sprechen Sie Deutsch? *Do you speak German?*
Sprechen Sie langsam, bitte. *Please speak slowly.*
Wen wünschen Sie zu sprechen? *Whom do you want to see?*
Sprecher *m. speaker.*
Sprechstunde *f. office hours, office (doctor).*
Sprechstundenhilfe *f. doctor's receptionist.*
Sprechweise *f. diction.*
Sprechzimmer *n. consulting room.*
sprengen *to burst, blow up, blast, spray.*
Sprengung *f. blowing up.*
Sprichwort *n. proverb.*
Springbrunnen *m. fountain.*
SPRINGEN *to jump, skip, spring, play.*
Das ist der springende Punkt. *That is the crucial point.*
in die Augen springen *to be obvious.*
spritzen *to spray, splash, sprinkle.*
spröde *reserved, shy.*
Sprosse *f. rung (ladder).*
Sprössling *m. sprout, shoot, offshoot.*
Spruch *m. aphorism, saying.*
spruchreif *ripe for decision.*
sprudeln *to bubble up.*
sprühen *to spark.*
Sprühregen *m. drizzle, drizzling rain.*
SPRUNG *m. leap, jump, crack.*
Es ist nur ein Sprung von meinem Haus. *It is only a stone's throw from my house.*
Ich war auf dem Sprung auszugehen. *I was just going to leave.*
Sprungschanze *f. ski-jump.*
spucken *to spit.*
Spucken Verboten! *No spitting!*
Spuk *m. ghost.*
Spülbecken *n. washtub.*
spülen *to rinse.*
Spülwasser *n. dishwater.*
Spund *m. plug, stopper.*
SPUR *f. trace, trail, track, footprint.*
einem auf die Spur kommen *to be on a person's tracks.*
Keine Spur! *Not in the least!*
spüren *to feel, perceive, experience.*
spüren nach *to track, follow.*
spurlos *trackless.*
Spürsinn *m. shrewdness.*
Spürsinn haben *to have a flair.*
STAAT *m. state, government, pomp, parade, show.*
in vollem Staat *in full dress.*
Staat machen *to show off.*
staatlich *public, political.*
Staatsaktion *f. political event.*
Staatsangehörige *m. & f. subject, national.*

Staatsangehörigkeit *f. nationality, citizenship.*
Staatsanwalt *m. public prosecutor.*
Staatsdienst *m. civil service.*
Staatsmann *m. statesman, politician.*
staatsmännisch *statesmanlike.*
Stab *m. stick, rod, bat, condemn.*
  den Stab brechen über *to condem.*
stabil *stable.*
stabilisieren *to stabilize.*
Stachel *m. thorn, prickle, sting, spur.*
Stachelbeere *f. gooseberry.*
Stacheldraht *m. barbed wire.*
Stadion *n. stadium, arena.*
Stadium *n. phase, stage.*
STADT *f. town, city.*
Stadtbahn *f. city railway.*
stadtbekannt *known all over town.*
Städter *m. townsman.*
Stadtgespräch *n. talk of the town.*
städtisch *municipal, urban.*
Stadtteil *m. quarter (of a town).*
Stahl *m. steel.*
stählern *steely.*
Stahlguss *m. steel.*
Stall *m. stable.*
Stamm *m. stem, root, trunk.*
Stammbaum *m. genealogical tree.*
stammeln *to stammer.*
stammen *to spring from, come from.*
Stammgast *m. regular customer.*
Stammhalter *m. eldest son.*
stämmig *sturdy, strong, vigorous.*
stampfen *to stamp, mash, crush.*
Stand *m. standing position.*
  einen schweren Stand haben *to have a tough job.*
  guten Stand haben *to be in good condition.*
Standbild *n. statute.*
Ständchen *n. serenade.*
Standesamt *n. registrar's office.*
Standesbeamte *m. registrar.*
Standesehe *f. marriage for position or rank.*
standesgemäss *in accordance with one's rank.*
Standesgericht *n. court martial.*
Standesunterschied *m. difference of class.*
standhaft *steady, constant.*
standhalten *to hold firm.*
ständig *permanent.*
Standort *m. station, position.*
Standpunkt *m. point of view.*
Standuhr *f. grandfather's clock.*
Stange *f. pole, bar, perch.*
  eine Stange Gold *a bar of gold.*
  von der Stange *ready-made.*

Stanze *f. stanza.*
stanzen *to stamp.*
STARK *strong, stout, considerable, hard.*
  Das ist denn doch zu stark! *That is too much!*
  stark auftragen *to exaggerate, boast.*
Stärke *f. strength, force, vigor, intensity, energy, violence.*
stärken *to strengthen, fortify, starch, confirm.*
Starkstrom *m. power current.*
Starkstromleitung *f. power-circuit.*
starr *stiff, hard, paralyzed.*
  starren vor Staunen *to be dumbfounded.*
starren *to stare, be numb.*
starrköpfig *stubborn.*
Starrsinn *m. obstinacy.*
Start *m. start.*
Startbahn *f. runway.*
starten *to start.*
startklar *ready for the take off.*
Station *f. station, stop, ward.*
  freie Station *free board and lodging.*
Stationsarzt *m. resident physician.*
Stationsvorsteher *m. station master.*
Statistik *f. statistics.*
statistisch *statistical.*
STATT *f. place.*
  an Kindesstatt annehmen *to adopt a child.*
STATT (anstatt) *prep. (gen.) instead of.*
stattfinden *to take place.*
stattgeben *to permit, allow.*
statthaft *admissible, legal.*
stattlich *stately, magnificent, imposing.*
Stattlichkeit *f. dignity, magnificence.*
Statue *f. statute.*
Staub *m. dust, powder.*
  in den Stabu ziehen *to depreciate.*
  Staub wischen *to dust.*
stauben *to be dusty.*
staubig *dusty.*
Staublappen *m. duster.*
Staubsauger *m. vacuum-cleaner.*
staunen *to be surprised.*
STECHEN *to stick, bite, sting.*
  sich stechen *to prick oneself.*
  in die Augen stechen *to take one's fancy.*
Stechfliege *f. horse-fly.*
Steckdose *f. wall-plug, socket.*
STECKEN *to stick, pin up, fasten, fix, plant, stuff.*
  Dahinter steckt etwas. *There is something behind this.*
  in Brand stecken *to set fire.*
steckenbleiben *to be stuck.*

Steckenpferd n. hobby, pet project.
Stecker m. plug.
Stecknadel f. pin.
STEHEN to stand, stop, be, suit, become.
  gut stehen to be becoming. (Rot steht ihr. Red is becoming to her.)
  gut stehen mit to be on good terms with
  geschrieben stehen to be written.
stehenbleiben to stop, remain standing.
stehend standing, stationary, permanent.
  stehenden Fusses at once.
stehenlassen to leave (standing).
Stehlampe f. floor lamp.
STEHLEN to steal, rob, take away.
steif stiff.
Steig m. path.
STEIGEN to climb, go up, ascend, rise, increase.
  zu Kopf steigen to go to one's head.
steigend growing, increasing.
steigern to raise, increase, intensify.
  sich steigern in to intensify, work up.
Steigerung f. raising, increase, gradation, climax.
steil steep, precipitous.
Steilhang m. steep slope.
STEIN m. stone, rock, jewel.
  Das hat den Stein ins Rollen gebracht. That started the ball rolling.
  Das ist nur ein Tropfen auf den heissen Stein. That's only a drop in the bucket.
  einen Stein im Brett haben bei to be in favor with.
  Mit fällt ein Stein vom Herzen! I feel so relieved!
  Stein des Anstosses stumbling block.
  Stein und Bein schwören to swear by all the gods.
Steinbruch m. quarry.
steinern of stone.
steinhart as hard as stone.
steinig stony, rocky.
Steinobst n. stone-fruit.
steinreich very wealthy.
Steinzeit f. Stone Age.
STELLE f. spot, place, position, situation, passage.
  auf der Stelle on the spot.
  offene Stelle vacancy.
  von der Stelle kommen to make progress.
  zur Stelle sein to be present.
  an Stelle von instead of.
STELLEN to put, place, set, arrange, regulate, provide, furnish.

  auf den Kopf stellen to turn upside down.
  auf sich selbst gestellt sein to be dependent on oneself.
  eine Bedingung stellen to make a condition.
  eine Frage stellen to ask a question.
  Er ist sehr gut gestellt. He is very well off.
  sich stellen to stand.
  kalt stellen to put in a cool place.
  sich gut stellen mit to be on good terms with.
  sich stellen zu to behave toward.
  zur Verfügung stellen to place at one's disposal.
Stellengesuch n. application for a position.
stellenlos unemployed.
Stellennachweis m. employment reference.
Stellenvermittlung f. employment agency.
STELLUNG f. position, situation, stand, job.
  Stellung nehmen zu to express one's opinion.
Stellungnahme f. opinion, comment.
Stellungsgesuch n. application for a position.
stellungslos unemployed.
Stellungswechsel m. change of position.
Stellvertreter m. representative.
Stempel m. stamp, postmark.
Stempelkissen n. ink-pad.
stempeln to stamp, mark.
stenografieren to write in shorthand.
stenografisch stenographic.
Stenogramm n. shorthand.
  Stenogramm aufnehmen to take down in shorthand.
Stenotypist m. (**-istin,** f.) stenotypist.
Steppdecke f. quilt.
Sterbebett n. deathbed.
Sterben n. death.
  im Sterben liegen to be dying.
STERBEN to die.
sterblich mortal.
  sterblich verliebt madly in love.
Sterblichkeit f. death rate.
steril sterile.
sterilisieren to sterilize.
Stern m. star.
Sternbild n. constellation.
Sterndeuter m. astrologer.
Sternschnuppe f. shooting-star.
stets always, forever.
Steuer n. rudder, helm, steering wheel.

Steuer f. tax.
steuerfrei tax-free.
steuern to steer, pilot, drive.
steuerpflichtig subject to taxation.
Steuerrad n. steering wheel.
Steuerzahler m. taxpayer.
Stich m. sting, prick, stitch.
  im Stich lassen to forsake.
Stichtag m. fixed day.
Stichwort n. catchword, cue.
Stiefbruder m. stepbrother.
Stiefmutter f. stepmother.
Stiefmütterchen n. pansy.
Stiefschwester f. stepsister.
Stiefsohn m. stepson.
Stieftochter f. stepdaughter.
Stiefvater m. stepfather.
Stiel m. handle, stick, stem.
Stier m. bull.
Stierkämpfer m. bullfighter.
Stift m. pencil, crayon.
stiften to donate; to found, establish.
Stifter m. founder; donor.
Stiftung f. foundation.
Stil m. style, manner.
stilgerecht in good style, taste.
STILL still, quiet, silent, secret.
  Seien Sie still! Be quiet!
STILLE f. silence, calm, quietude,
  peace.
  im Stillen secretly.
  in aller Stille privately, secretly.
stillen to quiet, appease, satisfy,
  quench, nurse.
stillhalten to keep still.
Stillleben n. still life (art).
stilllegen to shut down, close,
  discontinue.
stillschweigen to be silent.
stillschweigend silent.
Stillstand m. standstill, stop.
stillstehen to stand still, stop.
  Still gestanden! Attention!
stilvoll in good style, taste.
Stimmabgabe f. vote, voting.
stimmberechtigt entitled to vote.
STIMME f. voice, part, comment, vote.
  Stimme abgeben to vote.
STIMMEN to tune, vote, be correct,
  impress someone, influence someone's
  mood.
  Das stimmt! That is correct!
  Werden Sie für oder dagegen
   stimmen? Are you going to vote for
   or against?
Stimmrecht n. right to vote.
STIMMUNG f. tuning, pitch, key, mood,
  humor, impression, atmosphere.
  Stimmung machen für to create a
   mood for, to make propaganda for.

Stimmungsmensch m. moody person.
stimmungsvoll impressive.
Stimmzettel m. ballot.
Stirn f. forehead, front, imprudence.
  die Stim runzeln to frown.
  einem die Stirne bieten to show a bold
   front.
Stock m. stick, rod, cane, floor (story).
  über Stock und Stein up hill and down
   dale.
  Welcher Stock? What floor?
stockdumm utterly stupid.
stocken to stop, stand still.
  ins Stocken geraten to get tied up.
stockfinster pitch-dark.
Stockfisch m. dried cod.
Stockwerk n. story, floor.
Stoff m. matter, substance.
stöhnen to groan.
stolpern to stumble, trip over.
stolz proud.
stopfen to darn, fill, stuff.
Stopfgarn n. darning thread.
Stopfnadel f. darning needle.
stoppen to stop.
Stoppuhr f. stop-watch.
Stöpsel m. stopper, cork.
stöpseln to cork.
Storch m. stork.
STÖREN to disturb, trouble,
  inconvenience.
  Nicht stören! Do not disturb!
störrisch stubborn.
Störung f. disturbance, upset.
  geistige Störung mental disorder.
Stoss m. push, poke, pile, jerk, shock.
stossen to push, shove, hit, kick, knock.
  stossen auf to run into.
Stosseufzer m. deep sigh, groan.
Stosstange f. bumper.
stottern to shutter, stammer.
Strafanstalt f. penitentiary.
strafbar liable to punishment.
Strafe f. punishment, penalty, fine.
  bei Strafe von on pain of.
strafen to punish.
Straferlass m. amnesty.
straff stretched, tense, tight, strict.
straffällig punishable.
straffen to tighten.
sträflich criminal, punishable.
straffrei exempt from punishment,
  unpunished.
Strafgefangene m. convict.
Strafgericht n. criminal court.
Strafporto n. extra postage, surcharge.
Strafpredigt f. reprimand.
Strafprozess m. criminal case.
strafwürdig punishable.
STRAHL m. ray, beam, stream.

strahlen *to radiate, beam, shine.*

stramm *tight, close.*
  stramm stehen *to stand at attention.*

STRAND *m. seashore, beach, strand.*

Strandbad *n. seaside, resort.*

stranden *to run around or ashore.*

Strandschuhe *pl. beach shoes.*

STRANG *m. rope, cord, track.*
  am gleichen Strang ziehen *to act in concert.*
  über die Strange schlagen *to kick over the traces.*
  wenn alle Stränge reissen *if the worst comes to the worst.*
  zum Strang verurteilen *to condemn to the gallows.*

Strapaze *f. fatigue.*

strapazieren *to tire, enervate.*

STRASSE *f. street, highway, road.*
  an der Strasse *by the wayside.*
  auf der Strasse *in the street.*

Strassenarbeiter *m. roadman.*

Strassenbahn *f. tramway.*

Strassenfeger *m. street cleaner.*

sträuben *to ruffle up, bristle.*

Strauch *m. shrub, bush.*

streben *to endeavor, aspire, aim at.*

Streber *m. climber, careerist.*

Strecke *f. distance, way, route, tract.*
  auf freier Strecke *on the road.*

strecken *to stretch, extend, stretch out.*
  die Waffen strecken *to lay down arms.*
  sich strecken *to stretch.*

Streich *m. stroke, blow.*
  einem einen Streich spielen *to play a trick on a person.*

streichen *to spread, rub, strike, erase, cancel, paint, wander, stroll, migrate.*
  Frisch gestrichen! *Wet paint!*

Streichholz *m. match.*

Streichmusik *f. string music.*

Streichquartett *n. string quartet.*

Streife *f. patrol, raid.*

streifen *to touch lightly, stripe, brush, wander.*

Streik *m. strike.*
  in den Streik treten *to go on strike.*

streiken *to strike.*

STREIT *m. fight, quarrel, dispute.*

streitbar *valiant.*

streiten *to fight, quarrel.*

Streitfall *m. quarrel, controversy.*

Streitfrage *f. matter in dispute.*
  einem etwas streitig machen *to contest a person's right to a thing.*

STRENG *strict, stern, severe.*
  streng genommen *strictly speaking.*

Strenge *f. severity, strictness.*

strengläubig *orthodox.*

streuen *to strew, scatter, spread.*

Strich *m. dash, stroke, line, compass point.*
  Machen wir einen Strich darunter. *Let's put an end to that.*
  nach Strich und Faden *thoroughly.*

Strichpunkt *m. semicolon.*

Strick *m. cord, rope.*
  wenn alle Stricke reissen *if everything else fails.*

stricken *to knit.*

Stroh *n. straw.*

Strohhalm *m. straw (for drinking).*

STROM *m. large river, stream, current.*
  Es regnet in Strömen. *It's pouring.*

stromabwärts *downstream.*

stromaufwärts *upstream.*

strömen *to stream, flow, pour.*

Strömung *f. current, stream.*

Stromzähler *electric meter.*

Strudel *m. whirlpool.*

Strumpf *m. stocking, sock.*

Strumpfband *n. garter.*

Strumpfhalter *m. garter (woman's)*

struppig *bristly, unkempt.*

STUBE *f. room, chamber, living room.*

Stubenhocker *m. stay-at-home.*

stubenrein *house-broken.*

STÜCK *n. piece, play, extract, morsel.*
  aus einem Stück *all of a piece.*
  aus freien Stücken *of one's own free will.*
  ein starkes Stück *a bit stiff.*
  ein Stück Arbeit *a stiff job.*
  ein Stück mitnehmen *to give a lift.*
  Er hält grosse Stücke auf ihn. *He thinks a lot of him.*
  in allen Stücken *in every respect.*

stückweise *piece by piece, by the piece.*

Student *m. (-in, f.) student.*

Studie *f. study, sketch (art).*

studieren *to study.*

Studium *n. study, university education.*

Stufe *f. step, stair, level.*
  auf gleicher Stufe mit *on a level with.*

stufenweise *by degrees, gradually.*

STUHL *m. chair, seat.*

stumm *dumb, silent, mute.*

Stummheit *f. dumbness.*

stumpf *blunt, obtuse, dull.*
  mit Stumpf und Stiehl *root and branch.*

Stumpfsinn *m. stupidity.*

stumpfsinning *stupid, dull.*

STUNDE *f. hour; lesson, period.*

stundenlang *for hours.*

Stundenplan *m. timetable.*

Stundenzeiger *m. hour-hand.*

stündlich *hourly.*

Stundung *f. delay of payment.*
STURM *m. storm, gale.*
stürmen *to take by storm.*
stürmisch *stormy, impetuous.*
Sturz *m. fall, crash, tumble, overthrow, collapse.*
  zum Sturz bringen *to overthrow.*
stürzen *to overthrow, throw down, fall down, plunge into, crash.*
  Nicht stürzen! *Handle with care!*
Stütze *f. stay, support, help.*
stutzen *to trim, cut short, stop short.*
stützen *to support, base, prop up.*
Stutzer *m. dandy.*
Stützpfeiler *m. pillar, support.*
Stützpunkt *m. base, strong point.*
Subjekt *n. subject.*
Substantiv *n. substantive, noun.*
Substanz *f. substance.*
substrahieren *to subtract.*
Suche *f. search, quest.*
  auf die Suche gehen *to go in search of.*
  auf der Suche nach *in search of.*
SUCHEN *to look for, try, seek.*
  das Weite suchen *to run away.*
  nach Worten suchen *to be at a loss for words.*
  Sie hat hier nichts zu suchen. *She has no business here.*
Sucht *f. passion, rage.*
Süden *m. south.*
Südfrüchte *pl. tropical fruits.*
südlich *southern, (to the) south.*
Südpol *m. south pole.*
Sühne *f. expiation.*
sühnen *to expiate.*
Summe *f. sum, amount.*
summieren *to add up.*
Sumpf *m. swamp.*
Sünde *f. sin.*
Sünder *m. (-in. f.) sinner.*
süundhaft *sinful.*
sündigan *to sin.*
Suppe *f. soup, broth.*
suspendieren *to suspend.*
SÜSS *sweet, fresh, lovely.*
Süsse *f. sweetness.*
süsslich *sweetish, mawkish.*
Symbol *n. symbol.*
symbolisch *symbolical.*
Sympathie *f. sympathy.*
sympathisch *nice, likable, congenial.*
Symphonie *f. symphony.*
Symptom *n. symptom.*
Synagoge *f. synagogue.*
System *n. system.*
Szene *f. scene.*
Szenerie *f. scenery, settings.*

T

Tabak *m. tobacco.*
Tabelle *f. table, index, schedule.*
Tablett *n. tray.*
Tablette *f. tablet.*
Tadel *m. reprimand, blame.*
tadellos *excellent, perfect.*
tadeln *to blame, find fault.*
TAFEL *f. board, blackboard, bar, plate, table.*
  die Tafel aufheben *to rise from table.*
TAG *m. day, daylight; life (one's days).*
  alle acht Tage *every week.*
  alle Tage *every day.*
  am Tag *during the day, in the daytime.*
  an den Tag bringen *to bring to light.*
  auf ein paar Tage *for a few days.*
  auf seine alten Tage *in his old age.*
  bei Tage *in the daytime.*
  den ganzen Tag *all day long.*
  dieser Tage *one of these days.*
  einen um den andern Tag *every other day.*
  eines Tages *some day.*
  Er lebt in den Tag hinein. *He lives from hand to mouth.*
  Guten Tag! *Good morning!*
  in acht Tagen *in a week.*
  Tag aus, Tag ein *day in, day out.*
  Tag für Tag *day by day.*
  unter Tage arbeiten *to work underground.*
  vierzehn Tage *two weeks.*
  vor acht Tagen *a week ago.*
Tagebuch *n. diary.*
tagelang *for days.*
Tagesgesprach *n. topic of the day.*
Tageszeitung *f. daily paper.*
Tagewerk *n. day's work.*
taghell *as light as day.*
täglich *daily.*
tagsüber *during the day.*
Tagung *f. conference, meeting.*
Taille *f. waist.*
Takt *m. time measure (music).*
Taktgefühl *n. tact.*
Taktik *f. tactics.*
taktisch *tactical.*
taktlos *tactless.*
Taktlosigkeit *f. tactlessness, indiscretion.*
Taktstock *m. baton.*
taktvoll *tactful, discreet.*
Tal *n. valley.*
Talent *n. talent, ability.*
talentiert *talented.*
talentvoll *talented.*

Talk *m. talcum powder.*
Talsperre *f. river dam.*
talwärts *downhill.*
Tank *m. tank (car).*
tanken *to fill up (car).*
Tanne *f. fir tree.*
Tannenadeln *pl. fir needles.*
Tannenbaum *m. fir tree.*
Tannenzapfen *m. fir cone.*
Tante *f. aunt.*
Tanz *m. dance, ball.*
   Darf ich um den nächsten Tanz bitten?
   May I have the next dance?
TANZEN *to dance.*
Tänzer *m. (-in, f.) dance partner.*
Tapete *f. wallpaper.*
Tapezier *m. paperhanger, upholsterer.*
tapezieren *to paper.*
tapfer *brave, gallant.*
Tapferkeit *f. bravery, gallantry.*
Tarif *m. rate, tariff.*
tarifmässig *in accordance with the
   tariff.*
tarnen *to camouflage, disguise.*
Tarnung *f. camouflage.*
TASCHE *f. pocket, bag, purse.*
   jemandem auf der Tasche liegen *to
   be a financial drain to a person.*
Taschenbuch *n. pocketbook.*
Taschendieb *m. pickpocket.*
Taschenlampe *f. flashlight.*
Taschenmesser *n. pocket knife.*
Taschentuch *n. handkerchief.*
Taschenuhr *f. pocket-watch.*
TASSE *f. cup.*
   eine Tasse Kaffee *a cup of coffee.*
Taste *f. key (music and typewriter).*
tasten *to touch, feel.*
TAT *f. deed, act, fact, achievement,
   feat.*
   auf frischer Tat *in the very act.*
   in der Tat *indeed, as a matter of fact.*
tatenlos *inactive, idle.*
Täter *m. perpetrator.*
tätig *active.*
   tätig sein *to be active.*
Tätigkeit *f. activity, job.*
tatkräftig *energetic.*
Tatsache *f. fact.*
tatsächlich *real, actual.*
Tau *m. dew.*
Tau *n. rope.*
taub *deaf, empty, hollow.*
Taube *f. pigeon.*
Taubheit *f. deafness.*
taubstumm *deaf and dumb.*
Taubstumme *m. deaf-mute.*
tauchen *to dive, dip, plunge.*
Taucher *m. diver.*

tauen *to thaw.*
Taufe *f. baptism, christening.*
   aus der Taufe heben *to be godfather
   (or godmother).*
taufen *to baptize.*
taugen *to be of use.*
Taugenichts *m. good-for-nothing.*
Tauglichkeit *f. fitness, suitability.*
Tausch *m. exchange.*
tauschen *to exchange, swap.*
täuschen *to delude, deceive,
   disappoint.*
   Mich können Sie nicht täuschen. *You
   can't fool me.*
   sich täuschen *to be mistaken, fool
   oneself.*
   sich täuschen lassen *to let oneself be
   fooled.*
Täuschung *f. deception.*
TAUSEND *thousand.*
tausendmal *a thousand times.*
Tauwetter *n. thaw.*
Taxe *f. tax, rate, duty.*
Taxi *n. taxi.*
   ein Taxi holen *to call a cab.*
taxieren *to appraise, value.*
Technik *f. technology.*
technisch *technical.*
Tee *m. tea.*
Teelöffel *m. teaspoon.*
Teer *n. tar.*
Teich *m. pond.*
Teig *m. dough.*
TEIL *m. & n. part, share, portion.*
   ich für mein Teil *as for me.*
   sich sein Teil denken *to have one's
   own ideas.*
   zum Teil *partly.*
   zum grössten Teil *for the most part.*
teilbar *divisible.*
Teilchen *n. particle.*
TEILEN *to divide, share, distribute, deal
   out.*
   geteilte Gefühle *mixed feelings.*
   geteilter Meinung sein *to be of a
   different opinion.*
   sich teilen in *to divide, split.*
Teilhaber *m. partner, participant.*
Teilhaberschaft *f. partnership.*
Teilnahme *f. participation, condolences.*
   Meine aufrichtige Teilnahme *my
   sincere condolences.*
teilnahmslos *indifferent.*
teilnahmsvoll *sympathetic.*
teilnehmen *to take part in.*
Teilnehmer *m. participant, subscriber.*
teilweise *partial.*
Teilzahlung *f. part-payment, installment.*
TELEFON *n. telephone.*

Telefonanruf *m. telephone call.*
Telefonbuch *n. telephone directory.*
TELEFONIEREN *to telephone.*
telefonisch *telephonic, by telephone.*
Telefonist *m. (-in, f.) telephone operator.*
Telefonnummer *f. telephone number.*
Telefonzelle *f. telephone booth.*
Telefonzentrale *f. telephone exchange.*
Telegrafie *f. telegraphy.*
TELEGRAFIEREN *to telegraph.*
telegrafisch *by telegram.*
TELEGRAMM *n. telegram.*
Telegrammformular *n. telegraph form.*
Teller *m. plate.*
Temperament *n. temperament, character, disposition.*
Temperatur *f. temperature.*
Temperaturschwankungen *pl. variations in temperature.*
Tempo *n. time, measure, speed.*
Tendenz *f. tendency, inclination.*
Tennis *n. tennis.*
Tennisplatz *m. tennis court.*
Tennisschläger *m. tennis racket.*
Tenor *m. tenor.*
Teppich *m. carpet.*
Termin *m. deadline.*
Terrasse *f. terrace.*
Territorium *n. territory.*
Testament *n. testament.*
TEUER *expensive, high, costly.*
Teuerung *f. dearness, scarcity, high cost of living.*
Teufel *m. devil.*
    Den Teufel an die Wand malen. *Speak of the devil and there he is.*
teuflisch *devilish, diabolical.*
Text *m. text, libretto.*
    aus dem Text kommen *to lose the thread.*
Textbuch *n. words, libretto.*
Textilien *pl. textiles.*
Textilwaren *pl. textiles.*
THEATER *n. theater, stage.*
Theaterbesuch *m. playgoing.*
Theaterbesucher *m. playgoer.*
Theaterdirektor *m. manager of a theater.*
Theaterkasse *f. box office.*
theatralisch *theatrical.*
Theke *f. counter, bar.*
Thema *n. theme, subject.*
Theologe *m. theologian.*
Theoretiker *m. theoretician.*
Thermometer *n. thermometer.*
Thermometerstand *m. thermometer reading.*
Thron *m. throne.*

Thronbesteigung *f. accession to the throne.*
TIEF *deep, low, deeply, far.*
    Das lässt tief blicken. *That tells a tale.*
    in tiefer Nacht *late at night.*
Tiefe *f. depth, profundity.*
tiefgründig *deep, profound.*
tiefliegend *sunken.*
Tiefsee *f. deep sea.*
tiefsinnig *profound, pensive, melancholy.*
Tiefstand *m. lowness, low level.*
TIER *n. animal, beast.*
Tierarzt *m. veterinary.*
Tiergarten *m. zoo.*
Tiger *m. tiger.*
Tinte *f. ink.*
    in der Tinte sitzen *to be in a mess.*
Tintenfass *n. inkwell.*
Tintenfleck *m. blot, ink spot.*
TISCH *m. table.*
    bei Tisch *during the meal.*
    Bitte, zu Tisch! *Dinner is ready!*
    Er ist gerade zu Tisch gegangen. *He has just gone out to lunch.*
    reinen Tisch machen *to make a clean sweep.*
    unter den Tisch fallen *to be ignored.*
Tischdecke *f. tablecloth.*
Tischler *m. cabinet-maker.*
Tischplatte *f. table top.*
Tischrede *f. after-dinner talk.*
Tischtennis *n. table tennis, ping-pong.*
Tischtuch *n. tablecloth.*
Tischzeit *f. dinner-time.*
Titel *m. title, claim.*
Titelbild *n. frontispiece.*
Titelblatt *n. title page.*
Titelhalter *m. title-holder.*
Toast *m. toast.*
toasten *to drink toasts.*
toben *to rage, rave.*
Tobsucht *f. raving madness.*
tobsüchtig *raving mad.*
TOCHTER *f. daughter.*
TOD *m. death, decease.*
    des Todes sein *to be doomed.*
Todesanzeige *f. death notice.*
Todeskampf *m. death agony.*
Todesstrafe *f. capital punishment, death penalty.*
Todestag *m. death anniversary.*
todkrank *very ill.*
tödlich *fatal, deadly, mortal.*
todmüde *dead tired.*
Toilette *f. toilet, dress, dressing table, lavatory.*
    Toilette machen *to dress, get dressed.*
tolerant *tolerant.*

toll *mad, insane, raving, awful.*
tölpisch *clumsy.*
Ton *m. sound, note, stress, accent.*
tönen *to sound, resound.*
Tonfall *m. musical intonation.*
Tonfilm *m. sound film.*
Tonkunst *f. music, musical art.*
Tonleiter *f. scale.*
tonlos *soundless, voiceless.*
Tonne *f. barrel, ton.*
Tönung *shading.*
Topf *m. pot.*
Tor *n. gate.*
Tor *m. fool.*
Torheit *f. foolishness, folly.*
töricht *foolish, silly.*
Torte *f. layer cake.*
tosen *to rage, roar.*
TOT *dead, dull.*
   tote Zeit *dead season.*
   toter Punkt *deadlock.*
totarbeiten (sich) *to kill oneself with work.*
Tote *m. dead person, deceased.*
TÖTEN *to kill.*
   sich töten *to commit suicide.*
   sich totlachen *to die laughing.*
Totenbett *n. deathbed*
totenbleich *deadly pale.*
totenstill *still as death.*
Tötung *f. killing, slaying.*
Tour *f. tour, excursion.*
   in einer Tour *without stopping.*
Tournee *f. tour (theater).*
Trab *m. trot.*
   im Trab *quickly.*
Tracht *f. dress, costume.*
trachten *to strive, seek after.*
   einem nach dem Leben trachten *to make an attempt on a person's life.*
traditionell *traditional.*
Trage *f. barrow, litter.*
TRAGEN *to carry, bear, wear, take, endure, suffer, produce.*
   die Schuld tragen an *to carry the blame for.*
   Sie trägt Trauer. *She is in mourning.*
TRÄGER *m. porter.*
Tragfähigkeit *f. capacity.*
Tragfläche *f. wing of aircraft.*
Tragflügel *m. wing of aircraft.*
Tragik *f. tragic (art).*
tragisch *tragic.*
Tragödie *f. tragedy.*
trainieren *to train.*
Träne *f. tear.*
Trank *m. drink.*
tränken *to water, soak.*
transpirieren *to perspire.*

Transport *m. transport.*
Traube *f. grape, bunch of grapes.*
Traubenlese *f. grape harvest.*
Traubenmost *m. grape juice.*
trauen *to marry, give in marriage, join, trust, rely.*
   Ich traue ihm alles zu. *I believe him capable of everything.*
   sich trauen lassen *to get married.*
Trauer *f. sorrow, grief, affliction.*
Traueranzeige *f. announcement of a death.*
Trauermarsch *m. funeral march.*
trauern *to mourn, grieve.*
Trauerspiel *n. tragedy.*
Traufe *f. gutter.*
   vom Regen in die Traufe *out of the frying pan into the fire.*
träufeln *to drop.*
traulich *intimate, cosy.*
TRAUM *m. dream, fancy, illusion.*
   Träume sind Schäume. *All dreams are lies.*
träumen *to dream.*
Träumer *m. dreamer.*
träumerisch *dreamy.*
traumhaft *dreamlike.*
TRAURIG *sad, sorrowful, mournful.*
Traurigkeit *f. sadness.*
Trauschein *m. marriage certificate.*
Trauung *f. marriage ceremony.*
Trauzeuge *m. witness to a marriage.*
TREFFEN *to meet, hit, strike, affect, touch, fall upon.*
   Alle nötigen Vorbereitungen sind getroffen worden. *All the necessary arrangements have been made.*
   sich getroffen fühlen *to feel hurt.*
   sich gut treffen *to be lucky.*
   sich treffen *to meet.*
   Vorsichtsmassregeln treffen *to take all the necessary precautions.*
treffend *to the point.*
Treffer *m. target, luck, winning ticket, prize.*
trefflich *excellent, admirable.*
Trefflichkeit *f. excellence.*
treiben *to drive, set in motion, float, drift.*
   Wintersport treiben *to practice winter sports.*
Treibhaus *n. conservatory.*
trennbar *sparable, divisible.*
TRENNEN *to separate, divide, dissolve.*
   getrennt leben *to live separately.*
   sich trennen *to part.*
   sich trennen von *to part from.*
Trennung *f. separation.*
Treppe *f. stairway, stairs.*

Treppenabsatz *m. landing.*
Treppengeländer *n. banisters, railing.*
Tresor *m. treasury.*
TRETEN *to step, tread, walk, go.*
in jemandes Fusstapfen treten *to follow one's footsteps.*
in Kraft treten *to go into effect.*
in Verbindung treten *to get in touch.*
mit Füssen treten *to trample under foot.*
zu nahe treten *to hurt one's feelings.*
TREU *faithful, true, loyal.*
treubrüchig *faithless, perfidious.*
Treue *f. fidelity, faithfulness, loyalty.*
treuherzig *frank, naive.*
treulich *faithfully.*
treulos *unfaithful.*
Treulosigkeit *f. faithlessness.*
Tribüne *f. tribune.*
Trieb *m. sprout, shoot, motive power.*
trinkbar *drinkable.*
TRINKEN *to drink, absorb.*
Trinker *m. drunkard.*
Trinkgeld *n. tip.*
Trinkspruch *n. toast.*
Tritt *m. step, footstep.*
Trittbrett *n. running board.*
Triumph *m. triumph, victory.*
triumphieren *to triumph.*
trocken *dry, arid, dull.*
im Trockenen sein *to be under cover.*
Trockenmilch *f. dry milk.*
trocknen *to dry up.*
Trommel *f. drum.*
trommeln *to beat the drum.*
Trompete *f. trumpet.*
Trompeter *m. trumpeter.*
Tropen *pl. tropics.*
tropfen *to drop, drip.*
tropfenweise *by drops, drop by drop.*
TROST *m. comfort.*
trostbedürftig *in need of consolation.*
trösten *to comfort, console, cheer up.*
sich trösten *to cheer up.*
tröstlich *consoling, comforting.*
trostlos *discouraged.*
Trostlosigkeit *f. despair, hopelessness.*
trostreich *comforting, consoling.*
Trottoir *n. pavement.*
TROTZ *prep. (gen.) in spite of.*
Trotz der Kälte ging ich jeden Tag spazieren. *In spite of the cold, I took a walk every day.*
Trotz *m. obstinacy, stubborness, defiance.*
jemandem zum Trotz *in defiance of someone.*
Trotz bieten *to defy.*
trotzdem *nevertheless, anyway, although.*

Trotzdem es sehr kalt ist, werde ich spazieren gehen. *Although it is very cold, I shall take a walk.*
trotzen *to defy, be obstinate.*
trotzig *defiant.*
trüb *dark, sad, gloomy.*
trüben *to dim, trouble, spoil.*
Der Himmel trübt sich. *The sky is clouding over.*
Trübsal *f. affliction.*
trübselig *sad, gloomy, dreary.*
trübsinnig *melancholy.*
trügen *to deceive.*
trügerisch *deceitful.*
Truhe *f. chest, trunk.*
Trümmer *f. ruins, debris.*
in Trümmer gehen *to be shattered.*
Trumpf *m. trump.*
trumpfen *to trump.*
Trunk *m. drink.*
Trunkenheit *f. drunkenness.*
Truppe *f. troop, company.*
Truthahn *m. turkey.*
Tube *f. tube.*
tuberkulös *tuberculous.*
TUCH *n. cloth, fabric, shawl.*
tüchtig *good, able, fit, qualified, competent, efficient.*
Tüchtigkeit *f. fitness, ability, efficiency.*
Tücke *f. malice, spite.*
tückisch *malicious, spiteful.*
TUGEND *f. virtue.*
tugendhaft *virtuous.*
tugendsam *virtuous.*
Tulpe *f. tulip.*
Tumult *m. tumult, commotion.*
TUN *to do, make, act, perform, execute.*
Das tut nichts. *That does not matter.*
des Guten zu viel tun *to overdo something.*
Er tut nur so. *He is only pretending.*
Es tut mir leid. *I am sorry.*
es zu tun bekommen mit *to have trouble with.*
Haben Sie sich weh getan? *Did you hurt yourself?*
Mir ist darum zu tun. *It is very important for me.*
tun als ob *to pretend.*
Tun Sie als ob Sie zu Hause wären. *Make yourself at home.*
Wir haben viel zu tun. *We are very busy.*
tunlich *feasible, practicable.*
Tunnel *m. tunnel.*
tupfen *to dot, touch lightly, dab.*
TÜR *f. door, doorway.*
vor der Tür stehen *to be imminent.*
Türgriff *m. doorknob.*

Türklinke f. latch (handle).
Turm m. tower, steeple.
Turmuhr f. church clock.
Turnen n. gymnastics.
turnen to do gymnastics.
Turnhalle f. gymnasium.
Turnier n. tournament.
Tusche f. India ink.
Tüte f. paper bag.
typisch typical.
Tyrann m. tyrant.
tyrannisieren to tyrannize.

U

Übel n. evil, ailment, misfortune,
inconvenience.
ÜBEL evil, wrong, bad, ill.
Das ist nicht übel. That is not bad.
Mir ist übel. I feel sick.
übel daran sein to be in a bad way.
übelgelaunt cross, grumpy.
übelgesinnt evil-minded.
Übelkeit f. nausea.
übelnehmen to mind.
übelnehmerisch touchy, susceptible.
Übelstand m. inconvenience, drawback.
Übeltäter m. evil-doer criminal.
üben to exercise, practise.
ÜBER 1. prep (dat. when answering
question, Wo?; acc. when answering
question Wohin?, and depending on
the idiom) higher, while, concerning,
via.
den Winter über the whole winter long.
Er schwamm über den See. He swam
across the lake.
Er zog sich die Decke über den Kopf.
He pulled the blanket over his head.
Ich wundere mich über ihre Einstellung.
I am surprised at her attitude.
Sie sprach über ihre Sorgen. She
spoke about her sorrows.
über Bord overboard.
Über der Erde ziehen Wolken. Clouds
are floating above the earth.
über kurz oder lang sooner or later.
über und über over and over.
Seine Liebe geht ihr über alles. She
places his love above everything.
überall all over.
von Berlin über Strassburg nach Paris
from Berlin to Paris via Strassburg.
2. adv. wholly, completely, in excess.
3. prefix a) separable (when meaning
above).

Das Flugzeug fliegt über dem Ozean.
The airplane flies above the ocean.
b) inseparable (in all uses where it
does not mean above.)
Er übersetzt ein Gedicht von Schiller.
He translates a poem by Schiller.
überaltert too old.
überanstrengen to overwork,
overstrain.
überarbeiten to review, go over.
sich überarbeiten to overwork oneself.
überbelichten to overexpose (photo).
überbieten to excel, surpass.
Überblick m. perspective, summary,
survey.
überblicken to survey, sum up.
überdachen to roof.
überdauern to outlast.
überdies besides, moreover.
Überdruss m. boredom, satiety, disgust.
zum Überdruss werden to become a
bore.
überdrüssig tired of, sick of, bored
with.
Übereifer m. excess zeal.
übereignen to transfer, assign, convey.
übereilen to rush, hurry, precipitate.
sich übereilen to be in a great hurry.
Übereilen Sie sich nicht! Don't rush!
Übereilung f. hastiness, rush.
übereinkommen to agree.
Übereinkunft f. agreement,
arrangement.
übereinstimmen to agree, coincide.
Übereinstimmung f. agreement,
conformity.
überessen to overeat.
überfahren to overrun (signal) run over.
Überfahrt f. crossing.
Überfall m. holdup.
überfallen to hold up.
überfällig overdue.
Überfallkommando n. flying squad
(police).
überfliegen to fly over, skim through.
überfliessen to overflow, run over.
überflügeln to surpass, outstrip.
Überfluss m. abundance, profusion.
im Überfluss abundantly.
zum Überfluss unnecessarily.
überflüssig superfluous, unnecessary.
überfordern to overcharge.
Überfracht f. excess freight,
overweight.
überführen to convey, transport.
Überführung f. conveying, transfer.
überfüllen to overload, crowd.
Überfüllung f. overloading.
Übergabe f. delivery, surrender.

Übergang m. passage, crossing.
übergeben to hand over, deliver.
übergehen (separable prefix) to cross, pass over.
übergehen (inseparable prefix) to pass by, omit.
Das Geschäft ist in andere Hände übergegangen. This store has changed hands.
Übergewicht n. overweight, excess weight.
das Übergewicht bekommen to lose one's balance.
übergiessen to spill.
Überhandnahme f. increase.
überhandnehmen to increase, spread.
Überhang m. curtain, hangings.
überhangen to hang over.
ÜBERHAUPT in general, altogether.
überhaupt nicht not at all.
überheben to save, spare, exempt.
überheblich presumptuous.
Überhelichkeit f. presumption, arrogance.
überholen to pass (car), surpass, overhaul.
überholt outdated.
überhören to miss, ignore.
Überkleid n. overdress, overall.
überkochen to boil over.
überladen to overload.
überlassen to leave, give up, cede.
überlasten to overload.
überlaufen to run over, boil over, desert.
Überläufer m. deserter.
überleben to survive, outlive.
sich überlebt haben to be outdated.
Überlebende m. survivor.
überlegen to reflect, consider.
sich überlegen to think over, consider.
überlegen adj. superior.
Ich habe es mir anders überlegt. I've changed my mind.
überlegen sein to be better than.
Überlegenheit f. superiority.
überliefern to deliver, transmit.
Überlieferung f. delivery, tradition, surrender.
überlisten to outwit.
ÜBERMACHT f. superiority, predominance.
Übermass n. excess.
im Übermass to excess, excessive.
übermässig excessive, immoderate.
Übermensch m. superman.
übermenschlich superhuman.
übermitteln to transmit.
Übermittlung f. transmission.

ÜBERMORGEN the day after tomorrow.
übermüden to overtire.
Übermüdung f. over-fatigue.
Übermut m. high spirits.
übermütig to be in high spirits.
übernachten to stay overnight, spend the night.
Übernahme f. taking over.
übernatürlich supernatural.
übernehmen to take over, seize.
sich übernehmen to overstrain oneself.
überordnen to set over.
überraschen to surprise.
Überraschung f. surprise.
überreden to persuade.
überreichen to hand over, present.
überreif overripe.
Überrest m. remainder.
überrumpeln to surprise, take by surprise.
Überrumpelung f. surprise, sudden attack.
überschätzen to overrate, overestimate.
überschauen to overlook, survey.
Überschlag m. estimate.
überschlagen to estimate; to skip.
überschneiden to intersect, overlap.
überschreiten to cross, exceed, overstep.
Überschreitung f. crossing, excess, transgression.
Überschrift f. heading, title.
Überschuh m. overshoe, galosh.
Überschuss m. surplus, excess.
überschüssig in excess.
überschwemmen to inundate.
Überschwemmung f. inundation, flood.
Übersee f. overseas.
übersehen to survey, overlook.
übersenden to send, transmit.
Übersender m. sender.
Übersendung f. transmission.
übersetzen to pass across.
ÜBERSETZEN to translate.
Übersetzer m. translator.
Übersetzung f. translation.
Übersicht f. view, review, summary.
übersichtlich clear, visible.
Übersichtlichkeit f. clearness, lucidity.
übersinnlich transcendental.
überspannen to stretch over, span.
überspannt eccentric.
Überspanntheit f. eccentricity.
überspitzt too subtle.
überspringen to jump across.
überstehen to endure, come through.
überstrahlen to shine upon, outshine.
überströmen to overflow.

Überstunden *pl. overtime.*
  Überstunden machen *to work overtime.*
ÜBERSTÜRZEN *to rush, hurry, act hastily.*
  Überstürzen Sie sich nicht! *Don't rush yourself!*
übertragbar *transferable.*
übertragen *to transfer, give up, entrust with, transmit, broadcast.*
Übertragung *f. transfer, transcription, transmission.*
übertreffen *to excell, surpass.*
übertreiben *to exaggerate.*
Übertreibung *f. exaggeration.*
übertreten *to go over, change over, violate.*
Übertretung *f. violation, transgression.*
übertrumpfen *to outdo.*
übervölkert *overpopulated.*
übervorteilen *to take advantage.*
überwachen *to watch over, supervise.*
Überwachung *f. observation, surprise.*
überwältigen *to overwhelm.*
Überwältigung *f. overwhelming.*
überweisen *to transfer, remit.*
  telegraphisch überweisen *to send a cable.*
Überweisung *f. transfer, remittance.*
überwiegen *to outweigh.*
überwiegend *preponderant, predominant.*
überwinden *to overcome.*
Überwindung *f. overcoming, conquest.*
Überzahl *f. numerical superiority, majority.*
überzählig *surplus.*
überzeugen *to convince.*
Überzeugung *f. conviction, belief.*
  der Überzeugung sein *to be convinced.*
überziehen *to cover, re-cover; to overdraw (bank account).*
  das Bett überziehen *to change the sheets.*
üblich *usual, customary.*
U-Boot *n. submarine.*
ÜBRIG *left over, remaining, other.*
  das Übrige *the rest.*
  ein übriges tun *to do more than necessary.*
  Haben Sie ein paar Minuten für uns übrig? *Can you spare us a few minutes?*
  im übrigen *otherwise.*
  nichts übrig haben für *to care little for.*
  übrig bleiben *to be left over.*
  übrig lassen *to leave.*
  zu wünschen übrig lassen *to leave much to be desired.*

ÜBRIGENS *besides, by the way.*
ÜBUNG *f. exercise, practice, drill.*
UFER *n. shore, bank (river).*
UHR *f. hour, clock, watch.*
  nach der Uhr sehen *to look at the time.*
  um halb fünf *at half past five.*
  Um wieviel Uhr? *At what time?*
  Wieviel Uhr ist es? *What time is it?*
Uhrmacher *m. watchmaker.*
Uhrzeiger *m. clock hand.*
UM 1. *prep. (acc.), at, about, around, because of, for the sake of, for, up.*
  Der Zug verlässt Düsseldorf um drei Uhr. *The train leaves Düsseldorf at three o'clock.*
  einer um den anderen *one after the other.*
  Ihre Zeit ist um. *Your time is up.*
  Tag um Tag *every day, day after day.*
  Wir ängstigen uns um sie. *We worry about her.*
  Wir sitzen um den Tisch. *We sit around the table.*
  Um Himmels willen! *For God's sake!*
  um jeden Preis *not at any cost.*
  um keinen Preis *not at any price.*
  um so besser *all the better.*
  um zwei Jahre älter *two years older.*
  2. *Adv. around.*
  um und um *around.*
  um herum *all around.*
  3. *Conj. (um. . .zu), in order to.*
  Um den Frieden zu erhalten, dankt der Prinz ab. *The prince abdicates in order to preserve peace.*
  4. *Prefix.* a) *inseparable (implies the meaning of around).*
  Gärten umgeben das Schloss. *The castle is surrounded by gardens.*
  b) *separable (implies the meaning of to upset, to transform).*
  Er warf den Stuhl um. *He overturned the chair.*
umadressieren *to redirect a letter.*
umändern *to change, alter.*
Umänderung *f. change, alteration.*
umarbeiten *to remodel.*
Umarbeitung *f. remodeling.*
umarmen *to embrace, hug.*
Umarmung *f. embrace, hug.*
Umbau *m. rebuilding, reconstruction.*
umbinden *to tie around, put on.*
umblättern *to turn over.*
umblicken *to look about.*
umdrehen *to turn, turn round.*
Umdrehung *f. turning round.*
umfahren *to drive around.*
Umfahrt *f. circular tour.*

umfallen _to topple over._
Umfang _m. circumference, extent, size._
umfangreich _comprehensive, extensive._
umfassen _to clasp, embrace, enclose._
umfassend _comprehensive, extensive, complete, full._
umformen _to transform, remodel._
Umfrage _f. inquiry._
Umgang _m. association, relations._
umgänglich _sociable._
Umgangsformen _pl. manners._
Umgangssprache _f. colloquial speech._
umgeben _to surround._
Umgebung _f. surroundings, environs._
Umgegend _f. neighborhood, vicinity._
UMGEHEN _to go around, circulate, haunt, evade._
  umgehend antworten _to answer by return._
umgekehrt _opposite, reverse, contrary._
umgestalten _to alter, transform, reform._
umgraben _to dig up._
umgruppieren _to regroup._
Umhang _m. cape, shawl._
UMHER _around, about, here and there._
umherblicken _to glance around, look around._
umhin _about._
  Ich kann nicht umhin. _I can't help (refrain from)._
umhüllen _to wrap, cover, veil._
Umkehr _f. return, change._
UMKEHREN _to turn back, turn around, turn upside down, invert, reverse._
Umkehrung _f. inversion, reversal._
umkleiden _to change clothes._
Umkreis _m. circle, circuit._
umkreisen _to revolve, circle around._
Umkreisung _f. encirclement._
Umlauf _m. rotation, revolution, circulation._
  in Umlauf setzen _to circulate._
umleiten _to divert (traffic)._
Umleitung _f. detour._
  Strassenbau! Umleitung! _Road under repair! Detour!_
umliegend _surrounding, neighboring._
umpflanzen _to transplant._
umreissen _to outline, sketch._
Umriss _m. sketch, outline, contour._
Umsatz _m. sale, turnover._
umschalten _to switch over._
Umschalter _m. switch, commutator._
UMSCHLAG _m. envelope, cover, wrapper, hem, compress, change._
umschlagen _to fell, knock down, put on, change._
umschliessen _to enclose._
umschwärmen _to swarm around._

Umschwung _m. change, revolution._
umsehen _to look back, round._
  Sie sehen sich nach einer neuen Wohnung um. _They are looking for a new apartment._
Umsicht _f. circumspection, prudence, caution._
umsichtig _cautious, prudent._
umsonst _gratis, for nothing; in vain._
UMSTAND _m. circumstances, fact._
  ohne Umstände _without ceremony._
  mildernde Umstände _extenuating circumstances._
  sich Umstände machen _to put oneself out._
  Sie ist in anderen Umständen. _She is expecting a baby._
  Umstände machen _to make a fuss._
  unter allen Umständen _in any case, by all means._
  unter keinen Umständen _on no account._
  unter gewissen Umständen _in certain circumstances._
umständlich _laborious._
Umsteige fahrschein _m. transfer-ticket._
  einen Umsteige fahrschein verlangen _to ask for a transfer._
umsteigen _to change trains._
umstimmen _to tune to another pitch._
umstritten _disputed, controversial._
Umsturz _m. downfall, revolution._
umstürzen _to throw down, overturn._
Umtausch _m. exchange._
umtauschen _to change for._
umtun _to drape around._
umwechseln _to exchange, change (money)._
Umweg _m. detour._
Umwelt _f. surroundings, environment._
umwenden _to turn, turn over._
umwerben _to court._
umwickeln _to wrap up._
umziehen _to change clothes._
Umzug _m. procession._
unabhängig _independent._
Unabhängigkeit _f. independence._
unabkömmlich _indispensable._
unablässig _incessant._
unabsehbar _incalculable._
unabsichtlich _unintentional._
unabwendbar _inevitable._
unachtsam _careless._
unangebracht _out of place._
unangefochten _undisputed._
unangemessen _inadequate, improper._
unangenehm _unpleasant, disagreeable._
unannehmbar _unacceptable._
Unannehmlichkeit _f. inconvenience, trouble._

Unansehnlichkeit *f. plainness.*
unanständig *improper, indecent.*
unappetitlich *unappetizing, uninviting.*
Unart *f. bad behavior, rudeness.*
unartig *naughty.*
unauffindbar *undiscoverable.*
unaufgefordert *unasked.*
unaufhaltsam *inevitable, impetuous.*
unaufhörlich *incessant, incessantly.*
unaufmerksam *inattentive.*
unaufrichtig *insincere.*
unausbleiblich *unfailing, certain.*
unausführbar *impracticable, not feasible.*
unaussprechlich *inexpressible.*
unausstehlich *intolerable, unbearable.*
unbarmherzig *unmerciful, pitiless, brutally.*
Unbarmherzigkeit *f. mercilessness.*
unbeabsichtigt *unintentional, undesigned.*
unbeachtet *unnoticed.*
unbeanstandet *not objected to, unopposed.*
unbeantwortet *unanswered.*
unbedachtsam *inconsiderate, thoughtless.*
unbedenklich *harmless.*
unbedeutend *insignificant, trifling.*
unbedingt *unconditional, absolute.*
    Sie müssen unbedingt dabei sein. *You must be there whatever may happen.*
unbeeinflusst *unprejudiced.*
unbefangen *impartial, unprejudiced.*
Unbefangenheit *f. impartiality; facility.*
unbefriedigend *unsatisfactory, unsatisfactorily.*
unbefriedigt *unsatisfied.*
unbefugt *incompetent.*
unbegabt *not gifted, not clever.*
unbegreiflich *inconceivable.*
unbegrenzt *unbounded, unlimited.*
unbegründet *unfounded, groundless.*
Unbehagen *n. discomfort.*
unbehaglich *uncomfortable.*
unbehelligt *undisturbed.*
unbehilflich *helpless.*
unbehindert *unrestrained.*
unbeholfen *clumsy.*
UNBEKANNT *unknown.*
    Er ist hier unbekannt. *He is a stranger here.*
unbekümmert *unconcerned.*
unbeliebt *unpopular.*
unbemerkt *unnoticed.*
UNBEQUEM *uncomfortable, inconvenient.*
Unbequemlichkeit *f. discomfort.*
unberechenbar *incalculable.*

unberechtigt *unauthorized, unjustified.*
unberührt *untouched, intact, innocent.*
unbeschädigt *undamaged, uninjured.*
unbescheiden *immodest, insolent.*
unbeschreiblich *indescribable.*
unbeschwert *light.*
unbesehen *without inspection, hesitation.*
unbesiegbar *invincible.*
Unbesonnenheit *f. indiscretion, imprudence.*
unbesorgt *unconcerned.*
    Seien Sie unbesorgt. *Don't worry.*
unbeständig *unstable, unsteady.*
unbestechlich *incorruptible.*
unbestimmt *undetermined, undefined, indefinite.*
unbestreitbar *indisputable.*
unbeträchtlich *inconsiderable.*
unbeugsam *inflexible, stubborn.*
unbewandert *inexperienced.*
unbeweglich *motionless.*
unbewohnt *uninhabited.*
unbewusst *unconscious.*
unbezahlbar *priceless.*
unbezwingbar *invincible.*
unbrauchbar *useless, of no use.*
UND *and*
    und so weiter *and so forth.*
Undank *m. ingratitude.*
undankbar *ungrateful.*
Undankbarkeit *f. ingratitude.*
undenkbar *unconceivable.*
undeutlich *indistinct, vague.*
undicht *leaky.*
Unding *n. absurdity, impossibility.*
unduldsam *intolerant.*
undurchdringlich *impenetrable.*
uneben *uneven, rough.*
unebenbürtig *inferior.*
unecht *not genuine, false, improper, artificial.*
unehelich *illegitimate.*
unehrbar *indecent, immodest.*
unehrenhaft *dishonorable.*
unehrlich *dishonest.*
uneigennützig *unselfish.*
uneinig *disunited.*
Uneinigkeit *f. discord, disagreement.*
uneins *divided.*
    uneins sein *to disagree.*
unempfindlich *insensible.*
UNENDLICH *infinite, endless, infinitely.*
    unendlich lang *endless.*
unentbehrlich *indispensable.*
unentgeltlich *free of charge.*
unentschieden *undecided.*
unentschlossen *irresolute.*
unentschuldbar *inexcusable.*

unerbittlich *inexorable.*
unerfahren *inexperienced.*
unerforschlich *impenetrable.*
unerfreulich *unpleasant, unsatisfactory.*
unerfüllbar *unrealizable.*
unerhört *unheard of, insolent.*
unerklärlich *inexplicable.*
unerlaubt *illicit, unlawful.*
unermesslich *boundless, infinite.*
unermüdlich *untiring.*
unerreichbar *inaccessible.*
unerreicht *unequaled.*
unerschrocken *fearless.*
unerschütterlich *imperturbable.*
unersetzlich *irreplaceable.*
unerträglich *unbearable, intolerable.*
unerwartet *unexpected.*
unerwünscht *undesired, unwelcome.*
unerzogen *uneducated, ill-bred.*
UNFÄHIG *incapable, unable.*
Unfähigkeit *f. inefficiency.*
Unfall *m. accident.*
Unfallversicherung *f. insurance against accidents.*
unfehlbar *certainly, surely.*
unfreiwillig *involuntary.*
unfreundlich *unfriendly, unpleasant.*
unfruchtbar *unproductive, sterile.*
Unfug *m. wrong, mischief, nonsense.*
ungebildet *uneducated.*
ungebührlich *indecent, improper.*
ungebunden *unbound, unrestrained.*
ungedeckt *uncovered (also for a check).*
ungeduldig *impatient, impatiently.*
ungeeignet *unsuitable, unfit.*
UNGEFÄHR *approximately, about, nearly.*
  von ungefähr *by chance.*
ungefährlich *harmless.*
ungehalten *angry.*
Ungeheuer *monster.*
ungeheuer *huge, enormous, vast, monstrous.*
ungehorsam *disobedient.*
ungekünstelt *unaffected, simple.*
ungelegen *inconvenient.*
ungelernt *unskilled.*
ungemütlich *uncomfortable.*
ungeniert *free and easy.*
ungeniessbar *inedible, unbearable.*
ungenügend *insufficient.*
ungepflegt *neglected, untidy.*
UNGERECHT *unjust.*
ungerechtfertigt *unjustified.*
Ungerechtigkeit *f. injustice.*
UNGERN *unwillingly, reluctant.*
ungeschehen *undone.*
Ungeschick *n. misfortune.*

Ungeschicklichkeit *f. awkwardness.*
ungeschickt *awkward, clumsy.*
ungesetzlich *illegal.*
ungestört *undisturbed.*
ungestüm *impetuous.*
ungesund *unhealthy.*
ungetreu *faithless.*
ungewiss *uncertain.*
Ungewissheit *f. uncertainty.*
ungewöhnlich *unusual, strange.*
ungewohnt *unaccustomed, unfamiliar.*
ungezogen *ill-bred, naughty.*
Unglaube *m. disbelief.*
ungläubig *incredulous.*
unglaublich *incredible.*
ungleich *unequal, unlike.*
UNGLÜCK *n. misfortune, bad luck, accident.*
unglücklich *unfortunate, unlucky.*
unglücklickerweise *unfortunately.*
Unglücksvogel *m. unlucky person.*
Ungnade *f. disgrace, displeasure.*
  in Ungnade fallen bei *to displease someone.*
ungültig *void, invalid.*
  für ungültig erkären *to annul.*
ungut
  Nichts für ungut. *No harm meant.*
Unheil *n. mischief, harm, disaster.*
unheilbar *incurable, irreparable.*
unheilvoll *disastrous.*
unheimlich *sinister.*
unhöflich *impolite, rude.*
Uniform *f. uniform.*
UNIVERSITÄT *f. university, college.*
unkenntlich *unrecognizable.*
Unkenntnis *f. ignorance.*
unklar *not clear.*
unklug *imprudent, unwise.*
Unkosten *pl. expenses.*
Unkraut *n. weeds.*
unleserlich *illegible.*
unliebenswürdig *unamiable, unkind.*
unlogisch *illogical.*
unmässig *immoderate, disproportionate.*
unmenschlich *inhuman.*
Unmenschlichkeit *f. inhumanity, cruelty.*
unmerklich *imperceptible.*
unmittelbar *immediate.*
UNMÖBLIERT *unfurnished.*
unmodern *old-fashioned, antiquated.*
UNMÖGLICH *impossible.*
Unmöglichkeit *f. impossibility.*
unmoralisch *immoral.*
unmündig *minor.*
  unmündig sein *to be a minor.*
unnachsichtig *strict, severe.*
unnahbar *unapproachable, inaccessible.*

unnatürlich *unnatural, affected.*
UNNÖTIG *unnecessary, needless.*
unordentlich *disorderly, untidy.*
UNORDNUNG *f. disorder.*
　in Unordnung bringen *to mess up.*
unparteiisch *impartial.*
unpassend *inappropriate.*
unpässlich *indisposed, ailing.*
unpersönlich *impersonal.*
unpraktisch *impractical.*
unpünktlich *unpunctual.*
Unrecht *n. injustice.*
　im Unrecht *in the wrong.*
　Unrecht haben *to be wrong.*
　zu Unrecht *unlawfully, unjustly.*
UNRECHT *wrong, unjust, unfair.*
unredlich *dishonest.*
unregelmässig *irregular.*
unreif *unripe.*
unrein *unclean.*
　ins Unreine schreiben *to make a*
　rough copy.
Unruhe *f. uneasiness.*
Unruhen *pl. riots.*
unruhig *restless, uneasy.*
Unruhstifter *m. agitator.*
UNS *acc. and dat. of the pers. pron.*
　wir; reflexive and reciprocal pron.: us,
　to us, ourselves, each other.
unsachlich *subjective, personal.*
unsagbar *unspeakable.*
unsauber *dirty, filthy.*
Unsauberkeit *f. dirt, filth.*
unschädlich *harmless.*
　unschädlich machen *to render*
　harmless, neutralize, disarm.
unschätzbar *invaluable.*
unscheinbar *insignificant, plain, homely.*
unschlüssig *wavering, irresolute.*
UNSCHULDIG *innocent.*
unselbständig *helpless, dependent.*
UNSER *Poss. adj. our.*
UNSER *(er, -e -es) Poss. pron. ours.*
unsereins *people like us.*
unsererseits *as for us, for our part.*
unseresgleichen *people like us.*
unseresthalben *for our sakes, on our*
　behalf.
unseretwegen *for our sakes.*
unseretwillen *for our sakes.*
UNSICHER *unsafe, uncertain, unsteady.*
Unsicherheit *f. insecurity, uncertainty.*
Unsinn *m. nonsense.*
Unsitte *f. bad habit, abuse.*
unsterblich *immortal.*
unstet *changeable, unsteady.*
unsympathisch *unpleasant.*
untätig *inactive.*
untauglich *useless; unfit (sports, army).*

UNTEN *below, beneath, underneath.*
　von oben bis unten *from top to*
　bottom, from head to foot.
UNTER 1. *Prep. (dat. when answering*
　question, Wo?; acc. when answering
　question, Wohin?, and depending on
　the idiom): under, underneath, below,
　beneath, among, during, by.
　Ich habe meine Schuhe unter das Bett
　gestellt. *I put my shoes under the*
　bed.
　Ich sass unter den Zuschauern. *I sat*
　among the spectators.
　Unter anderem hat sie mir gesagt . . .
　Among other things, she told me . . .
　unter freiem Himmel *in the open air.*
　unter uns gesagt *between us.*
　unter vier Augen *privately ("under four*
　eyes").
　2. *Prefix. a) separable (when meaning*
　under).
　Die Sonne geht im Westen unter. *The*
　sun sets in the West.
　b) *inseparable when not meaning*
　under.
　Wir unterhielten uns über die Ferien.
　We talked about the holidays.
unterbauen *to lay a foundation.*
unterbelichten *to underexpose (photo).*
Unterbewusstsein *n. sub-conscious.*
unterbieten *to undersell.*
UNTERBRECHEN *to interrupt,*
　disconnect, cut off.
　Fräulein, wir sind unterbrochen worden.
　Operator, we have been cut off.
Unterbrechung *f. interruption.*
unterbringen *to put up, accommodate,*
　place.
unterdessen *meanwhile, in the*
　meantime.
unterdrücken *to oppress, suppress.*
Unterdrückung *f. repression,*
　oppression.
untereinander *among ourselves,*
　reciprocally.
Unterernährung *f. malnutrition.*
Unterführung *f. underpass.*
Untergang *m. setting, going down,*
　destruction, fall; decline.
　der Sonnenuntergang *the sunset.*
Untergebene *m. & f. subordinate.*
UNTERGEHEN *to go down, set, sink.*
Untergrundbahn *f. subway.*
unterhalb *below.*
Unterhalt *m. maintenance, living.*
UNTERHALTEN *to support, maintain,*
　keep up.
　sich gut unterhalten *to have a good*
　time.

sich unterhalten *to converse, talk.*
unterhandeln *to negotiate.*
Unterhemd *n. vest.*
Unterhosen *pl. shorts, drawers.*
unterirdisch *underground.*
Unterkleidung *f. underwear.*
unterkommen *to find accommodation, find a situation.*
Unterkunft *f. accommodation.*
Unterlage *f. foundation, support, evidence, pad.*
Unterlass *m. stopping*
ohne Unterlass *incessantly.*
unterlassen *to omit, neglect, fail to.*
unterlegen *to lay under, put under.*
unterliegen *to be defeated.*
Unterlippe *f. lower lip.*
Untermieter *m. subtenant.*
UNTERNEHMEN *to undertake, attempt.*
unternehmend *enterprising.*
Unternehmer, *m. contractor.*
Unternehmung *f. enterprise, undertaking.*
unterordnen *to subordinate, submit.*
Unterordnung *f. subordination.*
unterreden *to converse, confer with.*
Unterredung *f. talk, conference.*
UNTERRICHT *m. instruction, teaching, education, lesson.*
unterrichten *to teach, instruct.*
Unterrock *m. slip, petticoat.*
unterschätzen *to underestimate, underrate.*
unterscheiden *to distinguish, differentiate, discriminate.*
sich unterscheiden *to differ.*
Unterscheidung *f. distinction, discrimination.*
UNTERSCHIED *m. difference.*
ohne Unterschied *alike.*
unterschiedlich *different, distinct.*
unterschiedslos *indiscriminately.*
unterschlagen *to embezzle.*
Unterschlagung *f. embezzlement.*
unterschreiben *to sign.*
Unterschrift *f. signature.*
Unterseeboot *n. submarine.*
unterstehen *to stand under, be subordinate.*
sich unterstehen *to dare.*
unterstützen *to support, aid, assist.*
Unterstützung *f. support, aid, relief.*
untersuchen *to examine, investigate.*
Untersuchung *f. examination, investigation.*
Untertasse *f. saucer.*
Untertitel *m. subtitle (movie).*
Unterwäsche *f. underwear.*
unterwegs *on the way.*

unterweisen *to instruct.*
Unterweisung *f. instruction.*
Unterwelt *f. underworld.*
unterwerfen *to subjugate.*
unterwürfig *submissive.*
unterzeichnen *to sign, ratify.*
Unterzeichner *m. signatory.*
Unterzeichnung *f. signature, ratification.*
untragbar *not transferable, not negotiable; unbearable.*
untrennbar *inseparable.*
UNTREU *untrue, unfaithful.*
untröstlich *disconsolate.*
Untugend *f. vice, bad habit.*
unübersehbar *immense, vast.*
unübertrefflich *unequaled.*
ununterbrochen *continuously.*
unverantwortlich *irresponsible.*
unverbesserlich *incorrigible.*
unverbindlich *not obligatory, without obligation.*
unverdient *undeserved.*
unverdorben *unspoilt, pure.*
unvergänglich *imperishable, immortal.*
unvergleichlich *incomparable.*
unverheiratet *unmarried.*
unverhofft *unexpected.*
unverkennbar *unmistakable.*
unverletzt *unhurt, uninjured.*
unvermeidlich *inevitable.*
Unvermögen *n. inability, incapacity.*
unvermutet *unexpected.*
unvernünftig *unreasonable.*
unverrichtet *unperformed.*
unverrichteter Sache *unsuccessfully.*
unverschämt *impudent, fresh.*
unversehens *unexpectedly.*
unversehrt *intact, safe.*
unverständlich *unintelligible, incomprehensible.*
unverwüstlich *indestructible, inexhaustible.*
unverzeihlich *unpardonable.*
unverzollt *duty unpaid.*
unverzüglich *immediate.*
unvollkommen *imperfect.*
unvollständig *incomplete, defective.*
unvorhergesehen *unforeseen.*
UNVORSICHTIG *careless.*
unvorteilhaft *unprofitable, unbecoming.*
unweiblich *unwomanly.*
unweit *not far off, near.*
Unwesen *n. mischief, abuse.*
sein Unwesen treiben *to be up to one's tricks.*
unwesentlich *unessential, immaterial.*
Das ist ganz unwesentlich. *That does not matter.*

Unwetter *n. storm, hurricane.*
unwiderruflich *irrevocable.*
unwiderstehlich *irrestisble.*
Unwille *m indignation.*
unwillkommen *unwelcome.*
unwillkürlich *instinctively, involuntarily.*
unwirksam *ineffective, inefficient.*
unwirtlich *inhospitable, dreary.*
unwirtschaftlich *uneconomic.*
unwissend *ignorant.*
UNWOHL *not well, indisposed.*
Unwohlsein *n. indisposition.*
unwürdig *unworthy.*
Unzahl *f. endless number.*
unzählig *countless.*
unzeitgemäss *inopportune, out of season.*
unzerbrechlich *unbreakable.*
unzivilisiert *uncivilized, barbarian.*
unzufrieden *dissatisfied.*
unzulänglich *inadequate.*
unzulässig *forbidden.*
unzureichend *insufficient.*
unzuverlässig *unreliable.*
unzweideutig *unequivocal, unambiguous.*
unzweifelhaft *undoubted, indubitable.*
üppig *luxuriant, abundant, voluptuous.*
Üppigkeit *f. luxury.*
uralt *very old, ancient.*
Uraufführung *f. first performance, opening night.*
Ureinwohner *m. original inhabitant.*
Urgrosseltern *pl. great-grandparents.*
Urkunde *f. deed, document, record.*
Urkundenfälscher *m. forger of documents.*
urkundlich *documentary, authentic.*
Urlaub *m. leave, furlough, vacation.*
der bezahlte Urlaub *the paid vacation.*
URSACHE *f. cause, reason.*
Keine Ursache! *Don't mention it!*
Ursprung *m. source, origin.*
ursprünglich *original, primitive.*
URTEIL *n. judgment, decision, sentence, opinion.*
urteilen *to judge, pass a sentence, give an opinion.*
urteilsfähig *competent to judge.*
urteilslos *without judgment.*
Urteilsspruch *m. sentence, verdict.*

V

Vagabund *m. vagabond.*
Vanille *f. vanilla.*

Variante *f. variant.*
Variation *f. variation.*
Varieté *n. music-hall.*
variieren *to vary.*
Vase *f. vase.*
Vaselin *n. vaseline.*
VATER *m. father.*
Vaterhaus *n. home.*
Vaterland *n. native land, fatherland.*
vaterländisch *national, patriotic.*
vaterlandsliebend *patriotic.*
väterlicherseits *on the father's side.*
vaterlos *fatherless.*
Vaterstadt *f. native town.*
vegetarisch *vegetarian.*
Veilchen *n. violet.*
Vene *f. vein.*
Ventil *n. valve.*
verabreden *to agree upon, make an agreement.*
verabredet sein *to have a date or appointment.*
Verabredung *f. agreement, engagement; appointment.*
verabreichen *to give, dispense.*
verabscheuen *to detest.*
verabschieden *to dismiss, discharge.*
sich verabschieden *to say good-bye.*
verachten *to despise, scorn, disdain.*
verächtlich *contemptuous, disdainful.*
Verachtung *f. contempt, scorn, disdain.*
verallgemeinern *to generalize.*
veraltet *old, obsolete.*
veränderlich *variable, unstable.*
VERÄNDERN *to change, alter, vary.*
Veränderung *f. change, alteration, variation.*
verängstigt *intimidated.*
veranlagt *inclined.*
gut veranlagt sein *to be talented.*
Veranlagung *f. talent.*
veranlassen *to cause.*
Veranlassung *f. reason, suggestion.*
veranschlagen *to estimate.*
zu hoch veranschlagen *to overrate.*
veranstalten *to arrange, organize, set up.*
Veranstaltung *f. arrangement, organization.*
verantworten *to answer for, account for.*
verantwortlich *responsible.*
VERANTWORTUNG *f. responsibility.*
auf seine Verantwortung *at his own risk.*
zur Verantwortung ziehen *to call to account.*
verantwortungslos *irresponsible.*
verarbeiten *to use, work up, manufacture.*

Verarbeitung f. manufacturing.
Verband m. bandage, association.
verbannen to banish, exile.
Verbannung f. banishment, exile.
VERBESSERN to improve, correct.
Verbesserung f. improvement, correction.
verbeugen to bow.
Verbeugung f. bow.
verbiegen to bend, twist.
verbieten to forbid.
  Rauchen verboten! No smoking!
  Strengstens verboten! Strictly forbidden!
verbinden to tie, bind, bandage, connect, combine, join.
  Fräulein, Sie haben mich falsch verbunden! Operator, you gave me the wrong number!
  sich verbinden to unite.
  sich zu Dank verbunden fühlen to feel indebted to.
verbindlich obligatory, courteous.
Verbindlichkeit f. obligation.
VERBINDUNG f. union, combination.
  sich in Verbindung setzen mit to get in touch with.
verblüffen to disconcert.
verblüffend amazing.
Verblüffung f. stupefaction, amazement.
verbluten to bleed to death.
verborgen hidden, concealed, secret.
Verborgenheit f. concealment, retirement, seclusion.
Verbot n. prohibition, ban.
verboten prohibited, forbidden.
Vorbrauch m. consumption.
verbrauchen to consume, use.
Verbraucher m. consumer.
Verbrechen n. crime.
  ein Verbrechen vergehen to commit a crime.
Verbrecher m. criminal.
verbrecherisch criminal.
verbreiten to spread, diffuse.
verbrennen to burn, cremate.
  sich verbrennen to burn oneself.
Verbrennung f. burning, combustion.
verbringen to spend, pass time.
verbunden obliged.
verbürgen to guarantee.
Verdacht m. suspicion.
verdächtig suspicious.
verdächtigen to distrust.
Verdächtigung f. insinuation, false charge.
verdammen to condemn.
verdammenswert damnable.

Verdammnis f. damnation.
Verdammung f. condemnation.
verdanken to owe something.
Verderb m. ruin.
Verderben n. ruin, destruction.
  jemanden ins Verderben stürzen to ruin a person.
VERDERBEN to spoil, ruin.
  Ich möchte es mir nicht mit ihm verderben. I don't want to displease him.
  sich den Magen verderben to upset one's stomach.
Verderber m. corrupter.
verderblich pernicious.
verdienen to earn, gain, deserve, merit.
Verdienst m. gain, profit.
Verdienst n. merit.
verdienstlich deserving.
verdienstvoll deserving.
verdient deserving.
  sich verdient machen um to deserve well of.
Verdikt n. verdict.
verdingen (sich) to take a situation.
verdolmetschen to interpret.
verdoppeln to double.
verdorben spoilt.
verdrängen to displace, push aside.
verdrehen to twist, sprain.
  einem den Kopf verdrehen to turn one's head.
verdummen to grow stupid.
verdünnen to thin, dilute.
Verdünnung f. attenuation, rarefaction, dilution.
verdunsten to evaporate.
Verdunstung f. evaporation.
verdursten to die of thirst.
veredeln to ennoble, improve, refine, finish.
verehren to respect, worship, adore.
Verehrer m. worshipper.
Verehrung f. respect.
vereidigen to swear in, put on oath.
Vereidigung f. swearing in, taking of an oath.
Verein m. union, association.
vereinbar compatible, consistent.
Vereinbarung f. agreement.
vereinfachen to simplify.
vereinigen to join, unite, reconcile.
  die Vereinigten Staaten von Amerika. The United States of America.
vereisen to turn to ice.
vereiteln to frustrate, thwart.
verelenden to sink into poverty.
vererben to bequeath, transmit, hand down.

verewigen to perpetuate, immortalize.
Verfall m. decay, ruin.
  im Verfall geraten to go to ruin, decay.
verfallen to decline, go to ruin, grow
  weaker, expire.
  einem verfallen to become dependent
    on a person.
  verfallen lassen to let go to waste.
  verfallene Züge sunken features.
verfassen to compose, write.
Verfasser m. author, writer.
Verfassung f. state, condition.
verfechten to stand up for.
verfliegen to fly away, disappear,
  vanish.
verfolgen to follow, pursue, prosecute.
  heimlich verfolgen to shadow.
  gerichtlich verfolgen to prosecute.
Verfolgung f. pursuit, prosecution.
verfügbar available.
verfügen to arrange, decree, obtain.
  verfügen über to dispose of, have at
    one's disposal.
  zur Verfügung stellen to place at
    one's disposal.
verführen to induce, prevail upon,
  seduce.
Verführer m. tempter, seducer.
verführerisch tempting, seductive.
Verführung f. temptation.
Vergangenheit f. past; past tense
  (grammar).
vergänglich transitory, perishable.
Vergaser m. carburetor.
vergeben to give away, dispose of,
  confer, forgive.
vergebens in vain, vainly.
Vergebung f. pardon, forgiveness.
vergelten to pay back, repay, retaliate.
Vergeltung f. return, recompense.
VERGESSEN to forget, neglect.
vergesslich forgetful.
Vergesslichkeit f. forgetfulness.
vergiften to poison.
Vergiftung f. poisoning.
Vergleich m. comparison, agreement,
  arrangement.
VERGLEICHEN to compare, check,
  settle.
VERGNÜGEN n. pleasure, joy, fun.
vergnügen (sich) to amuse, enjoy
  oneself.
VERGNÜGT pleased, glad.
  Ich komme mit Vergnügen. I'll be
    delighted to come.
  Viel Vergnügen! Have a good time!
  Vergnügungsreise, f. pleasure trip.
vergnügungssüchtig pleasure-seeking.
vergraben to bury, hide in the ground.

vergrössern to enlarge, magnify.
Vergrösserung f. enlargement.
Vergünstigung f. privilege.
Verhältnis n. relation, ratio, love-affair.
verhältnismässig relative, proportional.
verhasst hated, hateful, odious.
verheimlichen to conceal, keep secret.
verheiraten to marry off.
verherrlichen to glorify.
Verherrlichung f. glorification.
verhindern to hinder, prevent.
Verhinderung f. hindrance, draw-back.
Verhör n. examination.
verhören to examine, interrogate.
verhungern to die of hunger.
verirren to lose one's way, go astray.
VERKAUF m. sale.
VERKAUFEN to sell.
  billiger verkaufen to undersell.
  zu verkaufen for sale.
VERKÄUFER m. (-in, f.) sales person.
verkäuflich for sale.
VERKEHR m. traffic, circulation,
  communication, trade.
verkehren to associate, transform,
  convert, change, run (buses).
  verkehren mit to associate with, see a
    good deal of.
Verkehrsampel f. signal light.
Verkehrsschutzmann m. traffic
  policeman.
Verkehrsunfall m. traffic-accident.
verkehrt wrong, backwards, upside
  down, absurd.
  verkehrt gehen to go the wrong way.
verkennen to fail to recognize, mistake,
  misunderstand, undervalue.
verkleiden to disguise, camouflage.
Verkleidung f. disguise, camouflage.
verkommen to be ruined, become bad,
  degenerate.
Verkommenheit f. depravity,
  degeneracy.
verkörpern to personify, incarnate,
  embody.
Verlag m. publication, publishing firm.
verlangen to demand, desire, require.
  auf Verlangen by request, on demand.
  verlangen nach to long for.
verlängern to extend, prolong.
Verlängerung f. extension, prolonging.
Verlass m. trustworthiness.
  Auf ihn ist kein Verlass. He cannot be
    relied on.
VERLASSEN to leave, abandon, desert.
verlegen embarrassed, self-conscious,
  confused.
  um etwas verlegen sein to be at a
    loss for.

um Geld verlegen sein *to be short of money.*

Verlegenheit *f. embarrassment, difficulty.*

Verleger *m. publisher.*

verleihen *to lend out, confer, bestow, grant.*

verletzbar *vulnerable, susceptible.*

verletzen *to hurt, injure, offend.*

Verletzung *f. injury, offense, violation.*

verleugnen *to deny, injure, offend.*

Verleugnung *f. denial, denunciation.*

verleumden *to calumniate, slander.*

Verleumder *m. slanderer.*

verleumderisch *slanderous.*

Verleumdung *f. slander, defamation, libel.*

VERLIEBEN (sich) *to fall in love.*

verliebt *in love.*
  Sie ist verliebt bis über die Ohren.
  She is head over heels in love.

VERLIEREN *to lose, waste, disappear.*
  An ihm ist nicht viel verloren. *He's no great loss.*
  Ich habe keinen einzigen Augenblick zu verlieren. *I don't have a single moment to lose.*

verloben (sich) *to get engaged.*

Verlobte *m. & f. fiancé(e).*

Verlobung *f. engagement.*

Verlust *m. loss, waste, escape.*

vermehren *to increase.*

Vermehrung *f. increase.*

vermieten *to rent, let, hire out.*

Vermieter *m. landlord.*

vermissen *to miss.*

vermuten *to suppose, presume, suspect.*

vermutlich *presumable, probable.*

vernachlässigen *to neglect.*

Vernachlässigung *f. neglect.*

verneigen *to bow.*

Verneigung *f. bow.*

vernichten *to annihilate, destroy.*

Vernichtung *f. annihilation, destruction.*

VERNUNFT *f. reason, understanding, intelligence, good sense, judgment.*
  Vernunft annehmen *to listen to reason.*
  zur Vernunft bringen *to bring to one's senses.*

veröffentlichen *to publish.*

Veröffentlichung *f. publication.*

verordnen *to order, decree.*

Verordnung *f. order, decree, prescription.*

verpacken *to pack up, wrap up.*

Verpackung *f. packing up, wrapping up.*

verpfänden *to pawn, mortgage.*

verpflegen *to feed, board.*

Verpflegung *f. feeding, board, food.*
  Zimmer mit Verpflegung. *Room and board.*

verpflichten *to oblige, bind, engage.*
  sich verpflichten *to commit (bind) oneself.*
  verpflichtet sein *to be under obligation.*

Verpflichtung *f. obligation, duty, engagement.*

Verrat *m. treason, betrayal.*

verraten *to betray, disclose, reveal.*

Verräter *m. traitor.*

verräterisch *treacherous.*

verrechnen *to reckon up, charge, account; miscalculate.*

Verrechnung *f. settling of an account, reckoning.*

verreisen *to go away.*
  verreist sein *to be away.*

verrichten *to execute, perform, accomplish.*
  die Hausarbeit verrichten *to do the housework.*

Verrichtung *f. execution, performance, function, work.*

VERRÜCKT *crazy, mad.*

Vers *m. verse, stanza.*

versagen *to deny, refuse; fail, miss.*

VERSAMMELN *to assemble, bring together, gather.*
  sich versammeln *to gather.*

versäumen *to neglect, omit, miss.*

Versäumnis *f. n. neglect, omission.*

verschenken *to give away.*

verschicken *to send away, dispatch, evacuate.*

Verschickung *f. dispatch, transportation, evacuation.*

VERSCHIEDEN *different from, distinct, various.*

verschlafen *to oversleep, sleepy.*

verschlimmern *to aggravate.*

Verschlimmerung *f. deterioration.*

verschlissen *worn out, threadbare.*

verschlucken *to swallow the wrong way.*

Verschluss *m. lock, fastener, clasp, seal, plug, zipper.*

verschmachten *to languish.*

verschonen *to spare, exempt from.*

verschönern *to beautify, embellish, adorn.*

Verschönerung *f. embellishment.*

verschreiben *to prescribe, order in writing, write for.*
  sich verschreiben *to make a mistake in writing.*

verschwägert *related by marriage.*

verschwenden *to waste, lavish.*
Verschwender *m. spendthrift, extravagant person.*
verschwenderisch *wasteful, extravagant.*
verschwiegen *discreet, close.*
Verschwiegenheit *f. secrecy, discretion.*
verschwistert *like brothers and sisters, closely united.*
Versehen *n. mistake, oversight.*
VERSEHEN *to provide, furnish, supply with; to overlook.*
  ehe man sich's versieht *unexpectedly, suddenly.*
  sich versehen *to make a mistake.*
versehentlich *by mistake.*
VERSETZEN *to displace, transfer, pledge, pawn.*
  den Verstand verlieren *to go out of one's mind. Just put yourself in my place.*
Versetzung *f. transfer, moving up.*
VERSICHERN *to insure, affirm.*
Versicherung *f. insurance.*
versöhnen *to reconcile, conciliate.*
Versöhnung *f. reconciliation.*
versorgen *to provide, supply.*
Versorger *m. support, breadwinner.*
Versorgung *f. supply.*
verspätet *late.*
Verspätung *f. delay, lateness.*
  Verspätung haben *to be late.*
verspielen *to lose, gamble away.*
VERSPRECHEN *to promise.*
  Ich habe mich nur versprochen. *It was only a slip of the tongue.*
  sich etwas versprechen von *to expect much of.*
Versprechung *f. promise.*
VERSTAND *m. mind, sense, brain, intellect.*
  den Verstand verlieren *to go out of one's mind.*
  zu Verstand kommen *to arrive at the age of discretion.*
verständig *intelligent, sensible, wise.*
verständigen *to inform, notify.*
  sich verständigen *to come to an understanding with.*
verständlich *understandable, clear, comprehensible.*
  sich verständlich machen *to make oneself understood.*
Verständlichkeit *f. intelligibility, clearness.*
Verständnis *comprehension, understanding.*
  Verständnis haben für *to appreciate.*

verständnislos *unappreciative, stupid.*
verständnisvoll *understanding, appreciative.*
Versteck *n. hiding place.*
verstecken *to hide, conceal.*
versteckt *hidden, concealed.*
  versteckte Absichten *ulterior motives.*
VERSTEHEN *to understand, comprehend, know.*
  falsch verstehen *to misunderstand.*
  Ich verstehe nicht! *I don't understand!*
  sich verstehen *to understand each other.*
  sich von selbst verstehen *to go without saying.*
  Was verstehen Sie darunter? *What do you understand by that?*
  zu verstehen geben *to give to understand.*
versteifen *to stiffen.*
  sich versteifen auf *to insist on.*
versteigern *to sell at auction.*
Versteigerung *f. auction.*
verstellbar *adjustable.*
verstellen *to change order or position, block, disguise.*
  sich verstellen *to put on an act.*
Verstellung *f. dissimulation, disguise, hypocrisy.*
versteuern *to pay duty on.*
verstimmen *to annoy, upset.*
Verstimmung *f. ill humor, bad temper.*
Versuch *m. experiment, trial.*
VERSUCHEN *to try, attempt, taste, sample.*
  es versuchen mit *to give a trial to, put to the test.*
Versuchung *f. temptation.*
vertagen *to adjourn.*
vertauschen *to exchange.*
verteidigen *to defend.*
Verteidiger *m. defender, advocate, attorney.*
Verteidigung *f. defense.*
verteilen *to distribute, dispense, assign.*
Verteilung *f. distribution.*
Vertrag *m. contract, treaty, agreement.*
VERTRAGEN *to carry away, bear, stand, endure, tolerate, digest.*
  ich kann diese Speise nicht vertragen. *This food does not agree with me.*
  sich vertragen *to get along.*
  sich wieder vertragen *to settle one's differences.*
Vertrauen *n. confidence.*
vertrauen *to trust.*
vertrauensvoll *confident.*
vertrauenwürdig *trustworthy.*
vertraulich *confidential.*

vertraut *familiar.*
im Vertrauen *in confidence, confidentially.*
im Vertrauen auf *relying on, trusting to.*
sich vertraut machen *to become familiar.*
Vertraute *m. f. intimate friend.*
vertreten *to represent, substitute for; to sprain.*
Vertreter *m. representative, substitute.*
VERTRETUNG *f. representation, replacement.*
eine Vertretung übernehmen *to take the place of, represent.*
vertrösten *to put off, console.*
verunglücken *to have an accident.*
verurteilen *to sentence, condemn.*
Verurteilung *f. sentence, condemnation.*
vervielfältigen *to multiply, duplicate, reproduce.*
verwahren *to keep, put away.*
verwaisen *to become an orphan.*
verwaist *orphaned, deserted.*
verwandt *related, similar, allied.*
Verwandte *m. f. relation, relative.*
Verwandtschaft *f. relationship, relations.*
verwechseln *to take for, mistake for.*
Verwechslung *f. mistake, confusion.*
verweigern *to deny, refuse.*
Verweigerung *f. denial, refusal.*
Verweis *m. reproof, reprimand, reference.*
Verweisung *f. exile, banishment.*
VERWENDEN *to use, utilize, employ, expend.*
sich verwenden für *to put in a good word for.*
verwenden auf *to put in on, spend on.*
Verwendung *f. use, utilization, application.*
verwirklichen *to realize, materialize.*
Verwirklichung *f. realization, materialization.*
Verwöhnung *f. spoiling, pampering.*
verwunderlich *astonishing, surprising.*
verwundern *to surprise.*
Verwunderung *f. surprise, astonishment.*
verzagen *to lose heart, despair.*
VERZEIHEN *to pardon, forgive, excuse.*
Verzeihen Sie! *Excuse me!*
verzeihlich *excusable.*
VERZEIHUNG *f. pardon, excuse.*
Ich bitte Sie um Verzeihung! *Please excuse me!*
Verzicht *m. resignation, renunciation.*
verzichten *to renounce, resign, give up.*

verzinsen *to pay interest on.*
verzögern *to delay.*
verzollen *to pay duty on.*
Haben Sie etwas zu verzollen? *Have you anything to declare?*
Verzollung *f. payment of duty, clearance.*
verzweifeln *to despair.*
verzweifelt *desperate, despairing.*
Verzweiflung *f. despair, desperation.*
zur Verzweiflung bringen *to drive one mad.*
Veto *n. veto.*
Veto einlegen *to veto a thing.*
VETTER *m. cousin.*
Vieh *n. cattle.*
Viehhändler *m. cattle dealer.*
VIEL *much, a great deal, a lot of.*
ein bisschen viel *a little too much.*
in vielem *in many respects.*
noch einmal so viel *as much again.*
viele *many.*
sehr viele *many (people).*
Viel Glück! *Lots of luck!*
Viel Vergnügen! *Have a good time!*
vielerlei *many kind of.*
VIELLEICHT *perhaps.*
vielseitig *many-sided, versatile.*
VIER *four.*
zu vieren, zu viert *four of us.*
Viereck *n. square.*
viereckig *square, quadrangular.*
VIERTE *fourth.*
VIERTEL *n. quarter, fourth.*
Es ist viertel vor zwei. *It is a quarter to two.*
vierteljährlich *quarterly.*
Viertelstunde *f. a quarter of an hour.*
viertelstündlich *every quarter of an hour.*
VIERZEHN *fourteen*
vierzehn Tage *two weeks.*
VIERZEHNTE *fourteenth.*
VIERZIG *forty.*
VIERZIGSTE *fortieth.*
Viola *f. viola.*
Violine *f. violin.*
virtuos *masterly.*
Virtuose *m. virtuoso.*
Virtuosität *f. virtuosity.*
Vision *f. vision.*
Visite *f. visit.*
Visitenkarte *f. visiting-card.*
Vitrine *f. show-case.*
VOGEL *m. bird.*
den Vogel abschiessen *to carry off the prize.*
Vogelscheuche *f. scarecrow.*
Vokabel *f. word.*

Vokabelschatz *m. vocabulary (range).*

VOLK *n. people, nation, crowd.*

das arbeitende Volk *the working classes.*

das gemeine Volk *the mob.*

der Mann aus dem Volk *the man in the street.*

Volksabstimmung *f. plebiscite.*

Volkslied *n. folk song.*

Volksschule *f. elementary or primary school.*

volkstümlich *national, popular.*

volkstümliche Preise *popular prices.*

Volksversammlung *f. public meeting.*

Volkswagen *m. people's car.*

VOLL 1. *adj. & adv. full, filled, complete, whole, entire; fully, completely.*

aus vollem Herzen *from the bottom of the heart.*

aus voller Kehle *at the top of one's voice.*

den Mund voll nehmen *to boast.*

Die Rechnung ist voll bezahlt. *The bill is paid in full.*

in voller Fahrt *at full speed.*

Man kann ihn nicht für voll nehmen. *One cannot take him too seriously.*

2. *Prefix.* a) *separable (meaning to fill)*

Sie giesst die Gläser voll. *She fills up the glasses.*

b) *inseparable (meaning to accomplish, finish).*

Er vollführte eine gute Leistung. *He executed a good performance.*

Vollbart *m. beard.*

vollblutig *full-blooded.*

vollbringen *to finish, accomplish, complete.*

Volldampf *m. full steam.*

völlig *complete, entire, quite.*

volljährig *of age.*

Volljährigkeit *f. majority (of age).*

VOLLKOMMEN *perfect, complete.*

Vollkommenheit *f. perfection.*

Vollkraft *f. full vigor.*

Vollmacht *f. full power, power of attorney.*

Vollmilch *f. unskimmed milk.*

Vollmond *m. full moon.*

vollständig *complete.*

vollzählig *complete, full, completely, absolutely.*

VON 1. *prep. (dat.). from, by, with, of, on, upon, about.*

Amerika wurde von Kolumbus entdeckt. *America was discovered by Columbus.*

Der Platz war voll von Menschen. *The place was full of people.*

ein Gedicht von Heine *a poem by Heine.*

eine Feder von Gold *a gold pen.*

von heute ab *from today on.*

Von meinem Fenster sehe ich auf den Garten. *From my window I see the garden.*

2. *adv.: apart, separate.*

von einander *apart.*

von klein auf *from childhood (on).*

von mir aus *as far I am concerned.*

von selbst *by itself, automatically.*

von Nutzen sein *to be needful, necessary.*

VOR 1. *prep. (dat. when answering question, Wo?; acc. when answering question, Wohin?, and depending on the idiom). before, in front of, ahead of, for, with, against, from.*

Das Bild ist vor mir. *The picture is in front of me.*

Es ist ein viertel vor elf. *It is a quarter to eleven.*

Ich werde sie vor ihm warnen. *I will warn her against him.*

nach wie vor *as usual.*

nicht vor *not until.*

vor acht Tagen *a week ago.*

vor allem *above all, first of all.*

vor der Klasse *before class.*

vor Hunger sterben *to die of hunger.*

Vor ihm müssen Sie sich in Acht nehmen. *With him, you must be on your guard.*

vorzeiten *formerly*

vorab *above all.*

2. *separable prefix (implies movement forward, presentation, demonstration).*

Der Lehrer las ein Gedicht vor. *The teacher read a poem aloud.*

Die Soldaten rückten vor. *The soldiers moved forward.*

Wir bereiten uns auf die Prüfung vor. *We prepare ourselves for the examination.*

vorahnen *to have a presentiment.*

Vorahnung *f. presentiment.*

voran *ahead, before.*

vorangehen *to precede.*

mit gutem Beispiel vorangehen *to set a good example.*

Voranschlag *m. estimate.*

Voranzeige *f. preliminary advertisement.*

Vorarbeit *f. preliminary work.*

Vorarbeiter *m. foreman.*

VORAUS *in front of, ahead of.*

etwas voraus haben vor *to have an advantage over a person.*

im Voraus *in advance.*

weit voraus *way ahead.*

vorausgehen *to lead the way, precede.*

voraussetzen *to presuppose, assume.*

Voraussetzung *f. supposition, assumption.*

voraussichtlich *presumable, probable.*

Vorbehalt *m. reservation, proviso.*

ohne Vorbehalt *unconditionally*

unter Vorbehalt aller Rechte *all rights reserved.*

vorbehalten *to keep in reserve, withhold.*

sich vorbehalten *to reserve to oneself.*

vorbehaltlos *unconditional.*

vorbei *by, along, past, over, gone.*

vorbeireden (aneinander) *to be at cross-purposes.*

vorbereiten *to prepare, make ready.*

Vorbereitung *f. preparation.*

vorbeugen *to hinder, prevent.*

Vorbeugungsmassregel *f. preventive measure.*

Vorbild *n. model, pattern, standard.*

vorbildlich *model, ideal.*

Vorbildung *f. preparatory training, education.*

vorder *fore, forward, anterior.*

Vordergrund *m. foreground.*

Vorderhaus *n. front part of the house.*

vordringlich *urgent.*

voreilig *hasty.*

Voreiligkeit *f. precipitation, rashness.*

voreingenommen *prejudiced.*

Voreingenommenheit *f. prejudice.*

vorenthalten *to keep back, withhold.*

Vorfall *m. occurrence, event.*

vorfallen *to occur, happen, take place.*

Vorfreude *f. joy of anticipation.*

vorführen *to demonstrate, produce.*

Vorführung *f. demonstration.*

Vorgang *m. occurrence.*

Vorgänger *m. predecessor.*

VORGEHEN *to go on, go forward, go first, lead, take place, occur, act, be of special importance.*

Gehen Sie schon vor! *Go right ahead!*

Vorgeschichte *f. previous history.*

Vorgeschmack *m. foretaste.*

Vorgesetzte *m. & f. chief, boss*

VORGESTERN *the day before yesterday.*

vorhaben *to have on, wear, to intend, plan.*

Haben Sie morgen etwas vor? *Do you have any plans for tomorrow?*

Vorhang *m. curtain.*

vorher *before, beforehand, in advance, previously.*

vorherrschen *to predominate, prevail.*

vorherrschend *predominant, prevailing.*

Vorjahr *n. preceding year.*

Vorkenntnis *f. previous knowledge.*

vorkommen *to come forward, occur, happen.*

Es kommt Ihnen nur so vor. *You are just imagining that.*

Vorkommnis *n. occurrence, event.*

Vorlage *f. model, pattern, copy.*

vorlassen *to give precedence to.*

vorläufig *preliminary.*

Vorleger *m. mat, rug.*

vorlesen *to read aloud.*

Vorlesung *f. lecture, recital.*

vorletzt *one before the last.*

Vorliebe *f. predilection, preference.*

vormachen *to put, place before, impose on someone, fool.*

vormerken *to make a note of, put down.*

sich vormerken lassen *to book.*

Vormittag *m. morning ("before noon").*

Vormund *m. guardian.*

Vormundschaft *f. guardianship.*

VORN *in front, in front of.*

nach vorn *forward.*

nach vorne heraus wohnen *to live in the front part of a house.*

von vorn *from the front.*

von vorn anfangen *to start afresh.*

vor vorn herein *from the first.*

Vorname *m. Christian name.*

vornehm *of high rank, noble, distinguished.*

Vornehmheit *f. distinction, high rank.*

vornehmlich *principally, chiefly, especially.*

Vorort *m. suburb.*

Vorplatz *m. court, hall, vestibule.*

Vorrang *m. precedence, priority.*

Vorrat *m. store, stock, provision.*

vorrätig *in stock, on hand.*

nicht mehr vorrätig *out of stock.*

Vorratskammer *f. storeroom, panty.*

vorsagen *to dictate, say, prompt.*

Vorsatz *m. purpose.*

Vorschlag *m. proposal, proposition.*

vorschlagen *to propose, offer.*

vorschreiben *to set a copy.*

Vorschrift *f. copy, direction.*

vorschriftmässig *according to instructions.*

vorsehen *to provide for, consider, take care.*

Vorsehung *f. providence.*

VORSICHT *f. foresight, caution, prudence.*

Vorsicht! *Take care! Beware!*

Vorsicht Stufe! *Mind the step!*
vorsichtig *cautious, prudent.*
vorsichtshalber *as a precaution.*
Vorsichtsmassregel *f. precaution, measure.*
Vorsitz *m. presidency, chairman.*
den Vorsitz führen *to preside in the chair.*
Vorspeise *f. hors d'oeuvre, relish.*
vorsprechen *to pronounce, recite.*
vorsprechen bei *to call on.*
Vorsprung *m. projection, projecting part.*
Vorstadt *f. suburb.*
Vorstand *m. board of directors.*
vorstellen *to place before, put in front of, demonstrate, introduce, represent, act.*
sich etwas vorstellen *to imagine something.*
sich vorstellen *to introduce oneself.*
vorstellig *adj.*
vorstellig werden *to present a case, petition.*
VORSTELLUNG *f. introduction, presentation, performance, picture.*
Wann fängt die Vorstellung an? *When does the performance start?*
Vorstellungsvermögen *n. imagination.*
Vorteil *m. advantage, profit.*
VORTEILHAFT *advantageous, favorable.*
vorteilhaft sussehen *to look one's best.*
Vortrag *m. reciting, delivery, execution, lecture.*
vortragen *to carry forward, recite, declaim, execute, perform.*
vortrefflich *excellent, admirable, splendid.*
Vortrefflichkeit *f. excellence.*
vorüber *past, over, by, along.*
vorübergehen *to go by, pass.*
Vorurteil *n. prejudice.*
vorurteilslos *unprejudiced.*
Vorverkauf *m. booking in advance (theater); advance sale.*
vorvorgestem *three days ago.*
Vorwand *m. pretext, pretense, excuse.*
VORWÄRTS *forward, onward, on.*
Vorwärts! *Go on! Go ahead!*
vorwärtsgehen *to go on, advance, progress.*
vorwärtskommen *to get on, advance, prosper.*
vorwärtskommend *predominant.*
Vorwurf *m. reproach.*
Vorwürfe machen *to blame.*
vorwurfsvoll *reproachful.*

vorzeigen *to show, produce, exhibit, display.*
vorzeitig *premature, precocious.*
vorziehen *to draw forward, prefer.*
Vorzimmer *n. antechamber.*
Vorzug *m. preference, superiority.*
vorzüglich *excellent, superior, first-choice.*
Vorzüglichkeit *f. excellency, superiority.*
Vorzugspreis *m. special price.*

W

WAAGE (Wage) *f. balance, scales.*
einem die Waage halten *to be a match for.*
sich die Waage halten *to counterbalance each other.*
wagerecht *horizontal level.*
WACH *awake, alive, brisk.*
Wachdienst *m. guard duty.*
Wache *f. guard, watch, sentry.*
WACHEN *to be awake, remain awake.*
wachen über *to watch over.*
Wachs *n. wax.*
wachsam *vigilant, watchful.*
Wachsamkeit *f. vigilance.*
WACHSEN *to grow, increase, extend.*
ans Herz wachsen *to grow fond of.*
einem gewachsen sein *to be a match for one.*
einer Sache gewachsen sein *to be equal to a task.*
Wachstum *n. growth, increase.*
Wacht *f. guard, watch.*
Wächter *m. watchman, guard.*
Waffe *f. weapon, arm.*
Waffel *f. wafer, waffle.*
Waffeleisen *n. waffle-iron.*
Waffenschein *m. gun-license.*
Waffenstillstand *m. armistice.*
WAGEN *m. car, automobile, railroad car, cab, wagon.*
Wagen *to venture, risk, dare.*
gewagt *daring, risky, perilous.*
Wagnis *n. risk.*
WAHL *f. choice, selection, election.*
in engere Wahl kommen *to be on the short list.*
seine Wahl treffen *to make one's choice.*
vor die Wahl stellen *to let one choose.*
wahlberechtigt *entitled to vote.*
WAHLEN *to choose, select, pick out, elect, dial.*

Wahler *m. elector, selector.*
wahlerisch *particular, fastidious.*
Wahlkampf *m. election, contest.*
wahllos *indiscriminately.*
Wahlstimme *f. vote.*
Wahn *m. delusion, illusion.*
Wahnsinn *m. insanity, madness, craziness.*
wahnsinnig *insane, mad.*
WAHR *true, sincere, genuine, real, proper, veritable.*
  etwas nicht wahr haben wollen *not to admit a thing.*
  Nicht wahr? *Isn't it? Don't you think so?*
  so wahr ich lebe *as sure as I live.*
  wahr werden *to come true.*
WÄHREND 1. *prep. (gen.): during, for, in the course of.*
  Während des Winters verleben wir unsere Ferien in den Bergen. *During the winter we spend our vacations in the mountains.*
  2. *conj. while.*
  Sie kam während Sie weg waren. *She came while you were out.*
WAHRHEIT *f. truth.*
  Ich habe ihm gehörig die Wahrheit gesagt. *I really gave him a piece of my mind.*
wahrheitsgetreu *truthful, true.*
wahrheitslebend *truthful.*
wahrnehmbar *perceptible, noticeable.*
wahrsagen *to tell fortunes, prophesy.*
Wahrsagerin *f. fortune teller.*
WAHRSCHEINLICH *probable, likely.*
Wahrscheinlichkeit *f. probability.*
Währung *f. standard, currency.*
Waise *f. & m. orphan.*
Waisenhaus *m. orphanage.*
Wal *m. whale.*
WALD *m. forest, woodland.*
waldig *woody.*
Waldung *f. woodland, wood.*
Wall *m. rampart, dike.*
Walnuss *f. walnut.*
Walze *f. roller, barrel.*
walzen *to walz.*
Walzer *m. waltz.*
WAND *f. wall, partition.*
Wandel *m. change, alteration.*
  Handel und Wandel *trade, commerce.*
wandelbar *perishable, changeable, fickle.*
wandern *to wander.*
Wanderschaft *f. trip, tour, travels.*
Wanderung *f. excursion, trip, hike, migration.*
Wandgemälde *n. mural painting, fresco.*

Wandschrank *m. cupboard.*
Wankelmut *m. inconsistency, fickleness.*
WANN *when.*
  wann immer *whenever.*
  dann und wann *now and then.*
Wanne *f. tub, bath.*
Wannenbad *n. tub bath.*
WARE *f. article, goods, merchandise.*
Warenhaus *n. department store.*
Warenprobe *f. sample.*
WARM *warm.*
  Ist es Ihnen warm genug? *Are you warm enough?*
  warm stellen *to keep hot.*
Warme *f. heat, warmth.*
WÄRMEN *to warm, heat.*
Wärmflasche *f. hot-water bottle.*
warnen *to warn, caution.*
Warnung *f. warning.*
Warnungssignal *n. danger signal.*
WARTEN *to wait, attend to, nurse.*
  warten auf *to wait for.*
  warten lassen *to keep waiting.*
Warter *m. attendant.*
Wartesaal *m. waiting-room.*
Wartezimmer *n. doctor's waiting room.*
WARUM *why, for what reason.*
WAS *what, whatever, that which, which, that.*
  Ach was! *Nonsense!*
  Nein so was! *Well, I never!*
  was ... auch immer *no matter what, whatever.*
  was für ein *what sort of, what a.*
Waschbecken *n. wash basin.*
WÄSCHE *f. wash; linen, underclothing.*
  in die Wäsche geben *to send to the laundry.*
  grosse Wäsche haben *to have washing day.*
  schmutzige Wäsche *soiled linen, dirty clothes.*
waschecht *fast color.*
Wäschegeschäft *n. haberdashery, lingerie store.*
Wäscheklammer *f. clothespin.*
Wäscheleine *f. clothesline.*
waschen *to wash.*
Wäscherei *f. laundry.*
WASSER *n. water.*
  fliessendes Wasser *running water.*
  ins Wasser fallen *to end in smoke.*
  mit allen Wassern gewaschen sein *to be cunning.*
  sich über Wasser halten *to keep one's head above water.*
  zu Wasser und zu Lande *by land and sea.*
Wasserball *m. water polo.*

Wasserbehälter *m. reservoir, tank.*
wasserdicht *waterproof.*
Wasserfall *m. waterfall.*
Wasserforbe *f. water-color.*
Wasserflugzeug *n. sea plane.*
Wasserglas *n. glass, tumbler.*
wasserhältig *containing water.*
wässerig *watery.*
  einem den Mund wässerig machen *to make a person's mouth water.*
Wasserkanne *f. watering-can.*
Wasserleitung *f. water supply, water pipes, faucet, sink.*
Wasserspiegel *m. water-surface.*
Wasserstiefel *pl. rubber boots.*
Wasserstrahl *m. jet of water.*
Watte *f. wadding, cotton-wool.*
weben *to weave.*
Weber *m. weaver.*
Wechsel *m. change, alteration, succession, turn.*
  gezogener Wechsel *draft.*
Wechselgeld *n. change (money).*
  Bitte, zahlen Sie ihr Wechselgeld nach. *Please count your change.*
Wechselkurs *m. rate of exchange.*
WECHSELN *to change, exchange, alternate, shift.*
  seinen Wohnort wechseln *to move away.*
  den Besitzer wechseln *to change ownership.*
wechselseitig *reciprocal, mutual, alternate.*
WECKEN *to wake, awaken.*
Wecker *m. alarm-clock.*
weder *neither.*
  weder…noch *neither…nor.*
WEG *m. way, path, road, street, walk.*
  am Weg *by the roadside.*
  auf gütlichem Weg *in a friendly way.*
  auf halbem Weg *halfway.*
  aus dem Weg gehen *to make way for, stand aside.*
  in die Wege leiten *to prepare for.*
  seiner Wege gehen *to go one's way.*
  sich auf den Weg machen *to set out.*
WEG *1. adv. away, off, gone, lost, disappeared.*
  Hände weg! *Hands off!*
  Ich muss weg. *I must go.*
  2. separable prefix (implies a motion away from the speaker).
  Er warf das alte Buch weg. *He threw the old book away.*
  Geh weg! *Go away!*
wegbleiben *to stay away, be omitted.*
wegbringen *to take away, remove.*
WEGEN *prep. (gen.): because of, for*

the sake of, owing to.
  Wegen des Krieges konnte ich nicht von Europa zürückkommen. *Because of the war, I could not come back from Europe.*
wegfahren *to drive off, away.*
weggehen *to go away, depart, leave.*
weglegen *to put away.*
wegnehmen *to take away, carry off, confiscate, occupy.*
Wegweiser *m. signpost.*
wegwerfen *to throw away.*
wegwerfend *disparaging, contemptuous.*
WEH *sore, aching, painful.*
  weh tun *to ache, to hurt.*
wehleidig *plaintive.*
Wehmut *f. sadness, melancholy.*
wehmütig *sad, melancholy.*
Wehrdienst *m. military service.*
wehren *to hinder, forbid, arrest, defend.*
  sich seiner Haut wehren *to defend one's life.*
wehrfähig *able-bodied.*
wehrlos *unarmed, defenseless, weak.*
Wehrmacht *f. armed forces.*
Wehrpflicht *f. conscription.*
wehrpflichtig *liable to military service.*
Weib *n. woman.*
weibisch *effeminate.*
weiblich *female, feminine, womanly.*
Weiblichkeit *f. womanhood, femininity.*
WEICH *soft, mold, mellow, tender, smooth.*
  weiches Ei *soft-boiled egg.*
weichen *to retreat, give in, yield; soften, soak.*
weichherzig *soft-hearted.*
weichlich *soft, flabby, weak.*
weigern *to refuse.*
Weigerung *f. refusal.*
Weihe *f. consecration, initiation, inauguration.*
weihen *to consecrate, dedicate, devote.*
WEIHNACHTEN *pl. Christmas.*
weihnachtlich *of Christmas.*
Weihnachtsabend *m. Christmas Eve.*
Weihnachtsbaum *m. Christmas tree.*
Weihnachtslied *n. Christmas carol.*
WEIL *because, since.*
WEILE *f. while, space of time.*
  Damit hat es gute Weile. *There is no hurry.*
  Eile mit Weile. *Haste makes waste.*
WEIN *m. wine, vine.*
Weinberg *m. vineyard.*
WEINEN *to weep, cry.*
Weinessig *m. wine vinegar.*
Weinfass *n. wine cask.*

Weinkarte *f. winelist.*
Weinlese *f. Vintage.*
Weinprobe *f. wine-tasting.*
Weinrebe *f. vine.*
Weinstock *m. vine.*
Weintraube *f. grape, bunch of grapes.*
WEISE *f. manner, way, tune.*
  auf diese Weise *in this way.*
  in der Weise, dass *in such a way that, so that.*
WEISEN *to show, refer, direct, point out, point at.*
Weisheit *f. wisdom, prudence.*
Weismachen *to make one believe, hoax.*
WEISS *white, blank, clean.*
  Weisser Sonntag *Sunday after Easter.*
Weissagen *to predict, prophesy.*
Weissager *m. (-in, f.) prophet.*
WEIT *distant, far, vast, loose, wide, big.*
  bei weitem *by far, by much.*
  beit weitem nicht *by no means.*
  es weit bringen *to get on well, be successful.*
  nicht weither sein *not to be worth much.*
  von weitem *from a distance.*
  Weit gefehlt *quite wrong.*
  weit und breit *far and wide.*
  weit voraus *way ahead.*
  weit weg *far away.*
  wenn alles so weit ist *when everything is ready.*
Weitab *far away.*
Weitaus *by far.*
Weitblick *m. foresight.*
Weite *f. width, size, extent, distance, length.*
WEITER *further, farther, more, else, additional.*
  bis auf weiteres *until further notice.*
  des weiteren *furthermore.*
  nichts weiter *nothing more.*
  niemand weiter *no one else.*
  Nur weiter! *Go on!*
  ohne weiteres *immediately.*
  und so weiter *and so on.*
  was weiter *what else.*
  wenn's weiter nichts ist *if that's all there is to it.*
Weitere *n. rest, remaining part.*
weiterführen *to continue, carry on.*
weitergeben *to pass on to.*
Weiterreise *f. continuation of a trip.*
weitgehend *far-reaching, full, much.*
weither *from afar.*
weitläufig *distant, wide, extensive, roomy.*
weitschweifig *detailed, tedious.*

weitsichtig *far-sighted.*
Weizen *m. wheat, corn.*
WELCH (ein) *what (a)*
  Welch ein Zufall! *What a coincidence!*
WELCH(-ER, -E, -ES) 1. *inter. pron. & adj. what, who, whom, which.*
2. *rel. pron. what, which, that, who, whom.*
Welle *f. wave, surge.*
  Wellen schlagen *to rise in waves.*
Wellenlinie *f. wavy line.*
Wellenreiter *m. surf-rider.*
WELT *f. world, universe, people.*
  alle Welt *everybody, everyone in the world.*
  auf der Welt *on earth.*
  auf die Welt kommen *to come into the world, be born.*
  aus der Welt schaffen *to put out of the way.*
  in der ganzen Welt *on earth.*
  in die Welt setzen (zur Welt bringen) *to give birth to.*
Weltall *n. universe.*
Weltanschauung *f. world outlook.*
weltbekannt *world-famous.*
weltfremd *secluded, solitary.*
Weltmann *m. man of the world.*
Weltmeister *m. world champion.*
Weltraum *m. space, universe.*
Weltuntergang *m. end of the world.*
WEM *dat. of wer. to whom.*
WEN *acc. of wer. whom.*
Wende *f. turn, turning point.*
wenden *to turn, turn around.*
  Bitte wenden! *Please turn over!*
Wendepunkt *m. turning point.*
WENIG *little, few, a few.*
  ein wenig *a little, a bit.*
WENIGER *less, fewer, minus.*
  immer weniger *less and less.*
  nichts weniger als *anything but.*
  vier weniger eins *four minus one.*
wenigst(er,-e,-es) *least.*
wenigstens *at least.*
WENN *if, in case of, when.*
  auch wenn *even if.*
  immer wenn *whenever.*
  Rufen Sie mich an wenn Sie kommen wollen. *Call me when you want to come.*
  selbst wenn *even if, supposing that.*
  wenn auch (wenn gleich, wenn schon) *although.*
  Wenn das nur wahr wäre! *If it were only true!*
  wenn nur *provided that.*
  Wenn schon! *What of it!*
  wenn Sie kommen könnten *If you could come.*

WER *inter. pron. who, what.*
  wer anders *who else.*
  wer auch immer *whoever.*
  Wer da? *Who is it?*
werben *to recruit; to court, propose (marriage).*
WERDEN 1. *to become, turn out, prove, happen.*
  Was soll aus ihr werden? *What's to become of her?*
  2. *aux, verb to form future and passive. shall, will, is, are.*
werfen *to throw, cast, toss.*
WERK *n. work, labor, production, performance, deed.*
  ans Werk! *Go to it!*
  ins Werk setzen *to set going.*
  zu Werk gehen *to begin.*
Werkstatt *f. workshop.*
Werktag *m. working day.*
werktags *on weekdays.*
werktätig *active*
  die werktätige Bevölkerung *working classes.*
Werkzeug *m. utensil.*
WERT *worth, valuable, worthy, honored, esteemed.*
  im Werte von *at a price of.*
  nichts wert sein *to be no good.*
Wertangabe *f. declaration of value.*
Wertgegenstände *pl. valuables.*
wertlos *worthless.*
Wertpapier *n. security, bond.*
Wertsachen *p. valuables.*
wertvoll *valuable, precious.*
Wesen *n. creature, soul, personality.*
wesentlich *essential, substantial.*
WESSEN *gen. of wer. whose? whose.*
Weste *f. waistcoat, vest.*
Westen *m. the West, Occident.*
  nach Westen *west (direction).*
westlich *western, occidental.*
westwärts *westwards.*
Wette *f. bet, wager.*
  eine Wette eingehen *to make a bet.*
  um die Wette laufen *to race someone.*
wetteifern *to emulate; to vie.*
wetten *to bet, wager.*
WETTER *n. weather.*
  Alle Wetter! *My word!*
  Heute ist das Wetter wunderschön! *The weather is wonderful today!*
Wetterbericht *m. meteorological report.*
Wetterlage *f. weather conditions.*
Wettkampf *m. match, contest, prize fighting.*
Wettstreit *m. competition, match.*
WICHTIG *important.*
  sich wichtig machen *to act important.*

WIDER 1. *prep. (acc.). against, contrary to, versus.*
  Wider meinen Willen *against my will.*
  2. *inseparable prefix. (con-,re-, anti-, contra-)*
widerhallen *to echo, resound.*
widerlegen *to refute.*
Widerlegung *f. refutation.*
widerlich *repulsive, disgusting.*
Widerrede *f. contradiction.*
widerrufen *to revoke, withdraw, retract, cancel.*
Widersacher *m. adversary.*
widersetzen (sich) *to oppose, resist.*
widerspiegeln *to reflect, mirror.*
Widerstand *m. resistance, opposition.*
Widerwille *m. repugnance, disgust.*
widerwillig *reluctant, unwilling.*
widmen *to dedicate.*
Widmung *f. dedication.*
WIE *how, as, such, like.*
  so . . . wie *as . . . as.*
  wie auch immer *however.*
  Wie bitte? *What did you say?*
  wie dem auch sei *be that as it may.*
  Wie geht es Ihnen? *How are you?*
  wie gesagt *as has been said.*
WIEDER 1. *adv. again, anew, back, in return for.*
  hin und wieder *now and then.*
  immer wieder *again and again.*
  2. *prefix. a) inseparable. In verb wiederholen (to repeat). b) separable (implies the idea of repetition or opposition).*
wiederbekommen *to get back, recover.*
wiederbeleben *to revive, reanimate.*
Wiederbelebungsversuch *m. attempt at resuscitation.*
wiederfinden *to find, recover.*
wiedererkennen *to recognize.*
wiedererlangen *to get back.*
wiedererobern *to reconquer.*
Wiedergabe *f. return; reproduction, recital (work of art)*
wiedergeben *to give back, return.*
Wiedergutmachung *f. reparation.*
WIEDERHOLEN *to repeat, renew, reiterate, fetch, bring back.*
Wiederholung *f. repetition, reiteration.*
  im Wiederholungsfalle *if it should happen again.*
wiederhören *to hear again.*
  auf Wiederhören! *Good-bye! (radio, tel.).*
WIEDERSEHEN *to see again, meet again.*
  auf Wiedersehen! *Good-bye! So long!*
Wiege *f. cradle.*

wiegen *to rock, move to, shake, sway.*
Wiese *f. meadow.*
wieso *why.*
WIEVIEL *how much.*
  Der wievielte ist heute? *What date is today?*
wieviele *how many.*
WILD *wild, rough, angry, furious, savage, untidy.*
Wild *n. game (hunting).*
Wildbraten *m. venison.*
Wilddieb *m. poacher.*
Wildente *f. wild duck.*
Wildleder *n. deerskin, suede.*
Wildnis *f. wilderness, desert.*
WILLE *m. will, say, determination, purpose.*
  aus freiem Willen *voluntarily.*
  guter Wille *kind intention.*
  letzter Wille *last will.*
willenlos *lacking will power, irresolute.*
Willenlosigkeit *f. lack of will power.*
Willenskraft *f. will power.*
willfahren *to gratify, grant, please.*
Willkommen *n. welcome, reception.*
Willkür *f. discretion, arbitrariness.*
willkürlich *arbitrary, despotic.*
WIND *m. wind, breeze.*
  bei Wind und Wetter *in storm and rain.*
  guter Wind *fair wind.*
  in den Wind reden *to talk in vain.*
  in den Wind schlagen *to disregard.*
  vor dem Wind segeln *to run before the rain.*
Windel *f. baby's diaper.*
Windelkind *n. infant.*
windeln *to swaddle.*
winden *to wind.*
windig *windy, breezy.*
Windstille *f. calm.*
Wink *m. sign, nod, wink.*
Winkel *m. corner, angle, secret spot.*
winken *to wave, nod, wink.*
WINTER *m. winter.*
  im Winter *in winter.*
Winterfrische *f. winter resort.*
Winterschlaf *m. hibernation.*
Wintersport *m. winter sports.*
winzig *tiny, diminutive.*
Winzigkeit *f. tininess.*
Wirbel *m. whirlpool, eddy.*
Wirbelknochen *m. vertebra.*
wirbeln *to whirl.*
Wirbelsäule *f. spine.*
Wirbelsturm *m. tornado, hurricane.*
wirken *to act, do, work, produce.*
WIRKLICH *real, actual, true, genuine.*
Wirklichkeit *f. reality, actuality.*
wirksam *active, effective.*

Wirkung *f. action, working, operation.*
wirkungslos *ineffectual, inefficient.*
wirkungsvoll *effective, striking.*
Wirt *m. host, proprietor, landlord.*
wirtlich *hospitable.*
Wirtschaft *f. housekeeping, economy, tavern, public house.*
  die Wirtschaft führen *to keep house.*
wirtschaften *to manage.*
Wirtschaftsgeld *n. housekeeping money.*
Wirtschaftslage *f. economic situation.*
Wirtschaftsprüfer *m. general adviser, accountant.*
Wirtshaus *n. inn, public house.*
WISSEN *n. knowledge, learning.*
  meines Wissens *as far as I know.*
  nach bestem Wissen und Gewissen *most conscientiously.*
  wider besseres Wissen *against one's better judgment.*
WISSEN *to know, be aware of, understand, be acquainted with.*
  Ich weiss nicht. *I don't know.*
  nicht dass ich wüsste *not that I am aware of.*
Wissenschaft *f. science, knowledge.*
Wissenschaftler *m. scientist, scholar.*
wissenwert *worth knowing, interesting.*
Witwe *f. widow.*
Witwer *m. widower.*
Witz *m. wittiness, witticism, wit, joke, pun.*
witzig *witty.*
WO *where, in which; when.*
  wo auch immer *wherever.*
woanders *elsewhere.*
wobei *whereat, whereby, in which, upon which.*
WOCHE *f. week.*
  diese Woche *this week.*
  heute in einer Woche *a week from today.*
Wochenende *n. weekend.*
wochenlang *for weeks.*
wochentags *on weekdays.*
Wochenschau *newsreel; weekly publication.*
wöchentlich *weekly.*
wodurch *by which, whereby, how.*
wofür *for which, for what.*
WOHER *from where, from what place?*
  Woher wissen Sie das? *How do you know that?*
WOHIN *to where, to what place?*
WOHL *n. welfare, prosperity, good health.*
  sich wohl fühlen *to feel well.*
WOHL *well, all right, probably,*

presumably, very likely, indeed.

Ich verstehe wohl. *I can well understand.*

Leben Sie wohl! *Good-bye!*

wohl oder übel *willy nilly.*

Zum Wohl! *To you! (a toast)*

Wohlbehagen *n. comfort, ease.*

wohlbekannt *well-known, familiar.*

Wohlfahrt *f. welfare.*

Wohlgeruch *m. fragrance, sweet, perfume.*

wohlhabend *wealthy, well-off.*

Wohlklang *m. harmony, melody.*

wohlschmeckend *tasty, palatable.*

Wohlstand *m. well-being, wealth, fortune.*

wohltuend *comforting, pleasant.*

wohlverdient *well-deserved, merited.*

WOHNEN *to live, dwell, reside, stay.*

zur Miete wohnen *to live as a tenant, rent-payer.*

wohnhaft *living, dwelling.*

wohnlich *comfortable, cozy.*

WOHNUNG *f. house, dwelling, residence, flat.*

Wohnviertel *n. residential district.*

Wohnzimmer *n. sitting-room.*

Wolf *m. wolf.*

Wolke *f. cloud.*

aus allen Wolken fallen *to be thunderstruck.*

Wolkenbruch *m. cloudburst.*

Wolkenkratzer *m. skyscraper.*

WOLLE *f. wool.*

WOLLEN *to want, wish, will, desire, like, mean.*

Das will etwas heissen. *That means something.*

Das will was heissen. *That's really something.*

Er mag wollen oder nicht. *Whether he likes it or not.*

Wie Sie wollen. *As you like.*

WOMIT *with what, by which, with which.*

Womit kann ich dienen? *What can I do for you?*

womöglich *if possible.*

WORAN *whereon, by what.*

woran liegt es? *how is it that?*

WORAUF *on what, upon which.*

WORAUS *of what, out of which.*

WORIN *in which, in what.*

WORT *n. word, expression, saying, promise.*

aufs Wort gehorchen *to obey implicitly.*

das grosse Wort führen *to brag.*

das Wort ergreifen *to begin to speak.*

das Wort führen *to be spokesman.*

einen beim Wort nehmen *to take one at one's word.*

Er hat sein Wort gebrochen. *He broke his promise.*

Ich habe kein Wort davon gewusst. *I did not know a thing about it.*

ins Wort fallen *to interrupt, cut short.*

mit anderen Worten *in other words.*

Sie macht viele Worte. *She talks too much.*

ums Wort bitten *to ask for the floor.*

zu Wort kommen lassen *to let one speak.*

Wörterbuch · *n. dictionary.*

Wortschatz *m. vocabulary.*

wortwörtlich *word for word.*

WORÜBER *of what, about which, whereof.*

WORUNTER *among what, which.*

WOVON *about what, which.*

WOVOR *of what, for what, before what, which.*

WOZU *before what, of what, for what, which.*

wund *sore, wounded.*

Wunde *f. wound.*

Wunder *n. wonder, miracle.*

sein blaues Wunder erleben *to be amazed.*

WUNDERBAR *wonderful, marvelous.*

Wunderbar! *Wonderful! Splendid!*

wunderbarerweise *strange to say.*

Wunderkind *n. child prodigy.*

wunderlich *strange, odd.*

WUNDERN *to astonish, surprise.*

sich wundern *to be surprised, wonder.*

wunderschön *beautiful, lovely, exquisite.*

WUNSCH *m. wish, desire, request.*

auf Wunsch *by request, if desired.*

Haben Sie noch eine Wunsch? *Is there anything else you'd like?*

nach Wunsch *as one desires.*

WÜNSCHEN *to wish, desire, long for.*

Glück wünschen *to congratulate (wish luck).*

Was wünschen Sie? *May I help you?*

Würde *f. dignity, honor, title, rank.*

in Amt und Würden *holding a high office.*

würdelos *undignified.*

würdevoll *dignified.*

würdig *worthy, deserving of, respectable.*

würdigen *to value, appreciate.*

nicht eines Wortes würdigen *not to say a word.*

Würfel *m. die, cube.*

Der Würfel ist gefallen. *The die is cast.*

würfeln *to play dice.*
Würfelspiel *n. dice game.*
Würfelzucker *m. lump of sugar.*
würgen *to choke, strangle.*
Wurm *m. worm.*
Wurst *f. sausage.*
Würze *f. seasoning, spice, flavor.*
Wurzel *f. root.*
würzen *to season.*
würzig *spicy.*
wüst *waste, deserted, desolate, wild, dissolute.*
Wüste *f. desert.*
Wüstling *m. libertine, dissolute person.*
WUT *f. rage, fury.*
  in Wut geraten *to fly into a rage.*
wüten *to rage, be furious.*
wütend *enraged, furious.*

X

xmal *ever so often, any number of times.*

Y

Y *the twenty-fifth letter of the alphabet.*

Z

zagen *to be afraid, hesitate.*
zähe *tough, tenacious, stubborn.*
ZAHL *f. figure, number, numeral.*
zahlbar *payable, due.*
zahlen *to pay.*
ZÄHLEN *to count, number, calculate.*
  gezahlt *numbered.*
Zahlkarte *f. money-order form.*
zahllos *countless, innumerable.*
zahlreich *numerous.*
Zahltag *m. pay-day.*
Zahlung *f. payment.*
zahlungsfähig *solvent.*
zahm *tame, domestic.*
zähmen *to tame, break in.*
ZAHN *m. tooth.*
  ein schlechter Zahn *a bad tooth.*
  die Zähne putzen *to brush the teeth.*
  einem auf den Zahn fühlen *to sound a person.*

  künstliche Zähne *artificial teeth.*
Zahnarzt *m. dentist.*
Zahnbürste *f. toothbrush.*
Zahnfleisch *n. gum.*
Zahnfüllung *f. filling.*
zahnlos *toothless.*
Zahnpasta *f. toothpaste.*
Zahnschmerzen *pl. toothache.*
Zahnstein *m. tartar.*
Zahnstocher *m. toothpick.*
Zahnweh *n. toothache.*
Zange *f. pincers.*
Zank *m. quarrel.*
zanken *to quarrel.*
zänkisch *quarrelsome.*
zanksüchtig *quarrelsome.*
ZART *tender, soft, delicate, fragile, frail.*
zartfühlend *tactful, sensitive.*
Zartgefühl *n. delicacy of feeling.*
Zartheit *f. tenderness, delicacy.*
Zauber *m. magic, charm, spell.*
Zauberei *f. magic, witchcraft.*
Zauberflöte *f. magic flute.*
zauberhaft *magical, enchanting.*
zaubern *to practice magic, conjure.*
zaudern *to hesitate, delay.*
Zaun *m. hedge, fence.*
  Streit von Zaune brechen *to pick a quarrel.*
Zebra *n. zebra.*
Zehe *f. toe.*
Zehenspitze *f. point of the toe.*
  auf Zehenspitzen gehen *to tiptoe.*
ZEHN *ten.*
zehnfach *tenfold.*
ZEHNTE *tenth.*
Zeichen *n. sign, signal, token, brand.*
  zum Zeichen dass *as a proof that.*
Zeichensetzung *f. punctuation.*
Zeichensprache *f. sign language.*
ZEICHNEN *to draw, design, mark.*
ZEICHNUNG *f. drawing, sketch, design.*
Zeigefinger *m. forefinger, index.*
ZEIGEN *to show, point at, point out, exhibit, display.*
Zeiger *m. hand of the clock, pointer.*
ZEIT *f. time, duration, period, epoch, season.*
  Damit hat es Zeit. *There is no hurry.*
  die freie Zeit *leisure, spare time.*
  Es ist an der Zeit. *It is high time.*
  höchste Zeit *high time.*
  in der letzten Zeit *lately.*
  in jüngster Zeit *quite recently.*
  Lassen Sie sich Zeit! *Take your time!*
  mit der Zeit *gradually.*
  Zeit seines Lebens *during life.*
  zu gleicher Zeit *at the same time.*
  zur rechten Zeit *in the nick of time.*

zur Zeit *at present.*
Zeit ist Geld. *Time is money.*
Zeitalter *n. age, generation.*
zeitgemäss *timely, seasonable.*
Zeitgenosse *m. contemporary.*
zeitgenössisch *contemporary.*
ZEITIG *early, timely, mature, ripe.*
zeitlebens *for life.*
Zeitpunkt *m. time, moment.*
Zeitschrift *f. journal, periodical, magazine.*
ZEITUNG *f. newspaper, paper.*
Zeitungsausschnitt *m. press cutting.*
Zeitungskiosk *m. newsstand.*
Zeitungsnotiz *f. notice, item, paragraph.*
Zeitungsstand *m. newsstand.*
Zeitungsverkäufer *m. news vendor.*
Zeitvertreib *m. pastime, amusement.*
Zeitwort *n. verb.*
Zelle *f. cell, booth.*
Zelt *n. tent, canopy.*
Zement *m. cement.*
Zentimeter *m. & n. centimeter (.3937 inch).*
Zentrale *f. central office, station, telephone exchange.*
Zentralheizung *f. central heating.*
ZENTRUM *n. center.*
zerbrechen *to break, smash.*
sich den Kopf zerbrechen *to rack one's brains.*
zerbrechlich *fragile.*
Zerbrechlichkeit *f. fragility, brittleness.*
Zeremonie *f. ceremony.*
zerreissbar *tearable.*
zerreissen *to tear, lacerate.*
zerren *to drag, pull.*
zerschmettern *to crush, destroy.*
zerstören *to destroy, demolish, devastate, ruin.*
Zerstörer *m. destroyer, devastator.*
Zerstörung *f. devastation, demolition, destruction.*
zerstreuen *to disperse, scatter, dissipate, divert.*
zerstreut *absent-minded.*
Zerstreuung *f. dispersion, distraction, amusement.*
Zerwürfnis *n. disagreement, quarrel.*
Zettel *m. slip, note, label, ticket, poster, bill.*
Zeug *n. stuff, material, cloth, fabric, utensils, things.*
sich ins Zeug legen *to set to work.*
Zeuge *m. witness.*
zeugen *to testify, bear witness, give evidence.*
Zeugenaussage *f. evidence, deposition.*

Zeugenvernehmung *f. hearing of witnesses.*
Ziege *f. goat.*
Ziegel *m. brick, tile.*
Ziegelstein *m. brick.*
ZIEHEN *to pull, draw, haul, tug, tow, extract, move, migrate, weigh.*
den Kürzeren ziehen *to get the worst of it.*
nach sich ziehen *to have consequences.*
Er zieht den Hut. *He tips his hat.*
zur Rechenschaft ziehen *to call to account.*
Ziehung *f. drawing of lottery.*
Ziel *n. goal.*
sich ein Ziel setzen *to aim at.*
zielbewusst *systematic, methodical.*
zielen *to aim.*
ziellos *aimless.*
Zielscheibe *f. target.*
Zielscheibe des Spottes sein *to be a laughing stock.*
ziemen *to become, be suitable.*
ZIEMLICH *rather, pretty, fairly, quite, considerable.*
so ziemlich *about, pretty much.*
ziemlich viele *quite a few.*
Zierde *f. ornament, decoration.*
zieren *to decorate, adorn, embellish.*
zierlich *elegant, graceful, delicate.*
Ziffer *f. figure, cipher.*
Zifferblatt *n. dial, face.*
ZIGARETTE *f. cigarette.*
Zigarettenetui *n. cigarette-case.*
Zigarettenspitze *f. cigarette-holder.*
Zigarre *f. cigar.*
Zigarrenkiste *f. cigar-box.*
Zigeuner *m. gypsy.*
ZIMMER *n. room, apartment, chamber.*
Zimmerdecke *f. ceiling.*
Zimmermädchen *n. chambermaid.*
Zimmermann *m. carpenter.*
zimperlich *supersensitive, prudish, affected.*
Zimt *m. cinnamon.*
Zinn *n. tin, pewter.*
Zins *m. tax, duty, rent; interest.*
auf Zinsen ausleihen *to lend money at interest.*
mit Zins und Zinseszins *in full measure.*
Zinseszins *m. compound interest.*
Zinsfuss *m. rate of interest.*
Zirkel *m. circle, compasses.*
Zirkus *m. circus.*
Zitat *n. quotation.*
Zitrone *f. lemon.*
Zitronenlimonade *f. lemonade.*

Zitronenpresse f. lemon-press.
Zitronensaft m. lemon juice.
zittern to tremble, shake, quiver, shiver.
zivil civil, reasonable, moderate.
  in Zivil in plain clothes.
Zivilbevölkerung f. civilian population.
Zivilisation f. civilization.
zivilisieren to civilize.
Zivilist m. civilian.
zögern to hesitate, delay, linger.
ZOLL f. duty, toll, tariff, customs.
Zoll m. inch.
Zollabfertigung f. customs inspection.
ZOLLAMT n. customhouse.
Zollbeamte m. customhouse officer.
zollfrei free of duty.
Zollgebühr f. duty.
Zöllner m. customs collector.
zollpflichtig subject to customs.
Zollschranke f. customs barrier.
Zollstock m. yardstick.
Zollverschluss m. customs seal.
Zone f. zone.
Zopf m. braid, pigtail.
Zom m. anger, rage, wrath.
zornig angry.
ZU 1. prep. (dat.). to, at, by, near,
  beside, for, with, in front of, on.
  Die Deutschen essen immer Kartoffeln
  zum Fleisch. Germans always eat
  potatoes with meat.
  Et war nicht zu Hause. He was not at
  home.
  Ich gehe zu meiner Tante. I am going
  to my aunt's.
  Setzen Sie sich zu mir. Sit down by
  me.
  Wenn es friert, wird das Wasser zu Eis.
  When it freezes, water turns to ice.
  Wit essen Eier zum Frühstück. We eat
  eggs for breakfast.
  zu Fuss, zu Pferd on foot, on
  horseback.
  zu meinem Erstaunen to my surprise.
  zum König gekronht werden to
  become a king.
  zum Teil partly.
  zum "Weisses Rössi" at the "White
  Horse" (inn).
  2. adv. too (more than enough), toward.
  zu viel too much.
  3. before infinitive to.
  Si wussten nicht was zu tun. They did
  not know what to do.
  4. Separable prefix (implies direction
  toward the speaker, increase,
  continuation, closing, confession).
  Sie liefen dem Walde zu. They ran
  toward the forest.

  Der Verbrecher gab es zu. The
  criminal confessed.
  Ich darf nicht mehr zunehmen. I must
  not gain more weight.
  Mach die Tür zu! Close the door!
  Nur zu! Come on!
Zubehör m. & n. accessories,
  trimmings, belongings.
zubereiten to prepare, cook, mix.
Zubereitung f. preparation.
Zucht f. breeding, training, education;
  breed, race, stock.
züchten to breed, grow, cultivate, train.
züchtig chaste, modest.
züchtigen to punish, correct, chastise.
zucken to flash.
  mit den Achseln zucken to shrug
  one's shoulders.
ZUCKER m. sugar.
Zuckerguss m. icing.
zuckerhältig containing sugar.
zuckerkrank diabetic.
zuckern to sugar, sweeten.
Zuckerwerk n. confectionery, sweets.
zudem besides, moreover.
zudrücken to shut, close.
  ein Auge zudrücken to be indulgent.
zuerst at first, in the first place.
Zufahrt f. drive.
Zufall m. chance, accident, occurrence.
  durch Zufall by accident
zufällig casual, by accident, by chance.
zufällig tun to happen to do.
zufälligerweise by chance.
Zuflucht f. refuge, shelter.
  seine Zuflucht nehmen zu to take
  refuge with.
ZUFRIEDEN satisfied, content.
  sich zufrieden geben to rest content
  with.
  zufrieden lassen to let alone, leave in
  peace.
Zufriedenheit f. contentment,
  satisfaction.
zufriedenstellen to content, satisfy.
zufriedenstellend satisfactory.
ZUG m. train; drawing, draft; procession,
  march, impulse; feature, characteristic.
  Er liegt in den letzten Zügen. He is
  breathing his last.
  Zug um Zug without delay,
  uninterruptedly.
  Wann kommt der Schnellzug aus Berlin
  an? When does the express train
  from Berlin arrive?
Zugabe f. extra, addition, encore.
Zugang m. entrance, door, access.
zugänglich accessible, open to.
zugeben to add, allow, permit.

Zügel *m. bridle, rein.*

zügellos *unbridled, unrestrained.*

Zugeständnis *n. concession, admission.*

Zugluft *f. draught, current of air.*

zugunsten *in favor of, for the benefit of.*

zugute (halten) *to allow for, take into consideration, give credit for.*

   zugute kommen *to come in handy, be an advantage to.*

Zuhilfenahme *f. (unter Zuhilfenahme von) with the help of.*

zuhören *to listen to.*

Zuhörer *m. hearer, listener.*

Zuhörerschaft *f. audience.*

ZUKUNFT *f. future.*

zukünftig *future.*

zulächeln *to smile at.*

Zulage *f. addition, raise.*

zulangen *to hand, give.*

zulässig *admissible, permissible.*

Zulassung *f. admission, permission.*

ZULETZT *finally, ultimately,*

   zuletzt kommen *to arrive last.*

zuliebe (tun) *to do for someone's sake.*

   einem zuliebe tun *to please someone.*

zumachen *to close, shut, fasten; to hurry.*

zumal *especially, particularly.*

zumindest *at least.*

zumuten *to expect of.*

   sich zu viel zumuten *to attempt too much.*

Zumutung *f. unreasonable demand, imputation.*

zunächst *first, first of all, above all.*

zünden *to catch fire, inflame, arouse enthusiasm.*

zunehmen *to grow, increase, get fuller.*

zuneigen *to lean forward, incline.*

Zuneigung *f. liking, affection, sympathy. inclination.*

ZUNGE *f. tongue.*

   Das Wort liegt mir auf der Zunge. / *have the word on the tip of my tongue.*

   eine belegte Zunge *a fuzzy tongue.*

   eine feine Zunge haben *to be a gourmet.*

zurechnungsfähig *responsible, of sound mind.*

Zurechnungsfähigkeit *f. responsibility.*

zurecht *right, in order, in time.*

zurechtfinden *to find one's way about.*

zurechtsetzen (einem den Kopf zurechtsetzen) *to bring one to reason.*

Zurechtweisung *f. reprimand, reproach.*

ZURÜCK *1. adv. back, backwards, late, behind. 2. separable prefix (implies the*

idea of a return motion; back).

   Wir kamen erst um elf Uhr zurück. *We only came back at eleven.*

zurückbeben *to start back, recoil.*

zurückbehalten *to keep back, retain.*

zurückbekommen *to get back, recover.*

zurückbleiben *to stay behind.*

zurückbringen *to bring back.*

zurückfahren *to drive back, return.*

zurückfordern *to reclaim.*

zurückgehen *to go back, return, retreat, decrease, decline.*

zurückgezogen *retired, secluded, lonely.*

Zurückgezogenheit *f. retirement.*

zurückhalten *to hold back, delay, detain.*

zurückhaltend *reserved.*

zurückkehren *to return, go back, come back.*

zurücklassen *to leave behind.*

zurücknehmen *to take back, withdraw.*

zurücksetzen *to put back, replace, reduce, neglect.*

Zurücksetzung *f. neglect.*

zurückstellen *to put back, replace, reserve, put aside.*

zurücktreten *to step back, withdraw, resign.*

zurückversetzen *to put back, restore.*

   sich in eine Zeit zurückversetzen *to go back (in imagination) to a time.*

zurückweisen *to send away, send back, repulse.*

zurückzahlen *to pay back, repay.*

Zurückzahlung *f. repayment.*

zurückziehen *to draw back, take back.*

Zuruf *m. acclamation, shout, call.*

zurufen *to call to, shout to.*

Zusage *f. acceptance, promise.*

ZUSAGEN *to promise, please, appeal.*

   einem etwas auf den Kopf zusagen *to tell a person plainly.*

ZUSAMMEN *together, altogether.*

zusammenfassen *to sum up, summarize.*

zusammenfassend *comprehensive.*

zusammengehören *to belong together, match, be correlated.*

Zusammenhalt *m. holding together.*

Zusammenhang *m. connection.*

zusammenhangslos *disconnected.*

Zusammenkunft *f. meeting, reunion, assembly.*

Zusammenspiel *n. playing together, teamwork.*

Zusammenstoss *m. collision, clash.*

zusammenstossen *to smash, collide.*

zusammentreffen *to meet each other, coincide.*

zusammenzöhlen *to count up, add up.*
zusätzlich *additional.*
ZUSCHAUER *m. spectator.*
Zuschauerraum *m. theater auditorium.*
Zuschlag *m. addition, increase in price.*
zuschlagpflichtig *liable to additional payment.*
zuschliessen *to lock, lock up.*
Zuschrift *f. letter, communication.*
zuschulden *adv. guilty*
   sich etwas zuschulden kommen lassen *to be guilty of doing something.*
zusehan *to look on, watch for, wait.*
zusehends *visibly, noticeably.*
zusichern *to assure of, promise.*
Zusicherung *f. insurance.*
zuspitzen *to point, sharpen.*
zusprechen *to encourage.*
   Trost zusprechen *to comfort, console.*
Zuspruch *m. consolation, encouragement.*
ZUSTAND *m. state, condition, position, situation.*
   zustande bringen *to do, get done.*
zuständig *belonging to, responsible, authorized, competent.*
Zuständigkeit *f. competence.*
zustimmen *to consent, agree.*
Zustimmung *f. consent.*
Zustrom *m. influx, crowd, multitude.*
zutrauen *to believe (one) capable of.*
zutraulich *confiding, trusting.*
zutreffend *correct.*
ZUTRITT *m. admission, entrance.*
   Zutritt verboten! *No admittance!*
zuverlässig *reliable, trustworthy.*
Zuversicht *f. confidence, trust.*
zuversichtlich *confident.*
ZUVIEL *too much.*
zuvor *before, previously, formerly.*
zuvorkommen *to come first.*
zuvorkommend *obliging.*
Zuvorkommenheit *f. politeness, kindness.*
ZUWEILEN *sometimes, now and then, occasionally.*
zuwider *offensive, repugnant.*
zuwider (sein) *to be repugnant.*
   Das ist mir zuwider. *I hate it.*
zuzahlen *to pay extra.*
zuziehen *to draw together, call, invite, consult.*
zuzüglich *including, plus.*
Zwang *m. compulsion, constraint, pressure.*
   sich Zwang antun *to restrain oneself.*
   sich keinen Zwang antun *to be quite free and easy.*
zwanglos *free and easy.*

Zwanglosigkeit *f. freedom, ease.*
Zwangslage *f. condition of constraint.*
   sich in einer Zwangslage befinden *to be under compulsion.*
zwangsläufig *necessarily, inevitably.*
ZWANZIG *twenty.*
Zwanziger *m. figure 20, a 20-year old.*
   in den Zwanzigern sein *to be in one's twenties.*
ZWANZIGSTE *twentieth.*
ZWAR *indeed, although.*
   und zwar *in fact, namely.*
ZWECK *m. purpose, design, aim, object, end, goal.*
   keinen Zweck haben *to be of no use.*
   Zu welchem Zweck? *Why? What for?*
zwecklos *useless.*
Zwecklosigkeit *f. uselessness, aimlessness.*
zweckmässig *expedient.*
ZWEI *two.*
   zu zweien *by pairs, two by two.*
zweideutig *ambiguous.*
zweierlei *of two kinds, different.*
zweifach *twofold, double.*
ZWEIFEL *m. doubt, suspicion.*
zweifelhaft *doubtful.*
zweifellos *doubtless, indubitable.*
zweifeln *to doubt, question, suspect.*
Zweifelsfall *m. im Zweifelsfall in case of a doubt.*
zweifelsohne *without doubt, doubtless.*
Zweig *m. branch.*
Zweigstelle *f. branch office.*
Zweikampf *m. duel.*
zweimal *twice.*
zweireihig *double-breasted.*
zweischneidig *two-edged, ambiguous.*
Zweisitzer *m. two-seater.*
ZWEITE *second, next.*
   zu zweit *two by two.*
zweitens *secondly, in the second place.*
Zwerg *m. dwarf.*
Zwieback *m. rusk, biscuit.*
Zwiebel *f. onion, bulb (plant).*
Zwielicht *n. twilight, dusk.*
Zwietracht *f. discord.*
Zwilling *m. twin.*
zwingen *to compel, force, get through, finish.*
zwingend *forcible.*
zwinkern *to blink.*
Zwirn *m. thread, sewing-cotton.*
ZWISCHEN *prep. (dat. when answering question, Wo?; acc. when answering question, Wohin?, and depending on the idiom). among, between.*
   Zwischen den Städten Duisburg und Köln liegt Düsseldorf. *Between the*

cities of Duisburg and Cologne lies
Düsseldorf.
zwischen drei und vier *between three
and four.*
Zwischenbemerkung *f. digression.*
Zwischendeck *n. lower deck.*
zwischendurch *through, in the midst of.*
Zwischenfall *m. incident, episode.*
Zwischenlandung *f. intermediate
landing or stop (flight).*
Zwischenpause *f. interval, break.*

Zwischenraum *m. space, gap, interval.*
Zwischenzeit *f. interval.*
in der Zwischenzeit *in the meantime.*
zwitschern *to twitter.*
ZWÖLF *twelve.*
ZWÖLFTE *twelfth.*
Zyklus *m. cycle, course, series.*
Zylinder *m. cylinder.*
Zyniker *m. cynic.*
zynisch *cynical.*
Zynismus *m. cynicism.*

GLOSSARY OF PROPER NAMES

Albrecht *Albert.*
Alfred *Alfred.*
Andreas *Andrew.*
Anne *Ann.*
Anton *Anthony.*
August *August.*
Barbara *Barbara.*
Bernhard *Bernard.*
Bertha *Bertha.*
Eduard *Edward.*
Elisabeth (Else) *Elizabeth.*
Emilie *Emily.*
Emma *Emma.*
Erich *Eric.*
Ernst *Ernest.*
Eugen *Eugene.*
Franz *Frank.*
Franziska *Frances.*
Friedrich *Frederick.*

Fritz *Fred.*
Genoveva. *Genevieve.*
Georg *George.*
Gertrud (Trudchen) *Gertrude.*
Gretchen *Margaret.*
Gustav *Gustave.*
Heinrich *Henry.*
Helene *Helen.*
Ilse *Elsie.*
Jakob *James.*
Johann *John.*
Johanna *Jane, Joan.*
Josef *Joseph.*
Karl *Charles.*
Katharina (Kätchen) (Käthe)
(Kate). *Katherine*
Klaus *Nicholas.*
Lotte *Charlotte.*
Ludwig *Lewis.*

Luise *Louise.*
Maria *Mary.*
Martha *Martha.*
Michael *Michael.*
Minna *Wilhelmina.*
Moritz *Maurice.*
Otto *Otto.*
Paul *Paul.*
Paula *Paula.*
Peter *Peter.*
Richard *Richard.*
Robert *Robert.*
Rosa *Rose.*
Rüdiger *Roger.*
Rudolph *Ralph.*
Susanne *Susan.*
Theodor *Theodore.*
Therese *Theresa.*
Thomas *Thomas.*
Wilhelm *William.*

GLOSSARY OF GEOGRAPHICAL NAMES

Aachen *n. Aix-la-Chapelle.*
Afrika *n. Africa.*
Agypten *n. Egypt.*
Alpen *pl. Alps.*
Amerika *n. America.*
  die Vereinigten Staaten *pl. the United States.*
  Nord Amerika *n. North America.*
  Süd Amerika *n. South America.*
  Mittel-Amerika *n. Central America.*
Antwerpen *n. Antwerp.*
Asien *n. Asia.*
Atlantik *m. (der Atlantische Ozean)*
Atlantic (the Atlantic Ocean).
Australien *n. Australia.*
Belgien *n. Belgium.*
Berlin *n. Berlin.*
Bonn *n. Bonn.*
Brasilien *n. Brazil.*
Brüssel *n. Brussels.*
Dänemark *n. Denmark.*
Deutschland *n. Germany.*
Europa *n. Europe.*
Frankfurt *n. Frankfort.*
Frankreich *n. France.*
Griechenland *n. Greece.*
Haag (den) *The Hague.*
Hamburg *n. Hamburg.*
Holland *n. Holland.*
Indien *n. India.*

Irland *n. Ireland.*
Italien *n. Italy.*
Japan *n. Japan.*
Jugoslavien *n. Yugoslavia.*
Kanada *n. Canada.*
London *n. London.*
Mexico *n. Mexico.*
Moskau *n. Moscow.*
München *n. Munich.*
Norwegen *n. Norway.*
Nürnberg *n. Nuremberg.*
Österreich *n. Austria.*
Polen *n. Poland.*
Portugal *n. Portugal.*
Preussen *n. Prussia.*
Rhein *m. Rhine.*
Rheinland *n. Rhineland.*
Rumänien *n. Rumania.*
Russland *n. Russia.*
Saar *f. Saar.*
Sachsen *n. Saxony.*
Schlesien *n. Silesia.*
Schottland *n. Scotland.*
Schweden *n. Sweden.*
Schweiz *f. Switzerland.*
Stille Ozean (der) *Pacific Ocean.*
Tschechoslovakei *f. Czechoslovakia.*
Türkei *f. Turkey.*
Ungarn *n. Hungary.*
Wien *n. Vienna.*

ENGLISH-GERMAN

A

a *(an) ein, eine.*
abandon *(to) verlassen.*
abbreviate *(to) abkürzen.*
abbreviation *abkürzung, f.*
ability *Fähigkeit, f.*
able *fähig.*
able *(to be) können.*
abolish *(to) abschaffen.*
about *ungefähr, um (acc.) (around).*
above *über.*
abroad *im Ausland.*
absence *Abwesenheit, f.*
absent *abwesend.*
absolute *unbedingt.*
absorb *(to) aufsaugen.*
abstain *(to) sich enthalten.*
abstract *abstrakt.*
absurd *unvernünftig.*
abundant *reichlich.*
abuse *Missbrauch, m.*
academy *Akademie, f.*
accent *Akzent, m.*
accent *(to) betonen.*
accept *(to) annehmen.*
acceptance *Annahme, f.*
accident *Unfall, m.; Zufall, m. (chance).*
accidental *zufällig.*
accidentally *nebenbei.*
accommodate *(to) unterbringen.*
accommodation *Unterkunft, f.*
accompany *(to) begleiten.*
accomplish *(to) vollführen.*
accord *Übereinstimmung, f.*
according to *zu (dat.); zufolge dem.*
account *Rechnung, f.; Konto, n.*
   (balance).
   on no account *auf keinen Fall.*
   to pay the account *die Rechnung*
   bezahlen.
accuracy *Genauigkeit, f.*
accurate *genau, richtig, akkurat.*
accuse *(to) anklagen, beschuldigen.*
accustom *(to) gewöhnen.*
ace *Ass, n.*
ache *Schmerz, m.*
ache *(to) schmerzen.*
achieve *(to) vollbringen.*
achievement *Vollbringung, f.; Leistung*
   (result).
acid *sauer*
acknowledge *(to) anerkennen.*
acknowledgment *Anerkennung, f.*
acquaintance *Bekannte, m. & f.*
acquire *(to) erwerben.*
across *gegenüber.*

act *Handlung, f.; Akt, m. (of a play);*
   Gesetz, n. (law).
active *tätig.*
activity *Tätigkeit, f.*
actor *Schauspieler, m.*
actress *Schauspielerin, f.*
actual *wirklich.*
acute *akut.*
adopt *(to) anpassen.*
add *(to) zufügen.*
addition *Zusatz, m.; Addition, f. (math).*
   in addition to *Zusätlich zu (dat.).*
address *Adresse, f.; Anschrift, f.;*
   Ansprache, f.; Anrede, f. (speech).
address *(to) adressieren; anreden,*
   ansprechen, sich wenden an (speech).
adequate *angemessen.*
adjective *Eigenschaftswort, n.*
adjoining *angrenzend.*
administer *(to) verwalten.*
admiral *Admiral, m.*
admiration *Bewunderung, f.*
admire *(to) bewundern.*
admission *Eintritt, m.*
admit *(to) einlassen; zugeben*
   (concede).
admittance *Zutritt, m.*
   no admittance *Zutritt verboten.*
adopt *(to) adoptieren (child); annehmen*
   (idea).
adult *Erwachsene(r) noun, m. & f.;*
   erwachsen (adj.).
advance *(to) vorangehen (lead); steigen*
   (price).
   in advance *im Voraus.*
advantage *Vorteil, m.*
adventure *Abenteuer, n.*
adverb *Adverb, n.*
advertise *(to) anzeigen; Reklame*
   machen.
advertisement *Anzeige, f.; Reklame, f.*
advice *Rat, m.*
advise *(to) raten.*
affair *Geschäft, n. (business); Sache, f.*
   (thing).
affect *(to) betreffen.*
affected *geziert, affektiert (pretentious);*
   gerührt (moved).
affection *Zuneigung, f.*
affectionate *herzlich, zärtlich, liebevoll.*
affirm *(to) bestätigen, bekräftigen.*
affirmation *Bestätigung, f.;*
   Bekräftigung, f.
afloat *schwimmend.*
afraid *ängstlich.*
after *nach (dat.).*
afternoon *Nachmittag, m.*
afterward *nachher.*
again *wieder.*
against *gegen (acc.); wider (acc.).*

age *Alter, n. (also old age); Epoche, f. (history).*
agency *Vertretung, f.*
agent *Agent, m.*
aggravate *(to) verschlimmern; ärgern (annoy).*
ago *vor (dat.).*
three days ago *vor drei Tagen.*
agree *(to) übereinstimmen.*
agreeable *angenehm.*
agreed *abgemacht.*
agreement *Übereinstimmung, f.; Vertrag, m. (contract).*
agricultural *landwirtschaftlich.*
agriculture *Landwirtschaft, f.*
ahead *voran, voraus.*
aid *Hilfe, f.*
first aid *Erste Hilfe.*
aid *(to) helfen.*
aim *Ziel, n.; Zweck, m.*
aim *(to) erreichen; zielen (shooting).*
air *Luft, f.*
air force *Luftwaffe, f.*
air mail *Luftpost, f.*
airfield *Flugplatz, m.*
airplane *Flugzeug, n.*
airport *Flughafen, m.*
aisle *Seitenschiff, n.*
alarm *Alarm, m.*
alarm clock *Wecker, m.*
alcohol *Alkohol, m.*
alike *gleich, ähnlich.*
all *ganz, alles.*
all right *in Ordnung, bestimmt.*
not at all *keineswegs.*
alliance *Verbindung f.; Allianz, f. (pact).*
allow *(to) erlauben, gestatten.*
allowed *gestattet.*
ally *Verbündete, m.*
almost *fast, beinahe.*
alone *allein.*
along *entlang.*
already *schon, bereits.*
also *auch.*
altar *Altar, m.*
alter *(to) ändern, verwandeln.*
alternate *abwechselnd.*
alternate *(to) abwechseln.*
although *obwohl, obgleich.*
altitude *Höhe, f.*
altogether *zusammen; gänzlich (wholly).*
always *immer*
amaze *(to) erstaunen.*
amazement *Verwunderung, f.*
ambassador *Botschafter, m.*
ambassadress *Botschafterin, f.*
ambitious *ehrgeizig.*
amend *(to) berichtigen.*

American *Amerikaner (noun, m.); amerikanisch (adj.).*
among *mitten; unter (dat. or acc.).*
amount *Betrag, m.*
ample *geräumig.*
amuse *(to) amüsieren.*
amusement *Unterhaltung, f.*
amusing *amüsant.*
analyze *(to) analysieren.*
ancestors *Vorfahren, pl.*
anchor *Anker, m.*
ancient *alt.*
and *und.*
anecdote *Anekdote, f.*
angel *Engel, m.*
anger *Ärger, m.*
angry *ärgerlich, bös.*
animal *Tier, n.*
animate *(to) beleben.*
annex *Nebengebäude, n.*
annihilate *(to) vernichten.*
anniversary *Hochzeitstag, m.*
announce *(to) ansagen.*
announcement *Anzeige, f.*
annoy *(to) ärgern.*
annual *jährlich.*
annul *(to) annulieren; ungültig machen.*
anonymous *anonym.*
another *ein anderer.*
answer *Antwort, f.*
answer *(to) antworten.*
anterior *vorhergehend.*
anticipate *(to) vorhersehen (foresee); erwarten (expect).*
antique *altertümlich, antik.*
anxiety *Unruhe, f.*
anxious *unruhig.*
any *etwas (some); irgend ein (whatever).*
anybody *irgendjemand.*
anyhow *sowieso.*
anyway *irgenwie.*
anything *irgendetwas.*
anywhere *irgendwo.*
apart *abseits.*
apartment *Wohnung, f.*
apiece *jeder; jedes Stück.*
apologize *(to) sich entschuldigen.*
apparent *scheinbar.*
appeal *(to) gefallen.*
appear *(to) erscheinen.*
appearance *Erscheinung, f.*
appease *(to) besänftigen.*
appendix *Anhang, m.*
appetite *Appetit, m.*
applaud *(to) applaudieren; klatschen.*
applause *Applaus, m.*
apple *Apfel, m.*
application *Antrag, m. (request);*

Gewissenhaftigkeit, f. (diligence).

apply *(to) sich bewerben (for a job); auftragen (use).*

appoint *(to) ernennen.*

appointment *Verabredung, f.*

appreciate *(to) schätzen.*

appreciation *Anerkennung, f.*

appropriate *angemessen.*

approve *(to) genehmigen.*

April *April, m.*

apron *Schürze, f.*

arbitrary *eigenwillig.*

arcade *Arkade, f.*

architect *Architekt, m.; Baumeister, m.*

architecture *Architektur, f.*

ardent *feurig, glühend.*

area *Gebiet, n.*

argue *(to) verhandeln, diskutieren.*

argument *Wortwechsel, m.*

arise *(to) aufsteigen; aufstehen (get up).*

arm *Arm, m.*
  firearms Waffen, pl.

arm *(to) bewaffnen.*

army *Heer, n.; Armee, f.*

around *herum, um (acc.).*

arouse *(to) erregen (revolt); erwecken (suspicion); aufwecken (wake up).*

arrange *(to) ordnen.*

arrangement *Ordnung, f. (order); Anordnung, f. (preparation).*

arrest *Verhaftung, f.*

arrest *(to) verhaften.*

arrival *Ankunft, f.*

arrive *(to) ankommen.*

art *Kunst, f.*

article *Artikel, m.*

artificial *künstlich.*

artist *Künstler, m.*

artistic *künstlerisch.*

as *als (when); so (as much); da (because).*
  as. . .as so. . .wie.
  as long as so lange wie.
  as soon as sobald.
  as to mit Bezug auf (business); was. . .anbetrifft.
  as well sowohl, auch.
  as yet bis jetzt.

ascertain *(to) feststellen.*

ash *Asche, f.*

ashamed *beschämt, verschämt (shy).*

aside *beiseite, abseits.*

ask *(to) fragen.*

asleep *schlafend.*

aspire *(to) sich sehnen.*

aspirin *Aspirin, n.*

assault *Angriff, m.*

assemble *(to) versammeln.*

assembly *Versammlung, f. (congress);*

Gesellschaft, f.

assign *(to) zuteilen.*

assist *(to) beistehen.*

assistant *Gehilfe, m.*

associate *(to) vereinigen.*

assume *(to) annehmen.*

assurance *Versicherung, f.*

assure *(to) versichern.*

astonish *(to) erstaunen.*

astound *(to) verblüffen.*

asylum *Asyl, n.*

at an, *in (dat. or acc.); bei, zu (dat.).*
  at home zu Hause.
  at first zuerst.
  at last endlich.
  at once sofort.
  at times zuweilen.

athlete *Athlet, m.*

athletics, *Gymnastik, f.*

atmosphere *Atmosphäre, f.*

attach *(to) anhängen.*

attain *(to) erreichen.*

attempt *(to) versuchen.*

attend *(to) beiwohnen.*

attendant *Gehilfe, m.*

attention *Aufmerksamkeit, f.*

attic *Dachkammer, f.*

attitude *Haltung, f.; Einstellung, f. (mental).*

attorney *Anwalt, m.*

attract *(to) anziehen.*

attraction *Anziehung, f.*

attractive *schön, anziehend.*

audience *Zuhörer, pl.*

August *August, m.*

aunt *Tante, f.*

author *Autor, m.*

authority *Autorität, f.*

authorize *(to) ermächtigen.*

automatic *automatisch.*

automobile *Auto, n.*

autumn *Herbst, m.*

available *verügbar.*

average *Durchschnitt, m. . .*

avoid *(to) vermeiden.*

awake *wach.*

awake *(to) wecken; erwachen (oneself).*

award *Belohnung, f.*

award *(to) zuerkennen.*

aware *gewahr.*

away *fort, weg.*
  to go away weggehen.

awful *furchtbar.*

awkward *ungeschickt.*

B

baby *Kind, n.*
back *Rücken (noun, m.) (body); zurück (adv.).*
background *Hintergrund, m.*
backwards *rückwärts.*
bacon *Speck, m.*
bad *schlecht.*
badge *Marke, f.*
bag *Beutel, m.*
baggage *Gepäck, n.*
baker *Bäcker, m.*
bakery *Bäckerei, f.*
balance *Gleichgewicht, n.*
balcony *Balkon, m.*
ball *Ball, m.*
balloon *Ballon, m.*
banana *Banane, f.*
band *Band, n.; Musikkapelle, f.*
bandage *Verband, m.*
banister *Treppengeländer, n.*
bank *Bank, f.*
bank note *Banknote, f.*
bankruptcy *Bankrott, m.*
banquet *Bankett, n.*
bar *Barre, f. (metal); Bar, f. (for drinks).*
barber *Frisör, m.*
bare *bloss, bar.*
barefoot *barfuss.*
barge *Barke, f. Lastschiff, n.*
barn *Scheune, f.*
barrel *Fass, n.*
barren *unfruchtbar.*
basin *Becken, n.*
basis *Grundlage, f.*
basket *Korb, m.*
bath *Bad, n.*
bathroom *Badezimmer, n.*
bathe *(to) baden.*
battle *Schlacht, f.*
bay *Bucht, f.*
be *(to) sein.*
    to be hungry *hungrig sein.*
    to be right *Recht haben.*
    to be thirsty *Durst haben.*
    to be tired *müde sein.*
    to be wrong *Unrecht haben.*
beach *Strand, m.*
bean *Bohne, f.*
bear *(to) aushalten.*
beard *Bart, m.*
beat *(to) schlagen.*
beautiful *schön, wunderschön.*
beauty *Schönheit, f.*
beauty parlor *Schönheitssalon, m.*
because *weil.*
become *(to) werden.*

becoming *passend, vorteilhaft.*
bed *Bett, n.*
beef *Rindfleisch, n.*
beer *Bier, n.*
beet *Rübe, f.*
before *vor (dat. or acc.); bevor (conj.).*
beg *(to) betteln.*
beggar *Bettler, m.*
begin *(to) beginnen, anfangen.*
beginning *Anfang, m.*
behave *(to) sich betragen, sich benehmen.*
behavior *Verhalten, n.*
behind *hinter (dat. or acc.).*
belief *Glaube, m.*
believe *(to) glauben.*
bell *Glocke, f.*
belong *(to) gehören.*
below *unter (dat. or acc.).*
belt *Gürtel, m.*
bench *Bank, f.*
bend *(to) biegen.*
beneath *unten; unter (dat. or acc.).*
benefit *Vorteil, m.*
beside *neben (dat. or acc.).*
besides *ausserdem.*
best *beste (der, die, das) (adj.); am besten (adv.).*
bet *Wette, f.*
bet *(to) wetten.*
betray *(to) verraten.*
better *besser.*
between *zwischen (dat. or acc.).*
beware *(to) sich hüten.*
    Beware! *Achtung!*
beyond *jenseits (gen.).*
bicycle *Fahrrad, n.*
bid *(to) bieten; befehlen (order).*
big *gross.*
bill *Rechnung, f.*
    bill of fare *Speisekarte, f.*
billion *Billion, f.*
bind *(to) binden.*
bird *Vogel, m.*
birth *Geburt, f.*
birthday *Geburtstag, m.*
biscuit *Zwieback, m.*
bishop *Bischof, m.*
bit *Stück, n. Gebiss, n. (horse).*
bite *Biss, m.*
bite *(to) beissen.*
bitter *bitter.*
bitterness *Bitterkeit, f.*
black *schwarz.*
blade *Klinge, f. (razor); Blatt, n. (grass).*
blame *Schuld, f.; Tadel, m.*
blame *(to) tadeln.*
blank *unbeschrieben (page); verwundert (expression).*
blanket *Decke, f.*

bleed (to) bluten.
bless (to) segnen.
blessing Segnung, f.; Segen, m.
blind blind.
block Block, m.
block (to) versperren.
blood Blut, n.
blotter Loschpapier, n.
blouse Bluse, f.
blow Schlag, m.
blow (to) blasen; putzen (nose).
blue blau.
blush (to) erröten.
board Brett, n. (plank); Verpflegung, f. (food).
boarding house Pension, f.
boast (to) prahlen.
boat Boot, n.
body Körper, m.
boil (to) kochen, sieden.
boiler Kessel, m.
bold kühn.
bomb Bombe, f.
   atom bomb. Atombombe, f.
bond Aktie, f. (stock).
bone Knochen, m.
book Buch, n.
bookseller Buchhändler, m.
bookstore Buchhandlung, f.
border Grenze, f.
boring langweilig.
born geboren.
borrow (to) borgen, leihen.
both beide.
bother (to) ärgern, plagen, bemühen.
   Don't bother! Bemühen Sie sich nicht!
bottle Flasche, f.
bottle opener Flaschenöffner, m.
bottom Boden, m.
bounce (to) aufspringen.
bowl Schale, f.
box Schachtel, f.
boy Junge, m.; Knabe, m.
bracelet Armband, n.
braid Borte, f.; Zopf, m. (hair).
brain Gehirn, n.
brake Bremse, f.
branch Ast, m. (tree); Filiale, f. (business).
brave tapfer.
brassiere Büstenhalter, m.
bread Brot, n.
break (to) brechen; lösen (engagement).
breakfast Frühstück, n.
   have breakfast frühstücken.
breath Atem, m.
breathe (to) atmen.
breeze Wind, m.; Brise, f.
bribe (to) bestechen.

brick Backstein, m.
bride Braut, f.
   bridegroom Bräutigam, m.
bridge Brücke, f.
brief kurz.
bright hell, klar.
brighten (to) erheitern; sich aufklären (weather).
brilliant glänzend.
bring (to) bringen.
bring up (to) erziehen.
British britisch.
broad weit, breit.
broil (to) braten.
broken zerbrochen.
brook Bach, m.
broom Besen, m.
brother Bruder, m.
brother-in-law Schwager, m.
brown braun.
bruise (to) quetschen.
brush Bürste, f.
bubble Blase, f.
buckle Schnalle, f.
bud Knospe, f.
budget Budget, n.
build (to) bauen.
building Gebäude, n.
bulletin Bulletin, n.
bundle Bündel, n.
burn (to) brennen.
burst (to) bersten.
bus Autobus, m. Omnibus, m.
bush Busch, m.
business Geschäft, n.
businessman Geschäftsmann, m.
busy beschäftigt.
but aber; sondern (neg.).
butcher Metzger, m.
butcher shop Metzgerei, f.
butter Butter, f.
button Knopf, m.
buy (to) kaufen.
buyer Käufer, m.
by von (dat.); durch (acc.); neben (dat. & acc.) (close to); um (acc.) (time).

C

cab Taxi, n.
cabbage Kohl, m.; Kraut, n.
cable Kabel, n.
cage Käfig, m.
cake Kuchen, m.
calendar Kalender, m.
calf Kalb, n.

call *Ruf, m.*
call *(to) rufen; anrufen; telefonieren (telephone); heissen (name).*
calm *ruhig.*
camera *Kamera, f.*
camp *Lager, n.*
camp *(to) lagern.*
can *Büchse, f.; Dose, f.*
can *(to be able) konnen.*
can opener *Büchsenöffner, m.*
cancel *(to) rückgängig machen, annulieren.*
candidate *Kandidat, m.*
candle *Kerze, f.*
candy *Bonbons, pl.*
cap *Mütze, f.*
capital *Hauptstadt, f. (city); Kapital, n. (finance).*
capricious *launisch; eigensinning (temperamental).*
captain *Hauptmann, n. (army); Kapitän, m. (navy).*
captive *Gefangene, m.*
capture *(to) fangen; einnehmen.*
car *Wagen, m.*
carbon paper *Durchschlagpapier, n.*
card *Karte, f.*
care *Sorge, f. (anxiety); Sorgfalt, f. (caution).*
care of *bei*
take care of *pflegen*
care *(to) sich sorgen.*
care about *sich kümmern.*
care for (to like) *gern haben.*
I don't care. *Das ist mir gleich.*
career *Laufbahn, f.*
careful *vorsichtig, sorgfältig.*
careless *nachlässig, sorglos.*
caress *Liebkosung, f.*
carpenter *Zimmermann, m.*
carpet *Teppich, m.*
carry *(to) tragen.*
carve *(to) schnitzen.*
case *Fall, m.; Aktentasche, f. (container).*
in case *im Falle.*
cash *Bargeld, n.*
to pay cash *bar zahlen.*
cash *(to) einlösen, kassieren.*
cashier *Kassierer, m.*
castle *Schloss, n.*
cat *Katze, f.*
catch *(to) fangen.*
category *Kategorie, f.*
cathedral *Dom, m.*
Catholic *katholisch.*
cattle *Vieh, n.*
cause *Grund, m.; Ursache, f.*
cause *(to) verursachen.*

cavalry *Reiterei, f.*
cease *(to) aufhören.*
ceiling *Decke, f.*
celebrate *(to) feiern.*
cellar *Keller, m.*
cement *Zement, m.*
cemetery *Kirchhof, m.; Friedhof, m.*
center *Zentrum, n.*
central *zentral.*
central heating *Zentralheizung, f.*
century *Jahrhundert, n.*
cereal *Getreide, n. (grain); Mehlspeise, f. (prepared).*
ceremony *Zeremonie, f.*
certain *gewiss.*
certainty *Gewissheit, f.; Sicherheit, f.*
certificate *Zeugnis, n.*
chain *Kette, f.*
chair *Stuhl, m.*
chairman *Vorsitzende, m.; Präsident, m.*
chalk *Kreide, f.*
challenge *Herausforderung, f.*
challenge *(to) herausfordern.*
champion *Meister, m.*
world champion *Weltmeister, m.*
chance *Zufall, m.*
change *Veränderung, f.; Kleingeld, n. (money).*
change *(to) ändern; wechseln (money).*
chapel *Kapelle, f.*
chapter *Kapitel, n.*
character *Charakter, m.*
characteristic *charakteristisch.*
charge *(to) beladen; berechnen (price).*
charitable *wohltätig.*
charity *Wohltätigkeit, f.*
charming *reizend.*
chase *(to) jagen.*
chat *(to) plaudern.*
cheap *billig.*
cheat *(to) betrügen.*
check *Scheck, m.; Rechnung, f. (in a restaurant).*
check *(to) knotrollieren; aufgeben (baggage).*
cheek *Wange, f.*
cheer *(to) aufheitern.*
cheerful *heiter, freudig, fröhlich.*
cheese *Käse, m.*
chemical *chemisch.*
cherish *(to) schätzen.*
cherry *Kirsche, f.*
chest *Brust, f.; Kiste, f. (box).*
chest of drawers *Kommode, f.*
chestnut *Kastanie, f.*
chew *(to) kauen.*
chicken *Huhn, n.; Hühnchen, n.*
chief *Leiter, m.*
chief *(adj.) haupt-.*

chime *Glockenspiel, n.*
chimney *Schornstein, m.*
chin *Kinn, n.*
china *Porzellan, n.*
chip *Span, m.; Splitter, m.*
chocolate *Schokolade, f.*
choice *Wahl, f.*
choir *Chor, m.*
choke *(to) ersticken.*
choose *(to) auswählen.*
chop *Kotelett, n.*
Christian *Christ (noun, m.); christlich (adj.).*
Christmas *Weihnachten, f.*
church *Kirche, f.*
cigar *Zigarre, f.*
cigarette *Zigarette, f.*
circle *Kreis, m.*
circular *rund.*
circulate *(to) kreisen.*
circumstances *Umstände, pl.*
citizen *Bürger, m.*
city *Stadt, f.*
city hall *Rathaus, m.*
civil *zivil.*
civilization *Zivilisation, f.*
civilize *(to) zivilisieren.*
claim *Forderung, f.*
claim *(to) fordern.*
clamor *Geschrei, n.*
clap *(to) klatschen.*
class *Klasse, f.*
classify *(to) klassifizieren.*
clause *Klausel, f.*
clean *rein, sauber.*
clean *(to) reinigen.*
cleaners *Reinigungsanstalt, f.*
cleanliness *Reinlichkeit, f.*
clear *klar.*
clerk *Angestellte, m.*
clever *klug, schlau.*
climate *Klima, n.*
climb *(to) klimmen, steigen (stairway); besteigen (mountain).*
clip *Klammer, f.*
clip *(to) beschneiden (cut); zusammenfügen (attach).*
clock *Uhr, f.*
close *nahe.*
close *(to) zumachen, schliessen.*
closed *geschlossen.*
closet *Schrank, m.*
cloth *Tuch, n.*
clothes *Kleider, pl.*
cloud *Wolke, f.*
cloudy *bewölkt.*
clover *Klee, m.*
club *Klub, m.; Keule, f. (cards).*
coal *Kohle, f.*

coarse *roh.*
coast *Küste, f.*
coat *Mantel, m. (overcoat); Anzug, m. (suit).*
code *Gesetzbuch, n. (law); Code, m.*
coffee *Kaffee, m.*
coffin *Sarg, m.*
coin *Münze, f.*
cold *kalt.*
coldness *Kälte, f.*
collaborate *(to) zusammenarbeiten.*
collar *Kragen, m.; Halsband, n. (dog).*
collect *(to) sammeln.*
collection *Sammlung, f.*
collective *gesamt.*
college *Universität, f.*
colonial *kolonial.*
colony *Kolonie, f.*
color *Farbe, f.*
color *(to) färben.*
column *Spalte, fl., Kollonne, f. (military); Säule, f. (arch).*
comb *Kamm, m.*
comb *(to) kämmen.*
combination *Verbindung, f.*
combine *(to) verbinden.*
come *(to) kommen.*
    come back *zurückkommen.*
comedy *Komödie, f.*
comet *Komet, m.*
comfort *Behaglichkeit, f.; Trost, m. (moral).*
comfort *(to) trösten.*
comfortable *bequem.*
comma *Komma, n.*
command *Befehl, m.*
command *(to) befehlen.*
commander *Befehlshaber, m.*
commercial *geschäftsmässig.*
commission *Kommission, f.; Offizierspatent, n.*
commit *(to) begehen.*
common *gemein, gewöhnlich.*
communicate *(to) mitteilen.*
communication *Mitteilung, f.*
community *Gemeinde, f.*
companion *Genosse, m.*
company *Gesellschaft, f. (social); Kompanie, f. (military).*
compare *(to) vergleichen.*
comparison *Vergleich, m.*
compete *(to) konkurrieren.*
competition *Konkurrenz, f.; Tournier, n. (sports).*
complain *(to) sich beklagen.*
complaint *Klage, f.*
complete *vollenden.*
complex *Komplex, (noun, m.); verwickelt (adj.).*

complexion *Gesichtsfarbe, f.*
complicate *(to) verwickeln, komplizieren.*
complicated *verwickelt, kompliziert.*
compliment *Kompliment, n.*
compose *(to) komponieren.*
composer *Komponist, m.*
composition *Komposition, f.*
compromise *Kompromiss, m.; Vergleich, m.*
compromise *(to) einen Kompromiss machen, kompromittieren.*
conceit *Einbildung, f.*
conceited *eingebildet.*
conceive *(to) ersinnen.*
concentrate *(to) konzentrieren.*
concern *Angelegenheit, f. (matter); Sorge, f. (anxiety); Geschäft, n. (business).*
concern *(to) betreffen.*
concert *Konzert, n.*
concrete *konkret.*
condemn *(to) verurteilen, verdammen.*
condense *(to) kondensieren.*
condition *Zustand, m.*
conduct *Benehmen, n.*
conduct *(to) führen; dirigieren (music).*
conductor *Führer, m. (guide); Schaffner, m. (vehicle); Dirigent, m. (music).*
confess *(to) gestehen; beichten (church).*
confession *Geständnis, n.; Beichte, f. (church).*
confidence *Vertrauen, n.*
confident *vertrauend, vertrauensvoll.*
confidential *vertraulich.*
confirm *(to) bestätigen.*
confirmation *Bestätigung, f.*
congratulate *(to) gratulieren.*
congratulations *Glückwunsch, m.*
connect *(to) verbinden.*
connection *Verbindung, f.*
conquer *(to) erobern, besiegen.*
conquest *Eroberung, f.; Sieg, m.*
conscience *Gewissen, n.*
conscientious *gewissenhaft.*
conscious *bewusst.*
consent *Einwilligung, f.*
conservative *konservativ.*
consider *(to) betrachten (look); bedenken (think).*
considerable *beträchtlich.*
consideration *Betrachtung, f.*
consist of *(to) bestehen (aus - dat.).*
consistent *übereinstimmend.*
constant *beständig.*
constitution *Verfassung, f.; Gesundheit, f. (health).*

constitutional *verfassungsmässig.*
consul *Konsul, m.*
contagious *ansteckend.*
contain *(to) enthalten.*
container *Behälter, m.*
contemporary *Zeitgenosse, (noun, m.); zeitgenössisch (adj.).*
content *zufrieden.*
content *(to) befriedigen.*
contents *Inhalt, m.; Gehalt, m.*
continent *Kontinent, m.*
continual *fortwährend.*
continue *(to) fortfahren.*
contract *Vertrag, m.*
contractor *Untermehmer, m.*
contradict *(to) widersprechen.*
contradiction *Widerspruch, m.*
contradictory *widersprechend.*
contrary *Gegenteil (noun, n.); entgegengesetzt (adj.).*
on the contrary *im Gegenteil.*
contrast *Gegensatz, m.*
contrast *(to) abstechen.*
contribute *(to) beitragen.*
contribution *Beitrag, m.*
control *Kontrolle, f.*
control *(to) kontrollieren.*
controversy *Meinungsverschiedenheit, f.*
convenience *Bequemlichkeit, f.*
convenient *passend; bequem (practical).*
convent *Kloster, n.*
convention *Versammlung, f.*
conversation *Gespräch, n.; Unterhaltung, f.*
converse *(to) sich unterhalten.*
convert *(to) verwandeln.*
convict *(to) verurteilen.*
conviction *Verurteilung, f.*
convince *(to) überzeugen.*
cook *Koch, m.; Köchin, f.*
cook *(to) kochen.*
cool *kühl.*
cool *(to) kühlen.*
copy *Kopie, f.*
cork *Kork, m.*
corkscrew *Korkenzieher, m.*
corn *Mais, m.*
corner *Ecke, f.*
corporation *Körperschaft, f.*
correct *richtig.*
correct *(to) berichtigen, korrigieren.*
correction *Berichtigung, f.*
correspond *(to) korrespondieren.*
correspondence *Briefwechsel, m.*
correspondent *Korrespondent, m.*
corresponding *entsprechend.*
corrupt *(to) verderben.*

corruption *Verdorbenheit, f.*
cost *Kosten, f.*
costume *Kostüm, n.*
cottage *Häuschen, n.*
cotton *Baumwolle, f.; Watte, f. (pharmacy).*
couch *Sofa, n.*
cough *Husten, m.*
count *Graf, m. (nobility); Zählung, f.*
count *(to) zählen.*
counter *Ladentisch, m.*
countess *Gräfin, f.*
countless *zahllos.*
country *Land, n; Vaterland, n. (fatherland).*
countryman *Landsmann, m.*
couple *Paar, n.*
courage *Mut, m.*
course *Lauf, m. (direction); Kursus, m. (studies).*
court *Gericht, n.*
courteous *zuvorkommend.*
courtesy *Höflichkeit, f.*
courtyard *Hof, m.*
cousin *Vetter, m.; Cousine, f.*
cover *Decke, f.*
cow *Kuh, f.*
crack *Riss, m.*
crack *(to) knacken.*
cradle *Wiege, f.*
crash *Zusammenbruch, m.*
crazy *verrückt.*
cream *Sahne, f.*
create *(to) schaffen.*
creature *Geschöpf, n.; Wesen, n.*
credit *Kredit, m.*
creditor *Gläubiger, m.*
crime *Verbrechen, n.*
crisis *Krise, f.*
crisp *knusperig.*
critic *Kritiker, m.*
critical *kritisch.*
criticize *(to) kritisieren.*
crooked *krumm.*
crop *Ernte, f.*
cross *Kreuz, n.*
crossing *Übergang, m.*
crossroads *Strassenkreuzung, f.*
crouch *(to) sich ducken.*
crow *Krähe, f.*
crowd *Menge, f.*
crowd *(to) überfüllen.*
crowded *überfüllt.*
crown *Krone, f.*
crown *(to) krönen.*
cruel *grausam.*
cruelty *Grausamkeit, f.*
crumb *Krume, f.*
crumble *(to) zerbröckeln.*

crust *Kruste, f.*
crutch *Krücke, f.*
cry *Ruf, m.; Geschrei, n.*
cry *(to) weinen (weep); schreien (shout).*
cuff *Manschette, f.*
cunning *gerissen.*
cup *Tasse, f.*
cure *Heilung, f.*
curiosity *Neugier, f.*
curious *neugierig.*
curl *Locke, f.*
current *Strom (noun, m.); laufend (adj.).*
curtain *Vorhang, m.*
curve *Kurve, f.*
cushion *Kissen, n.*
custom *Sitte, f.*
customary *gebräuchlich.*
customer *Kunde, m.*
customhouse *Zollamt, m.*
customs official *Zollbeamter, m.*
cut *Schnitt, m.*
cut *(to) schneiden.*

D

dagger *Dolch, m.*
daily *täglich.*
dainty *zierlich.*
dairy *Milchgeschäft, n.*
dam *Damm, m.*
damage *Schaden, m.*
damage *(to) beschädigen.*
damp *feucht.*
dance *Tanz, m.*
dance *(to) tanzen.*
danger *Gefahr, f.*
dangerous *gefährlich.*
dark *dunkel.*
darkness *Dunkelheit, f.*
dash *(to) sich beeilen.*
date *Datum, n.; Verabredung, f. (meeting).*
daughter *Tochter, f.*
dawn *Morgendämmerung, f.*
day *Tag, m.*
  day after tomorrow *übermorgen.*
  day before yesterday *vorgestern.*
  yesterday *gestern.*
dazzle *(to) blenden.*
dead *tot.*
deaf *taub.*
deal *Teil, m.; Geschäft, n. (business).*
deal *(to) ausgeben (cards).*
dealer *Händler, m.; Geber, m. (cards).*

dear *lieb; teuer (also expensive).*
death *Tod, m.*
debate *Debatte, f.*
debt *Schuld, f.*
debtor *Schuldner, m.*
decanter *Karaffe, f.*
decay *Verfall, m. (ruin); Fäulnis, f. (rot).*
decay *(to) verfallen, verfaulen.*
deceased *verstorben.*
deceit *Falschheit, f.*
deceive *(to) betrügen.*
December *Dezember, m.*
decent *anständig.*
decide *(to) entscheiden.*
decided *entschieden.*
decision *Entscheidung, f.; Entschluss, m.*
decisive *entscheidend.*
deck *Deck, n.*
declare *(to) erklären.*
decline *Abnahme, f.; Fall, m.*
decline *(to) verfallen, abweisen; deklinieren (grammar).*
decrease *Abnahme, f.; Verminderung, f.*
decrease *(to) abnehmen, vermindern.*
decree *Verordnung, f.*
dedicate *(to) widmen.*
deed *Tat, f.*
deep *tief.*
deer *Hirsch, m.*
defeat *Niederlage, f.*
defeat *(to) besiegen.*
defect *Fehler, m.*
defend *(to) verteidigen.*
defense *Verteidigung, f.*
defiance *Trotz, m.*
define *(to) definieren.*
definite *bestimmt.*
defy *(to) trotzen.*
degree *Grad, m.*
delay *Verzögerung, f.*
delay *(to) aufhalten.*
delegate *Delegierter, m.*
delegate *(to) delegieren.*
deliberate *(to) erwägen.*
deliberately *absichtlich.*
delicacy *Delikatesse, f.*
delicate *zart.*
delicious *köstlich.*
delight *Freude, f.*
delighted *erfreut.*
deliver *(to) liefern.*
deliverance *Befreiung, f.*
delivery *Ablieferung, f.*
demand *Forderung, f.; Nachfrage, f. (business).*
demand *(to) fordern.*
democracy *Demokratie, f.*
demonstrate *(to) demonstrieren.*

demonstration *Kundgebung, f.; Demonstration, f.*
denial *Verleugnung, f.*
denounce *(to) denunzieren.*
dense *dicht.*
density *Dichte, f.*
dentist *Zahnarzt, m.*
deny *(to) ableugnen, verleugnen.*
departure *Abreise, f.*
department *Abteilung, f.*
depend *(to) abhängen.*
dependent *abhängig.*
deplore *(to) beweinen.*
deposit *Anzahlung, f.*
depress *(to) niederdrücken.*
depression *Depression, f.*
deprive *(to) berauben, entziehen.*
depth *Tiefe, f.*
deride *(to) verlachen, verhöhnen.*
derive *(to) ableiten.*
descend *(to) abstammen.*
descendant *Nachkomme, m.*
descent *Abstieg, m.; Abstammung, f. (family).*
describe *(to) beschreiben.*
description *Beschreibung, f.*
desert *Wüste, f.*
desert *(to) verlassen.*
deserve *(to) verdienen.*
design *Zeichnung, f. (drawing); Absicht, f. (intention).*
designer *Zeichner, m.*
desirable *wünschenswert.*
desire *(to) wünschen.*
desire *Wunsch, m.*
desirous *begierig.*
desk *Pult, n.*
desolate *trostlos.*
despair *Verzweiflung, f.*
despair *(to) verzweifeln.*
desperate *verzweifelt.*
despise *(to) verachten.*
despite *trotz (gen.).*
dessert *Nachtisch, m.*
destiny *Schicksal, n.*
destroy *(to) zerstören.*
destruction *Zerstörung, f.*
detach *(to) lösen.*
detail *Einzelheit, f.*
detain *(to) aufhalten.*
detect *(to) entdecken.*
detective *Detektiv, m.*
detective story *Kriminalgeschichte, f.; Detektivroman, m.*
determination *Entschlossenheit, f.*
determine *(to) bestimmen.*
detest *(to) verabscheuen.*
detour *Umweg, m.*
detract *(to) abziehen.*

detrimental *schädlich.*
develop *(to) entwickeln.*
development *Entwicklung, f.*
device *Kunstgriff, m.*
devil *Teufel, m.*
devise *(to) ersinnen.*
devoid *bar (gen.); ohne (acc.)*
devote *(to) widmen.*
devour *(to) verschlingen.*
dew *Tau, m.*
dial *Zifferblatt, n. (clock).*
dial *(to) wählen.*
dialect *Dialekt, m.*
dialogue *Dialog, m.*
diameter *Durchmesser, m.*
diamond *Diamant, m.*
diary *Tagebuch, n.*
dictate *(to) diktieren.*
dictation *Diktat, n.*
dictionary *Wörterbuch, n.*
die *(to) sterben.*
diet *Diät, f.*
differ *(to) sich unterscheiden.*
difference *Unterschied, m.*
different *verschieden.*
difficult *schwierig.*
difficulty *Schwierigkeit, f.*
dig *(to) graben.*
digest *(to) verdauen.*
dignity *Würde, f.*
dim *trübe.*
dimension *Dimension, f.; Mass, n.*
diminish *(to) vermindern.*
dining room *Speisesaal, m.*
dinner *Abendessen, n.*
dine *(to) essen, speisen.*
dip *(to) senken, (ein)tauchen.*
diplomacy *Diplomatie, f.*
diplomat *Diplomat, m.*
direct *direkt.*
direct *(to) den Weg zeigen (show the way).*
direction *Richtung, f.*
director *Direktor, m.*
directory *Adressbuch, n.*
dirt *Schmutz, m.*
dirty *schmutzig.*
disability *Unfähigkeit, f.*
disabled *unfähig.*
disadvantage *Nachteil, m.*
disagree *(to) uneinig sein.*
disagreeable *unangenehm.*
disagreement *Meinungsverschiedenheit, f.*
disappear *(to) verschwinden.*
disappearance *Verschwinden, n.*
disappoint *(to) enttäuschen.*
disapprove *(to) missbilligen, ablehnen.*
disaster *Unglück, n.; Katastrophe, f.*

disastrous *unheilvoll.*
discharge *Entlassung, f. (dismissal); Abfeuern, n. (gun).*
discharge *(to) entlassen (person); abfeuern (firearm).*
discipline *Zucht, f.*
disclaim *(to) bestreiten.*
disclose *(to) enthüllen.*
disclosure *Enthüllung, f.*
discomfort *Unbehaglichkeit, f.*
disconnect *(to) trennen.*
discontent *unzufrieden.*
discontinue *(to) aufhören.*
discord *Zwietracht, f.*
discount *Diskonto, m. (financial); Rabatt, m.*
discourage *(to) entmutigen.*
discouragement *Entmutigung, f.*
discover *(to) entdecken.*
discovery *Entdeckung. f.*
discreet *diskret, vorsichtig.*
discretion *Klugheit, f.; Urteil, n.*
discuss *(to) besprechen, erörtern.*
discussion *Erörterung, f.; Diskussion, f.*
disdain *Verachtung, f.*
disdain *(to) verschmähen, verachten.*
disease *Krankheit, f.*
disgrace *Schande, f. (shame); Ungnade, f.*
disguise *Verkleidung, f.*
disguise *(to) verkleiden.*
disgust *Ekel, m.*
disgust *(to) (an)ekeln.*
disgusted *ekelhaft, angeekelt.*
dish *Speise, f. (food); Schüssel, f. (plate).*
dishonest *unehrlich.*
disk *Scheibe, f.*
dislike *Widerwille, m.*
dislike *(to) nicht mögen.*
dismiss *(to) entlassen.*
dismissal *Entlassung, f.*
disobey *(to) nicht gehorchen.*
disorder *Unordnung, f.*
dispense *(to) verteilen.*
display *Entfaltung f. (unfold); Schau, f. (exposition).*
displease *(to) missfallen.*
displeasure *Missfallen, n.*
disposal *Verfügung, f.*
dispose *(to) anordnen, verfügen.*
dispute *Streit, m.*
dispute *(to) steiten.*
dissolve *(to) auflösen.*
distance *Entfernung, f.*
distant *entfernt.*
distinct *deutlich.*
distinction *Auszeichnung, f.; Unterschied, m. (difference).*

distinguish *(to) unterscheiden.*
distort *(to) verdrehen.*
distract *(to) verwirren.*
distress *Not, f.*
distress *(to) betrüben.*
distribute *(to) verteilen.*
district *Distrikt, m.*
distrust *Misstrauen, n.*
distrust *(to) misstrauen.*
disturb *(to) stören.*
disturbance *Störung, f.*
ditch *Graben, m.*
dive *(to) tauchen.*
divide *(to) verteilen.*
divine *göttlich.*
division *Teilung, f.*
divorce *(to) scheiden.*
divorced *geschieden.*
dizziness *Schwindel, m.*
dizzy *schwindlig.*
do *(to) run, machen.*
dock *Dock, n.*
doctor *Arzt, m.*
doctrine *Lehre, f.*
document *Urkunde, f. Dokument, n.*
dog *Hund, m.*
doll *Puppe, f.*
dome *Kuppel, f.*
domestic *Häuslich; einheimisch (native).*
domestic animal *Haustier, n.*
dominate *(to) beherrschen.*
door *Tür, f.*
dose *Dosis, f.*
dot *Punkt, m.*
double *doppelt.*
doubt *Zweifel, m.*
doubt *(to) zweifeln.*
doubtful *zweifelhaft.*
doubtless *ohne Zweifel.*
dough *Teig, m.*
down *unter (dat. or acc.); hinunter, herunter.*
dozen *Dutzend, n.*
draft *Wechsel, m. (money); Zeichnung, f. (drawing).*
drag *(to) schleppen.*
drain *(to) entwässern.*
drama *Drama, n.*
draught *Zug, m.*
draw *(to) zeichen.*
draw back *(to) schleppen.*
drawer *Schublade, f.*
drawing-room *Gesellschaftszimmer; n.; Salon, m.; Wohnzimmer, n.*
dread *Furcht, f.*
dread *(to) fürchten.*
dreadful *furchtbar, schrecklich.*
dream *Traum, m.*
dream *(to) träumen.*
dreamer *Träumer, m.*

dress *Kleid, n.*
dress *(to) sich anziehen.*
dressmaker *Schneiderin, f.*
drink *Getränk, n.*
drink *(to) trinken.*
drip *(to) tropfen.*
drive *(to) fahren.*
driver *Chauffeur, m.*
drop *Fall, m.; Tropfen, m. (liquid).*
drown *(to) ertrinken.*
drug *Droge, f.*
drugstore *Apotheke, f.; Drogerie, f.*
drum *Trommel, f.*
drunk *betrunken.*
dry *trocken.*
dry *(to) trocknen.*
dryness *Trockenheit, f.*
duchess *Herzogin, f.*
duck *Ente, f.*
due *Gebühr, f.*
duke *Herzog, m.*
dull *trüb (weather); matt (color); dumpf (sound).*
dumb *stumm; dumm (stupid).*
   deaf and dumb taubstumm.
during *während (gen.).*
dust *Staub, m.*
dust *(to) abstäuben.*
dusty *staubig.*
Dutch *holländisch.*
duty *Pflicht, f.; Dienst, m. (service); Zoll, m. (customs).*
dwarf *Zwerg, m.*
dwell *(to) wohnen.*
dye *Farbe, f.*
dye *(to) färben.*

E

each *jeder.*
   each other einander.
   each time jedesmal.
eager *eifrig.*
eagle *Adler, m.*
ear *Ohr, n.*
early *früh.*
earn *(to) verdienen.*
earnest *ernst.*
earth *Erde, f.*
ease *Bequemlichkeit, f. (comfort); Ruhe, f. (calm); Linderung, f. (relief); Leichtigkeit, f. (facility).*
ease *(to) lindern, erleichtern.*
easily *leicht.*
east *Osten, m.*
Easter *Ostern, pl.*

eastern *östlich.*
easy *leicht.*
eat *(to) essen.*
echo *Echo, n.*
echo *(to) widerhallen.*
economical *wirtschaftlich; sparsam.*
economize *(to) sparen.*
edge *Schneide, f. (blade); Rand, m. (rim).*
edition *Ausgabe, f.; Auflage, f.*
editor *Redakteur, m.*
editorial *Leitartikel (noun, m.); redaktionell (adj.).*
education *Bildung, f.*
effect *Wirkung, f.*
effective *wirkungsvoll.*
efficiency *Leistungsfähigkeit, f.*
effort *Anstrengung, f.; Bestreben, n. (endeavor).*
egg *Ei, n. (Eier, pl.)*
egoism *Egoismus, m.; Selbstsucht, f.*
eight *acht.*
eighteen *achtzehn.*
eighteenth *achtzehnte.*
eighth *achte.*
eightieth *achtzigste.*
eighty *achtzig.*
either *oder.*
  either...or *entweder...oder.*
elastic *elastisch.*
elbow *Ellbogen, m.*
elder *älter.*
elderly *älterer, ältlich.*
eldest *Älteste, m. & f.*
elect *(to) erwählen.*
election *Wahl, f.*
elector *Wähler, m.*
electrical *elektrisch.*
electricity *Elektrizität, f.*
elegant *elegant.*
element *Element, n.*
elementary *elementar.*
elephant *Elefant, m.*
elevator *Aufzug, m.*
eleven *elf.*
eleventh *elfte.*
eliminate *(to) ausscheiden.*
eloquence *Beredsamkeit, f.*
eloquent *beredt.*
else *ander, anders; sonst (otherwise).*
  anyone else *irgend ein anderer.*
  elsewhere *anderswo.*
  everybody else *jeder andere.*
  nobody else *sonst niemand.*
  someone else *ein anderer.*
elude *(to) ausweichen.*
embark *(to) (sich) einschiffen.*
embarrass *(to) in Verlegenheit bringen.*
embarrassing *unangenehm, beschämend.*

embarrassment *Verlegenheit, f.*
embassy *Botschaft, f.*
embody *verkörpern.*
embrace *(to) umarmen.*
embroidery *Stickerei, f.*
emerge *(to) herauskommen.*
emergency *Notfall, m.*
eminent *hervorragend.*
emotion *Aufregung, f.*
emperor *Kaiser, m.*
emphasis *Nachdruck, m.*
emphasize *(to) betonen.*
emphatic *nachdrücklich.*
empire *Reich, n.*
employee *Angestellte, m. or f.*
employer *Arbeitgeber, m.*
employment *Arbeit, f.; Beschäftigung, f.*
empty *leer.*
enable *(to) befähigen.*
enamel *Email, n.*
enclose *(to) einschliessen.*
enclosure *Anlage, f. (letter); Einzäunung, f. (fence).*
encourage *(to) ermutigen.*
encouragement *Ermutigung, f.*
end *Ende, n.*
end *(to) enden, aufhören.*
endeavor *Bestreben, n.; Bemühung, f.*
endeavor *(to) sich bemühen.*
endorse *(to) unterzeichnen.*
endure *(to) ertragen.*
enemy *Feind, m.*
energy *Energie, f.*
enforce *(to) durchsetzen.*
engage *(to) anstellen.*
engaged *beschäftigt (busy); verlobt (affianced).*
engagement *Verabredung, f. (appointment); Beschäftigung, f. (business); Verlobung, f. (marriage)*
engine *Maschine, f.; Lokomotive, f. (train).*
engineer *Ingenieur. m.*
English *englisch.*
engrave *(to) eingravieren.*
enjoy *(to) geniessen, amüsieren.*
  enjoy oneself *sich amüsieren.*
enjoyment *Vergnügen, n.*
enlarge *(to) vergrössern.*
enlist *(to) anwerben.*
enormous *ungeheuer.*
enough *genug.*
enter *(to) hineingehen.*
  Enter! *Herein!*
entertain *(to) unterhalten.*
entertainment *Unterhaltung, f., Schau, f. (show).*
enthusiasm *Begeisterung, f.*
enthusiastic *begeistert.*

entire *ganz.*
entitle *(to) berechtigen.*
entrance *Eingang, m.*
entrust *(to) anvertrauen.*
enumerate *(to) aufzählen.*
envelope *Umschlag, m.*
envious *neidisch.*
envy *Neid, m.*
envy *(to) beneiden.*
episode *Episode, f.; Begebenheit, f.*
equal *gleich.*
equal *(to) gleichen.*
equality *Gleichheit, f.*
equator *Äquator, m.*
equilibrium *Gleichgewicht, n.*
equip *(to) ausrüsten.*
equipment *Ausrüstung, f.*
era *Zeitalter, n.*
erase *(to) ausstreichen.*
eraser *Gummi, m.*
erect *(to) errichten.*
err *(to) sich irren.*
errand *Auftrag, m.*
error *Irrtum, m.*
escalator *Rolltreppe, f.*
escape *Flucht, f.*
escape *(to) entlaufen.*
escort *(to) begleiten, eskortieren.*
especially *besonders.*
essay *Aufsatz, m.*
essence *Essenz, f. (extract); Wesen, n.*
essential *wesentlich.*
establish *(to) errichten, gründen.*
establishment *Gründung, f.*
estate *Vermögen, n. (wealth); Gut, n. (land).*
esteem *Achtung, f.*
esteem *(to) schätzen.*
estimate *Kostenanschlag, m. (cost); Schätzung, f. (appraise).*
estimate *(to) veranschlagen.*
eternal *ewig.*
eternity *Ewigkeit, f.*
European *Europäer (noun, m.); europäisch. (adj.)*
evade *(to) entfliehen.*
evasion *Ausflucht, f.*
eve *Vorabend, m.*
even *eben (adj.); sogar (adv.)*
evening *Abend, m.*
  good evening! *Guten Abend!*
evening clothes *Gesellschaftsanzug, m.*
evening dress *Abendkleid, n. (woman's).*
event *Ereignis, n.*
ever *je, jemals.*
every *jeder.*
  everybody *jedermann.*

  everything *alles.*
  everywhere *überall.*
evidence *Beweis, m.*
evident *offenbar.*
evil *Übel (noun, n.); schlecht (adj.).*
evoke *(to) hervorrufen.*
evolve *(to) herausarbeiten, sich entwickeln.*
exact *genau.*
exaggerate *(to) übertreiben.*
exaggeration *Übertreibung, f.*
exalt *(to) erheben.*
exaltation *Erhebung, f.*
examination *Prüfung, f.*
examine *(to) prüfen.*
example *Beispiel, n.*
exceed *(to) überschreiten.*
excel *(to) übertreffen.*
excellence *Vortrefflichkeit, f.*
excellent *vortrefflich, ausgezeichnet*
except *ausgenommen; ausser (dat.).*
except *(to) ausnehmen.*
exception *Ausnahme, f.*
exceptional *aussergewöhnlich.*
exceptionally *ausnahmsweise.*
excess *Übermass, n.*
excessive *übermässig.*
exchange *Tausch, m.*
exchange *(to) wechseln.*
excite *(to) aufregen.*
excitement *Aufregung, f.*
exclaim *(to) ausrufen.*
exclamation *Ausruf, m.*
exclude *(to) ausschliessen.*
exclusive *auschliesslich.*
excursion *Ausflug, f.*
excuse *Verzeihung, f.*
excuse *(to) verzeihen, entschuldigen.*
  Excuse me *Verzeihung! (Entschuldigung!)*
execute *(to) ausführen (carry out); hinrichten (put to death).*
execution *Ausführung, f. (of plan or idea); Hindrichtung, f. (of person).*
exempt *(to) befreien.*
exercise *Übung, f.*
exercise *(to) üben.*
exert *(to) sich anstrengen.*
exertion *Anstrengung, f.*
exhaust *(to) erschöpfen.*
exhaustion *Erschöpfung, f.*
exhibit *(to) ausstellen.*
exhibition *Ausstellung, f.*
exile *Verbannung, f.*
exile *(to) verbannen.*
exist *(to) existieren.*
existence *Existenz, f.*
exit *Ausgang, m.*
expand *(to) ausdehnen.*

expansion   Ausdehnung, f.
expensive   teuer.
experience   Erfahrung, f.
experience   (to) erfahren.
experiment   (to) experimentieren.
expert   Fachmann, m.
expire   (to) verscheiden, ablaufen.
explain   (to) erklären.
explanation   Erklärung, f.
explanatory   erklärend.
explode   (to) explodieren.
exploit   Heldentat, f.
exploit   (to) ausnützen.
explore   (to) erforschen.
explosion   Explosion, f.
export   (to) ausführen, exportieren.
export   Ausfuhr, f.; Export, m.
expose   (to) aussetzen.
express   Schnellzug, m.
express   (to) ausdrücken.
expression   Ausdruck, m.
expressive   ausdrucksvoll.
expulsion   Ausstossung, f.
exquisite   vorzüglich.
extend   (to) verlängern, ausdehnen.
extensive   ausgedehnt.
extent   Weite, f. (distance);
    Verlängerung, f. (time).
exterior   Äussere (noun, n); äusserlich
    (adj.).
exterminate   (to) ausrotten.
external   äusserlich, auswärtig.
extinction   Erlöschen, n.
extinguish   (to) erlöschen.
extra   extra.
extraordinary   aussergewöhnlich.
extravagant   verschwenderisch.
extreme   äusserst.
eye   Auge, n.
eyebrow   Augenbraue, f.
eyeglasses   Brille, f.
eyelash   Wimper, f.
eyelid   Augenlid, n.
eyesight,   Gesicht, n.; Sehkraft, f.

F

fable   Fabel, f.
face   Gesicht, n.
face   (to) unter die Augen treten,
    gegenüberstehen
facilitate   (to) erleichtern.
facility   Leichtigkeit, f.
fact   Tatsache, f.
    in fact   in der Tat.
    as a matter of fact   im übrigen.

factory   Fabrik, f.
faculty   Fähigkeit, f. (ability); Fakultät, f.
    (school).
fade   (to) welken.
faded   verschossen (color).
fail   (to) fehlen; unterlassen (neglect);
    durchfallen (exam).
    without fail   ganz gewiss.
failure   Misserfolg, m.
faint   (to) ohnmächtig werden.
fainting spell   Ohnmacht, f.
fair   schön (weather); hell (complexion);
    ehrlich (just).
    fair play   ehrliches Spiel.
faith   Glaube, m. (religion); Treue, f.
faithful   treu.
fall   Fall, m.; Sturz, m.; Herbst, m.
    (autumn).
fall   (to) fallen, stürzen.
false   falsch.
fame   Ruhm, m.
familiar   vertraut.
family   Familie, f.
famine   Hungersnot, f.
famous   berühmt.
fan   Fächer, m.; Ventilator, m.
    (ventilator).
fancy   Neigung, (noun, f.); bunt (adj.).
fantastic   fantastisch.
far   weit, fern.
farce   Posse, f.
fare   Fahrpreis, m.
farewell   Abschied, m.
    Farewell!   Lebe wohl!
farm   Bauernhof, m.
farmer   Landwirt, m.
farming   Landwirtschaft, f.
farther   weiter, ferner.
fashion   Mode, f.
fashionable   elegant, modisch, modern.
fast   schnell.
fasten   (to) befestigen.
fat   Fett (noun, n.); fett, dick (adj.).
fatal   tödlich, fatal.
fate   Schicksal, m.
father   Vater, m.
father-in-law   Schwiegervater, m.
faucet   Knopf, m.; Hahn, m.
fault   Fehler, m.
favor   Gunst, f.
    Do me a favor.   Tun Sie mir einen
    Gefallen.
favor   (to) begünstigen.
favorable   günstig.
favorite   Günstling, m.; Liebling, m.;
    lieblings (adj.)
fear   Furcht, f.
fear   (to) fürchten.
fearless   furchtlos.

feather *Feder, f.*
feature *(Gesichts)zug, m.; Merkmal, n.;*
　Film, m. (movie).
February *Februar, m.*
federal *Bundes.*
federation *Verband, m.*
fee *Gebühr, f.*
feeble *schwach.*
feed *(to) füttern.*
feel *(to) fühlen.*
feeling *Gefühl, n.*
fellow *Kamerad, m.*
fellowship *Kameradschaft, f.;*
　Gemeinschaft, f.
female *weiblich.*
feminine *fraulich.*
fence *Zaun, m.*
fencing *Fechten, n.*
fender *Kotflügel, m.*
ferocious *wild.*
ferry *Fähre, f.*
fertile *fruchtbar.*
fertilize *(to) befruchten.*
fertilizer *Düngemittel, n.; Dünger, m.*
fervent *inbrünstig.*
fervor *Inbrunst, f.*
festival *Fest, n.*
fetch *(to) holen.*
fever *Fieber, n.*
few *wenige.*
　a few ein paar.
fiction *Dichtung, f.*
field *Acker, m.; Feld, n.*
fierce *wild.*
fiery *feurig.*
fifteen *fünfzehn.*
fifteenth *fünfzehnte.*
fifth *fünfte.*
fiftieth *fünfzigste.*
fifty *fünfzig.*
fig *Feige, f.*
fight *Kampf, m.*
fight *(to) kämpfen.*
figure *Figur, f.; Ziffer (number).*
file *Feile, f. (tool); Ablage, f. (office).*
fill *(to) füllen.*
filling *(tooth) Füllung, f.*
film *Film, m.*
filthy *schmutzig.*
final *endgültig.*
finance *Finanz, f.*
finance *(to) finanzieren.*
financial *finanziell.*
find *(to) finden.*
fine *Geldstrafe (noun, f.); fein (adj.)*
　(opp. of coarse); schön (adj.) (elegant).
finger *Finger, m.*
finish *(to) beenden.*
fire *Feuer, n.*
fireman *Feuerwehrmann, m.*

fireplace *Kamin, m.*
firm *Firma, (noun, f.); fest, stark (adj.).*
first *erster.*
　at first zuerst.
fish *Fisch, m.*
fish *(to) fischen.*
fisherman *Fischer, m.*
fishing *Fischen, n.*
fist *Faust, f.*
fit *Anfall, (noun, m.); passend (adj.)*
　(becoming); tauglich (adj.) (capable).
fitness *Tauglichkeit, f.*
five *fünf.*
fix *(to) reparieren.*
flag *Fahne, f.*
flame *Flamme, f.*
flank *Seite, f.*
flash *Blitz, m. (lightning).*
flashlight *Blitzlicht, n.*
flat *flach.*
flatter *(to) schmeicheln.*
flatterer *Schmeichler, m.*
flattery *Schmeichelei, f.*
flavor *Aroma, n.*
fleet *Flotte, f.*
flesh *Fleisch, n.*
flexibility *Biegsamkeit, f.*
flexible *biegsam.*
flight *Flug, m.*
fling *(to) werfen.*
flint *Kieselstein, m.*
float *(to) treiben.*
flood *Überschwemmung, f.*
flood *(to) überschwemmen.*
floor *Boden, m.; Stock, m. (story).*
flourish *(to) blühen.*
flourishing *blühend.*
flow *(to) strömen.*
flower *Blume, f.*
fluid *flüssig.*
fly *Fliege, f.*
fly *(to) fliegen.*
foam *Schaum, m.*
fog *Nebel, m.*
fold *Falte, f.*
fold *(to) falten.*
foliage *Laubwerk, n.*
follow *(to) folgen.*
following *folgend.*
fond *zärtlich, liebevoll.*
fondness *Zärtlichkeit, f.*
food *Essen, n.*
fool *Narr, m.*
foolish *töricht, lächerlich.*
foot *Fuss, m.*
football *Fussball, m.*
footstep *Schritt, m.*
for *für (acc.); zu (dat.); wegen (gen.)*
　(on account of); denn (because).
　as for me was mich betrifft.

for a year *während eines Jahres.*
for example *zum Beispiel.*
word for word *Wort für Wort.*
forbid *(to) verbieten.*
force *Kraft, f.*
force *(to) zwingen.*
ford *Furt, f.*
foreground *Vordergrund, m.*
forehead *Stirn, f.*
foreign *fremd, ausländisch.*
foreigner *Fremder, m.; Ausländer, m.*
forest *Wald, m.*
forget *(to) vergessen.*
forgetfulness *Vergesslichkeit, f.*
forget-me-not *Vergissmeinnicht, n.*
forgive *(to) vergeben, verzeihen.*
forgiveness *Vergebung, f.*
fork *Gabel, f.*
form *Form, f.*
formal *offiziell, formell.*
formation *Bildung, f.*
former *früher; erster (as opposed to latter).*
formerly *vormals.*
formula *Formel, f.*
forsake *(to) verlassen.*
fort *Festung, f.*
fortieth *vierzigste.*
fortunate *glücklich.*
fortunately *glücklicherweise.*
fortune *Vermögen, n.; Glück, n. (luck).*
forty *vierzig.*
forward *vorwärts.*
forward *(to) absenden.*
foster *(to) pflegen.*
foul *faul.*
found *(to) gründen.*
foundation *Gründung, f.*
founder *Gründer, m.*
fountain *Brunnen, m.*
fountain pen *Füllfeder, f.*
four *vier.*
fourteen *vierzehn.*
fourteenth *vierzehnte.*
fourth *vierte.*
fowl *Geflügel, n.*
fox *Fuchs, m.*
fragile *zerbrechlich.*
fragment *Bruchstück, n.*
fragrance *Duft, m.*
fragrant *duftig.*
frail *zart.*
frame *Rahmen, m.*
frame *(to) rahmen.*
frank *aufrichtig, freimütig.*
frankness *Offenheit, f.*
free *frei.*
freedom *Freiheit, f.*
freeze *(to) frieren.*
freight *Fracht, f.*

French *französisch.*
frequent *häufig.*
frequently *oft, oftmals.*
fresh *frisch.*
friction *Reibung, f.; Friktion, f. (hair).*
Friday *Freitag, m.*
fried *gebraten.*
friend *Freund, m.*
friendly *freundlich.*
friendship *Freundschaft, f.*
frighten *(to) erschrecken.*
frightening *schrecklich, erschreckend.*
fringe *Rand, m.*
frivolity *Leichtsinn, f.*
frog *Frosch, m.*
from *von, aus (dat); nach (dat.) (according to).*
  from morning till night *von früh bis spät.*
  from time to time *von Zeit zu Zeit.*
  from top to bottom *von oben bis unten.*
front *Vorderseite, f.; Front, f. (military).*
frozen *gefroren.*
fruit *Frucht, sing. f.; Obst, coll., n.*
fry *(to) braten*
  fried eggs *Spiegeleier, pl.*
  fried potatoes *Bratkartoffeln, pl.*
frying pan *Bratpfanne, f.*
fuel *Brennstoff, m.*
fulfill *(to) erfüllen.*
full *voll.*
fully *voll.*
fun *Scherz, m; Spass, m.*
  to have fun *sich amüsieren.*
  to make fun *sich lustig machen.*
function *Funktion, f.*
function *(to) funktionieren.*
fund *Fonds, m.*
fundamental *grundlegend; wesentlich.*
funeral *Begräbnis, n.*
funny *komisch.*
fur *Pelz, m.*
furious *wütend, rasend.*
furnace *Ofen, m.*
furnish *(to) möblieren.*
furniture *Möbel, n.*
furrow *Furche, f.*
further *weiter.*
fury *Wut, f.*
future *Zukunft (noun, f.); zukünftig (adj.).*

G

gaiety *Fröhlichkeit, f.*
gain *Gewinn, m.*

gain *(to) gewinnen.*
gallant *tapfer, ritterlich.*
gallery *Galerie, f.*
gallop *Galopp, m.*
gamble *(to) spielen.*
game *Spiel, n.*
garage *Garage, f.*
garbage *Abfälle, pl.*
garden *Garten, m.*
gardener, *Gärtner, m.*
garlic *Knoblauch, n.*
gas *Gas, n.*
gasoline *Benzin, n.*
gate *Tor, n.*
gather *(to) sammeln.*
gay *lustig.*
gear *Getriebe, n.*
gem *Edelstein, m.*
general *General, m. (military); allgemein
(adj.).*
generality *Allgemeinheit, f.*
generalize *(to) verallgemeinern.*
generation *Geschlecht, n.*
generosity *Freigebigkeit, f.; Grossmut,
f. (magnanimity).*
generous *grosszügig.*
genius *Genie, n.*
genteel *fein, vornehm.*
gentle *artig, vornehm, sanft.*
gentleman *Herr, m.*
gentleness *Sanftheit, f.*
genuine *echt.*
geographical *geographisch.*
geography *Geographie, f.*
germ *Keim, m.*
German *Deutscher (noun, m.); deutsch
(adj.).*
gesture *Gebärde, f.*
get *(to) bekommen, erwerben, holen
(fetch); werden (become);*
get down *hinunterkommen.*
get off *absteigen.*
get up *aufstehen.*
ghastly *grässlich.*
ghost *geist, m.*
giant *Riese, m.*
gift *Geschenk, n.*
gifted *begabt.*
girl *Mädchen, n.*
give *(to) geben.*
to give back *zurückgeben*
glad *froh.*
gladly *gern.*
glance *Blick, m.*
glass *Glas, n.*
looking glass *Spiegel, m.*
glasses *Brille, f.*
gleam *Schein, m; Schimmer, m.*
gleam *(to) scheinen.*
glitter *Glanz, m; Glitzen, n.*

globe *Kugel, f.*
gloomy *düster.*
glorious *glorreich.*
glory *Ruhm, m.*
glove *Handschuh, m.*
glow *Glut, f.; Glühen, n.*
glue *Leim, m.*
go *(to) gehen*
to go away *weggehen.*
to go back *zurückgehen.*
to go in *hineingehen.*
to go out *herausgehen, ausgehen.*
to go to bed *zu Bett gehen.*
God *Gott, m.*
godchild *Patenkind, n.*
godfather, *Pate, m.*
godmother *Patin, f.*
gold *Gold, n.*
golden *golden.*
golf *Golf, m.*
good *gut.*
Good afternoon! *Guten Tag!*
Good evening! *Guten Abend!*
Good morning! *Guten Morgen!*
Good night! *Gute Nacht!*
good-bye *Auf Wiedersehen!*
good-looking *gut aussehend.*
goodness *Güte, f.*
goods *Waren, pl.*
goodwill *guter Wille, m.*
goose *Gans, f.*
gossip *Klatsch, m.*
gossip *(to) klatschen.*
govern *(to) regieren.*
grace *Gnade, f; Anmut, f. (charm).*
graceful *anmutig.*
grade *Grad, m.*
grain *Korn, n.*
grammar *Grammatik, f.*
grand *grossartig.*
grandchild *Enkelkind, n.*
granddaughter *Enkelin, f.*
grandfather *Grossvater, m.*
grandmother *Grossmutter, f.*
grandson *Enkel, m.*
grant *Bewilligung, f.; Schenkung, f.*
grant *(to) bewilligen.*
grape *Weintraube, f.*
grapefruit *Pompelmuse, f.*
grasp *Griff, m.*
grasp *(to) greifen.*
grass *Gras, n.*
grateful *dankbar.*
gratitude *Dankbarkeit, f.*
grave *Grab, (noun, n.); ernst (adj.).*
gravy *Sauce, f.*
gray *grau.*
grease *Fett, n.*
great *gross.*
greatness *Grösse, f.*

greedy *gierig, gefrässig.*
green *grün.*
greet *(to) grüssen.*
greeting *Gruss, m.*
grief *Kummer, m.*
grieve *(to) sich grämen.*
grin *(to) grinsen.*
grind *(to) mahlen.*
groan *Stöhnen, n.*
groan *(to) stöhnen.*
grocer *Kolonialwarenhändler, m.*
grocery store *Kolonialwarenladen, m.*
gross *grob.*
ground *Boden, m.*
group *Gruppe, f.*
group *(to) gruppieren.*
grow *(to) wachsen; bauen (crops).*
growth *Gewächs, n.*
grudge *Groll, m.*
guaranteed *garantiert.*
guess *Vermutung, f.*
guess *(to) raten.*
guide *Führer, m.*
gum *Zahnfleisch, n. (teeth).*
  chewing gum *Kaugummi, n.*
gun *Gewehr, n.*
gush *Erguss, m.*
gush *(to) hervorströmen.*

H

habit *Gewohnheit, f.*
habitual *gewöhnlich.*
hail *Hagel, m.*
hair *Haar, n.*
hairdo *Frisur, f.*
hairdresser *Frisör, m.*
hairpin *Haarnadel, f.*
half *halb.*
hall *Halle, f.; Saal, m. Diele, f.*
ham *Schinken, m.*
hammer *Hammer, m.*
hand *Hand, f.*
hand *(to) reichen.*
handbag *Handtasche, f.*
handful *Handvoll, f.*
handkerchief *Taschentuch, n.*
handle *Griff, m.*
handle *(to) tun.*
handsome *stattlich.*
handy *handlich.*
hang *(to) hängen.*
happen *(to) geschehen.*
happiness *Glück, n.*
happy *glücklich.*

harbor *Hafen, m.*
hard *hart.*
harden *(to) härten.*
hardly *kaum.*
hardness *Härte, f.*
hardware *Eisenwaren, pl.*
hardware store *Eisenwarengeschäft, n.*
hardy *abgehärtet.*
hare *Hase, m.*
harm *Schaden, m.*
harm *(to) schädigen.*
harmful *schädlich.*
harmless *harmlos.*
harmonious *harmonisch.*
harmony *Harmonie, f.*
harsh *barsch*
harvest *Ernte, f.*
haste *Eile, f.*
hasten *(to) eilen.*
hat *Hut, m.*
hate *Hass, m.*
hate *(to) hassen.*
hateful *gehässig.*
hatred *Hass, m.*
haughty *stolz.*
have *(to) haben.*
haven *Hafen, m.*
hay *Heu, n.*
he *er.*
head *Kopf. m. (of a person); Chef, m.*
  (of a firm); Haupt, n (of a government).
headache *Kopfschmerzen, pl.*
heal *(to) heilen.*
health *Gesundheit, f.*
healthy *gesund.*
heap *Haufen, m.*
heap *(to) (auf)häufen.*
hear *(to) hören.*
hearing *Gehör, n.*
heart *Herz, n.*
heaven *Himmel, m.*
heavy *schwer.*
hedge *Hecke, f.; Zaun, m.*
heel *Ferse, f. (of the foot); Absatz, m.*
  (of a shoe).
height *Höhe, f.*
heir *Erbe, m.*
hell *Hölle, f.*
helm *Ruder, n.*
help *Hilfe, f.*
help *(to) helfen.*
helpful *behilflich.*
hem *Saum, m.*
hen *Huhn, n.; Henne, f.*
her *ihr (pers. pr., dat.; poss. adj.); sie*
  (pers. pr., acc.).
herb *Kraut, n.*
herd *Herde, f.*
here *hier.*
herewith *hiermit.*

hero *Held, m.*
heroic *heldenhaft, heroisch.*
heroine *Heldin, f.*
herring *Hering, m.*
hers *ihr(er, -e, -es).*
herself *sie (ihr) selbst; sich.*
hesitate *(to) zögern.*
hide *(to) verstecken.*
hideous *scheusslich.*
high *hoch.*
higher *höher.*
hill *Hügel, m.*
him *ihn (acc.); ihm (dat.).*
himself *er (ihm, ihn) selbst; sich.*
hinder *(to) hindern.*
hint *Wink, m.*
hint *(to) andeuten.*
hip *Hüfte, f.*
hire *(to) mieten.*
his *sein (poss. adj.); sein(er, -e, -es) (pron.).*
hiss *(to) zischen.*
historian *Geschichtsschreiber, m.*
historical *historisch.*
history *Geschichte, f.*
hoarse *heiser.*
hoe *Hacke, f.*
hold *Halt, m.*
hold *(to) halten.*
hole *Loch, n.*
holiday *Feiertag, m.*
holidays *Ferien, pl.*
holy *heilig.*
homage *Huldigung, f.*
home *Heim, n.*
honest *ehrlich.*
honesty *Ehrlichkeit, f.*
honey *Honig, m.*
honeymoon *Flitterwochen, pl.*
honor *Ehre, f.*
honor *(to) ehren.*
honorable *ehrenvoll.*
hood *Kapuze, f.; Dach, n. (car).*
hoof *Huf, m.*
hook *Haken, m.*
hope *Hoffnung, f.*
hope *(to) hoffen.*
hopeful *hoffnungsvoll.*
hopeless *hoffnungslos.*
horizon *Horizont, m.*
horizontal *horizontal.*
horn *(auto) Hupe, f.*
horrible *schrecklich.*
horse *Pferd, n.*
horseback *(on) zu Pferde.*
hosiery *Strümpfe, f.*
hospitable *gastfrei.*
hospital *Krankenhaus, n.*
host *Gastgeber, m.; Wirt, m.*

hostess *Gastgeberin, f.; Wirtin, f.*
hostile *feindlich.*
hot *heiss.*
hotel *Hotel, n.; Gasthof, m.*
hour *Stunde, f.*
house *Haus, n.*
household *Haushalt, m.*
housekeeper *Haushälterin, f.*
housemaid *Hausmädchen, n.*
how *wie*
    How are you? *Wie geht's?*
however *dennoch.*
howl *Heulen, n.*
howl *(to) heulen.*
human *menschlich.*
humane *human.*
humanity *Menschlichkeit, f.*
humble *demütig.*
humid *feucht.*
humiliate *erniedrigen, demütigen.*
humility *Demut, f.*
humor *Humor, m.*
hundred *hundert.*
hundredth *hundertste.*
hunger *Hunger, m.*
hungry *hungrig.*
hunt *Jagd, f.*
hunter *Jäger, m.*
hurricane *Orkan, m.*
hurry *Eile, f.*
    Hurry up! *Beeilen Sie sich!*
hurt *(to) verwunden; verletzen.*
husband *Mann, m.; Gatte, m.*
hush *(to) schweigen.*
hyphen *Bindestrich, m.*
hypocrite *Heuchler, m.*

I

I *ich.*
ice *Eis, n.*
ice cream *Eis, n.*
icy *eisig.*
idea *Idee, f.; Einfall, m.*
ideal *Ideal, (noun, n.); ideal (adj.).*
idealism *Idealismus, m.*
idealist *Idealist, m.*
identical *identisch.*
identity *Identität, f.*
idiot *Idiot, m.*
idle *müssig.*
idleness *Müssigkeit, f.*
if *wenn, ob.*
ignoble *unedel.*
ignorance *Unwissenheit, f.*
ignorant *unwissend.*

ignore *(to) ignorieren.*
ill *krank.*
illegal *gesetzwidrig, ungesetzlich.*
illness *Krankheit, f.*
illusion *Täuschung, f.*
illustrate *(to) illustrieren.*
illustration *Abbildung, f.*
image *Einbildungskraft, f.; Ebenbild, n.; Bild, n.*
imagination *Fantasie, f.*
imagine *(to) sich einbilden.*
imitate *(to) nachahmen.*
imitation *Nachahmung, f.*
immediate *unmittelbar.*
immediately *sogleich, sofort.*
immigrant *Immigrant, m.*
imminent *bevorstehend.*
immobility *Unbeweglichkeit, f.*
immoral *unmoralisch.*
immorality *Unsittlichkeit, f.*
immortal *unsterblich.*
immortality *Unsterblichkeit, f.*
impartial *unparteiisch.*
impassible *gefühllos.*
impatience *Ungeduld, f.*
imperfect *Vergangenheit (noun, f.) (in grammar); unvollkommen (adj.).*
impertinence *Unverschämtheit, f.*
impetuosity *Ungestüm, n.*
import *Einfuhr, f.; Import, m.*
import *(to) einführen, importieren.*
important *wichtig.*
imported *importiert.*
importer *Importeur, m.*
impossible *unmöglich.*
impress *(to) Eindruck machen.*
impression *Eindruck, m.*
imprison *(to) einsperren.*
improve *(to) verbessern.*
improvement *Verbesserung, f.*
improvise *(to) improvisieren.*
imprudence *Unvorsichtigkeit, f.*
imprudent *unklug.*
impulse *Antrieb, m.*
impure *unrein.*
in *in (dat.).*
inadequate *unzulänglich.*
inaugurate *(to) eröffnen.*
incapable *unfähig.*
incapacity *Unfähigkeit, f.*
inch *Zoll, m.*
incident *Vorfall, m.*
include *(to) einschliessen.*
included *eingeschlossen.*
income *Einkommen, n.*
income tax *Einkommensteuer, f.*
incomparable *unvergleichlich.*
incompatible *unvereinbar.*
incompetent *untauglich; unzulänglich.*

incomplete *unvollständig.*
inconvenient *lästig, unbequem.*
incorrect *unrichtig.*
increase *Erhöhung, f.*
increase *(to) sich vermehren, erhöhen.*
incredible *unglaublich.*
indebted *verschuldet; verpflichtet.*
indecision *Unentschlossenheit, f.*
indeed *tatsächlich.*
independence *Unabhängigkeit, f.*
independent *unabhängig.*
index *Inhaltsverzeichnis, n.*
index finger *Zeigefinger, m.*
indicate *(to) zeigen.*
indicative *Indikativ (noun, m.) (in grammar); anzeigend (adj.).*
indifference *Gleichgültigkeit, f.*
indifferent *gleichgültig.*
indigestion *Verdauungsstörung, f.*
indignant *entrüstet.*
indignation *Entrüstung, f.*
indirect *indirekt.*
indiscreet *indiskret.*
indiscretion *Unbedachtsamkeit, f.*
indispensable *unentbehrlich.*
individual *einzeln.*
indolent *träge.*
indoors *im Hause.*
induce *(to) veranlassen.*
indulge *(to) sich hingeben.*
indulgence *Nachsichtigkeit, f.*
indulgent *nachsichtig.*
industrial *industriell.*
industrious *fleissig.*
industry *Industrie, f.*
inefficient *unfähig.*
infancy *Kindheit, f.*
infant *kleines Kind, n.*
infantry *Infanterie, f.*
infection *Infektion, f.*
inferior *minderwertig.*
infernal *höllisch.*
infinite *unendlich.*
infinity *Unendlichkeit, f.*
influence *Einfluss, m.*
influence *(to) beeinflussen.*
inform *(to) benachrichtigen.*
information *Auskunft, f.; Nachricht, f. (news).*
ingenious *geistig.*
ingenuity *Scharfsinn, m.*
inhabit *(to) bewohnen.*
inhabitant *Einwohner, m.*
inherit *(to) erben.*
inheritance *Erbgut, n.*
inhuman *unmenschlich.*
initial *Anfangsbuchstabe, m.*
initiate *(to) einweihen.*
initiative *Initiative, f.*

injection *Einspritzung, f.*
injury *Verletzung, f.*
injustice *Ungerechtigkeit, f.*
ink *Tinte, f.*
inkwell *Tintenfass, n.*
inland *Binnenland, n.*
inn *Gasthof, m.*
innkeeper *Gastwirt, m.*
innocent *unschuldig.*
innocence *Unschuld, f.*
inquire *(to) sich erkundigen.*
inquiry *Erkundigung, f.; Auskunft, f.*
insane *geisteskrank.*
inscription *Inschrift, f.*
insect *Insekt, n.*
insensible *unempfindlich.*
inseparable *unzertrennlich.*
inside *drinnen.*
insight *Einsicht, f.*
insignificant *unbedeutend.*
insincere *unaufrichtig.*
insinuate *(to) andeuten.*
insist *(to) bestehen auf.*
insistence *Beharren, n.*
inspect *(to) besichtigen.*
inspection *Besichtigung, f.*
inspiration *Inspiration, f.*
install *(to) einstellen, installieren.*
installment *Rate, f.; Teilzahlung, f.*
instance *Beispiel, n.; Fall, m.*
instant *Augenblick, m.*
instantly *sofort.*
instead of *anstatt (gen.).*
institute *(to) herbeiführen.*
institution *Anstalt, f.*
instruct *(to) unterrichten.*
instructor *Lehrer, m.*
instruction *Anweisung, f.; Unterricht, m. (teaching).*
instrument *Instrument, n.*
insufficient *ungenügend.*
insult *Beleidigung, f.*
insult *(to) beleidigen.*
insurance *Versicherung, f.*
insure *(to) versichern.*
intact *unversehrt.*
intellectual *intellektuell.*
intelligence *Intelligenz, f.*
intelligent *intelligent.*
intend *(to) beabsichtigen.*
intense *intensiv.*
intensity *Heftigkeit, f.*
intention *Absicht, f.*
interest *Interesse, n.*
interesting *interessant.*
interfere *(to) sich einmischen.*
interior *Innere, n.*
intermediate *mittel.*
intermission *Pause, f.*
international *international.*

interpret *(to) interpretieren, übersetzen; deuten (emotion).*
interpreter *Dolmetscher, m.*
interrupt *(to) unterbrechen.*
interval *Pause, f.; Zwischenzeit, f.*
interview *Interview, n.*
intimacy *Vertrautheit, f.*
intimate *vertraut.*
into *in (dat. or acc.).*
intolerant *unduldsam.*
intonation *Tonfall m.*
introduce *(to) vorstellen.*
introduction *Vorstellung, f.*
intuition *Einfühlungsgabe, f.*
invade *(to) einfallen.*
invent *(to) erfinden.*
invention *Erfindung, f.*
inventor *Erfinder, m.*
invert *(to) umkehren, umdrehen.*
invest *(to) investieren; anlegen (money).*
investment *Kapitalanlage, f.*
invisible *unsichtbar.*
invitation *Einladung, f.*
invite *(to) einladen.*
invoice *Faktura, f.*
invoke *(to) anrufen.*
involve *(to) verwickeln.*
iodine *Jod, n.*
Irish *irländisch.*
iron *Eisen, n. (metal); Bügeleisen, n. (for ironing).*
iron *(to) bügeln.*
irony *Ironie, f.*
irregular *unregelmässig.*
irresistible *unwiderstehlich.*
irritate *(to) reizen, ärgern.*
island *Insel, f.*
isolate *(to) absondern, isolieren.*
issue *Ausgabe, f.*
it *es.*
Italian *Italiener (noun, m.); italienisch (adj.).*
itch *(to) jucken.*
its *sein (poss. adj.); sein(er, -e, -es), (poss. pron.).*
itself *es (ihm) selbst, sich.*
ivory *Elfenbein, n.*
ivy *Efeu, n.*

J

jacket *Jacke, f.*
jail *Gefängnis, n.*
jam *Marmelade, f.*
January *Januar, m.*

Japanese *Japaner (noun, m.); japanisch (adj.).*
jar *Krug, m.*
jaw *Kiefer, m.*
jealous *eifersüchtig.*
jealousy *Eifersucht, f.*
jelly *Gelee, n.*
jewel *Juwel, m.*
jeweler *Juwelier, m.*
Jewish *jüdisch.*
job *Arbeit, f.*
join *(to) binden.*
joint *Gelenk, n.*
joke *Witz, m.; Scherz, m.; Spass, m.*
joke *(to) scherzen.*
jolly *lustig.*
journalist *Journalist, m.*
journey *Reise, f.*
joy *Freude, f.*
joyous *freudig.*
judge *Richter, m.*
judge *(to) urteilen.*
judgment *Urteil, n.*
judicial *gerichtlich.*
juice *Saft, m.*
July *Juli, m.*
jump *Sprung, m.*
jump *(to) springen.*
June *Juni, m.*
junior *jünger.*
jungle *Dschungel, m.*
just *recht (fair); gerecht (justice); gerade (recent).*
justice *Gerechtigkeit, f.*
justify *(to) rechtfertigen.*

K

keen *scharf.*
keep *(to) halten (retain); hindern (hinder).*
  keep off *abhalten.*
  keep on *fortfahren.*
  keep up *aufrechterhalten.*
kernel *Kern, m.*
kettle *Kessel, m.*
key *Schlüssel, m.*
kick *Fusstritt, m.*
kick *(to) ausschlagen.*
kidneys *Nieren, pl.*
kill *(to) töten.*
kin *Blutsverwandtschaft, f.*
kind *Art (noun, f.); gütig (adj.).*
kindly *freundlich.*
kindness *Güte, f.; Freundlichkeit, f.*
king *König, m.*

kingdom *Königreich, n.*
kiss *Kuss, m.*
kiss *(to) küssen.*
kitchen *Küche, f.*
kite *Drache, m.*
knee *Knie, n.*
kneel *(to) knieen.*
knife *Messer, n.*
knight *Ritter, m.*
knit *(to) stricken.*
knock *Schlag, m.; Hieb, m. (beating); Klopf, m.; Griff, m. (door).*
knock *(to) klopfen, schlagen, hauen, stossen; anklopfen (door).*
knot *Knoten, m.*
know *(to) wissen (have knowledge of); kennen (be acquainted with).*
knowledge *Kenntnis, f.*

L

label *Zettel, m.*
labor *Arbeit, f.*
laboratory *Laboratorium, n.*
laborer *Arbeiter, m.*
lace *Spitze, f. (ornamental); Senkel, m. (of a shoe).*
lack *Mangel, m.*
lack *(to) mangeln.*
lady *Dame, f.*
lake *See, m.*
lamb *Lamm, n .*
lame *lahm.*
lamp *Lampe, f.*
land *Land, n.*
land *(to) landen.*
landscape *Landschaft, f.*
language *Sprache, f.*
languish *(to) schmachten.*
languor *Schlaffheit, f.*
lantern *Latern, f.*
large *gross.*
last *letzt.*
  last year *voriges Jahr.*
last *(to) dauern.*
lasting *dauernd.*
latch *Klinke, f. (knob); Drücker.*
late *spät.*
lately *kürzlich.*
latter *letzter.*
laugh *(to) lachen.*
laughter *Gelächter, n.*
lavish *freigebig.*
lavish *(to) überhäufen.*
law *Gesetz, n.; Recht, n. (code).*
lawful *rechtmässig.*

lawn *Rasenplatz, m.*
lawyer *Rechtsanwalt, m.*
lay *(to) legen.*
layer *Schicht, f.*
lazy *faul.*
lead *Blei, n.*
lead *(to) führen.*
leader *Führer, m.*
leadership *Führung, f.*
leaf *Blatt, n.*
leak *Leck, n.*
lean *(to) lehnen.*
leap *(to) springen.*
leap *Sprung, m.*
learn *(to) lernen.*
learned *gelehrt.*
learning *Gelehrsamkeit, f.*
least *wenigste.*
  at least *mindestens.*
leather *Leder, n.*
leave *(to) verlassen (abandon);*
  weggehen (on foot); wegfahren (by
  vehicle).
lecture *Vortrag, m.*
left *linke.*
  to the left *links.*
leg *Bein, n.*
  leg of lamb *Hammelkeule, f.*
legal *gesetzmässig.*
legend *Sage, f.*
legislation *Gesetzgebung, f.*
legislator *Gesetzgeber, m.*
legitimate *legitim.*
leisure *Freizeit, f.*
lemon *Zitrone, f.*
lemonade *Limonade, f.*
lend *(to) leihen.*
length *Länge, f.*
lengthen *(to) verlängern.*
less *weniger.*
lesson *Stunde, f.; Lektion, f. (in book).*
let *(to) lassen; gestatten (allow);*
  vermieten (rent).
letter *Buchstabe, m. (alphabet); Brief,*
  m. (correspondence).
level *Niveau, n.*
liable *haftbar.*
liar *Lügner, m.; Lügnerin, f.*
liberal *liberal.*
liberty *Freiheit, f.*
library *Bibliothek, f.*
license *Erlaubnis, f.*
lick *(to) lecken.*
lie *Lüge, f.*
lie *(to) lügen (falsify); liegen (rest).*
lieutenant *Leutnant, m.*
life *Leben, n.*
lift *(to) heben.*
light *Licht (noun, n.); leicht (adj.).*

light *(to) anzünden.*
  to light up *erleuchten.*
lighten *(to) erhellen (brightness);*
  erleichtern (weight).
lighter *Feuerzeug, n.*
lighthouse *Leuchtturm, m.*
lighting *Beleuchtung, f.*
lightning *Blitz, m.*
like *wie (as); ähnlich (similar).*
like *(to) gern haben, mögen, gefallen.*
  I'd like to *ich möchte.*
likely *wahrscheinlich.*
likeness *Ähnlichkeit, f.*
likewise *gleichfalls.*
liking *Vorliebe, f.*
limb *Glied, n.*
limit *Grenze, f.*
limit *(to) begrenzen.*
limp *hinken.*
line *Linie, f.*
line up *(to) sich anstellen.*
linen *Wäsche, f. (household); Leinwand,*
  f. (fabric).
linger *(to) weilen.*
lingerie *Damenwäsche, f.*
lining *Futter, n.*
link *Glied, n.*
link *(to) verbinden.*
lion *Löwe, m.*
lip *Lippe, f.*
lipstick *Lippenstift, m.*
liquid *Flüssigkeit (noun, f.); flüssig (adj.).*
liquor *Alkohol, m.; Likör, m. (liqueur).*
list *Liste, f.*
literary *literarisch.*
literature *Literatur, f.*
little *klein.*
  a little *ein wenig.*
live *lebend.*
live *(to) leben.*
lively *lebhaft, lebendig.*
liver *Leber, f.*
load *Last, f. (burden); Ladung, f.*
  (cargo).
load *(to) laden.*
loan *(ver)leihen.*
lobby *Vorhalle, f.*
local *lokal.*
locate *(to) orientieren, finden.*
location *Platz, m; Gegend, f.*
lock *Schloss, n.*
lock *(to) zuschliessen.*
locomotive *Lokomotive, f.*
log *Klotz, m.*
logic *Logik, f.*
logical *logisch.*
loneliness *Einsamkeit, f.*
lonely *einsam.*
long *lang.*

long ago *vor langer Zeit; längst.*
a long time *lange.*
long *(to) sehnen.*
longer *länger.*
longing *Sehnsucht, f.*
look *Blick, m.*
look *(to) schauen; aussehen (appear).*
Look! *Sehen Sie her!*
Look out! *Passen Sie auf!*
to look forward *entgegensehen; sich freuen auf (rejoice).*
loose *lose.*
loosen *(to) lösen.*
lose *(to) verlieren.*
loss *Verlust, m.; Schaden, m.*
lost *verloren.*
lot *(a) viel (much).*
loud *laut.*
love *Liebe, f.*
love *(to) lieben.*
lovely *schön, reizend.*
low *niedrig.*
lower *(to) niederholen.*
loyal *treu.*
loyalty *Treue, f.*
luck *Glück, n.*
lucky *glücklich.*
luggage *Gepäck, n.*
luminous *leuchtend.*
lump *Klumpen, m.*
lunch *Mittagessen, n.*
lung *Lunge, f.*
luxurious *prächtig.*
luxury *Luxus, m.*

M

machine *Maschine, f.*
mad *verrückt.*
madam *gnädige Frau.*
made *gemacht.*
madness *Wahnsinn, m.*
magazine *Zeitschrift, f.*
magistrate *Magistrat, m.*
magnificent *prachtvoll.*
maid *Dienstmädchen, n. (servant).*
mail *Post, f.*
main *haupt*
the main thing *die Hauptsache.*
maintain *(to) erhalten; unterhalten (support).*
maintenance *Unterhalt, m.*
majesty *Majestät, f.*
major *Major, m.*
majority *Mehrheit, f.*

make *(to) machen.*
man *Mann, m.; Mensch, m. (human being).*
manage *(to) führen, verwalten.*
management *Leitung, f.*
manager *Leiter, m.*
manicure *Maniküre, f.*
mankind *Menschheit, f.*
manner *Art, f.; Weise, f.*
manners *Bildung, f.*
manufacture *Fabrikation, f.*
manufactured *hergestellt.*
many *viele.*
map *Karte, f.*
marble *Marmor, m.*
March *März, m.*
march *Marsch, m.*
march *(to) marschieren.*
margin *Rand, m.*
marine *Marine, f.*
mark *Kennzeichen, n.*
mark *(to) markieren.*
market *Markt, m.*
marketplace *Marktplatz, m.*
marriage *Heirat, f.*
married *verheiratet.*
marry *(to) heiraten, sich verheiraten; trauen (perform the ceremony).*
to marry off *verheiraten.*
marvel *Wunder, n.*
marvel *(to) sich wundern.*
marvelous *wunderbar.*
masculine *männlich*
mask *Maske, f.*
mask *(to) maskieren.*
mason *Maurer, m.*
mass *Masse, f.; Messe, f. (church).*
massage *Massage, f.*
master *Meister, m.*
master *(to) meistern.*
masterpiece *Meisterwerk, n.; Meisterstück, n.*
match *Streichholz, n. (incendiary); Gleiche, n. (comparative).*
match *(to) zusammenpassen.*
material *Material, n.*
maternal *mütterlich.*
mathematics *Mathematik, f.*
matter *Angelegenheit, f. (affair); Stoff, m. (substance).*
What's the matter? *Was ist los?*
mattress *Matratze, f.*
mature *erwachsen.*
May *Mai, m.*
may *dürfen (to be allowed); mögen (to be likely).*
mayor *Bürgermeister, m.*
me *mich (acc.); mir (dat.).*
meadow *Wiese, f.*

meal *Mahl, n.*

mean *übel (unkind).*

mean *(to) meinen (to be of the opinion); bedeuten (to signify).*
What does it mean? *Was bedeutet das?*

meaning *Bedeutung, f. (significance).*

means *Mittel, n.*

meanwhile *inzwischen.*

measure *Mass, n.*

measure *(to) messen.*

meat *Fleisch, n.*

mechanic *Mechaniker, m.*

mechanical *mechanisch.*

medal *Medaille, f. (jewel); Orden, m.*

medical *ärztlich.*

medicine *Medizin, f. (science); Arznei, f. (medication).*

mediocre *mittelmässig.*

mediocrity *Mittelmässigkeit, f.*

meditate *(to) grübeln, sinnen, nachdenken.*

meditation *Nachdenken, n.*

medium *mittel.*

meet *(to) treffen.*
Pleased to meet you *Seht erfreut Sie kennenzulernen.*

meeting *Versammlung, f.*

melon *Melone, f.*

melt *(to) schmelzen.*

member *Mitglied, n.*

memorize *(to) auswendig lernen.*

memory *Gedächtnis, n.*

mend *(to) reparieren.*

mental *geistig.*

mention *(to) erwähnen.*

menu *Speisekarte, f.*

merchandise *Ware, f.*

merchant *Kaufmann, m.*

merciful *barmherzig.*

merciless *unbarmherzig.*

mercury *Quecksilber, n.*

mercy *Barmherzigkeit, f.*

merit *Verdienst, n.*

merit *(to) verdienen.*

merry *fröhlich, heiter, lustig.*

message *Nachricht, f.*

messenger *Bote, m.*

metal *Metall, n.*

metallic *metallisch.*

method *Methode, f.*

Mexican *Mexicaner (noun, m.); mexikanisch (adj.).*

microphone *Mikrofon, n.*

middle *Mitte, f.*

middle age *mirtleres Alter, n.*

Middle Ages *Mittelalter, n.*

midnight *Mitternacht, f.*

midway *halbwegs.*

might *Macht, f.*

mighty *mächtig.*

mild *leicht, mild, sanft.*

mildness *Milde, f.*

mile *Meile, f.*

military *militärisch.*

milk *Milch, f.*

milkman *Milchhändler, m.*

milky way *Milchstrasse, f.*

mill *Mühle, f.*

miller *Müller, m.; Müllerin, f.*

milliner *Modistin, f.*

million *Million, f.*

millionaire *Millionär, m.*

mind *Verstand, m.; Sinn, m.*

mind *(to) beachten (to pay heed); aufpassen (also to watch over).*

mine *Grube, f. (coal).*

mine *(poss. pr.) mein(er, -e, -es).*

miner *Bergmann, m.*

mineral *mineralisch.*

mineral *Mineral, n.*

minister *Minister (state), m.; Geistliche, m. (church).*

ministry *Ministerium, n. (state); Amt, n. (church).*

mink *Nerz, m.*

minor *jüngere.*

minority *Minderheit, f.*

minute *Minute, f.*
Just a minute! *Einen Augenblick!*
Wait a minute! *Warten Sie einen Augenblick!*
Any minute now! *Jeden Augenblick!*

miracle *Wunder, n.*

mirror *Spiegel, m.*

miscellaneous *gemischt, verschieden.*

mischief *Unfug, m.*

mischievous *boshaft.*

miser *Geizhals, m.*

miserly *geizig.*

misfortune *Unglück, n.*

Miss *Fräulein, n.*

miss *(to) versäumen.*

mission *Mission, f.*

mist *Nebel, m.*

mistake *Fehler, m.*

mistaken *irrtümlich.*
You are mistaken. *Sie sind im Irrtum.*

Mister *Herr.*

mistrust *(to) misstrauen.*

misunderstand *(to) missverstehen.*

misunderstanding *Missverständnis, n.*

misuse *(to) missbrauchen.*

mix *(to) mischen.*

mixture *Mischung, f.*

mob *Pöbel, m.*

mobile *beweglich.*

mobilization *Mobilmachung. f.*

mobilize *(to) mobilisieren.*
mock *(to) verspotten.*
mockery *Gespött, n.*
mode *Mode, f.*
model *Modell, n.*
moderate *mässigen.*
moderation *Mässigkeit, f.*
modern *modern.*
modest *bescheiden.*
modesty *Bescheidenheit, f.*
modification *Veränderung, f.*
modify *(to) verändern.*
moist *feucht.*
moisten *anfeuchten.*
moment *Augenblick, m.; Moment, m.*
  Just a moment *Einen Augenblick.*
monarchy *Monarchie, f.*
monastery *Kloster, n.*
Monday *Montag, m.*
money *Geld, n.*
monk *Mönch, m.*
monkey *Affe, m.*
monologue *Monolog, m.*
monotonous *eintönig.*
monotony *Eintönigkeit, f.*
monster *Ungeheuer, n.*
monstrous *ungeheuer.*
month *Monat, m.*
monthly *monatlich.*
monument *Denkmal, n.*
monumental *monumental.*
mood *Stimmung, f.; Laune, f. (temper).*
moody *launisch.*
moon *Mond, m.*
moonlight *Mondschein, m.*
mop *Mop, m.*
moral *Moral, f.*
morality *Sittlichkeit, f.*
more *mehr.*
moreover *darüber hinaus.*
morning *Morgen, m.*
morsel *Bissen, m.*
mortal *sterblich.*
mortality *Sterblichkeit, f.*
mortgage *Hypothek, f.*
mortgage *(to) verpfänden.*
mosquito *Mücke, f.*
most *am meisten.*
  most of *die meisten.*
mostly *meistens.*
moth *Motte, f.*
mother *Mutter, f.*
mother-in-law *Schwiegermutter, f.*
motion *Bewegung, f.*
motionless *bewegungslos.*
motivate *(to) beweisen, begründen.*
motor *Motor, m.*
mount *Hügel, m.*
mountain *Berg, m.*

mountainous *bergig.*
mourn *(to) trauern.*
mournful *traurig.*
mourning *Trauer, f.*
mouse *Maus, f.*
mouth *Mund, m.*
move *(to) bewegen.*
movement *Bewegung, f.*
movies *Kino, n.*
moving *rührend.*
much *viel*
  How much? *Wieviel?*
mud *Schlamm, m.*
muddy *schlammig.*
mule *Maultier, n.*
multiply *(to) multiplizieren.*
multitude *Menge, f.*
mumble *(to) murmeln.*
municipal *städtisch.*
munition *Munition, f.*
murder *Mord, m.*
murder *(to) ermorden.*
murderer *Mörder, m.*
murmur *(to) murren.*
muscle *Muskel, m.*
museum *Museum, n.*
mushroom *Pilz, m.*
music *Musik, f.*
musical *musikalisch.*
musician *Musiker, m.*
must *müssen.*
mustache *Schnurrbart, m.*
mustard *Senf, m.*
mute *stumm.*
mutton *Hammelfleisch, n.*
my *mein*
myself *ich (mich, mir) selbst.*
mysterious *geheimnisvoll.*
mystery *Geheimnis, n.*

N

nail *Nagel, m.*
nail *(to) nageln.*
naive *harmlos, naive.*
naked *nackt.*
name *Name, m.*
  first name *Vorname, m.*
  last name *Zuname, m.*
  What is your name? *Wie heissen Sie?*
namely *nähmlich.*
nap *Schläfchen, n.*
napkin *Serviette, f.*
narrow *eng.*

nasty *garstig.*
nation *Nation, f.*
national *national.*
nationality *Nationalität, f.*
native *Eingeborene, m., f., n.*
  native country *Heimat, f.*
natural *natürlich.*
naturally *natürlich.*
nature *Natur, f.*
naughty *unartig.*
naval *see-.*
navy *Flotte, f.*
near *nah.*
nearly *beinahe.*
neat *nett, ordentlich.*
neatness *Niedlichkeit, f.; Sauberkeit, f.*
necessary *notwendig.*
necessity, *Notwendigkeit, f.*
neck *Hals, m.*
necklace *Halsband, n.*
necktie *Krawatte, f.; Schlips, m.*
  (colloquial).
need *Not, f.; Bedürfnis, f.*
need *(to) brauchen.*
needle *Nadel, f.*
needless *unnötig.*
needy *dürftig, bedürftig.*
negative *Negative, m.*
neglect *Vernachlässigung, f.*
neglect *(to) vernachlässigen.*
negotiate *(to) unterhandeln.*
negotiation *Unterhandlung, f.*
Negro *Neger, m.*
neighbor *Nachbar, m.*
neighborhood *Nachbarschaft, f.*
neither *kein(er,-e,-es).*
  neither... nor *weder...noch.*
nephew *Neffe, m.*
nerve *Nerv, m.*
  What a nerve! *So eine Frechheit!*
nervous *nervös.*
nest *Nest, n.*
net *Netz, n.*
neuter *Neutrum, n.*
neutral *neutral.*
never *niemals, nie*
  Never mind! *Das macht nichts!*
nevertheless *trotzdem; auf alle Fälle.*
new *neu*
news *Nachrichten, pl.*
newspaper *Zeitung, f.*
next *nächst.*
nice *nett.*
nickname *Spitzname, m.*
niece *Nichte, f.*
night *Nacht, f.*
nightgown *Nachthemd, n.*
nightmare *Alpdrücken, n.*
nine *neun.*

nineteen *neunzehn*
ninety *neunzig.*
ninth *neunte.*
no *nein; kein (adj)*
  no longer *nicht mehr.*
  no matter *ungeachtet (gen.)*
nobility *Adel, m.*
noble *adlig.*
nobody *niemand.*
noise *Geräusch, n.*
noisy *geräuschvoll.*
nominate *(to) ernennen.*
nomination *Ernennung, f.*
none *kein(e, -er, -es).*
nonsense *Unsinn, m.*
noon *Mittag, m.*
nor *noch.*
normal *normal.*
north *Norden, m.*
northern *nordisch, nördlich.*
northeast *Nordosten, m.*
northwest *Nordwesten, m.*
nose *Nase, f.*
nostril *Nasenloch, n.*
not *nicht.*
note *Note, f.*
note (to) *notieren.*
notebook *Notizbuch, n.*
nothing *nichts.*
notice *Benachrichtung, f.*
notice *(to) bemerken*
notify *(to) benachrichtigen.*
notion *Idee, f.; Begriff, m.*
noun *Name, m.*
nourish *(to) nähren.*
nourishment *Nahrung, f.*
novel *Roman, m.*
novelty *Neuheit, f.*
November *November, m.*
now *jetzt.*
  now and then. *dann und wann;*
    manchmal.
nowadays *heutzurage.*
nowhere *nirgendwo.*
nude *nackt, bloss.*
nuisance *Unfug, m.*
null *null.*
  null and void *null und nichtig.*
numb *gefühllos.*
number *Nummer, f.*
numerous *zahlreich.*
nun *Nonne, f.*
nurse *Krankenschwester, f. (for the*
    sick); Kindermädchen (for children).
nursery *Kinderstube, f. (children);*
    Gärtnerei, f. (trees)
nursery rhyme *Kinderlied, n.*
nut *Nuss, f.*
nutcracker *Nussknacker, m.*

o

oak *Eiche, f.*
oar *Ruder, n.*
oat *Hafer, m.*
oath *Eid, m.*
obedience *Gehorsam.*
obedient *gehorsam.*
obey *(to) gehorchen.*
object *(to) einwenden, dagegen sein.*
objection *Einwand, m.*
objective *objektiv.*
objectively *sachlich.*
obligation *Verpflichtung, f.*
oblige *(to) verpflichten.*
obliging *gefällig.*
obscure *verdunkelt; verworren (meaning).*
obscurity *Dunkelheit, f.*
observation *Beobachtung, f.*
observatory *Sternwarte, f.*
observe *(to) beobachten.*
obstacle *Hindernis, n.*
obstinacy *Eigensinn, m.*
obstinate *eigensinnig.*
obvious *klar.*
obviously *offenbat, deutlich.*
occasion *Gelegenheit, f.*
occasional *gelegentlich.*
occasionally *zuweilen.*
occupation *Beschäftigung, f.*
occupy *(to) besitzen; besetzen (military).*
occur *(to) vorkommen (an event); einfallen (a thought).*
occurrence *Vorfall, m.*
ocean *Ozean, m.*
October *Oktober, m.*
odd *ungerade (uneven); sonderbar (unusual).*
odor *Geruch, m.*
of *von (dat.); aus (dat.) (made of).*
  of course *natürlich.*
off *fort, weg.*
  off and on *ab und zu.*
offend *(to) beleidigen.*
offense *Beleidigung, f.*
offensive *beleidigend.*
offer *(to) anbieten.*
offering *Gabe, f.*
office *Büro, n.*
official *offiziell.*
often *oft, oftmals.*
oil *Öl, n.*
old *alt.*

olive *Olive, f.*
olive oil *Olivenöl, n.*
on *auf (dat. or acc.); an (dat. or acc.) (date).*
once *einmal; vormals, einst (formerly).*
  at once *sofort.*
  once in a while *manchmal.*
  once more *noch einmal.*
one *ein(er, -e, -es).*
one *(pr.) man.*
oneself *sich, sich selbst.*
onion *Zwiebel, f.*
only *nur.*
open *offen.*
open *(to) öffnen.*
opener *Öffner, m.*
opening *Öffnung, f.*
opera *Oper, f.*
operate *(to) operieren.*
operation *Operation, f.*
opinion *Meinung, f.*
opponent *Gegner, m.*
opportune *gelegen.*
opportunity *Gelegenheit, f.*
oppose *(to) sich widersetzen.*
opposite *gegenüber.*
opposition *Widerstand, m.*
oppress *(to) unterdrücken.*
oppression *Unterdrückung, f.*
optician *Optiker, m.*
optimism *Optimismus, m.*
optimistic *optimistisch.*
or *oder.*
orange *Apfelsine, f.*
orange juice *Apfelsinensaft, m.*
orator *Redner, m.*
orchard *Obstgarten, m.*
orchestra *Orchester, n.*
ordeal *Prüfung, f.*
order *Ordnung, f. (neatness); Bestellung, f. (commercial); Befehl, m. (command); Orden, m. (decoration).*
  out of order *kaputt.*
  to put in order *in Ordnung bringen.*
order *(to) ordnen (regulate); bestellen (commercial); befehlen (command).*
ordinary *gewöhnlich.*
organ *Orgel, f. (music); Organ, n. (anatomy).*
organization *Organisation, f.*
organize *(to) organisieren.*
Orient *Orient, m.*
oriental *orientalisch.*
origin *Ursprung, m. (source); Herkunft, f. (descent).*
original *original.*
originality *Originalität, f.*
ornament *Ornament, n.*
orphan *Waisenkind, n.*

orthodox *orthodox.*
other *anderer.*
ought *(to) sollen.*
ounce *Unze, f.*
our *unser.*
ours *unser(er, -e, -es).*
out *aus (dat); hinaus.*
  out of *ausser (dat.)*
outcome *Folge, f.; Ergebnis, n.*
outdo *(to) übertreffen.*
outdoors *im Freien.*
outer *äusser.*
outlast *überdauern.*
outlaw *Geächtete, m.*
outlaw *(to) achten.*
outlay *Auslage, f.*
outlet *Auslass, m.; Absatz, m. (market)*
outline *Umriss, m.*
outlook *Aussicht, f.*
output *Produktion, f.; Leistung, f. (machine).*
outrage *Schandtat, f.*
outrageous *schändlich.*
outside *Aussenseite (noun, f.); draussen (outdoors); ausserhalb (besides).*
oval *oval*
oven *Ofen, m.*
over *über (acc.); vorbei (finished).*
  over and over *wieder und wieder.*
overboard *über Bord.*
overcoat *Mantel, m.*
overcome *(to) überwinden.*
overflow *(to) überfliessen.*
overlook *(to) übersehen.*
overrun *überrennen.*
overseas *übersee.*
overthrow *umstürzen.*
overwhelm *(to) überwältigen.*
owe *(to) schulden.*
owl *Eule, f.*
own *eigen.*
own *(to) besitzen (possess); bekennen (admit).*
owner *Eigentümer, m.*
ox *Ochse, m.*
oxygen *Sauerstoff, m.*
oyster *Auster, f.*

P

pace *Schritt, m.*
pace *(to) schreiten.*
pacific *friedlich.*
pack *Kartenspiel, n. (cards).*
pack *(to) einpacken.*

package *Paket, n.*
page *Seite, f.*
pain *Schmerz, m.*
pain *(to) schmerzen.*
painful *schmerzhaft.*
painless *schmerzlos.*
paint *Farbe, f.*
paint *(to) malen (art); anstreichen (a wall).*
painter *Maler, m. (artist); Anstreicher (workman).*
painting *Gemälde, n.*
pair *Paar, n.*
pajamas *Pyjama, m.*
palace *Palast, m.*
pale *blass.*
palm *Palme, f.*
pamphlet *Broschüre, f.*
pan *Pfanne, f.*
pancake *Pfannkuchen, m.*
pane *Scheibe, f.*
panel *Füllung, f.; Liste, f. (persons).*
panic *Panik, f.*
panorama *Panorama, n.*
panties *Schlüpfer, m.*
pants *Hose, f.*
paper *Papier, n.*
parachute *Fallschirm, m.*
parade *Parade, f.*
paragraph *Paragraph, m; Absatz, m.*
parallel *parallel.*
paralysis *Lähmung, f.*
paralyzed *gelähmt.*
parcel *Paket, n.*
pardon *Verzeihung, f.*
pardon *(to) vergeben.*
parenthesis *Klammer, f.*
parents *Eltern, pl.*
Parisian *Pariser, m.*
park *Park, m.*
park *(to) parken.*
parliament *Parlament, n.*
parrot *Papagei, m.*
parsley *Petersilie, f.*
part *Teil, n. (share); Ersatzteil (machinery).*
part *(to) teilen; sich trennen (separate); scheiteln (hair).*
partial *teilweise.*
partiality *Vorliebe, f.*
particular *besonder(er, -e, -es).*
particularly *besonders.*
partner *Partner, m.*
party *(political) Partei, f.; Gesellschaft, f. (society).*
pass *Ausweis, m.*
pass *(to) durchgehen, vorbeigehen; passen (cards); bestehen (exam).*
passage *Durchgang, m.; Überfahrt, f. (travel).*

passenger *Passagier, m.*
passion *Leidenschaft, f.*
passionately *leidenschaftlich.*
passive *Passiv, n.*
passport *Pass, m.*
past *Vergangenheit (noun, f.); vorbei, vorige (time); nach (on the clock). ten past six zehn nach sechs.*
paste *Kleister, m.*
paste *(to) kleistern.*
pastry *Gebäck, n.*
pastry shop *Konditorei, f.*
patch *Flicken, m.*
patch *(to) flicken.*
patent *Patent, n.*
paternal *väterlich.*
path *Weg, m.*
pathetic *pathetisch.*
patience *Geduld, f.*
patient *Patient (noun, m.); geduldig (adj.).*
patriot *Patriot, m.*
patriotic *patriotisch.*
patron *Gönner, m.*
patronage *Gönnerschaft, f.*
patronize *(to) unterstützen.*
pattern *Muster, n.*
pause *Pause, f.*
pave *(to) pflastern.*
pavement *Pflaster, n.*
paw *Pfote, f.*
pay *Lohn, m.; Löhnung, f.; Sold, m. (military).*
pay *(to) zahlen.*
payment *Bezahlung, f.*
pea *Erbse, f.*
peace *Frieden, m.*
peaceful *friedlich.*
peach *Pfirsich, m.*
peak *Gipfel, m.*
peanut *Erdnuss, f.*
pear *Birne, f.*
pearl *Perle, f.*
peasant *Bauer, m.*
pebble *Kieselstein, m.*
peculiar *sonderbar.*
pedal *Pedal, n.*
pedantic *pedantisch.*
pedestrian *Fussgänger, m.*
peel *Rinde, f.; Schale, f.*
peel *(to) schälen.*
pen *Feder, f.*
   fountain pen *Füllfeder, f.*
penalty *Strafe, f.*
pencil *Bleistift, m.*
penetrate *(to) durchdringen.*
peninsula *Halbinsel, f.*
penitence *Reue, f.*
pension *Pension, f.*

people *Leute, pl.*
pepper *Pfeffer, m.*
peppermint *Pfefferminz, m.*
per *pro.*
perceive *(to) wahrehmen.*
percentage *Prozentsatz, m.*
perfect *vollkommen.*
perfection *Vollkommenheit, f.*
perfectly *gänzlich.*
perform *(to) verrichten; aufführen (theater or surgery).*
performance *Vorstellung, f.*
perfume *Parfüm, n.*
perfume *(to) parfümieren.*
perhaps *vielleicht.*
period *Periode, f.*
periodical *periodisch.*
permanent *ständig.*
permission *Erlaubnis, f.*
permit *Erlaubnisschein, m.*
permit *(to) erlauben.*
peroxide *Hyperoxyd, n.*
perpetual *immerwährend.*
perplex *verwirren.*
persecute *(to) verfolgen.*
persecution *Verfolgung, f.*
perseverance *Ausdauer, f.*
persist *(to) beharren.*
person *Person f.*
personal *persönlich.*
personality *Persönlichkeit., f.*
perspective *Perspektive, f.*
perspiration *Schweiss, m.*
persuade *(to) überreden.*
pertaining *gehören (zu).*
petrol *Petroleum, n.*
petticoat *Unterrock, m.*
petty *kleinlich.*
pharmacist *Apotheker, m.*
pharmacy *Apotheke, f.*
phenomenon *Phänomen, n.*
philosopher *Philosoph, m.*
philosophical *philosophisch.*
philosophy *Philosophie, f.*
phonograph *Plattenspieler, m.*
photograph *Fotografie, f.*
photograph *(to) aufnehmen.*
photographer *Fotograf, m.*
photostat *Lichtpause, f.*
phrase *Frase, f.*
physical *körperlich.*
physician *Arzt, m; Doktor, m.*
piano *Klavier, n.*
pick *(to) pflücken.*
pick up *(to) aufheben.*
picnic *Piknik, n.*
picture *Bild, n.*
picturesque *malerisch.*
pie *Torte, f.*

piece *Stück, n.*
pier *Mole, f.*
pig *Schwein, n.*
pigeon *Taube, f.*
pile *Haufen, m.*
pile *(to) aufhäufen.*
pilgrim *Pilger, m.*
pill *Pille, f.*
pillar *Säule, f.*
pillow *Kissen, n.*
pilot *Pilot, m.*
pin *Stecknadel, f.*
pinch *(to) kneifen.*
pink *rosa.*
pious *fromm.*
pipe *Pfeife, f. (tobacco); Rohr, n. (plumbing).*
pirate *Seeräuber, m.; Pirat, m.*
pistol *Pistole, f.*
pitiful *mitleidig.*
pity *Mitleid, n.*
place *Platz, m.; Stelle, f. (spot, situation); Ort, m. (locality).*
take place *stattfinden.*
place *(to) stellen.*
plain *Ebene (noun, f.); einfach (adj.).*
plan *Plan, m. (project); Grundriss, m.*
plan *(to) ausdenken.*
plane *Flugzeug, n.*
planet *Planet, m.*
plant *Pflanze, f.*
plant *(to) pflanzen.*
plaster *Verputz, m.*
plastic *Kunststoff (noun, m.); plastisch (adj.).*
plate *Teller, m.*
platform *Bahnsteig, m. (station).*
platter *Platte, f.*
play *Spiel, n.; Stück, n. (theater).*
play *(to) spielen.*
plea *Gesuch, n.*
plead *(to) plädieren.*
pleasant *angenehm.*
please *bitte.*
please *(to) gefallen.*
pleasure *Vergnügen, n.*
pledge *Pfand, n.*
plenty *genug (enough); reichlich (abundance).*
plot *Verschwörung, f. (conspiracy); Handlung, f. (of a story).*
plot *(to) anstiften.*
plow *Pflug, m.*
plow *(to) pflügen.*
plum *Pflaume, f.*
plumber *Klempner, m.*
pneumonia *Lungenentzündung, f.*
pocket *Tasche, f.*
poem *Gedicht, n.*

poet *Poet, m.*
poetic *poetisch.*
poetry *Dichtung, f.*
point *Punkt, m.; Spitze, f.*
point *(to) spitzen.*
pointed *spitz.*
poise *Gleichgewicht, n.*
poison *Gift, n.*
poison *(to) vergiften.*
poisonous *giftig*
polar *pol-.*
pole *Pol, m.*
police *Polizei, f.*
policeman *Schutzmann, m.; Polizist, m.*
policy *Politik, f.; Police, f. (insurance).*
Polish *polnisch.*
polish *Glanz, m.*
polish *(to) glänzend machen; polieren.*
polite *höflich.*
politeness *Höflichkeit, f.*
political *politisch.*
pond *Teich, m.*
pool *Pfuhl, m.*
poor *arm.*
Pope *Papst, m.*
popular *volkstümlich.; beliebt (liked).*
population *Bevölkerung, f.*
pork *Schweinefleisch, n.*
port *Hafen, m.*
porter *Träger, m.*
portrait *Bild, n.*
Portuguese *Portugiese (noun, m.); portugiesisch (adj.).*
position *Stellung, f. (job); Lage, f. (site).*
positive *bestimmt.*
possibility *möglicherweise.*
possible *möglich.*
post *Post, f.; Stelle, f. (job).*
postage *Porto, n.*
postcard *Postkarte, f.*
poster *Plakat, n.*
posterity *Nachwelt, f.*
post office *Postamt, n.*
pot *Topf, m.*
potato *Kartoffel, f.*
pound *Pfund, n.*
pour *(to) giessen.*
poverty *Armut, f.*
powder *Pulver, n.; Puder, m. (cosmetic).*
powder *(to) pudern.*
power *Macht, f.*
powerful *mächtig.*
practical *praktisch.*
practice *(to) üben.*
praise *Lob, n.*
praise *(to) loben.*
prank *Prank, m.; Streich, m.*
pray *(to) beten.*

prayer *Gebet, n.*
preach *(to) predigen.*
preacher *Prediger, m.*
precaution *Vorsicht, f.*
precede *(to) vorangehen.*
preceding *vorangehend.*
precept *Vorschrift, f.; Beispiel, n. (example).*
precious *kostbar.*
precise *genau; steif (formal).*
precision *Genauigkeit, f.*
predecessor *Vorgänger, m.*
preface *Vorwort, n.*
prefer *(to) vorziehen.*
preference *Vorzug, m.*
pregnant *schwanger.*
prejudice *Vorurteil, n.*
preliminary *einleitend.*
preparation *Vorbereitung, f.*
prepare *(to) vorbereiten.*
prepay *(to) vorauszahlen.*
prescribe *(to) verschreiben.*
prescription *Rezept, n.*
presence *Gegenwart, f.; Anwesenheit, f.*
present *Gegenwart, f. (grammar); Geschenk, n. (gift); anwesend (adj.).*
preserve *(to) erhalten; konservieren (food).*
preserves *Konserven, f.; Eingemachte, n.*
preside *(to) präsidieren.*
president *Präsident, m.*
press *Presse, f.*
press *(to) drücken; bügeln (clothes).*
pressing *dringend.*
pressure *Druck, m.; Andrang, m. (blood-).*
prestige *Prestige, n.; Ansehen, n.*
presume *(to) vermuten.*
pretend *(to) vorgeben.*
pretext *Vorwand, m.*
pretty *hübsch, nett.*
prevail *(to) vorherrschen.*
prevent *(to) verhindern.*
prevention *Verhinderung, f.*
previous *frühere.*
prey *Raub, m.*
price *Preis, m.*
pride *Stolz, m.*
priest *Priester, m.*
prince *Prinz, m.*
principal *haupt-(adj.)*
principle *Grundsatz, m.*
print *(to) drucken.*
prison *Gefängnis, n.*
prisoner *Gefangene, m.*
private *privat.*
privilege *Vorrecht, r.*

prize *Preis, m.*
prize *(to) schätzen.*
probable *wahrscheinlich.*
problem *Problem, n.*
procedure *Verfahren, n.*
proceed *(to) fortschreiten.*
process *Verfahren, n.; Prozess, m.*
procession *Prozession, f.*
proclaim *(to) bekanntmachen.*
produce *(to) erzeugen.*
product *Erzeugnis, n.*
production *Erzeugung, f.; Produktion, f.*
productive *fruchtbar.*
profession *Beruf, m.*
professional *berufsmässig.*
professor *Professor, m.; Lehrer, m. (school).*
profile *Profil, n.*
profit *Gewinn, m.*
profit *(to) gewinnen.*
program *Programm, n.*
progress *Fortschritt, m.*
progress *(to) vorwärtskommen.*
progressive *fortschrittlich.*
prohibit *(to) verbieten.*
prohibition *Verbot, n.*
project *Projekt, n.*
project *(to) hervorstehen.*
promise *(to) versprechten.*
prompt *schnell.*
pronoun *Fürwort, n.*
pronounce *(to) aussprechen.*
pronunciation *Aussprache, f.*
proof *Beweis, m.*
propaganda *Propaganda, f.*
proper *passend; anständig (decent).*
property *Eigentum, n.*
proportion *Verhältnis, n.*
proposal *Vorschlag, m.*
propose *(to) vorschlagen.*
prose *Prosa, f.*
prospect *(to) Aussicht, f.*
prosper *(to) gedeihen.*
prosperity *Wohlstand, m.*
prosperous *gedeihlich, blühend.*
protect *(to) schützen.*
protection *Schutz, m.*
protector *Beschützer, m.*
protest *Einspruch, m.*
protest *(to) protestieren.*
Protestant *Protestant, m.*
proud *stolz.*
prove *(to) probieren.*
proverb *Sprichwort, n.*
provide *(to) versorgen.*
provided that *vorausgesetzt dass.*
province *Provinz, f.*
provincial *provinziell.*

provision *Provision, f.*
provoke *(to) herausfordern, reizen.*
proximity *Nähe, f.*
prudence *Vorsicht, f.*
prudent *klug, vorsichtig.*
prune *Backpflaume, f.*
psychological *psychologisch.*
psychology *Psychologie, f.*
public *Publikum (noun, n.); öffentlich (adj.).*
publication *Herausgabe, f. (literary); Veröffent. lichtung, f. (notification)*
publish *(to) herausgeben (book); veröffentlichen (announcement).*
publishing house *Verlag, m.*
publisher *Verleger, m.*
pull *(to) ziehen.*
pump *Pumpe, f.*
punish *(to) bestrafen.*
punishment *Strafe, f.*
pupil *Schüler, m.; Schülerin, f.*
purchase *(to) kaufen.*
purchase *Einkauf, m.*
pure *rein.*
purity *Reinheit, f.*
purple *Purpur, m.*
purpose *Absicht, f.*
purse *Geldtasche, f.*
pursue *(to) verfolgen.*
push *(to) stossen.*
put *(to) legen (lay); setzen (set); stellen (place).*
    put down *aufschreiben.*
    put off *aufschieben.*
    put on *anziehen.*
    put up *aufstellen.*
puzzle *Rätsel, n.*
puzzle *(to) verwirren.*

Q

quaint *seltsam.*
qualify *berechtigen.*
quality *Qualität, f.*
quantity *Quantität, f.*
quarrel *Streit, m.*
quarter *Viertel, n.*
queen *Königin, f.*
queer *seltsam.*
quench *(to) löschen.*
question *Frage, f.*
question *(to) fragen.*
quick *schnell.*
quiet *ruhig.*

quit *(to) verlassen.*
quite *ganz.*
quote *(to) anführen.*

R

rabbit *Kaninchen, n.*
race *Rennen, n. (contest); Rasse, f. (species).*
radiator *Heizkörper, m.*
radio *Radio, n.*
rag *Fetzen, m.*
rage *Wut, f.*
ragged *zerlumpt.*
rail *Schiene, f.*
railroad *Eisenbahn, f.*
railroad car *Eisenbahnwagen, m.*
rain *Regen, m.*
rain *(to) regnen.*
rainbow *Regenbogen, m.*
raincoat *Regenmantel, m.*
rainy *regnerisch.*
raise *(to) erhöhen.*
raisin *Rosine, f.*
rake *Rechen, m.*
rank *Rang, m.*
rapid *schnell.*
rapidly *schnell.*
rapture *Entzücken, n.*
rash *Hautausschlag (noun, m.) (skin); hastig (adj.).*
rat *Ratte, f.*
rate *Kurs, m. (exchange); Verhältnis, n.*
rate *(to) schätzen.*
rather *ziemlich, lieber, eher.*
ration *Ration, f.*
rational *vernünftig.*
rave *(to) schwärmen.*
raw *roh.*
ray *Strahl, m.*
razor *Rasiermesser, n.*
razor blade *Razierklinge, f.*
reach *(to) erreichen.*
reach *Bereich, m; Reichweite, f.*
react *(to) rückwirken, reagieren.*
read *(to) lesen.*
reading *Lesen, n.; Lektüre, f.*
ready *fertig.*
real *wirklich.*
realization *Verwirklichung, f.*
realize *(to) verwirklichen.*
really *wirklich.*
rear *Hintergrund (noun, m.); hinter (adj.).*
rear *(to) grossziehen.*

reason *Grund, m. (cause); Vernunft, f. (intelligence).*
reason *(to) besprechen.*
reasonable *vernünftig.*
reasoning *Schlussfolgerung, f.*
reassure *(to) beruhigen.*
rebel *Rebell, m.*
rebel *(to) sich auflechnen.*
rebellion *Empörung, f.*
recall *(to) sich erinnern (memory); zurückrufen (to summon back).*
receipt *Quittung, f.*
receive *(to) empfangen*
receiver *Empfäger, m.*
recent *neu.*
recently *neulich.*
reception *Empfang, m.*
recess *Nische, f.*
reciprocal *gegenseitig.*
recite *(to) aufsagen; rezitieren (drama).*
recognize *(to) erkennen.*
recollect *(to) sich erinnern.*
recollection *Erinnerung, f.*
recommend *(to) empfehlen.*
recommendation *Empfehlung, f.*
reconcile *(to) versöhnen.*
record *Ordner, m.*
   phonograph record (Schall)platte, f.
recover *(to) sich erholen.*
recruit *Rekrut, m.*
recruit *(to) reknutieren.*
red *rot.*
Red Cross *Rote Kreuz, n.*
redeem *(to) erlösen.*
reduce *(to) herabsetzen; abnehmen (weight).*
reduction *Nachlass, m.*
reed *Schilf, m.*
reef *Riff, n.*
refer *(to) sich beziehen.*
reference *Bezugnahme, f.*
referring to *bezugnehmen auf.*
refine *(to) verfeinern.*
refinement *Bildung, f.*
reflect *(to) zurückstrahlen.*
reflection *Widerschein, m. (image); Überlegung, f. (thoughts).*
reform *Besserung, f.*
reform *(to) sich bessern.*
refrain *(to) sich enthalten.*
refresh *(to) erfrischen.*
refreshment *Erfrischung, f.*
refrigerator *Kühlschrank, m.*
refuge *Zufluchtsort, m.*
   take refuge flüchten.
refugee *Flüchtling, m.*
refund *Rückzahlung, f.*
refund *(to) zurückzahlen.*
refusal *Verweigerung, f.*

refuse *(to) ablehnen, verweigern.*
refute *(to) widerlegen.*
regard *Ansehen, n.*
regardless *unbeachtet.*
regime *Regime, n.*
regiment *Regiment, n.*
register *(to) eintragen (membership); einschreiben (letter).*
regret *Bedauern, n.*
regret *(to) bedauern.*
regular *regelmässig.*
regulate *regulieren.*
regulation *Vorschrift, f.*
rehearsal *Probe, f.*
rehearse *(to) Probe halten.*
reign *Regierung, f.*
reign *(to) regieren.*
reinforce *(to) verstärken.*
reject *(to) verwerfen.*
rejoice *(to) sich freuen.*
relapse *Rückfall, m.*
relate *(to) erzählen.*
relation *Verwandtschaft, f.*
relationship *verwandtschaftliche Beziehung, f.*
relative *Verwandte, m.*
relax *(to) entspannen.*
relaxation *Entspannung, f.*
release *Befreiung, f.*
release *(to) freilassen.*
reliable *zuverlässig.*
relic *Überbleibsel, n.; Relique, f.; (religious).*
relief *Erleichterung, f.; Linderung, f. (of pain).*
relieve *(to) erleichtern, lindern.*
religion *Religion, f.*
religious *religiös.*
relinquish *(to) aufgeben.*
relish *(to) munden.*
relish *Geschmack, m.*
reluctance *Widerwille, n.*
reluctant *widerwillig.*
rely *(to) sich verlassen.*
remain *(to) bleiben.*
remainder *Rest, m.*
remark *Bemerkung, f.*
remark *(to) bemerken.*
remarkable *bemerkenswert.*
remedy *Arznei, f. (medicine); Hilfsmittel, n. (cure).*
remember *(to) sich erinnern.*
remembrance *Erinnerung, f.*
remind *(to) mahnen.*
remorse *Reue, f.*
remote *entfernt (distance); rückständig (antiquated).*
removal *Beseitigung, f.*
remove *(to) entfernen.*

renew *(to) erneuern.*
renewal *Erneuerung, f.*
rent *Miete, f.*
rent *(to) mieten.*
repair *Reparatur, f.*
repay *(to) zurückzahlen.*
repeat *(to) wiederholen.*
repent *(to) bereuen.*
repetition *Wiederholung, f.*
reply *Antwort, f.*
reply *(to) antworten.*
report *Bericht, m.; Zeugnis, n.*
report *(to) berichten.*
reporter *Reporter, m.*
represent *(to) vertreten.*
representation *Vertretung, f.*
representative *Vertreter, m.*
repress *(to) unterdrücken.*
repression *Unterdrückung, f.*
reprimand *Verweis, m.*
reprimand *(to) tadeln.*
reprisal *Gegenmassregel, f.*
reproach *Vorwurf, m.*
reproach *(to) vorwerfen.*
reproduce *(to) reproduzieren.*
reproduction *Reproduktion, f.*
republic *Republik, f.*
reputation *Ruf, m.; Ansehen, n.*
request *Bitte, f.*
request *(to) bitten.*
require *(to) benötigen.*
requirement *Bedarf, m.*
rescue *(to) retten.*
research *Forschung, f.*
resent *(to) verübeln.*
resentful *empfindlich.*
resentment *Verdruss, m.*
reservation *Reservation, f.*
reserve *(to) reservieren.*
reservoir *Behälter, m.*
residence *Wohnstätte, f.*
resident *Bewohner, m.*
resign *(to) aufgeben.*
resignation *Rücktritt, m.*
resist *(to) widerstehen.*
resistance *Widerstand, m.*
resolute *entschlossen.*
resolution *Beschluss, m.*
resolve *(to) sich entschliessen (decide); lösen (problem).*
resort *Kurort, m. (health); Luftkurort, m. (vacation); Zuflucht, f. (recourse).*
resource *Hilfsmittel, n.*
respect *Achtung, f.*
respectful *ehrfürchtig, achtungsvoll.*
respective *bezüglich.*
responsibility *Verantwortlichkeit, f.*
responsible *verantwortlich.*
rest *Ruhe, f.*

rest *(to) ruhen.*
restaurant *Restaurant, n.*
restless *unruhig.*
restoration *Wiederherstellung, f.*
restore *(to) wiederherstellen, restaurieren.*
restrain *(to) zurückhalten.*
restraint *Zurückhaltung, f.*
restrict *(to) beschränken.*
restriction *Einschränkung, f.*
result *Resultat, n.*
result *(to) folgen.*
resume *(to) wiederaufnehmen, wieder anfangen.*
retail *Einzelverkauf, m.; Kleinhandel, m.*
retail *(to) im Kleinhandel verkaufen.*
retain *(to) behalten.*
retaliate *(to) vergelten.*
retaliation *Vergeltung, f.*
retire *(to) sich zurückziehen.*
retirement *Zurückgezogenheit, f.*
retract *widerrufen; zurückziehen.*
retreat *Rückzug, m.*
retreat *(to) sich zurückziehen.*
return *Rückkehr, f.*
return *(to) zurückkehren.*
reveal *(to) offenbaren, enthüllen.*
revelation *Offenbarung, f.*
revenge *Rache, f.*
revenge *(to) rächen.*
revenue *Einkommen, n.*
reverence *Ehrerbietung, f.*
reverend *erwürdig.*
reverse *Rückseite, f.*
reverse *(to) umkehren.*
review *(to) betrachten; mustern (inspect); rezensieren (critical).*
review *Überblick, m. Parade, f. (army);Revue, f. (theater), Rezension, f.*
revise *(to) revidieren (critique).*
revive *neubeleben.*
revival *Wiederbelebung, f.*
revoke *(to) widerrufen.*
revolt *Aufstand, m.*
revolt *(to) sich empören.*
revolution *Revolution, f.*
revolve *(to) sich drehen.*
reward *Belohnung, f.*
reward *(to) belohnen.*
rhyme *Reim, m.*
rhyme *(to) reimen.*
rib *Rippe, f.*
ribbon *Band, n.*
rice *Reis, m.*
rich *reich.*
richness *Reichtum, m.*
rid *(to get) loswerden.*
riddle *Rätsel, n.*
ride *Fahrt, f.*

ridiculous *lächerlich.*
rifle *Gewehr, n.*
right *richtig (correct); rechts (position).*
  all right *ganz gut.*
righteous *gerecht.*
rigid *steif, fest, starr.*
rigor *Strenge, f.*
rigorous *streng, scharf, hart.*
ring *Ring, m.*
  wedding ring *Ehering, m.*
ring *(to) ringen.*
rinse *(to) spülen, ausspülen.*
riot *(to) Aufruhr, f.; Sfchwelgerei, f.*
  (army).
ripe *reif.*
ripen *(to) reifen.*
rise *Steigung, f.*
rise *(to) aufstehen (get up); steigen*
  (increase, mount); aufgehen (sun).
risk *Gefahr, f.*
risk *(to) riskieren.*
rite *Ritus, m.*
ritual *rituell.*
rival *Rivale, m.*
rivalry *Mitbewerbung, f.; Konkurrenz, f.*
river *Fluss, m.*
roach *Schabe, f.*
road *Weg, m.*
roar *(to) brüllen.*
roast *Braten, m.*
roast *(to) braten.*
rob *(to) rauben.*
robber *Räuber, m.*
robbery *Diebstahl, m.*
robe *Morgenrock, m.*
robust *stark, rüstig.*
rock *Felsen, m.*
rock *(to) wiegen.*
rocky *felsig.*
rocket *Rakete, f.*
rod *Rute, f.*
roll *Rolle, f. (cylinder); Brötchen, n.*
  (bread).
roll *(to) rollen.*
Roman *Römer (noun, m.); römisch*
  (adj.).
romantic *romantisch.*
roof *Dach, n.*
room *Zimmer, n. (of a house); Raum,*
  m. (space).
  There is no room. *Da ist kein Platz.*
roomy *geräumig.*
root *Wurzel, f.*
rope *Seil, n.*
rose *Rose, f.*
rot *(to) faulen; vermodern.*
rough *rauh (coarse); roh (crude);*
  stürmisch (stormy).
round *Runde (noun, f.); rund (adj.).*

round *um (acc.); herum.*
rouse *(to) aufwecken; erzümen (anger).*
routine *Routine, f.; Erfahrung, f.*
row *Reihe, f.*
row *(to) rudern.*
royal *königlich.*
rub *(to) reiben.*
rubber *Gummi, m.*
ruby *Rubin, m.*
rude *grob.*
ruffle *(to) verwirren.*
ruin *Ruine, f.*
ruin *(to) ruinieren.*
rule *Regel, f.*
rule *(to) regieren, beherrschen.*
ruler *Lineal, n.*
rum *Rum, m.*
rumor *Gerücht, n.*
run *(to) rennen, laufen.*
  run away *weglaufen.*
rural *ländlich.*
rush *(to) Sturz, m.; Andrang, m.*
  (crowd).
Russian *Russe (noun, m.); russisch*
  (adj.)
rust *(to) verrosten.*
rusty *rostig.*
rye *Roggen, m.*

S

sacred *heilig.*
sacrifice *Opfer, n.*
sacrifice *(to) opfern.*
sacrilege *Entweihung, f.*
sad *traurig.*
sadden *(to) trauern.*
saddle *Sattel, m.*
sadness *Traurigkeit, f.*
safe *Schliessfach (noun, m.) (of a*
  bank);' wohlbehalten (adj.) (in
  safekeeping); sicher (adj.) (secure).
safety *Sicherheit, f.*
sail *(to) segeln.*
sail *Segel, n.*
sailor *Matrose, m.*
saint *Heilige, m. & f.*
  patron saint *Schutzheilige, m. & f.*
sake *(for the - of) um (gen.) willen.*
salad *Salat, m.*
salami *Salami, f.*
salary *Gehalt, n.*
sale *Verkauf, m.; Ausverkauf, m.*
  (bargain).
saleslady *Verkäuferin, f.*
salesman *Verkäufer, m.*

salmon *Lachs, m.*
salt *Salz, n.*
salute *Gruss, m.*
salute *(to) grüssen.*
salvation *Rettung, f.*
Salvation Army *Heilsarmee, f.*
same *der (die-, das-). selbe*
  the same as *derselbe wie.*
  all the same *es spielt keine Rolle.*
sample *Muster, n.*
sanctuary *Zufluchtsort, m.*
sand *Sand, m.*
sandal *Sandale, f.*
sandwich *Butterbrot, n.*
sandy *sandig.*
sanitary *hygienisch.*
sap *Saft, m.*
sapphire *Saphir, m.*
sarcasm *Sarkasmus, m.*
sarcastic *sarkastisch.*
sardine *Sardine, f.*
satiate *(to) sättigen.*
satin *Seidenatlas, m.*
satisfaction *Befriedung, f.*
satisfactory *zufriedenstellend.*
satisfy *(to) befriedigen.*
saturate *(to) durchtränken.*
Saturday *Samstag, m.*
sauce *Sauce, f.*
saucer *Untertasse, f.*
sausage *Wurst, f.*
savage *wild.*
save *(to) sparen (hoard); retten*
  (rescue).
saving *Ersparnis, f.*
savior *Erretter, m.*
Savior *Heiland, m.*
say *(to) sagen.*
scale *Schuppe, f.; Tonleiter, f. (music).*
scales *Massstab, m.; Waage, f.*
scalp *Skalp, m.*
scan *(to) überblicken.*
scandal *Skandal, m.*
scanty *knapp, dürftig.*
scar *Narbe, f.*
scarce *knapp.*
scarcely *kaum.*
scare *(to) erschrecken.*
scarf *Schal, m.*
scarlet *scharlachrot.*
scattered *verstreut.*
schedule *Stundenplan, m. (time).*
scheme *Schema, n.; Entwurf, m.*
scholar *Gelehrte, m. & f.*
school *Schule, f.*
schoolteacher *Lehrer, m.; Lehrerin, f.*
science *Wissenschaft, f.*
scientific *wissenschaftlich.*
scientist *Wissenschaftler, m.*

scissors *Schere, f.*
scold *(to) schelten.*
scorn *Verachtung, f.*
scorn *(to) verachten.*
scornful *verächtlich.*
Scottish *schottisch.*
scrape *(to) kratzen; schaben*
  (vegetables).
scraper *Schaber, m.*
scratch *Schramme, f.*
scratch *(to) kratzen.*
scream *Schrei, m.*
scream *(to) schreien.*
screen *Schirm, m.*
  movie screen *Leinwand, f.*
screw *Schraube, f.*
scribble *(to) kritzeln.*
scruple *Skrupel, m.*
scrupulous *gewissenhaft.*
scrutinize *(to) prüfen.*
sculptor *Bildhauer, m.*
sculpture *Bildhauerei, f.*
sea *Meer, n.*
seal *Siegel, n.; Seehund, m. (animal).*
seal *(to) siegeln.*
seam *Naht, f.*
search *Suche, f.; Untersuchung, f.*
  (customs).
search *(to) suchen; untersuchen.*
seashore *Seeküste, f.*
seasickness *Seekrankheit, f.*
season *Jahreszeit, f.; Saison, f.*
  (events).
seat *Sitz, m.*
seat *(to) setzen; stellen.*
second *zweit(er, -e, -es).*
secret *Geheimnis, noun, n.; geheim,*
  (adj.).
secretary *Sekretär, m.; Sekretärin, f.*
sect *Sekte, f.*
section *Teil, m.*
secure *sicher.*
secure *(to) sichern.*
security *Sicherheit, f.*
see *(to) sehen.*
seed *Samen, m.*
seek *(to) suchen.*
seem *(to) scheinen.*
seize *(to) ergreifen, fassen.*
seldom *selten, rar.*
select *(to) wählen.*
selection *Auswahl, f.*
selfish *selbstsüchtig.*
selfishness *Selbstsucht, f.*
sell *(to) verkaufen.*
semicolon *Semikolon, n.*
senate *Senat, m.*
senator *Senator, m.*
send *(to) senden.*

senior *Ältere.*
sensation *Gefühl, n. (feeling);*
  Sensation, f. (excitement).
sense *Sinn, m.*
senseless *sinnlos.*
sensibility *Vernünftigkeit, f.*
sensible *vernünftig.*
sensitive *empfindlich.*
sensitivity *Empfindlichkeit, f.*
sensual *wollüstig.*
sensuality *Wollust, f. Sinnlichkeit, f.*
sentence *Urteil, n. (legal); Satz, m.*
  (grammar).
sentiment *Gefühl, n.*
sentimental *sentimental.*
sentimentality *Sentimentalität, f.*
separate *einzeln.*
separate *(to) trennen.*
separately *besonders.*
separation *Trennung, f.*
September *September, m.*
serene *heiter.*
sergeant *Sergeant, m.*
series *Serie, f.*
serious *ernst.*
seriousness *Ernst, m.*
servant *Diener, m.*
serve *(to) dienen.*
service *Dienst, m.; Gottesdienst, m.*
  (church).
session *Sitzung, f.*
set *festgelegt.*
set *Sammlung, f. (collection);*
  Untergang, m. (sun); Satz, m. (series);
  Service, n. (dishes).
set *(to) setzen; stellen (clock).*
settle *(to) begleichen (accounts);*
  erledigen (conclude).
settlement *Begleichung, f.; Erledigung,*
  f.; Siedlung f. (houses).
seven *sieben.*
seventeen *siebzehn.*
seventeenth *siebzehnte.*
seventh *siebte.*
seventieth *siebzigste.*
seventy *siebzig.*
several *mehere.*
  several times *mehrmals.*
severe *streng (stern, rigorous); hettig*
  (pain).
severity *Strenge, f.*
sew *(to) nähen.*
sewer *Abzugskanal, m.*
sex *Geschlecht, n.*
shabby *schäbig.*
shade *Schatten, m.*
shadow *Schatten, m.*
shady *schattig.*
shake *(to) schütteln; zittern (tremble).*

handshake *Händedruck, m.*
shallow *seicht.*
shame *Schande, f. (disgrace); Scham, f.*
  (modesty).
shameful *schändlich.*
shameless *schamlos.*
shampoo *Shampoo, n.*
shape *Form, f.*
share *Teil, m.; Anteil, m.; Aktie, f.*
  (stock).
share *(to) teilen.*
shareholder *Aktionär, m.*
sharp *scharf.*
sharpen *(to) schärfen.*
shave *(to) sich rasieren.*
she *sie.*
shed *(to) vergiessen (spill); abwerfen*
  (discard).
sheep *Schaf, n.*
sheer *rein, lauter.*
sheet *(Bett)laken, n. (linens); Blatt, n.*
  (paper).
shelf *Brett, n.*
shell *Muschel, f.; Geschoss, n.*
  (artillery).
shelter *Unterkunft, f.; Luftschutzraum,*
  m. (air raids).
shelter *unterstellen (from exposure);*
  schützen (from danger).
shepherd *Schäfer, m.;*
shield *Schild, n.*
shield *(to) schützen.*
shift *Schicht, f. (workers).*
shift *(to) schieben.*
shine *(to) scheinen; putzen (shoes).*
ship *Schiff, n.*
ship *(to) senden, befördern.*
shipment *Verladung, f.; Verschiffung, f.;*
  Beförderung, f.
shirt *Hemd, n.*
shiver *Schauer, m.*
shiver *(to) (er)schauern.*
shock *Schlag, m. (blow); Stoss, m.*
shock *(to) anstossen (scandalize);*
  erschüttern.
shoe *Schuh, m.*
schoemaker *Schuhmacher, m.*
shoot *(to) schiessen.*
shop *Laden, m.; Geschäft, n.*
short *kurz.*
shorten *(to) kürzen.*
shorthand *Kurzschrift, f.; Stenographie,*
  f.
shorts *Unterhosen, pl. (men's).*
shot *Schuss, m.*
shoulder *Schulter, f.*
shout *Schrei, m.*
shout *(to) schreien.*
shovel *Schaufel, f.*

show *Vorstellung, f. (play); Ausstellung, f. (exhibition).*
show *(to) zeigen.*
shower *Schauer, m. (rain); Dusche, f. (shower-bath).*
shrill *schrill.*
shrimp *Krabbe, f.*
shrink *(to) einlaufen.*
shrub *Strauch, m.*
shrubbery *Gebüsch, n.*
shun *(to) meiden.*
shut *geschlossen.*
shut *(to) schliessen.*
shy *schüchtern.*
sick *krank.*
sickness *Krankheit, f.*
side *Seite, f.*
sidewalk *Bürgersteig, m.*
siege *Belagerung, f.*
sigh *Seufzer, m.*
sigh *(to) seufzen.*
sight *Aussicht, f.; Anblick, m.*
sign *Zeichen, n.*
sign *(to) zeichnen.*
signal *Signal, n.*
signal *(to) signalisieren.*
signature *Unterschrift, f.*
significance *Bedeutung, f.*
significant *bezeichnend.*
signify *(to) bezeichnen (indicate); bedeuten (mean).*
silence *Schweigen, n.*
silent *still, schweigend.*
silk *Seide, f.*
silken *seiden.*
silly *ausgelassen, dumm.*
silver *Silber, n.*
silvery *silbern.*
similar *ähnlich.*
similarity *Ähnlichkeit, f.*
simple *einfach.*
simplicity *Einfachheit, f.*
simply *nur (only).*
simulate *(to) erheucheln, vortäuschen.*
simultaneous *gleichzeitig.*
sin *Sünde, f.*
sin *(to) sündigen.*
since *seit (dat.); da, weil (because).*
sincere *aufrichtig.*
sincerity *Aufrichtigkeit, f.*
sing *(to) singen.*
singer *Sänger, m.; Sängerin, f.*
single *einzeln; ledig (unmarried).*
singular *einzigartig; seltsam (strange).*
sinister *unheilvoll.*
sink *Gussstein, m.; Ausguss, m.*
sink *(to) sinken.*
sinner *Sünder, m.; Sünderin, f.*
sip *(to) nippen.*

sip *Schluck, m.*
sir *Herr, m.*
sister *Schwester, f.*
sister-in-law *Schwägerin, f.*
sit *(to) sitzen (be seated); sich setzen (sit down).*
site *Lage, f.; Bauplatz, m.*
situation *Lage, f.*
six *sechs.*
sixteen *sechzehnte.*
sixteenth *sechzehnte.*
sixth *sechate.*
sixtieth *sechzigste.*
sixty *sechzig.*
size *Grösse, f.*
skate *Schlittschuh, m.*
skate *(to) Schlittschuh laufen.*
skeleton *Gerippe, n.*
sketch *Skizze, f.*
sketch *(to) skizzieren.*
skill *Geschicklichkeit, f.*
skillful *geschickt, kundig.*
skin *Haut, f.*
skirt *Rock, m.*
skull *Schädel, m.*
sky *Himmel, m.*
skyscraper *Wolkenkratzer, m.*
slander *(to) verleumden.*
slap *Klaps, m.*
slate *Schiefer, m.*
slaughter *(to) schlachten.*
slave *Sklave, m.; Sklavin, f.*
slavery *Sklaverei, f.*
sleep *Schlaf, m.*
sleep *(to) schlafen.*
sleeve *Ärmel, m.*
sleigh *Schlitten, m.*
slender *schlank.*
slice *Schnitte, f.*
slice *(to) in Scheiben schneiden.*
slide *(to) schleifen, gleiten.*
slight *gering.*
slip *entschlüpfen.*
slip *Fehler, m. (mistake); Unterrock, m. (lingerie).*
slope *Abhang, m.*
slot *Einwurf, m.; Schlitz, m. (mail).*
slow *langsam.*
slumber *Schlummer, m.*
slumber *(to) schlummern.*
sly *schlau.*
small *klein.*
smart *elegant (clothes); gescheit (clever).*
smash *(to) zerschmettern.*
smear *(to) schmieren.*
smell *Geruch, m.*
smell *(to) riechen.*
smile *Lächeln, n.*

smile *(to) lächeln.*
smoke *Rauch, m.*
smoke *(to) rauchen.*
smooth *glatt.*
smother *(to) ersticken.*
smuggle *(to) schmuggeln.*
snail *Schnecke, f.*
snake *Schlange, f.*
snapshot *(Moment)aufnahme, f.*
snatch *(to) ergreifen.*
sneer *(to) (ver)höhnen.*
sneeze *(to) niessen.*
snore *(to) schnarchen.*
snow *Schnee, m.*
snowstorm *Schneesturm, m.*
so *so.*
  and so on *und so weiter*
soak *(to) einweichen; durchnäss.*
  (drench).
soap *Seife, f.*
sob *Schluchzen, n.*
sob *(to) schluchzen.*
sober *nüchtern.*
social *gesellschaftlich.*
society *Gesellschaft, f.*
sock *Sock, m.*
soda *Sodawasser, n.*
soft *weich.*
soften *(to) erweichen, aufweichen.*
soil *(to) beschmutzen.*
soil *Erde, f.; Boden, m.*
soiled *schmutzig.*
soldier *Soldat, m.*
sole *Sohle, f.*
solemn *feierlich.*
solemnity *Feierlichkeit, f.*
solicit *(to) bitten; nachsuchen.*
solid *fest.*
solitary *einsam (lonely); einzeln (one).*
solitude *Einsamkeit, f.*
solution *Lösung, f.*
solve *lösen.*
some *einige (a few); etwas (partial).*
somebody *jemand.*
somehow *irgendwie.*
something *etwas.*
sometimes *zuweilen.*
somewhat *etwas.*
somewhere *irgendwo.*
son *Sohn, m.*
song *Lied, n.*
son-in-law *Schwiegersohn, m.*
soon *bald.*
soot *Russ, m.*
soothe *(to) besänftigen; lindern (pain).*
sore *Geschwür (noun, n.); wund,*
  schmerzhaft (adj.); empfindlich,
  verärgert (annoyed).
  sore throat *Halsschmerzen, pl.*

sorrow *Kummer, m.*
sorry *bekümmert.*
  I am sorry. *Es tut mir leid.*
sort *Sorte, f.*
sort *(to) sortieren.*
sound *Laut, m.*
sound *(to) lauten.*
soup *Suppe, f.*
sour *sauer.*
source *Quelle, f. (spring); Ursprung, m.*
  (origin).
south *Süden, m.*
southeast *Südost, m.; Südosten, m.*
southern *Süd-; südlich.*
southwest *Südwest, m.; Südwesten, m.*
sovereign *Herrscher, m.*
sow *(to) säen.*
space *Raum, m.; Zwischenraum, m.*
  (space between).
spacious *(ge)räumig.*
spade *Spaten, m.; Pik, n. (cards).*
Spanish *spanisch.*
spare *spärlich.*
spare *(to) entbehren.*
spark *Funke, m.*
sparkle *(to) funkeln, glänzen.*
sparrow *Sperling, Spatz, m.*
speak *(to) sprechen.*
special *besonders, extra.*
speciality *Spezialität, f.*
specific *eigen, spezifisch, genau.*
specify *(to) spezifizieren.*
spectacle *Schauspiel, n.*
spectator *Zuschauer, m.*
speculate *(to) spekulieren.*
speech *Sprache, f.; Rede, f.*
speed *Geschwindigkeit, f.*
speedy *schnell.*
spell *Zauber, m. (charm).*
spell *(to) buchstabieren, schreiben.*
spelling *Buchstabieren n.*
spend *(to) ausgeben.*
sphere *Sphäre, f.*
spice *Gewürz, n.*
spice *(to) würzen.*
spicy *würzig.*
spider *Spinne, f.*
spill *(to) verschütten.*
spin *(to) spinnen.*
spine *Rückgrat, n.*
spirit *Geist, m.*
spiritual *geistig.*
spit *(to) spucken.*
spite *Bosheit, f.*
  in spite of *trotz (gen.), trotzdem (gen.*
  or dat.).
splash *(to) (be)spritzen.*
splendid *prachtvoll.*
  Splendid! *Wunderbar!*

splendor *Pracht, f.; Glanz, m.*

split *Spalt, m.*

split *(to) spalten.*

spoil *(to) verderben; verwöhnen (child).*

sponge *Schwamm, m.*

spontaneous *spontan.*

spoon *Löffel, m.*

spoonful *Löffelvoll, m.*

sport *Sport, m.*

spot *Fleck, m. (stain); Stelle, f. (place).*

spread *(to) verbreiten; bestreichen (on bread).*

spring *Frühling, m. (season); Sprung, m. (jump); Quelle, f. (source).*

spring *(to) springen.*

sprinkle *sprenkeln.*

sprout *Sprössling, m.*

spur *Sporn, m.*

spur *(to) anspornen.*

spurn *(to) verschmähen.*

spy *Spion, m.*

spy *(to) spionieren.*

squadron *Schwadron, f.*

square *Quadrat, n.*

squeeze *(to) (aus)drücken.*

squirrel *Eichhörnchen, n.*

stabilize *(to) stabilisieren.*

stable *fest (adj.); stabil.*

stack *Stoss, m. (wood).*

stack *(to) aufstrapeln.*

stadium *Stadion, n.*

staff *Stab (military), m.; Personal, n. (business).*

stage *Bühne, f. (theater).*

stain *Fleck, m.*

stain *(to) (be)flecken.*

stairs *Treppe, f.*

stammer *(to) stottern.*

stamp *Briefmarke, f.; Stempel, m.*

stand *Stand, m.*

    Stand still! *Stillgestanden!*

star *Stern, m.*

starch *Stärke, f.*

stare *(to) starren.*

start *Anfang, m.*

start *(to) beginnen, anfangen.*

starve *(to) (ver)hungern.*

state *Staat, m. (country); Zustand, m. (condition).*

state *(to) angeben.*

stately *stattlich.*

statement *Erklärung, f.; Aufstellung, f. (account).*

stateroom *Kabine, f.*

station *Bahnhof, m. (railroad); Stellung, f. (position).*

statistics *Statistik, f.*

statue *Statue, f.*

stay *Aufenthalt, m.*

stay *(to) bleiben.*

steady *fest.*

steak *Beefsteak, n.*

steal *(to) stehlen.*

steam *Dampf, m.*

steamer *Dampfer, m.*

steel *Stahl, m.*

steep *steil.*

steer *(to) steuern.*

stem *Stiel, m.*

stenographer *Stenotypistin, f.*

stenography *Kurzschrift, f.; Stenographie, f.*

step *Schritt, m.; Stufe, f. (stairs).*

step *(to) schreiten.*

sterilized *sterilisiert.*

stern *ernst.*

stew *Ragout, n.*

stew *(to) schmoren.*

steward *Steward, m.*

stick *Stock, m.*

stick *(to) stecken; ankleben (paste).*

stiff *steif.*

stiffen *(to) (ver)steifen; verstärken.*

stiffness *Steifheit, f.*

still *still, ruhig (adj.); jedoch, noch (adv.)*

still *(to) stillen.*

stimulant *Anregungsmittel, n.*

stimulate *(to) anregen.*

sting *Stich, m.*

sting *(to) stechen.*

stinginess *Geiz, m.*

stingy *geizig.*

stir *(to) rühren, bewegen.*

stirrup *Steigbügel, m.*

stitch *Stich, m.; Masche, f.*

stitch *(to) heften; nähen (sew).*

stock *Warenbestand, m.; Stamm, m.*

stocking *Strumpf, m.*

stomach *Magen, m.*

stone *Stein, m.*

stool *Schemel, m.*

stop *Haltestelle, f.*

stop *(to) halten.*

    Stop! *Halt!*

store *Laden, m.; Warenhaus, n.*

stork *Storch, m.*

storm *Sturm, m.*

story *Geschichte, f.*

stove *Ofen, m.*

straight *gerade.*

    straight on *gerade aus.*

straighten *gerade machen, aufrichten.*

strain *Anstrengung, f.*

strange *seltsam, sonderbar.*

stranger *Ausländer, m.; Fremde, m.*

strap *Riemen, m.*

straw *Stroh, n.; Strohhalm, m. (for drinking).*

strawberry *Erdbeere, f.*

stream *Strom, m.*

street *Strasse, f.*
streetcar *Strassenbahn, f.*
strength *Kraft, f.*
strengthen *verstärken; kräftigen.*
strenuous *angestrengt.*
stress *Druck, m.; Betonung, f. (accentuation).*
stretch *Strecke, f.*
stretch *(to) strecken.*
strict *streng.*
stride *Schritt, m.*
string *Bindfaden, m.*
strip *(to) streifen; entkleiden (of clothes).*
stripe *Streifen, m.*
strive *(to) streben.*
stroke *Schlag, m.; Zug, m. (pen).*
stroll *Spaziergang, m.*
stroll *(to) spazierengehen.*
strong *stark.*
structure *Bau, m.*
struggle *kampf, m.*
struggle *(to) kämpfen.*
stubborn *hartnäckig.*
student *Schüler, m.; Schülerin, f.; Student, m. & f.*
studio *Studio, n.*
studious *lernbegierig, lerneifrig.*
study *Studium, n.*
study *(to) studieren.*
stuff *Stoff, m.*
stuff *(to) stopfen.*
stumble *(to) stolpern.*
stump *Stumpf, m.*
stun *(to) betäuben.*
stunt *Sensation, f.*
stupendous *fantastisch.*
stupid *dumm.*
stupidity *Dummheit, f.*
stupor *Betäubung, f.*
sturdy *kräftig.*
stutter *(to) stottern.*
style *Stil, m.*
subdue *(to) unterwerfen.*
subject *Angelegenheit, f.; Fach, n. (school).*
subjugate *(to) beherrschen.*
subjunctive *Konjunktiv, m.*
sublime *erhaben.*
submission *Unterwerfung, f.*
submissive *unterwürfig.*
submit *(to) unterwerfen.*
subordinate *untergeordnet.*
subordination *Unterordnung, f.*
subscribe *(to) abonnieren.*
subscription *Abonnement, n.*
subsist *(to) bestehen.*
substance *Substanz, f.*
substantial *beträchtlich.*

substitute *(to) ersetzen.*
substitution *Ersatz, m.*
subtle *scharfsinnig, fein, spitzfindig.*
subtract *abziehen.*
subtraction *Abzug, m.*
suburb *Vorstadt, f.*
subway *Untergrundbahn, f.*
succeed *(to) nachfolgen; gelingen (achieve).*
success *Erfolg, m.*
successful *erfolgreich.*
succession *Nachfolge, f.*
successor *Nachfolger, m.*
such *solch.*
  Such a scandal! *Solch ein Skandal!*
sudden *plötzlich.*
sue *(to) verklagen.*
suffer *(to) leiden.*
suffering *Leiden, n.*
sufficient *genügend.*
sugar *Zucker, m.*
suggest *(to) andeuten, vorschlagen.*
suggestion *Anregung, f.*
suicide *Selbstmord, m.*
suit *Anzug, m.; Kostüm, n. (lady's).*
suitable *passend.*
sulk *(to) schmollen.*
sullen *mürrisch.*
sum *Summe, f.*
summary *Auszug, m.*
summer *Sommer, m.*
summit *Gipfel, m.*
summon *(to) vorladen; einberufen.*
sumptuous *prächtig, kostbar.*
sum up *(to) abkürzen, zusammenfassen.*
sun *Sonne, f.*
sunbeam *Sonnenstrahl, m.*
Sunday *Sonntag, m.*
sunny *sonnig.*
sunrise *Sonnenaufgang, m.*
sunset *Sonnenuntergang, m.*
sunshine *Sonnenschein, m.*
superb *herrlich.*
superficial *oberflächlich.*
superfluous *überflüssig.*
superintendent *Inspektor, m.*
superior *Vorgesetzte, m. & f.*
superiority *Überlegenheit, f.*
superstition *Aberglaube, m.*
supervise *(to) beaufsichtigen.*
supper *Abendessen, n.*
supplement *Nachtrag, m.; Beilage, f.*
supplementary *ergänzend.*
supply *(to) versorgen.*
support *stütze, f.; Unterstützung, f.*
support *(to) (unter)stützen.*
suppose *(to) vermuten, annehmen.*
suppress *(to) unterdrücken.*

supreme *höchst, oberst.*
sure *gewiss, sicher.*
surety *Sicherheit, f.*
surface *Oberfläche, f.*
surgeon *Chirurg, m.*
surgery *Chirurgie, f.*
surname *Zuname, m.; Nachname, m.*
surpass *übertreffen.*
surprise *Überraschung, f.*
surprise *(to) überraschen.*
surrender *Übergabe, f.*
surrender *(to) aufgeben, übergeben.*
surroundings *Umgebung, f.*
survey *Übersicht, f.; Vermessung, f.*
survey *(to) besichtigen, vermessen.*
survive *(to) überleben.*
susceptibility *Empfänglichkeit, f.*
susceptible *empfänglich.*
suspect *(to) verdächtigen.*
suspense *Ungewissheit, f.; Spannung, f.*
suspicion *Verdacht, m.*
suspicious *verdächtig.*
sustain *(to) ernähren.*
swallow *Schluck, m. (gulp); Schwalbe, f. (bird).*
swallow *(to) verschlucken.*
swamp *Sumpf, m.*
swan *Schwan, m.*
swear *(to) schwören.*
sweat *Schweiss, m.*
sweat *(to) schwitzen.*
sweep *(to) kehren; fegen.*
sweet *süss.*
sweetness *Süsse, f.*
swell *(to) (an)schwellen.*
swift *schnell, rasch.*
swim *(to) schwimmen.*
swindle *(to) schwindeln.*
swindler *Schwindler, m.*
swing *(to) schwingen.*
Swiss *Schweizer (noun, m.); schweizerisch (adj.).*
switch *Schalter, m.*
sword *Schwert, n.*
syllable *Silbe, f.*
symbol *Symbol, n.*
symbolic *symbolisch.*
symbolize *symbolisieren.*
symmetrical *symmetrisch.*
sympathetic *mitfühlend.*
sympathize *(to) mitfühlen.*
sympathy *Sympathie, f.; Verständnis, n.*
symptom *Symptom, n.*
syrup *Sirup, m.*
system *System, n.*
systematic *systematisch.*

T

table *Tisch, m.*
tablecloth *Tischtuch, n.*
tacit *stillschweigend.*
taciturn *schweigsam.*
tact *Takt, m.*
tactful *taktvoll.*
tactless *taktlos.*
tail *Schwanz, m.*
tailor *Schneider, m.*
take *(to) nehmen.*
tale *Erzählung, f.*
talent *Talent, n; Begabung, f.*
talk *Gespräch, n.*
talk *(to) reden, plaudern.*
talkative *gesprächig.*
tall *hoch; gross (people).*
tame *zahm.*
tame *(to) zähmen.*
tangle *(to) verwickeln.*
tank *Tank, m.*
tapestry *Wandteppich, m.*
tar *Teer, m.*
tardy *spät.*
target *(Ziel)scheibe, f.*
tarnish *(to) trüben.*
task *Aufgabe, f.*
taste *Geschmack, m.*
taste *(to) schmecken.*
tax *Steuer, f.*
taxi *Taxi, n.*
tea *Tee, m.*
teach *(to) unterrichten.*
teacher *Lehrer, m.; Lehrerin, f.*
team *Gruppe, f.; Mannschaft, f. (sports).*
tear *Träne, f. (teardrop); Riss, m. (rip).*
tear *(to) (zer)reissen.*
tease *(to) necken.*
teaspoon *Teelöffel, m.*
technical *technisch.*
technique *Technik, f.*
tedious *langweilig, ermüdend.*
telegram *Telegramm, n.*
telegraph *(to) telegrafieren.*
telephone *Telefon, n.*
　telephone operator *Telefonistin, f.*
telephone *(to) telefonieren, anrufen.*
tell *(to) sagen.*
temper *Laune, f.*
temperate *gemässig, mässig.*
temperature *Temperatur, f.*
tempest *Sturm, m.*
temple *Tempel, m.; Schläfe, f. (head).*
temporary *vorübergehend.*

tempt *(to) versuchen, verlocken.*
temptation *Versuchung, f.*
ten *zehn.*
tenacious *zäh.*
tenacity *Zähigkeit, f.*
tenant *Mieter, m.*
tend *(to) sich neigen zu.*
tendency *Neigung, f.*
tender *zart, empfindlich.*
tennis *Tennis, n.*
tense *gespannt.*
tense *Zeitform, f. (grammar).*
tension *Spannung, f.*
tent *Zelt, n.*
tenth *Zehntel (noun, n.) (fraction); zehnt (adj.).*
tepid *lauwarm.*
term *Ausdruck, m.*
terrace *Terrasse, f.*
terrible *schrecklich.*
terrify *(to) (er)schrecken.*
territory *Gebiet, n.*
terror *Schrecken, m.*
test *Prüfung, f.*
test *(to) prüfen.*
testify *(to) bezeugen.*
testimony *Zeugnis, n.*
text *Text, m.*
textbook *Lehrbuch, n.*
than *als.*
thank *(to) danken.*
     Thank you! *Danke schön!*
thankful *dankbar.*
that *das (demonstrative); der, die, das, welch (er, -e, -es) (relative); dass, damit (conjunction).*
thaw *Tauwetter, n.*
thaw *(to) tauen.*
the *der, die, das.*
theater *Theater, n.*
their *ihr.*
theirs *ihr(er, -e, -es).*
them *sie (acc.); ihnen (dat.).*
theme *Thema, n.*
themselves *sie (ihnen) selbst, sich.*
then *dann.*
theory *Theorie, f.*
there *dort.*
     there is, there are *es gibt.*
thereafter *danach.*
thereby *dadurch.*
therefore *deshalb, daher.*
thereupon *darauf.*
thermometer *Fiebermesser, n.*
these *diese.*
thesis *These, f.*
they *sie.*
thick *dick.*
thief *Dieb, m.*

thigh *Schenkel, m.*
thimble *Fingerhut, m.*
thin *dünn.*
thing *Sache, f.; Ding, n.*
think *(to) denken.*
third *dritte.*
thirst *Durst, m.*
thirteen *dreizehn.*
thirteenth *dreizehnte.*
thirtieth *dreissigste.*
thirty *dreissig.*
this *dieser.*
thorn *Dorn, m.*
thorough *gründlich, gänzlich.*
though *zwar, obwohl, obgleich.*
thought *Gedanke, m.*
thoughtful *nachdenklich.*
thoughtless *rücksichtslos.*
thousand *tausend.*
thrash *(to) dreschen.*
thread *Faden, m.*
threat *Drohung, f.*
threaten *(to) drohen.*
three *drei.*
threshold *Schwelle, f.*
thrift *Sparsamkeit, f.*
thrifty *sparsam.*
thrill *Schauer, m.; Begeisterung, f.*
thrill *(to) schauern.*
thrilling *ergreifend, begeisternd.*
thrive *(to) gedeihen.*
thriving *ergreifend.*
throat *Kehle, f.; Hals, m.*
throb *(to) schlagen.*
throne *Tron, m.*
throng *Menge, f.*
through *durch (acc.); durchaus.*
throughout *durchaus.*
throw *(to) werfen.*
thumb *Daumen, m.*
thunder *Donner, m.*
thunder *(to) donnern.*
Thursday *Donnerstag, m.*
thus *so.*
thwart *(to) vereiteln.*
ticket *Karte, f.; Fahrkarte, f. (train).*
ticket window *Schalter, m.*
tickle *(to) kitzeln.*
ticklish *kitzlig.*
tide *Flut, f. (high); Ebbe, f. (low).*
tidiness *Ordentlichkeit, f.*
tidy *ordentlich.*
tie *Band, n.; (bond); Krawatte, f. (necktie).*
tie *(to) binden.*
tiger *Tiger, m.*
tight *eng.*
tile *Ziegel, m. (roof); Kachel, f. (wall); Fliese, f. (kitchen).*

till *bis.*
  till now *bisher.*
tilt *(to) kippen.*
timber *Bauholz, n.*
time *Zeit, f.*
  from time to time *von Zeit zu Zeit.*
  on time *pünktlich.*
  to have a good time *sich vergnügen,*
  sich amüsieren.
  what time is it? *Wie spät ist es?*
timid *zaghaft, furchtsam.*
timidity *Furchtsamkeit, f.*
tin *Zinn, n.*
tinkle *(to) klingeln.*
tiny *winzig.*
tip *Spitze, f. (end); Trinkgeld, n.*
  (money).
tip *(to) Trinkgeld geben.*
tire *Reifen, m.*
tire *(to) ermüden.*
tired *müde.*
tireless *unermüdlich.*
tiresome *langweilig.*
title *Titel, m.*
to *zu (with infinitive); nach, zu (dat); an*
  (dat. or acc.).
toad *Kröte, f.*
toast *Toast, m.*
tobacco *Tabak, m.*
today *heute.*
toe *Zehe, f.*
together *zusammen.*
toil *(to) schwer arbeiten.*
toilet *Toilette, f.*
token *Andenken, n; Münze, f. (coin).*
tolerable *erträglich.*
tolerance *Toleranz, f.; Duldung, f.*
tolerant *duldsam.*
tolerate *(to) dulden.*
toll *(to) läuten.*
tomato *Tomate, f.*
tomb *Grab, n.*
tomorrow *morgen.*
ton *Tonne, f.*
tone *Ton, m.*
tongs *Zange, f.*
tongue *Zunge, f.*
tonight *heute abend.*
too *auch (also); zu (excessive).*
tool *Werkzeug, n.*
tooth *Zahn, m.*
toothbrush *Zahnbürste, f.*
toothpaste *Zahnpasta, f.*
toothpick *Zahnstocher, m.*
toothpowder *Zahnpulver, n.*
top *Gipfel, m.; Oberst, n.*
topic *Gesprächsstoff, m.; Thema, n.*
torch *Fackel, f.*
torment *Qual, f.*

torment *(to) quälen*
torture *Folter, f.*
torture *(to) foltern.*
toss *(to) werfen.*
toss *Wurf, m.*
total *Gesamtsumme, f.; gesamt (adj.).*
totally *gänzlich.*
touch *(to) berühren.*
touching *rührend.*
touchy *empfindlich.*
tough *hart.*
tour *Reise, f.; Rundreise, f.*
tour *(to) herumreisen, bereisen.*
tourist *Tourist, m.*
tournament *Turnier, n.*
toward *zu, nach (dat.); gegen (acc.).*
towel *Handtuch, n.*
tower *Turm, m.*
town *Stadt, f.*
toy *Spielzeug, n.*
trace *Spur, f.*
trace *(to) zeichnen (drawing);*
  nachspüren.
track *Spur, f.*
trade *Handel, m.*
tradition *Überlieferung, f.*
traditional *herkömmlich, überliefert.*
traffic *Verkehr, m.*
tragedy *Tragödie, f.*
tragic *tragisch.*
trail *Fährte, f.*
train *Zug, m.*
train *(to) erziehen.*
training *Erziehung, f.*
traitor *Verräter, m.*
trample *(to) niedertreten.*
tranquil *ruhig.*
tranquillity *Ruhe, f.*
transaction *Verhandlung, f.;*
  Transaktion, f.
transfer *(to) übertragen.*
transit *Durchgang, m.*
transition *Übergang, m.*
transitory *vergänglich.*
translate *(to) übersetzen.*
translation *Übersetzung, f.*
translator *Übersetzer, m.*
transmission *Übersendung, f.*
transmit *(to) übersenden.*
transparent *durchsichtig.*
transport *Transport, m.*
Transport *(to) transportieren.*
transportation *Beförderung, f.*
trap *Falle, f.*
trap *(to) fangen, ertappen.*
trash *Plunder, m.*
travel *Reise, f.*
travel *(to) reisen.*
traveler *Reisende, m. & f.*

tray *Tablett, n.*
treacherous *treulos.*
treachery *Treulosigkeit, f.*
treason *Verrat, m.*
treasure *Schatz, m.*
treasurer *Schatzmeister, m.*
treasury *Schatzamt, n.*
treat *Bewirtung, f.*
treat *(to) behandeln.*
treatment *Behandlung, f.*
treaty *Vertrag, m.*
tree *Baum, m.*
tremble *(to) zittern.*
trembling *Zittern, n.*
tremendous *ungeheuer.*
trench *Graben, m.; Schützengraben, m. (military).*
trend *Neigung, f.*
trial *Probe, f.*
triangle *Dreieck, n.*
tribe *Stamm, m.*
tribunal *Tribunal, n.*
tribune *Tribüne, f.*
tribute *Abgabe, f.*
trick *Kniff, m.*
trifle *Kleinigkeit, f.*
trifling *kleinlich (petty); gering (minor).*
trim *(to) besetzen (sewing); stutzen (hair).*
trimming *Verzierung, f.; Besatz, m. (clothes).*
trip *Fahrt, f.*
trip *(to) stolpern.*
triple *dreifach.*
triumph *Triumph, m.*
triumph *(to) siegen.*
trivial *geringfügig.*
trolley car *Strassenbahnwagen, m.*
troop *Truppe, f.*
trot *Trab, m.*
trot *(to) traben.*
trouble *Unannehmlichkeit, f.*
trousers *Hose, f.*
truck *Lastwagen, m.*
true *wahr.*
truly *wahrhaftig; aufrichtig.*
trump *Trumpf, m.*
trump *(to) trumpfen.*
trumpet *Trompete, f.*
trunk *Koffer, m.*
trust *Vertrauen, n.*
trust *(to) trauen.*
trustworthy *zuverlässig.*
truth *Wahrheit, f.*
truthful *wahrhaft.*
truthfully *aufrichtig.*
truthfulness *Aufrichtigkeit, f.*
try *(to) versuchen, probieren.*
tube *Rohr, n.*

tumble *(to) stürzen.*
tumult *Aufruhr, m.*
tune *Melodie, f.*
tune *(to) stimmen.*
tunnel *Tunnel, m.*
turf *Rasen, m.*
turkey *Truthahn, m.*
turmoil *Aufruhr, f.; Unruhe, f.*
turn *(to) drehen.*
  turn back *zurückkehren*
  Turn left. *Biegen Sie links ein.*
turnip *weisse Rübe, f.*
twelfth *zwölfte.*
twelve *zwölf.*
twentieth *zwanzigste.*
twenty *zwanzig.*
twice *zweimal.*
twilight *Zwielicht, n.*
twin *Zwilling (noun, m.); doppelt (adj.).*
twist *(to) drehen.*
two *zwei.*
type *Modell, n.*
type *(to) mit der Schreibmaschine schreiben.*
typewriter *Schreibmaschine, f.*
tyranny *Tyrannei, f.*
tyrant *Tyrann, m.*

U

ugliness *Hässlichkeit, f.*
ugly *hässlich.*
utlimate *letzt.*
umbrella *(Regen)schirm, m.*
umpire *Schiedsrichter, m.*
unable to *unfähig.*
unanimity *Einmütigkeit, f.*
unanimous *einstimmig.*
unawares *unversehens.*
unbearable *unerträglich.*
unbelievable *unglaublich.*
unbutton *(to) aufknöpfen.*
uncertain *unsicher.*
uncertainty *Unsicherheit, f.*
unchangeable *unveränderlich.*
uncle *Onkel, m.*
uncomfortable *unbequem.*
uncommon *ungewöhnlich.*
unconscious *bewusstlos.*
unconsciousness *Ohnmacht, f.*
uncouth *ungebildet.*
uncover *(to) aufdecken.*
undecided *unentschieden.*
undefinable *undefinierbar.*
undeniable *unleugbar.*
under *unter (dat. or acc.).*

undergo *(to) durchmachen; erleiden (suffer).*
underground *Untergrund (noun, n.); unterirdisch (adj.)*
underline *(to) unterstreichen.*
underneath *unten.*
understand *(to) verstehen.*
understanding *Verständnis, n.; Einverständnis, n.*
undertake *(to) unternehmen.*
undertaker *Leichenbestatter, m.*
underwear *Unterwäsche, f.*
undesirable *unerwünscht.*
undignified *würdelos.*
undo *(to) aufmachen; auflösen (untie).*
undress *(to) sich ausziehen.*
uneasy *beunruhigt.*
uneasiness *Beunruhigung, f.*
unemployed *arbeitslos.*
unequal *ungleich; unvergleichlich.*
uneven *uneben.*
uneventful *öde.*
unexpected *unerwartet.*
unfair *ungerecht.*
unfaithful *untreu.*
unfavorable *ungünstig.*
unforgettable *unvergesslich.*
unfortunate *unglücklich.*
unfortunately *unglücklicherweise.*
ungrateful *undankbar.*
unhappily *leider.*
unhappy *unglücklich.*
unharmed *unverletzt.*
unhealthy *ungesund.*
unheard *(of) unerhört.*
uniform *Uniform (noun, f.); gleichförmig (adj.).*
uniformity *Gleichförmigkeit, f.*
uniformly *gleichförmig.*
unify *(to) vereinigen.*
unimportant *unwichtig.*
unintentional *unabsichtlich.*
union *Vereinigung, f.; Verband, m.*
universal *universal.*
universe *Weltall, n.*
university *Universität, f.*
unjust *ungerecht.*
unkind *unfreundlich.*
unknown *unbekannt.*
unlawful *ungesetzlich.*
unless *es sei denn dass.*
unlike *unähnlich, anders als.*
unlikely *unwahrscheinlich.*
unlimited *unbeschränkt.*
unload *(to) abladen, ausladen.*
unluckily *unglücklicherweise.*
unnecessary *unnötig.*
unoccupied *unbesetzt; unbeschäftigt.*
unpack *(to) auspacken.*

unpleasant *unangehehm.*
unpublished *unveröffentlicht.*
unquestionably *fraglos.*
unravel *(to) lösen.*
unreal *unwirklich.*
unreasonable *unvernünftig.*
unreliable *unzuverlässig.*
unrestrained *ungezwungen.*
unroll *(to) abwickeln, entrollen.*
unsafe *unsicher.*
unsatisfactory *unbefriedigend.*
unsatisfied *unbefriedigt.*
unscrupulous *bedenkenlos, skrupellos.*
unselfish *selbstlos.*
unsteady *unbeständig.*
unsuccessful *erfolglos.*
unsuitable *unpassend.*
untidy *unordentlich.*
untie *(to) lösen; aufbinden.*
until *bis, an, zu (dat.).*
  until now bisher.
untrue *unwahr; untreu (faithless).*
unusual *ungewöhnlich.*
unwell *unwohl.*
unwholesome *ungesund.*
unwilling *widerwillig.*
unwise *unklug.*
unworthy *unwürdig.*
up *auf (dat. or acc.); aufwärts; oben.*
uphold *(to) stützen.*
upkeep *Instandhaltung, f.*
upon *auf, über (dat. or acc.).*
upper *ober.*
upright *aufrecht.*
uprising *Aufstand, m.*
upset *beunruhigt.*
upset *(to) umkehren; aufregen (distress).*
upside down *drunter and drüber.*
upstairs *oben.*
upward *steigend, aurwarts.*
urge *(to) dringen, drängen.*
urgent *dringend.*
us *uns.*
use *Gebrauch, m.; Verwendung, f. (utility).*
use *(to) gebrauchen; verwenden.*
used to *(to be) gewöhnt sein*
useful *nützlich.*
useless *nutzlos.*
usual *gewöhnlich.*
utensil *Werkzeug, n.; Gerät, n.*
utility *Nützlichkeit, f.*
utilize *(to) nutzbar machen.*
utmost *äussert.*
  to the utmost aufs äusserste.
utter *(to) äussern, aussprechen.*
utterly *durchaus.*

V

vacant *frei.*
vacation *Ferien, pl.*
vaccination *Impfung, f.*
vaccination certificate *Impfschein, m.*
vaguely *unbestimmt.*
vain *eitel.*
  in vain *vergebens, umsonst.*
valiant *tapfer.*
valid *gültig.*
validity *Gültigkeit, f.*
valley *Tal, n.*
valuable *wertvoll.*
value *Wert, m.*
value *(to) schätzen.*
valued *geschätzt.*
valve *Ventil, n.*
vanilla *Vanille, f.*
vanish *(to) verschwinden.*
vanity *Eitelkeit, f.*
vanquish *(to) besiegen.*
vapor *Dampf, m.*
variable *veränderlich.*
variation *Abweichung, f.; Variation, f.*
varied *verschieden.*
variety *Abwechslung, f.;*
  Mannigfaltigkeit, f.
various *verschieden.*
varnish *(to) lackieren.*
vary *(to) verschieden.*
vase *Vase, f.*
vast *ungeheuer.*
vault *Gewölbe, n.*
veal *Kalbfleisch, n.*
vegetable *Gemüse, n.*
vehicle *Fahrzeug, n.*
veil *Schleier, m.*
veil *(to) verschleiern.*
vein *Ader, f. (body and mineral); Laune,*
  f. (luck).
velvet *Samt, m.*
venerable *ehrwürdig.*
venerate *(to) verehren.*
veneration *Verehrung, f.*
vengeance *Rache, f.*
ventilation *Lüftung, f.*
ventilator *Ventilator, m.; Englüftung, f.*
venture *(to) wagen.*
verb *Zeitwort, n.*
verdict *Urteil, n.*
verge *Rand, m.*
  on the verge of *am Rand (gen).*
verification *Bestätigung, f.*
verify *(to) bestätigen.*

verse *Vers, m.; Dichtung, f. (poetry).*
version *Version, f. (translation);*
  Darstellung, f. (account.)
very *sehr.*
vest *Weste, f.*
veterinarian *Tierarzt, m.*
vice *Laster, n.*
vice-president *Vizepräsident, m.*
vice versa *umgekehrt.*
vicinity *Nähe, f.; Nachbarschaft, f.*
victim *Opfer, n.*
victor *Sieger, m.*
victorious *siegreich.*
victory *Sieg, m.*
view *Aussicht, f.; Ansicht, f. (opinion).*
vigorous *kräftig.*
vile *abscheulich.*
village *Dorf, n.*
vine *Weinstock, m.*
vinegar *Essig, m.*
vineyard *Weingarten, m.*
violence *Gewalttätigkeit, f.; Heftigkeit, f.*
violent *gewaltig, heftig.*
violet *Veilchen, n.*
violet *violett.*
violin *Geige, f.*
violinist *Geiger, m.*
virtue *Tugend, f.*
virtuous *tugendhaft.*
visible *sichtbar.*
vision *Sehen, n.; Erscheinung, f.*
  (ghost).
visit *Besuch, m.*
visit *(to) besuchen.*
visitor *Besucher, m.*
visualize *(to) sich vorstellen.*
vital *lebens-; vital.*
vitality *Lebenskraft, f.*
vivacious *lebhaft.*
vivacity *Lebhaftigkeit, f.*
vivid *lebendig.*
vocabulary *Wortschatz, m.*
vocal *stimmlich, stimmhaft.*
vocation *Beruf, m.*
vogue, *Mode, f.*
voice *Stimme, f.*
void *Leere (noun, f.); leer (empty);*
  ungültig (invalid).
volcano *Vulkan, m.*
volume *Umfang, m.*
voluntary *freiwillig.*
vote *(to) stimmen.*
vote *Stimme, f.*
vow *Gelübde, n.*
vow *(to) geloben.*
vowel *Vokal, m.*
vulgar *gemein, niedrig.*
vulnerable *verwundbar.*

W

wager *Wette, f.*
wager *(to) wetten.*
wages *Gehalt, n.*
waist *Taille, f.*
wait *(to) warten.*
  waiting room *Wartezimmer, n.*
waiter *Kellner, m.; Kellnerin, f.*
wake *(to) aufwecken.*
wake up *(to) erwachen.*
walk *Spaziergang, m.*
walk *(to) gehen.*
  take a walk *spazierengehen.*
wall *Wand, f.*
wallet *Brieftasche, f.*
walnut *Walnuss, f.*
wander *wandern.*
wanderer *Wanderer, m.*
want *Mangel, m.; Not, f. (poverty).*
want *(to) wollen.*
war *Krieg, m.*
ward *Saal, m. (hospital).*
wardrobe *Kleiderschrank, m.*
ware *Ware, f.*
warehouse *Warenhaus, n.*
warm *warm.*
warm *(to) wärmen.*
warmth *Wärme, f.*
warn *(to) warnen.*
warning *Warnung, f.*
warrior *Krieger, m.*
wash *(to) waschen.*
washroom *Waschraum, m.*
washstand *Waschbecken, n.*
waste *Verschwendung, f.*
waste *(to) verschwenden.*
watch *Uhr, f.*
watch *(to) wachen.*
watchful *wachsam.*
water *Wasser, n.*
waterfall *Wasserfall, m.*
waterproof *wasserdicht.*
wave *Welle, f.*
wave *(to) schwenken; winken; wellen (hair).*
wax *Wachs, n.*
way *Weg, m. (road); Weise, f. (manner).*
we *wir.*
weak *schwach.*
weaken *(to) schwächen.*
weakness *Schwachheit, f.*
wealth *Reichtum, m.*
wealthy *reich.*
weapon *Waffe, f.*
wear *(to) tragen.*

weariness *Müdigkeit, f.; Langweile, f.*
weary *müde.*
weather *Wetter, n.*
weave *(to) weben.*
wedding *Hochzeit, f.*
Wednesday *Mittwoch, m.*
weed *Unkraut, n.*
week *Woche, f.*
weekend *Wochenende, n.*
weekly *wöchendich.*
weep *(to) weinen.*
weigh *(to) wiegen.*
weight *Gewicht, n.*
welcome *Empfang, m.*
welfare *Wohlfahrt, f.*
well *gut.*
well *Brunnen, m.*
  oil well *Ölquelle, f.*
west *west; Westen, m.*
westwards *westwärts.*
wet *nass, feucht.*
whale *Walfisch, m.*
what *was; welch(er, -e, -es) (which).*
  what kind of *was für ein.*
whatever *was auch.*
wheat *Weizen, m.*
wheel *Rad, n.*
when *wenn, als; wann (interrogative).*
whenever *so oft wie.*
where *wo; wohin (whereto).*
whereas *da, nun.*
wherever *überall wo.*
whether *ob.*
which *der (die, das); welch(-er, -e,-es).*
  which one *welch(-er, -e, -es).*
while *Weile (noun, f.); indem, während (conj.).*
whim *Laune, f.; Einfall, m.*
whip *Peitsche, f.*
whisper *(to) flüstern.*
whistle *Pfeife, f.*
whistle *pfeifen.*
white *weiss.*
who *der (die, das), welch(er, -e, -es) (pron.); wer (inter. pron.).*
whoever *wer auch immer.*
whole *Ganze (noun, n.), ganz (adj.).*
wholesale *Grosshandel, m.*
wholesome *heilsam, gesund.*
whose *dessen (deren); wessen (inter.).*
why *warum.*
wicked *böse.*
wide *breit.*
widen *(to) breiten, erweitern.*
widow *Witwe, f.*
widower *Witwer, m.*
width *Weite, f. Breite, f.*
wife *Frau, f.*
wig *Perücke, f.*

wild *wild.*
wilderness *Wildnis, f.*
will *Wille, m.; Testament, n. (legal).*
will *(to) wollen.*
willing *gewillt.*
willingly *gern.*
win *(to) gewinnen.*
wind *Wind, m.*
wind *(to) winden.*
window *Fenster, n.*
windy *windig.*
wine *Wein, m.*
wing *Flügel, m.*
wink *Blinzeln, n.; Augenzwinkern, n.*
wink *(to) blinzeln, zwinkern.*
winner *Sieger, m.*
winter *Winter, m.*
wipe *(to) wischen; ausrotten (wipe out).*
wire *Draht, m.*
wire *(to) kabeln.*
wisdom *Weisheit, f.*
wise *weise.*
wish *Wunsch, m.*
wish *(to) wünschen.*
wit *Witz, m.; Geist, m.*
witch *Hexe, f.*
with *mit (dat.).*
withdraw *(to) zurückziehen; abheben.*
wither *(to) verwelken.*
within *drinnen.*
without *ohne (acc.).*
witness *Zeuge, m.*
witness *(to) bezeugen.*
witticism *Witz, m.*
witty *witzig, geistreich.*
woe *Weh, n.*
wolf *Wolf, m.*
woman, *Frau, f.*
wonder *Wunder, n.*
wonder *(to) sich wundern, sich fragen.*
wonderful *wunderbar.*
wood *Holz, n.*
woods *Wald, n.*
woodwork *Holzwerk, n.*
wool *Wolle, f.*
word *Wort, n.*
  word by word *Wort für Wort.*
work *Arbeit, f.*
  work of art *Kunstgegenstand, m.*
work *(to) arbeiten.*
worker *Arbeiter, m.*
workshop *Werkstatt, f.*
world *Welt, f.*
wordly *weltlich.*
worried *besorgt.*
worry *Sorge, f.; Plage, f.*
worry *(to) besorgen; plagen*
  Don't worry *Sorgen Sie sich nicht!*
  (Machen Sie sich keine Sorgen!)

worse *schlechter.*
worship *(to) anbeten.*
worst *schlechtest.*
worth *Wert, m.*
worthless *wertlos.*
worthy *würdig.*
wound *Wunde, f.*
wound *(to) verwunden.*
wounded *verwundet.*
wrap *(to) einschlagen, (ein)wickeln.*
wrath *Zorn, m.*
wreath *Kranz, m.*
wreck *Wrack, n. Schiffbruch, m.*
wreck *(to) zertrümmern, scheitern.*
wrestle *(to) (au)wringen.*
wrestler *Ringkämpfer, m.*
wrestling *Ringkampf, m.*
wretched *elend bän lich.*
wring *(to) ringen.*
wrist *Handgelenk, n.*
write *(to) schreiben.*
writer *Schreiber, m.;-Schriftsteller, m.*
writing *Schreiben, n.; Schrift, f. (work).*
  in writing *in Schrift, schriftlich.*
wrong *unrecht, falsch.*
  You are wrong. *Sie haben Unrecht.*

X

X-ray *Röntgenstrahlen, pl.*

Y

yacht *Yacht, f.*
yard *Hof, m. (courtyard).*
yam *Garn, m.*
yawn *Gähnen, n.*
yawn *(to) gähnen.*
year *Jahr, n.*
yearly *jährlich.*
yearn *(to) sich sehnen.*
yearning *Sehnen, n.; Sehnsucht, f.*
yeast *Hefe, f.*
yell *(to) schreien.*
yellow *gelb.*
yes *ja, doch.*
yesterday *gestern.*
yet *noch (also besides); doch, dennoch (however).*
yield *(to) aufgeben (give up); erzeugen (produce).*
yoke *Joch, n.*
yolk *(Ei) Dotter, n. (of an egg).*

you *Sie, du (familiar sing.); ihr (familiar pl.); Sie, dich, euch (acc.); Ihnen, dir, euch (dat.).*
young *jung.*
  young lady *junge Dame, f.; Fräulein, n.*
your *ihr, dein, ihr.*
yours *Ihr(-er, -e, -es); dein(-er, -e, -es).*
yourself *Sie (Ihnen) selbst; du (dich, dir) selbst; ihr (euch)*
youth *Jungend, f.*

Z

zeal *Eifer, m.*
zealous *eifrig.*
zebra *Zebra, n.*
zero *Null, f.*
zipper *Reissverschluss, m.*
zone *Zone, f.*
zoo *Tierpark, m.; Zoo, m.*
Zoology *Zoologie, f.*

GLOSSARY OF PROPER NAMES

Albert *Albrecht.*
Alfred *Alfred.*
Andrew *Andreas.*
Ann *Anna.*
Anthony *Anton.*
August *August.*
Barbara *Barbara.*
Bernard *Bernhard.*
Bertha *Bertha.*
Charles *Carl.*
Charlotte *Lotte.*
Edward *Eduard.*
Elisabeth *Elisabeth, Else.*
Elsie *Ilse.*
Emily *Emilie.*
Eric *Erich.*
Ernest *Ernst.*

Eugene *Eugen.*
Frances *Franziska.*
Frank *Franz.*
Frederick *Friedrich.*
Fred *Fritz.*
George *Georg.*
Gertrude *Gertrud, Trudchen.*
Gustave *Gustav.*
Helen *Helene.*
Henry *Heinrich.*
Jane *Johanna.*
John *Johann, Hans.*
Joseph *Josef.*
Katherine *Katharina,*
Kätchen, Käthe.
Lewis *Ludwig.*
Louise *Luise.*

Margaret *Gretchen, Margareta.*
Martha *Martha.*
Mary *Maria.*
Maurice *Mortiz.*
Michael *Michael.*
Nicolas *Nikolaus, Klaus.*
Otto *Otto.*
Paul *Paul.*
Peter *Peter.*
Ralph *Rudolf, Rolf.*
Roger *Rüdiger.*
Susan *Susanne.*
Theodore *Theodor.*
Theresa *Therese.*
Thomas *Thomas.*
William *Wilhelm.*

GLOSSARY OF GEOGRAPHICAL NAMES

Africa *Afrika, n.*
Aix-la-Chapelle *Aachen, n.*
Alps *Alpen, pl.*
America *Amerika, n.*
  North America *Nordamerika, n.*
  Central America *Zentralamerika, n.,*
  Mittelamerika, n.
  South America *Südamerika, n.*
Antwerp *Antwerpen, n.*
Arabia *Arabien, n.*
Asia *Asien, n.*
Atlantic *Atlantik, m.*
Australia *Australien, n.*
Austria *Österreich, n.*
Belgium *Belgien, n.*
Berlin *Berlin, n.*
Bonn *Bonn, n.*
Brazil *Brasilien, n.*
Brussels *Brüssel, n.*
Canada *Kanada, n.*
China *China, n.*
Czechoslavakia *Tschechoslovakei, f.*
Denmark *Dänemark, n.*
Egypt *Ägypten, n.*
England *England, n.*
Europe *Europa, n.*
France *Frankreich, n.*
Frankfort *Frankfurt, n.*
Germany *Deutschland, n.*
Hamburg *Hamburg, n.*
Greece *Griechenland, n.*
Hague *Haag, m.*

Holland *Holland, n.*
Hungary *Ungarn, n.*
India *Indien, n.*
Ireland *Irland, n.*
Italy *Italien, n.*
Japan *Japan, n.*
Jugoslavia *Jugoslavien, n.*
London *London, n.*
Mexico *Mexico, n.*
Moscow *Moskau, n.*
Munich *München, n.*
Norway *Norwegen, n.*
Nüremberg *Nürnberg, n.*
Pacific Ocean *Stille Ozean, m.*
Poland *Polen, n.*
Portugal *Portugal, n.*
Prussia *Preussen, n.*
Rhine *Rhein, m.*
Rhineland *Rheinland, n.*
Russia *Russland, n.*
Saar *Saar, f.*
Saxony *Sachsen, n.*
Scotland *Schottland, n.*
Silesia *Schlesien, n.*
Spain *Spanien, n.*
Sweden *Schweden, n.*
Switzerland *Schweiz, f.*
Turkey *Türkei, f.*
United States *die Vereinigten*
Staaten, pl.
Vienna *Wien, n.*

Advanced ($14.95)	**Cassette**	**Record**
French	☐ 558866	☐ 558874
Spanish	☐ 558831	☐ 55884X

For Foreign-Speaking, Who Wish to Learn English ($17.95)

	Cassette	**Record**
English for French	☐ 50202X	☐ 508192
English for Spanish	☐ 558793	☐ 558807
English for Italian	☐ 513234	☐ 502003
English for German	☐ 513226	☐ 501996
English for Portuguese		☐ 508206
English for Chinese	☐ 508176	☐ 508184

Children's Courses ($17.95)

French	☐ 563290	☐ 563304
Spanish	☐ 563339	☐ 563347

Business Skills
Keyboard Typing

cassette $17.95		☐ 542536
record $17.95		☐ 010852
manual $3.00		☐ 512831

Shorthand

cassette $17.95		☐ 542528
record $17.95		☐ 010860
Book I $3.00		☐ 512718
Book II $3.00		☐ 512726

Better Speech

cassette $17.95		☐ 542455
record $17.95		☐ 001373
correct speech $3.00		☐ 512505
correct usage $3.00		☐ 512513

Living Language Videocassette Program ($29.95)

French (60 minutes)	☐ VHS	555549
	☐ Beta	555611
Spanish (77 minutes)	☐ VHS	555557
	☐ Beta	55562X
German	☐ VHS	560151
(90 minutes)	☐ Beta	560143

Order Here
LIVING LANGUAGE, Dept. 849
34 Engelhard Avenue, Avenel, N.J. 07001

YES—rush me the LIVING LANGUAGE COURSES® I've checked.

Name (Please Print) _____

Address _____

City _____ State _____ Zip _____

_____ Courses @ $17.95			
_____ Courses @ $14.95			
_____ Manuals/Dictionaries @ $3.95			
_____ Manuals/Dictionaries @ $4.95			
_____ Books @ $3.00			
_____ Videocassettes @ $29.95			
	N.Y. and N.J. Residents add Sales Tax		
	Shipping & Handling Charge _____ Items @ $2.60 Each		
TOTAL ITEMS ORDERED	**Total Amount Due**		

☐ Check or Money Order Enclosed Made Payable to Crown Publishers, Inc.
(No cash or stamps, please)

Charge ☐ MasterCard ☐ Visa ☐ American Express

Account Number (include all digits)

Card Expires

MO		YR

Signature _____